1876 Facts About Custer
& The Battle of the Little Big Horn

Jerry. L. Russell

Savas Publishing Company

1876 Facts About Custer & the Battle of the Little Big Horn
by Jerry L. Russell

Copyright © 1999
Jerry L. Russell

Includes bibliographic references

Printing Number
10 9 8 7 6 5 4 3 2
First Edition

ISBN 1-882810-34-1
LCCN 99-64133

Savas Publishing Company
202 First Street SE, Suite 103A
Mason City, IA 50401

(515) 421-7135 (editorial offices)
(800) 732-3669 (distribution)

Cover art, "The Last Command: Custer and the 7th Cavalry at Little Big Horn, by Kirk Stirnweis, is courtesy of Americana Historical Art, 34 Sumner Place, Fort Leavenworth, KS 66027. Phone: (913) 682-2543. This beautiful print is available for purchase.

This book is printed on 50-lb. acid-free paper. It meets or exceeds the guidelines for permanence and durability of the Committee on Production Guidelines for Book Longevity of the Council on Library Resources

To my beloved wife, Alice Anne Russell

Lt. Col. George Armstrong Custer in dress uniform. Custer sat for this portrait in March 1876, just three months before his death at the Little Big Horn. *USAMHI*

Table of Contents

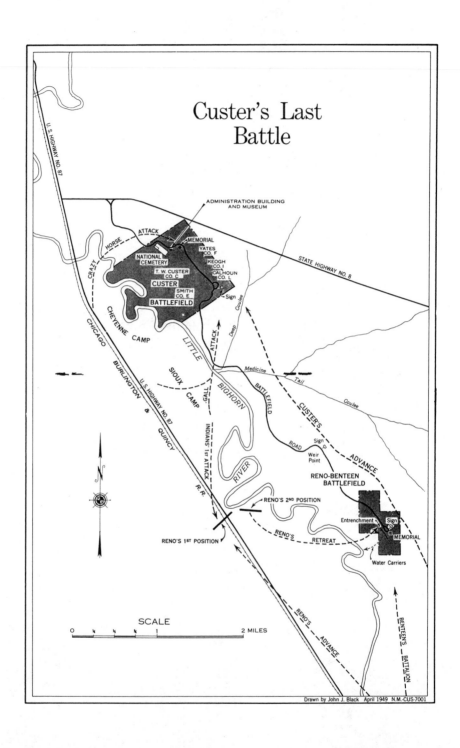

Custer's Last Battle

ADMINISTRATION BUILDING
AND MUSEUM

STATE HIGHWAY NO. 8

ATTACK

MEMORIAL

YATES
CO. F

NATIONAL
CEMETERY

KEOGH
CO. I

T. W. CUSTER
CO. C

CALHOUN
CO. L

CUSTER

SMITH
CO. E

BATTLEFIELD

Sign

CHEYENNE CAMP

CRAZY HORSE

ATTACK

Deep Coulee

LITTLE

Medicine

Tail

Coulee

SIOUX CAMP

BATTLEFIELD

BIGHORN

CUSTER'S

TAIL

ROAD

Sign

Weir
Point

ADVANCE

INDIANS 1st ATTACK

RIVER

RENO-BENTEEN
BATTLEFIELD

R. R.

RENO'S 2ND POSITION

Entrenchment

Sign

MEMORIAL

RENO'S 1ST POSITION

RENO'S

RETREAT

Water Carriers

U. S. HIGHWAY NO. 87

CHICAGO

BURLINGTON & QUINCY

U. S. HIGHWAY NO. 87

N

RENO'S

ADVANCE

BENTEEN'S BATTALION

SCALE

0   ¼   ½   1   2 MILES

Drawn by John J. Black   April 1949   N.M.-CUS-7001

Acknowledgments

I suppose the first acknowledgement should go to the publisher, Savas Publishing Company, and the distributor, Stackpole Books, for believing in the concept of a "Facts About" series in general and *1876 Facts About Custer & The Little Big Horn* in particular.

But my biggest acknowledgement is for my wife's invaluable contribution to the project. Without the help, suggestions, support, editing, and frequently-needed nudging of Alice Anne Russell, this book would never have made it to the printer. I can't overstate her importance.

Two other family members have been very helpful: daughter Leigh Anne Russell and her son, Chris Russell, who have read and re-read the manuscript for typos and other gremlin-induced occurrences that <u>will</u> crop up, no matter how hard you try; in Chris' case, he also kept the source books organized and itemized for the bibliography.

Reading for "historical accuracy" was done by Ronald L. Nichols, long-time president of the Custer Battlefield Historical & Museum Association, and editor of Dr. Kenneth Hammer's wonderful book, *Men With Custer: Biographies of the 7th Cavalry*; Michael J. Koury of the Old Army Press; and William W. Wells, a long-time board member of the CBH&MA and one of the leaders of Little Big Horn Associates. Dr. Michael Hughes, editor of *The Journal of the Indian Wars*, also checked the first draft. Thanks, also, to John Doerner, the Chief Historian at LBBNM, who helped greatly with hard-to-find minutiae.

But any mistakes found herein are solely my responsibility.

Moral support was given in large measure by Neil C. Mangum, Superintendent of the Little Bighorn Battlefield National Monument, and long-time chief historian at the predecessor Custer Battlefield National Monument; and James V. Court, long-time superintendent at Custer Battlefield National Monument.

Jim and Neil were responsible in the 1980s for the revitalization of the Custer Battlefield Historical Association, Inc., the long-time cooperating association for the Custer Battlefield National Monument and the Little Bighorn Battlefield National Monument.

Finally, I am grateful to all those many, many people who, over the years, wrote (sometimes accurately and sometimes not) about what happened on those hot late June days in the summer of our nation's Centennial Celebration, an event which resulted in a watershed change in the relationship between whites and Indians in the United States and its territories...and to you, for being interested.

jlr

Chapter 1

Basic Facts

How many soldiers from Greece (or Australia) died at the Little Big Horn?

How many Texans were in the 7th Cavalry at the Little Big Horn?

What was the temperature on the hills east of the Little Big Horn River near Minneconjou Ford on the afternoon of June 26, 1876?

Were Custer's men high on marijuana?

How did Custer get into (and out of) West Point?

All this and much more will be addressed, and sometimes answered, in the pages of this book.

But this is not an encyclopedia: "everything you ever wanted to know about Custer and the Battle of the Little Big Horn."

"My" 1876 "facts" might not be "your" 1876 "facts," because there are probably 187,600 "facts" to choose from.

The Battle of the Little Big Horn is the second most-written-about event in American history, second only to the Battle of Gettysburg, a "fact" you will find later in the book.

The following basic "facts" about that Battle were put forth by Col. W.A. Graham (US Army-Ret), one of the foremost of many military historians who have studied and written about the battle over the past 123 years, in *The Custer Myth* (Stackpole Books, 1953). They are as follows:

On June 25, 1876, General [Lt. Col.] George A. Custer and five troops of the Seventh United States Cavalry were completely wiped out by Indians at the Battle of the Little Big Horn River in Montana. The remainder of the regiment, under Major [Marcus A.] Reno, after a short engagement in the valley of that river, in which his own battalion of three troops was routed, was besieged throughout the late afternoon and evening of the 25th and during most of the 26th, sustaining very heavy losses. The Indians withdrew and the survivors were relieved by forces under Generals [Alfred] Terry and [Col. John] Gibbon during the morning of June 27.

As Col. Graham put it, these are the bare facts, stripped to the bone, devoid of detail—and even this unadorned presentation calls for commentary: Custer's "real" rank was lieutenant colonel in the Regular Army; he had been given a brevet (temporary) rank of major general of volunteers during the Civil War, and other Army officers continued to use it as a courtesy. The same situation applies to Colonel John Gibbon, commander of the Montana Column, who had received the brevet rank of brigadier general during the Civil War. Others with temporary ranks, all Civil War-related, included Marcus Reno (Brig. Gen.), Frederick Benteen (Col.), W.W. Cooke (Col.), Tom Custer (Maj.), Myles Keogh (Lt. Col.), and Myles Moylan (Maj.). (There are half-a-dozen extra "facts" for you. . .)

The purpose of this book is to put the flesh on the bones, and bring out details of the Battle, its participants, and the environment in which they lived, fought, and died on those dusty Montana hills over 12 decades ago, while at the same time pointing out some discrepancies and disagreements over nomenclature, time sequence, strategy, tactics, and just about anything and everything else connected with a discussion of the Battle of the Little Big Horn. The writing is in a journalistic style rather than a "military" or "scholarly" style, to make for easier reading.

Some of the "facts" are undisputed, even indisputable, *facts.*

Other "facts" are, or may be, "opinions" or "recollections" published and/or presented as *facts.*

A list of the sources used in the compilation of these "facts" is included at the end of the book, and each "fact" can be tied to the specific source.

Some of the "facts" seem to be contradicted by other "facts," and, in some cases, are directly contradicted. This is due to differences of opinion, flaws in recollections, differences of perspective, differences of interpretation, etc., etc., etc.

Nevertheless, all of the "facts" have been presented as "facts" by one source or another, in one form or another, at some time or another.

This is not designed to be a "scholarly work" or a "literary work" on General George A. Custer and the Battle of the Little Big Horn. It is, rather, a simple compilation of some of the "facts" about the Battle and its participants, designed to stimulate the reader's interest and motivate the reader to do further, in-depth research on this important clash of cultures.

It is not necessarily designed to be read "in order," although it certainly may be. It is written for browsing, dipping, tasting the history and legends of the Battle of the Little Big Horn.

The book is divided into five "chapters"—this one and one each on four basic categories: *Army*, *Indians*, *Literature*, and *Aftermath*.

Each category is divided into subsets: **Individuals**, **Custer**, **Events**, **Environment**, and **Equipment**.

The **Individuals** subset is the largest, because it deals with the hundreds of individuals involved in the history of June 25, 1876: men serving with the 7th Cavalry on that date and their families, some other Army officers, some writers about the battle, and Indians involved before, during, and after the battle.

The **Environment** subset is next, in length, because it deals with:

Time Environment (generally what was referred to in those days before "standard" time and "time zones" as "Chicago time"; as well as Time, The Passage of); Distance Environment; Geographic Environment; Weather/Climate Environment; Terrain/Topographical Environment; Cultural/Sociological Environment; Psychological Environment; Resource Environment (Men, Weapons, Supplies, etc.)

Custer and **Events** are self-explanatory.

Equipment deals with weapons, gear, paraphernalia, animals—the implements and accessories of war.

Within the subsets, the "facts" have been randomized and are not in any particular order. However, each "fact" has been written so as to stand alone within the overall context of the book.

The variations in spelling (Little Bighorn, Little Big Horn; Ogalalla, Oglala; Mineconjou, Minneconjou, Miniconjou, etc.) occur because of the variations in spelling from the sources.

"Little Big Horn" is the compiler's personal preference because of its many years of use in connection with the battlefield. However, let it be noted that both the National Park Service and the National Geological Survey Service prefer "Little Bighorn."

The spellings within contemporary quotes have not been corrected, nor has [sic] been inserted every time. Please just assume that if a misspelling is found within a contemporary quote, it's because it is a "historically accurate misspelling."

A sincere effort has been made to achieve "balance" in the presentation of the "facts" but "balance" to one is "bias" to another.

We have done the best we can.

There are many other "facts" about Custer and the Battle of the Little Big Horn that are not touched on in this volume, leaving room, perhaps, for additional volumes. (Send suggestions to PO Box 7401, Little Rock AR 72217.)

Some acronyms that you will run across include LBH (Little Big Horn, referring to the Battle), LBBNM (Little Bighorn Battlefield National Monument), CBNM (Custer Battlefield National Monument), CBNC (Custer Battlefield National Cemetery), CBH&MA (Custer Battlefield Historical & Museum Association, Inc.), LBHA (Little Big Horn Associates), KIA (Killed In Action at LBH), MIA (Missing In Action at LBH), WIA (Wounded In Action at LBH), D.T. (Dakota Territory), M.T. (Montana Territory), W.T. (Wyoming Territory), O.T. (Oklahoma Territory [the western "half" of what later became the state of Oklahoma]), I.T. (Indian Territory [the eastern "half" of what later became the state of Oklahoma], or, in the case of Nez Perce-related actions, Idaho Territory), NW.T. (the Northwest Territory [what is now the upper Midwest; the St. Clair "massacre" occurred in Ohio]); and USCT (United States Colored Troops in the Union's Civil War forces).

The book also uses the standard United States Postal Service's two-letter designations for the states of the Union.

One bibliographic caveat: the *Custer Battlefield* handbook of 1978, referred to frequently in the book, was written by long-time Battlefield superintendent Edward S. Luce and his wife Evelyn S. Luce, but, for brevity's sake, we have consistently used "Luce" as the author's designation.

During the writing of *1876 Facts About Custer and the Battle of the Little Big Horn*, which has definitely been a family affair, some of my beliefs, attitudes, etc., have been altered by the "fact"-finding process.

Maybe some of yours will be, too.

Chapter 2

Facts About the Army

Individuals

Fact #1. The headquarters staff of the 7th Cavalry Regiment, under the field command of Lt. Col. George Armstrong Custer, consisted of Maj. Marcus A. Reno; 1st Lt. William W. Cooke, Adjutant; Assistant Surgeon George E. Lord, M.D.; Acting Assistant Surgeon James M. DeWolf, M.D.; Acting Assistant Surgeon Henry R. Porter, M.D.; Sgt. Maj. William H. Sharrow; and Chief Trumpeter Henry Voss.

Fact #2. Three hundred and seventy-nine immigrant soldiers and civilians saw action at the Little Big Horn, from 25 foreign countries: Australia, Austria, Bavaria, Canada, Denmark, England, France, Germany, Greece, Hungary, the Ionian Islands, Ireland, Italy, Norway, Poland, Prussia, Russia, Saxony, Scotland, Silesia, South Wales, Spain, Sweden, Switzerland, and Wales.

Fact #3. Many of the men who enlisted in the frontier Army used names, or were known by names other than their own. For instance, 7th Cavalry soldier William Cummings enlisted as William Braendle (Pvt., Co. C).

Fact #4. 1st Lt. Edward Settle Godfrey (Co. K) was the first officer to whom Capt. Frederick Benteen (commanding, Cos. D, H, K) showed the last message from Custer, "Benteen—come on."

Fact #5. Jacob Deihle (Pvt., Co. A, 22 at LBH), a bartender, was born in Germany. WIA.

Fact #6. Seventh Cavalry soldier Thomas Anderson enlisted as Thomas Murphy (Pvt., Co. K).

Fact #7. Uriah S. Lewis (Pvt., Co. D, 23 on June 25, 1876), a painter, was born in Pennsylvania.

Fact #8. Miles F. O'Hara (Sgt., Co. M, 24 at LBH), a laborer, was born in Ohio. KIA.

Captain Frederick Benteen

USAMHI

Fact #9. Only one soldier from Austria served in the 7th Cavalry at LBH: 1st Lt. Charles C. DeRudio (Co. E), who was in the valley fight and the Reno-Benteen position.

Fact #10. Seventh Cavalry soldier Charles Harry Reynolds enlisted as Henry M. Brinkerhoff (Pvt., Co. G).

Fact #11. Dewitt Winney was the 1st Sgt. of K Co., assigned to Benteen's battalion.

Fact #12. Two civilians—newspaper correspondent Mark Kellogg, and Custer's nephew Harry Armstrong (Autie) Reed—were assigned to the headquarters contingent of the 7th Cavalry Regiment on June 25, 1876.

Fact #13. The state of Massachusetts provided 44 men to the 7th Cavalry column which rode to the Little Big Horn on June 25, 1876. Twenty of those men were killed (45.4%), the highest casualty rate of any substantial state group.

Fact #14. Maj. Marcus A. Reno commanded Cos. A, G, and M in the valley fight on the morning of June 25, and commanded Cos. A, B, D, G, H, K, and M at the Reno-Benteen site June 25-26.

Fact #15. James M. DeWolf (Acting Asst. Surgeon, HQs, 33 at LBH) was born in Jenningsville (PA).

Fact #16. Seventh Cavalry soldier Jacob Emerich enlisted as Jacob Huff (Pvt., Band).

Fact #17. Col. Samuel Sturgis, the commanding officer of the 7th U.S. Cavalry at the time of LBH, was on semi-permanent detached duty in St. Louis (MO). Sturgis lost a son at the Little Big Horn.

Fact #18. Michael P. Madden (Saddler, Co. K, 40 at LBH) was born in Ireland. WIA.

Fact #19. Henry Rinaldo Porter (Acting Asst. Surgeon, HQs, 28 at LBH) was born in New York; graduated from Georgetown University School of Medicine in 1872 and became an Army contract surgeon in June 1872.

Fact #20. Otto Voit (Saddler, Co. H, 30 at LBH) was born in Baden (Germany). WIA.

Fact #21. The officers of Co. M, 7th Cavalry, in June 1876, included Capt. T.H. French, commanding; 1st Lt. E.G. Mathey, commanding pack train; 2d Lt. J.G. Sturgis, killed with Co. E. Replacement: 2d Lt. J.C. Gresham.

Fact #22. Seventh Cavalry soldier William H. Beardslee enlisted as Alexander Harrison (Pvt., Co. K).

Fact #23. ". . .everybody now lay down and spread himself out as thin as possible. After lying there a few minutes I was horrified to find myself wondering if a small sagebrush, about as thick as my finger, would turn a bullet, so I got up and walked along the line, cautioned the men not to waste ammunition; ordered certain men who were good shots to do the firing, and others to keep them supplied with loaded guns." Lt. Edward S. Godfrey (commanding Co. K), recounting his experiences at the Reno-Benteen site on the evening of June 25, 1876.

Fact #24. The officers of Co. H, 7th Cavalry, in June 1876, included Capt. F.W. Benteen, battalion commander; 1st Lt. F.M. Gibson, commanding Co. H; 2d Lt. E.A. Garlington, graduation leave of absence. Replacement: 2d Lt. A.J. Russell.

Fact #25. Company G, 7th Cavalry, assigned to Reno's battalion on June 25, 1876, was commanded by 1st Lt. Donald McIntosh and 2d Lt. George D. Wallace.

Fact #26. The 1st Sgt. of G Company, Edward Garlick, assigned to Reno's battalion, was on leave June 25, 1876, and missed the battle.

Fact #27. Joseph McCurry, 1st Sgt. of H Co., assigned to Benteen's battalion, was wounded in the left shoulder in the hilltop fight.

Fact #28. Seventh Cavalry soldier William Gardner enlisted as John Gardner (Pvt., Co. F).

Fact #29. Thomas P. Eagan wrote his sister from Fort Totten (D.T.), March 5, 1876: "We are to start the 10th of this month for the Big horn country. The Indians are getting bad again. i [sic] think that we will have some hard times this summer. The old Chief Sitting Bull says that he will not make peace with the whites as long as he had a man to fight. ...As soon as I get back of the campaign i [sic] will rite [sic] you. That is if i [sic] do not get my hair lifted by some Indian." Eagan was killed June 25, 1876.

Fact #30. Pvt. Thomas J. Callan (Co. B) was one of a number of volunteers who earned a Medal of Honor for fetching water for the wounded at the Reno-

Officers from the Seventh Cavalry. Seated from left to right: Lieutenant Charles Varnum, chief of scouts at Little Big Horn; Captain Frederick Benteen; Lieutenant Benjamin Hodges; a lieutenant identified only as "Bronson."

Little Bighorn Battlefield National Monument Archives

Benteen site by going down Water Carriers' Ravine to the Little Big Horn River on June 26, 1876.

Fact #31. Chief of Scouts Charles Varnum (2d Lt., Co. A) was informed by Custer on the evening of the 24th, "the Crows reported that between us and the Little Big Horn was a high hill with a sort of Crow nest in the top where the Crows watched the Sioux when they were on that river and the Crows were on a horse stealing trip. That their camp could be made out in the clear light of the morning when daylight broke. The Indian trail we were following led in that direction and the Crows believe their camp was on the Little Big Horn. Custer said that the Crows were going on at once and he wanted an intelligent white man to go with them and take some Rees [Arikaras] for messengers & Boyer as interpreter and send him [Custer] back word what we discovered. I said that meant me, but he said it was a tough, mean job, but I insisted that it was my place, only I would like to take Charley Reynolds with me. . ."

Fact #32. William M. Harris (Pvt., Co. D, 25 at LBH), a farmer, was born in Kentucky.

Fact #33. Frank C. Mann (civilian packer, age unknown) was employed in St. Paul (MN) as a civilian packer by the 7th Cavalry Quartermaster. KIA.

Fact #34. Seventh Cavalry soldier Henry M. Scollin enlisted as Henry M. Cody (Cpl., Co. M).

Fact #35. Harry Armstrong "Autie" Reed (civilian attached to Custer's column, 18 at LBH), the nephew of George, Tom, and Boston Custer, accompanied his uncles on a "great adventure" and was killed with the Custers on June 25, 1876.

Fact #36. Stanislaus Roy (Cpl., Co. A, 29 at LBH) was born in France.

Fact #37. James Weeks (Pvt., Co. M, 22 at LBH), a laborer, was born in Halifax, Nova Scotia (Canada).

Fact #38. Co. G, assigned to Reno's battalion, had two officers and 43 men.

Fact #39. Charles L. Anderson (Pvt., Co. C, 29 at the time of LBH), a sailor, enlisted in Boston (MA) in August 1875; deserted at the Powder River camp on June 20, 1876, owing $67.39 for ordnance stores.

Fact #40. Seventh Cavalry soldier Latrobe Brommell enlisted as Latrobe Bromwell (Pvt., Co. E).

Fact #41. Charles W. Campbell (Pvt., Co. G, 31 at LBH), a carpenter, was born in Iowa.

Fact #42. Frederic F. Girard (civilian interpreter, 46 at LBH) was employed May 12, 1876, by the 7th Cavalry Quartermaster to interpret for Arikara and Sioux Indian scouts.

Fact #43. Pvt. David W. Harris (Co. A) was one of a number of volunteers who earned a Medal of Honor for fetching water for the wounded at the Reno-Benteen site by going down Water Carriers' Ravine to the Little Big Horn River on June 26, 1876.

Fact #44. Seventh Cavalryman Charles Wrangel enlisted as Charles A. Windolph (Pvt., Co. H).

Fact #45. Benjamin (Bennie) Hubert Hodgson (2d Lt., Co. B, 27 at LBH) was born in Philadelphia (PA). KIA.

Fact #46. Seventh Cavalry soldier James Hood enlisted as James Hurd (Pvt., Co. D).

Fact #47. George M. McDermott (Sgt., Co. A, 28 at LBH), a laborer, was born in Ireland.

Fact #48. Charles Sanders (Pvt., Co. D, 32 at LBH) was born in Saxony (Germany).

Fact #49. Thomas Benton Weir (Capt., Co. D, 37 at LBH) was born in Ohio and was a Civil War veteran who worked his way up from the ranks, finishing his Civil War service as a brevet Lt. Col.

Fact #50. Seventh Cavalry soldier James Thomas enlisted as Thomas Jaynes Stowers (Pvt., Co. B).

Fact #51. Co. K, 7th Cavalry, assigned to Benteen's battalion, was commanded by 1st Lt. Edward S. Godfrey.

Fact #52. Frederick William Benteen (Capt., Co. H), a native of Petersburg (VA), enlisted in the Union Army at the beginning of the Civil War as a 1st Lt. in the 10th Missouri Volunteer Cavalry and reached the brevet rank of brigadier general. He was appointed Capt., 7th Cavalry, to rank from July 28, 1866, the date the regiment was organized.

Fact #53. 2d Lt. John J. Crittenden was serving with the 20th Infantry in October 1875 and exploded a cartridge with a knife, with the result that a small piece of the casing was lodged in his eye; the eye was removed a month later. He was assigned to the 7th Cavalry in May 1876.

Fact #54. The seven civilians who died at LBH included Boston Custer, younger brother of George and Tom; Harry Armstrong Reed (known as "Autie"), nephew of George, Tom and Boston Custer; Frank Mann, a packer; Mark Kellogg, a newspaperman; Charley Reynolds, a scout; Isaiah Dorman, a scout and the only Negro at the battle; and Mitch Boyer (Bouyer), a French/Santee Sioux interpreter and scout.

Fact #55. Cpl. John E. Hammon, 18 (Co. G), and Pvt. George W. Hammon, 25 (Co. F), were brothers.

Fact #56. Archibald McIlhargey (Pvt., Co. I, 31 at LBH) was born in Ireland. KIA.

Fact #57. Seventh Cavalry soldier Max Cernow enlisted as Otto Arndt (Pvt., Band).

Fact #58. William H. Sharrow (Sgt. Maj., HQs Co., 30 at LBH) was born at sea. KIA.

Fact #59. John R. Wilkinson (Sgt., Co. F, 28 at LBH), a farmer, was born in New York. KIA.

Fact #60. Co. D, assigned to Benteen's battalion, consisted of two officers and 52 enlisted men.

Fact #61. Pvt. Charles H. Welch (Co. D) was one of a number of volunteers who earned a Medal of Honor for fetching water for the wounded at the Reno-Benteen site by going down Water Carriers' Ravine to the Little Big Horn River on June 26, 1876.

Fact #62. Seventh Cavalry soldier Charles Laurse enlisted as William G. Hardy (Trumpeter, Co. A).

Fact #63. Rufus T. Hutchinson (Sgt., Co. B, 25 at LBH), a farmer, was born in Ohio.

Fact #64. Donald McIntosh (1st Lt., Co. G, 37 at LBH) was born in Canada and raised at various posts of the Hudson's Bay Co. KIA.

Fact #65. Thomas W. Stivers (Pvt., Co. D, 25 at LBH), a clerk, was born in Kentucky where he enlisted September 1871.

Fact #66. Company E, 7th Cavalry, assigned to Custer's battalion, was commanded by 1st Lt. Algernon E. Smith and 2d Lt. James G. Sturgis.

Fact #67. Seventh Cavalry soldier Frank May enlisted as Otto Voit (Saddler, Co. H).

Fact #68. Co. K, assigned to Benteen's battalion, consisted of one officer and 41 enlisted men.

Fact #69. Elihu F. Clear (Pvt., Co. K, 32 at LBH), born in Indiana, was an orderly for surgeon Dr. James DeWolf. KIA.

Fact #70. Pvt. George D. Scott (Co. D) was one of the volunteers who earned a Medal of Honor for fetching water for the wounded at the Reno-Benteen site by going down Water Carriers' Ravine to the Little Big Horn River on June 26, 1876.

Fact #71. Myles Walter Keogh (Capt., Co. I, 36 at LBH) was born in Ireland. KIA.

Fact #72. Seventh Cavalry soldier Michael Burke enlisted as George M. McDermott (Sgt., Co. A).

Fact #73. Myles Moylan (Capt., Co. A, 37 at LBH) was born in Massachusetts. KIA.

Fact #74. Peter Thompson (Pvt., Co. C, 21 at LBH), a miner, was born in Scotland and came to the U.S. in 1865.

Fact #75. Young Hawk (Pvt., Detachment of Indian Scouts, about 21 at LBH) enlisted as a 7th Cavalry scout May 1876 Fort Abraham Lincoln (D.T.).

Fact #76. Writing in "The Experience of a Private Soldier in the Custer Massacre," Pvt. Peter Thompson (Co. C) described how cavalry companies divided into "fours," with one soldier of each "four" designated to be the horse holder, taking charge of the horses of the other three and conducting them out of the line of fire. "The men composing the four with myself were [Blacksmith John] Fitzgerald [Co. C], [Pvt. John] Brennan [Co. C], and [Pvt. James] Watson [Co. C], and although composing one of the sets of fours that entered into action with Custer, not one of us ever reached the battlefield which proved fatal to Custer and his men."

Fact #77. Seventh Cavalry soldier John Bush enlisted as Henry P. Jones (Pvt., Co. I).

Major Marcus A. Reno

USAMHI

Fact #78. Maj. Marcus Reno had been severely criticized by Custer three days before LBH. In his June 22 dispatch, Custer wrote: "[Reno] returned, having inexcusably and inexplicably disobeyed and violated his orders and thereby embarrassed and marred hopes of future success of the expedition... Had he pursued and overtaken the village, this error would have been forgotten; but instead, he countermarched to the rear. . .to report his blunder to Gen. Terry who informed him that his disobedience would not bear investigation. A court martial is strongly hinted at."

Fact #79. John Jordan Crittenden, 2d Lt., Co. G, 20th Infantry, was placed on temporary duty to Co. L, 7th Cavalry, Dakota Column, having been commissioned in October 1875; killed June 25, 1876, at age 22.

Fact #80. Pvt. Thomas Meador (Co. H) and Pvt. Julien Jones (Co. H) were killed along the southeast end of the Reno-Benteen firing line. Skeletal remains, buttons, and scraps of uniform cloth discovered along the site of the line's L-shaped trench in 1958 revealed that two or three men were buried in the trench after the fight was over, and not recovered later. The remains were most likely those of Jones and Meador.

Fact #81. Maj. Marcus A. Reno, at LBH, was in command of a three-company battalion consisting of Cos. A, G, and M, after Custer divided the entire regimental command on June 25, 1876.

Fact #82. Pvt. Daniel Newell (Co. M) was told by his "bunkie," Cpl. Henry Scollin, of Scollin's premonition of death, and his real name—Henry Cody; ". . . in less than 24 hours he was lying dead on the bottom of the Little Big Horn, his body riddled with bullets," Newell said. Newell had seen Scollin when he was first shot: "He had been shot but was still alive when I got to him. I couldn't help him and he was beyond help anyway. All he could say was 'Goodbye, boys.'"

Fact #83. Seventh Cavalry soldier Edward H. Kelly enlisted as Patrick Kelly (Pvt., Co. I).

Fact #84. George August Finckle (Sgt., Co. C, 31 at LBH), a clerk, was born in Berlin, Germany. KIA.

Fact #85. "Corporal [George] Lell [Co. H]. . .was fatally wounded [in the abdomen] and dragged to the hospital [in the center of the Reno-Benteen site]. He was dying and knew it. 'Lift me up boys,' he said to some of the men, 'I want to see the boys again before I go.' So they held him up in a sitting position where he could see his comrades in action. . .then they laid him down and he died soon after. . .I will never forget Corporal Lell." Pvt. Charles Windolph, Co. H, writing about his experiences at the Reno-Benteen site June 25-26, 1876.

Fact #86. Pvt. Michael Madden (Co. K) was one of the volunteers who risked his life by fetching water for the wounded at the Reno-Benteen site by going down Water Carriers' Ravine to the Little Big Horn River on June 26, 1876; severely wounded, Pvt. Madden lost his leg, but survived for many years. For reasons unknown he was not awarded the Medal of Honor, one of three "water carriers" to be ignored by the awards board.

Fact #87. Charles H. Houghtaling (Pvt., Co. D, 32 at LBH), a druggist, was born in New York.

Fact #88. David McWilliams (Pvt., Co. H, 26 at LBH) was born in Scotland.

Fact #89. Seventh Cavalry soldier Jan Mollar (or James Moller) enlisted as Jan Moller (Pvt., Co. H).

Fact #90. The officers of Co. D, 7th Cavalry, in June 1876, included Capt. T.B. Weir, commanding; 1st Lt. J.M. Bell, leave of absence; 2d Lt. W.S. Edgerly. Replacements: 1st Lt. E.P. Eckerson; 2d Lt. D.C. Pearson, transferred; 2d Lt. E.P. Brewer.

Fact #91. 1st Lt. Donald McIntosh (Co. G), who was half-Indian and Canadian, was not completely accepted by his fellow officers in the 7th Cavalry. To add to his position of disfavor, Lt. McIntosh had put 2d Lt. George Wallace (Co. G) under arrest for insubordination over an incident which occurred on the troop train en route from the South to Fort Abraham Lincoln (D.T.).

Fact #92. Seventh Cavalry soldier Robert Nelson enlisted as Benjamin Brandon (Farrier, Co. F).

Fact #93. Mitchel (Mitch) Boyer [Bouyer], a 39-year-old half-Sioux, half-white Scout, was the only scout to die with Custer's main command at LBH.

Fact #94. Thomas Ward Custer, younger brother of George Armstrong Custer, was killed June 25, 1876, at age 31.

Fact #95. Charles Alexander Reynolds (Lonesome Charley), civilian guide, was killed at age 34 in the valley fight June 25, 1876.

Fact #96. Company M, 7th Cavalry, assigned to Reno's battalion on June 25, 1876, was commanded by Capt. Thomas French.

Fact #97. Thomas French (Capt., Co. M) was born in Maryland.

Fact #98. Seventh Cavalry soldier Henry Gross enlisted as John Green (Pvt., Co. D).

Fact #99. During the morning of June 26, several groups of volunteers went down to the river, through what is now known as Water Carriers' Ravine, to fill kettles and canteens for the wounded at the Reno-Benteen site. Dr. Henry Porter, Acting Assistant Surgeon, the only physician left alive atop the bluffs, had advised Maj. Reno and Capt. Benteen that some of the wounded would die unless they were given water.

Fact #100. Henry Klotzbucher (Pvt., Co. M, 27 at LBH), a cooper, born in Baden (Germany), enlisted October 1873 in Philadelphia (PA). KIA.

Fact #101. Thomas Murray (Sgt., Co. B, 39 at LBH) was born in Ireland.

Fact #102. Ludwick St. John (Pvt., Co. C, 28 at LBH) was born in Missouri. KIA.

Fact #103. The officers of Co. F, 7th Cavalry, in June 1876, included Capt. G.W. Yates, killed; 1st Lt. H. Jackson, detached service; 2d Lt. W.C. Larned, detached service. Replacements: Capt. J.M. Bell; 1st Lt. W.W. Robinson, Jr.; 2d Lt. C.B. Schofield, transferred; 2d Lt. H.J. Slocum.

Fact #104. Seventh Cavalry soldier James J. Tanner enlisted as Jacob Henry Gebhart (Pvt., Co. M).

Fact #105. Only one soldier from Greece served in the 7th Cavalry at LBH: Pvt. Alexander Stella (Co. E), who died with Custer.

Fact #106. J.C. Wagoner, Chief Packer, born 1836 New York, was in charge of 7th Cavalry, Dakota Pack Train. WIA.

Fact #107. Michael Kenney was the 1st Sgt. of F Co., assigned to Custer's battalion.

Fact #108. Abram B. Brant (Pvt., Co. D, 26 at LBH), a civil engineer, was born in New York City.

Fact #109. Theodore W. Goldin (Pvt., Co. G, 18 at LBH), a brakeman, was born in Wisconsin.

Fact #110. Seventh Cavalry soldier Michael Conlon enlisted as Martin Personeus (Pvt., Co. L).

Fact #111. Pvt. Peter Thompson (Co. C) was one of a number of volunteers who earned a Medal of Honor for fetching water for the wounded at the Reno-Benteen site by going down Water Carriers' Ravine to the Little Big Horn River on June 26, 1876.

Fact #112. Gustave Korn (Pvt., Co. I, 24 at LBH), a clerk, was born in Sprollow, Silesia (Germany).

Fact #113. Henry W.B. Mecklin (Blacksmith, Co. H, 24 at LBH), a blacksmith, was born in Pennsylvania.

Fact #114. George E. Smith (Pvt., Co. M, 25 at LBH), a shoemaker, was born in Maine. MIA.

Fact #115. Seventh Cavalry soldier John McKinney enlisted as John Noonan (Cpl., Co. L).

Fact #116. The officers of Co. B, 7th Cavalry, in June 1876 included Capt. T.M. McDougall, commanding; 1st Lt. W.T. Craycroft, detached service; 2d Lt. B.H. Hodgson, killed. Replacements: 2d Lt. W.W. Robinson, Jr., transferred; 2d Lt. W.J. Nicholson.

Fact #117. Col. John Gibbon, responding to critics who speculated "in sarcastic calculations as to how many millions of dollars are required to kill one Indian," wrote, ". . .in Indian wars the labor performed is far greater than in so-called civilized wars (as if war in any shape could be called civilized!), whilst the troops engaged have not even the poor consolation of being credited with 'glory,' a term which, upon the frontier, has long since been defined to signify being 'shot at by an Indian behind a rock, and having your name wrongly spelled in the newspapers!' Hence, if the American people do not wish to spend money they should not go to war."

Fact #118. Pvt. Charles Sanders of Company D served as Lt. W. S. Edgerly's orderly. Noticing during the fighting at Weir Point that Sanders "had a large grin on his face although he was sitting in a perfect shower of bullets," Edgerly reported later that he had asked Sanders what he was laughing about. Sanders replied: "I was laughing to see what poor shots those Indians were; they were shooting too low and their bullets were spattering dust like drops of rain."

Fact #119. Thomas French, Capt., Commanding Co. M, 7th Cavalry, Dakota Column, was 33 at the Little Big Horn.

Fact #120. Frank E. Varden was the 1st Sgt. of I Co., assigned to Custer's battalion.

Fact #121. Seventh Cavalry soldier Nicholas Kline enlisted as Nikolaus Klein (Pvt., Co. F).

Captain Thomas French

USAMHI

Fact #122. Charles Cunningham (Pvt., Co. B, 30 at LBH), a cooper, was born in Hudson (NY). WIA.

Fact #123. From the "Crow['s] nest," Chief of Scouts Charles Varnum (2d Lt., Co. A) could see a timbered stream, up which he and his scouts had advanced during the night, leading back to the Rosebud River, he wrote historian Walter Camp in 1909. "Another [tributary] led down to the Little Big Horn. On this were the two lodges that you know of and which I understand were filled with dead bodies of Indians, probably from Crook's fight of the 17th. . .I crawled up & watched the valley till the sun rose. All I could see was two lodges. The Crows tried to make me see smoke from villages behind the bluffs on the Little Big Horn & gave me a cheap spy glass but I could see nothing. They said there was an immense pony herd out grazing & told me to look for worms crawling on the grass & I could make out the herd; but I could not see worms or ponies either."

Fact #124. Jacob Horner (Pvt., Co. K) was born in New York City in 1854 of immigrant parents from Alsace-Lorraine (France) who returned to Europe when he was three. He came back to the U.S. at age 15.

Fact #125. Thomas McElroy (Trumpeter, Co. E, 32 at LBH) was born in Ireland. KIA.

Fact #126. Surgeons attached to the 7th Cavalry on the 1876 Sioux Expedition included Assistant Surgeon G.E. Lord, killed; Acting Assistant Surgeon J.M. DeWolf, killed; Acting Assistant Surgeon H.R. Porter.

Fact #127. Seventh Cavalry soldier Thomas Brown enlisted as John Dolan (Pvt., Co. M).

Fact #128. Francis (Frank) Marion Gibson, 1st Lt., Co. H, 7th Cavalry, Dakota Column, was commissioned 2d Lt. 7th Cavalry 1867; 1st Lt., 1871.

Fact #129. Company I, 7th Cavalry, assigned to Custer's battalion, was commanded by Capt. Myles W. Keogh and 1st Lt. James E. Porter.

Fact #130. James C. Bennett (Pvt., Co. C, 27 at LBH) was a laborer from Ohio. WIA.

Fact #131. George H. Geiger (Sgt., Co. H, 32 at LBH) was born in Cincinnati (OH).

Fact #132. Seventh Cavalry soldier Charles Miller enlisted as Frederick Shulte (Pvt., Co. F).

Fact #133. Sgt. Rufus D. Hutchinson (Co. B) was one of a number of volunteers who earned a Medal of Honor for fetching water for the wounded at the Reno-Benteen site by going down Water Carriers' Ravine to the Little Big Horn River on June 26, 1876.

Fact #134. William Heyn (1st Sgt., Co. A, 28 at LBH) was born in Bremen (Germany). WIA.

Fact #135. Edward Gustave Mathey (1st Lt., Co. M, 38 at LBH) was placed in command of the pack train June 22, 1876, and engaged in the fight at Reno-Benteen position June 25-26.

Fact #136. John M. Ryan (1st Sgt., Co. M, 30 at LBH), a carpenter and a Civil War veteran, first enlisted in the 7th Cavalry in 1866.

Fact #137. Seventh Cavalry soldier John Blanchard enlisted as John S. Wells (Sgt., Co. E).

Fact #138. James Wynn (Pvt., Co. D, 40 at LBH) (date and place of birth unknown) entered his second enlistment in Alabama March 1873.

Fact #139. All of the 7th Cavalry officers who died in the year 1876 perished at the Little Big Horn on June 25-26.

Fact #140. Only one soldier from the Ionian Islands served in the 7th Cavalry at the time of LBH: Lt. Henry James Nowland (Quartermaster) was not present at the Battle, being on detached service.

Fact #141. John Burkman (Pvt., Co. L, 37 at LBH) was born in Germany, not in Allegheny County, Pa. as he said on his 1861 enlistment record.

Fact #142. Benjamin C. Criswell (Sgt., Co. B, 27 at LBH) was born in Western Virginia. WIA.

Fact #143. Seventh Cavalry soldier James Hurd enlisted as Henry Holden (Pvt., Co. D).

Fact #144. David W. Harris (Pvt., Co. A, 23 at LBH), a laborer, was born in Indiana.

Fact #145. John Martin (Giovanni Martini) (Trumpeter, Co. H, 23 at LBH), a musician, was born in Italy, arrived in the U.S. in 1873, and enlisted June 1874; carried the famous "Last Message" from Custer to Capt. F.W. Benteen.

Fact #146. William J. Randall (Pvt., Co. D, 25 at LBH), a carpenter, was born in Pennsylvania.

Fact #147. Charles H. Welch (Pvt., Co. D., 31 at LBH), a laborer, was born in New York City.

Fact #148. Two Co. I enlisted men, Pvt. Archibald McIlhargey and Pvt. John Mitchell, were attached to Reno's column as it crossed the Little Big Horn River and prepared to attack the (southern) upper end of the Indian village on June 25, 1876. Both were sent with messages to Custer that Reno was encountering strong opposition. Both remained and died with Custer's column.

Fact #149. Seventh Cavalry soldier Garrett H. Niver enlisted as Garrett H. Van Allen (Pvt., Co. C).

Fact #150. George Edwin Lord, 1st Lt., Asst. Surgeon, 7th Cavalry, Dakota Column, entered military medical service in 1871 and was 30 at LBH. KIA.

Fact #151. Edwin Bobo was the 1st Sgt. of C Co., assigned to Custer's battalion.

Fact #152. Co. I, assigned to Custer's battalion, consisted of two officers and 46 enlisted men. All with Custer perished in the battle.

Fact #153. Fred Stressinger (Cpl., Co. M, 24 years and one day old at LBH), a laborer, was born in Ripley County (IN). KIA.

Fact #154. Otto Durselew (Pvt., Co. A, 25 at LBH), a clerk, was born in Germany.

Fact #155. Seventh Cavalry soldier Solomon Angst (or August) enlisted as John H. Meier (Pvt., Co. M).

Fact #156. Samuel James Foster (Pvt., Co. A, 29 at LBH) was born in Kentucky. WIA.

Fact #157. Pvt. Abram Brant (Co. D) was one of a number of volunteers who earned a Medal of Honor for fetching water for the wounded at the Reno-Benteen site by going down Water Carriers' Ravine to the Little Big Horn River on June 26, 1876.

Fact #158. James Pym (Pvt., Co. B, 23 at LBH), a laborer, was born in England. WIA.

Fact #159. William Van Wyck Reily (2d Lt., Co. E, 22 at LBH) was born in Washington (DC). KIA.

Fact #160. James Watson (Pvt., Co. C, 25 at LBH), a laborer, was born in New York.

Fact #161. Seventh Cavalry soldier Charles N. Hayes enlisted as Charles N. Hood (Pvt., Co. H).

Fact #162. Checking the 7th Cavalry company rosters, one finds a puzzling situation: a soldier named James Hurd was serving on June 25, 1876, under the name of Henry Holden (Pvt., Co. D), while another soldier, whose real name was James Hood, was serving on that day under the name of James Hurd (Pvt., Co. D).

Fact #163. Lt. John Jordan Crittenden, who died with L Company on Battle Ridge, was a 2d Lieutenant in Co. G of the 20th Infantry, but was placed on temporary duty with the 7th Cavalry where he served as a 1st Lieutenant.

Fact #164. Lt. James G. Sturgis (Co. M), the youngest officer to die at the Little Big Horn, was the son of the commanding officer of the 7th Cavalry, Col. (Bvt. Maj. Gen.) Samuel D. Sturgis, West Point 1846, who was on detached service in St. Louis (MO) at the time of the battle.

Fact #165. Only one soldier from Russia served in the 7th Cavalry at LBH: Pvt. Ygnatz Stungewitz (Co. C), who died with Custer.

Fact #166. Seventh Cavalry soldier Patrick Redican enlisted as Patrick Coakley (Pvt., Co. K).

Fact #167. The Pack Train Detachment of the 7th Cavalry Regiment, under the command of Lt. Col. George A. Custer, consisted of 1st Lt. Edward G.

Mathey and six mule-packers, employed by the Quartermaster Corps; plus Company B, 48 men under the command of Capt. Thomas M. McDougall.

Fact #168. Thomas J. Callan (Pvt., Co. B, 22 at LBH) was born in Ireland. His trade before the Army was that of "morocco dresser."

Fact #169. Charles Camilus DeRudio (1st Lt., Co. E, 43 at LBH), a native of Austria, was educated at the Austrian Military Academy and served on the staff of Italian patriot Giuseppe Garibaldi during an unsuccessful revolution.

Fact #170. Seventh Cavalry soldier John Folsom enlisted as Alonzo Jennys (Pvt., Co. K).

Fact #171. Pvt. Theodore W. Goldin (Co. G) was one of a number of volunteers who earned a Medal of Honor for fetching water for the wounded at the Reno-Benteen site by going down Water Carriers' Ravine to the Little Big Horn River on June 26, 1876.

Fact #172. Edward S. Godfrey (1st Lt., commanding Co. K at LBH) served in all four major Indian Wars battles which made the 7th Cavalry so famous in the Indian-fighting Army: the Washita in 1868, the Little Big Horn in 1876, Bear Paw Mountain in 1877, and Wounded Knee (SD) in 1890.

Fact #173. Daniel Newell (Pvt., Co. M, 29 at LBH), a blacksmith, was born in Ireland, one of 13 children. WIA.

Fact #174. The officers of Co. L, 7th Cavalry, in June 1876, included Capt. M.V. Sheridan, detached service; 1st Lt. C. Braden, sick leave; 2d Lt. E.P. Eckerson, detached service; 2d Lt. J.J. Crittenden, attached from 20th Infantry, killed. Replacements: 1st Lt. E.S. Godfrey, 2d Lt. L.S. McCormick.

Fact #175. Seventh Cavalry soldier Frank E. Noyes enlisted as Frank E. Varden (1st Sgt., Co. I).

Fact #176. Only one soldier from Spain served in the 7th Cavalry at LBH: Pvt. George Horn (Co. D), who fought at the Reno-Benteen position.

Fact #177. From Capt. Thomas Weir's position on "Weir Point," nearly a mile and a half northeast of the Reno-Benteen position, after midday on June 25, the Co. D commander saw action several miles beyond where Indians were moving about on the field and appeared to be shooting at something on the ground. Because of the distance, nothing else was distinguishable.

Fact #178. Boston Custer, 27, George Custer's younger brother, was a quartermaster employee assigned to the pack train on June 25, 1876. He left the pack train and joined Custer's headquarters command on the way to Last Stand Hill.

Fact #179. Isaiah Dorman (civilian Negro interpreter, age unknown), employed from May 15, 1876, by the 7th Cavalry Quartermaster, was killed in the valley fight June 25 but was not listed among the dead in the *Bismarck [D.T.] Tribune Extra* July 6, 1876. He is listed only as Isaiah on the battle monument.

Fact #180. Seventh Cavalry soldier Thomas Dean enlisted as Thomas F. O'Neill (Pvt., Co. G).

Fact #181. Frederick Deetline (blacksmith, Co. D, 30 at LBH) was an illiterate laborer, born in Germany.

Fact #182. Luther Rector Hare (2d Lt., Co. K, 24 at LBH) was born in Indiana.

Fact #183. By June 26, the men of Reno's command atop the bluffs were suffering desperately from lack of water; Pvt. Jacob Adams (Co. H) wrote later: ". . .the sun beat down on us and we became so thirsty that it was almost impossible to swallow."

Fact #184. George Edwin Lord (Asst. Surgeon, HQs, 30 at LBH) was "suffering from an indisposition" on June 25 and received a suggestion from Custer to "remain with the force to the rear." Dr. Lord insisted on going with the regimental staff and was killed with Custer's command.

Fact #185. Seventh Cavalry soldier Joseph C. Murphy enlisted as Joseph Bates (Pvt., Co. M).

Fact #186. Frank Neely (Pvt., Co. M, 26 at LBH), a painter, was born in Ohio.

Fact #187. George D. Scott (Pvt., Co. D, 25 at LBH), a farmer, was born in Kentucky.

Fact #188. Felix Villiet Vinatieri (Chief Musician, HQs, 42 on June 25, 1876) was born in Turin, Italy, and graduated from music school at the University of Naples.

Fact #189. The officers of Co. I, 7th Cavalry, in June 1876, included Capt. M.W. Keogh, killed; 1st Lt. J.E. Porter, killed; 2d Lt. A.H. Nave, sick leave. Replacements: Capt. H.J. Nowland; 1st Lt. L.R. Hare; 2d Lt. G.F. Chase, transferred; 2d Lt. H.L. Scott.

Fact #190. Seventh Cavalry soldier William A. Adams enlisted as William Teeman (Cpl., Co. F).

Fact #191. While Capt. Frederick W. Benteen has been criticized by many students of LBH for not proceeding with all haste to "bring packs" which Custer requested, some say that when Benteen joined with Maj. Marcus Reno's battalion, Reno, the ranking officer, was then in command of all seven companies (including the pack train escort), and he was in control of the decision whether or not to proceed to Custer. A sortie was thrown forward to Weir Point, but was driven back by advancing warriors and besieged at the Reno-Benteen position. Bringing the packs to Custer was not practicable.

Fact #192. There is some confusion about the birthdate of Marcus A. Reno: Kenneth Hammer, in his book *Men With Custer: Biographies of the 7th Cavalry* (edited by Ronald H. Nichols), suggests the year is "about 1832," and Reno's file in the National Archives indicates the same. However, John Upton Terrell, in *Faint the Trumpet Sounds*, gives the date as November 15, 1834, which date was confirmed by census records and by Maj. Reno's grand-nephew, the late Charles Reno.

Fact #193. George Lorentz (Pvt., Co. M) (also Lawrence, Lawerence) was killed in the valley fight, shouting "Oh, My God, I've got it," as he fell from his horse, after being struck in the back of the neck by a bullet which came out through his mouth; this occurred during the retreat from the timber on the afternoon of June 25.

Fact #194. George B. Herendeen (scout for Gibbon's column, attached to Custer's column, then Reno's command; 29 at LBH) was born in Ohio.

Fact #195. Seventh Cavalry soldier John Cassella enlisted as John James (Pvt., Co. E).

Fact #196. Only one soldier from Wales served in the 7th Cavalry at LBH: Sgt. William B. James (Co. E), who died with Custer.

Fact #197. Seventh Cavalry soldier Michael Vetter enlisted as Johann Vetter (Pvt., Co. L).

Fact #198. Thomas F. O'Neill (Pvt., Co. G), born in Ireland, was 30 at LBH.

Fact #199. William C. Slaper (Pvt., Co. M, 21 at LBH), a safemaker, was born in Cincinnati (OH) where he enlisted September 1875.

Fact #200. Seventh Cavalry soldier Aini Chreer enlisted as Ami Cheever (Pvt., Co. L).

Fact #201. J.C. Wagoner (Chief Packer, about 40 at LBH) was employed as Chief Packer for the Sioux Expedition pack train March 1876 by the 7th Cavalry Quartermaster at a pay of $100 a month. WIA.

Fact #202. Maj. Marcus A. Reno survived the 1879 Court of Inquiry in Chicago (IL) that he had requested, without blame.

Fact #203. In Peter Thompson's narrative, published in 1913-1914 as "The Experience of a Private Soldier in the Custer Massacre," the private from Co. C recalled the Officers' Call held shortly after Custer ascended the Crow's Nest, hoping to see the Indian village which his scouts had spied some 15 miles away at the Little Big Horn River. This gathering, Thompson said, ". . .gave me the opportunity of seeing the officers all together and noting their appearances. The most noticeable among them was Captain [Frederick] Benteen. He was a senior captain of the regiment. . ."

Fact #204. "There were also present [Capt. George W.] Yates, [Maj. Marcus] Reno, [Capt. Thomas] Custer, [Capt. Thomas McDougall] McDugal, [1st Lt. Algernon] Smith, [Capt. Thomas Weir] Ware, [Capt. Thomas] French, [Capt. Myles Moylan] Moline, Lieut. [W.W. Cooke] Cook. . .[1st Lt. James] Calhoun, [1st Lt. Donald McIntosh] MacIntosh, [2d Lt. Charles] Varnum," and others (at the Officers' Call held shortly after Custer ascended the Crow's Nest). (Pvt. Thompson in his published narrative)

Fact #205. Seventh Cavalry soldier John F. Duggan enlisted as John L. Crowley (Pvt., Co. L).

Fact #206. Winfield Scott Edgerly, 2d Lt., Co. D, 7th Cavalry, Dakota Column, was appointed to the U.S. Military Academy from New Hampshire. He retired as a Brigadier General in 1909, and died September 10, 1927, in Framingham (NH).

Fact #207. Only one soldier from South Wales served in the 7th Cavalry on June 25, 1876: Pvt. Thomas P. Herbert (Co. I) was on detached service from May 17, 1876, with the Quartermaster Dept.

Fact #208. Officers' Call was held after Custer had descended from the Crow's Nest on the morning of June 25, 1876, when his scouts had pointed out to him the large Indian village 15 miles away on the banks of the Little Big Horn. Peter Thompson (Pvt., Co. C), in his "The Experience of a Private Soldier in the Custer Massacre," listed the officers present: "[2d Lt. George] Wallace, [2d Lt. Henry Harington] Harrington, [2d Lt. Winfield S. Edgerly] Agerly, [2d Lt. James G.] Sturgis," and others, plus "other officers whose names I have entirely forgotten. It would be difficult to find a finer set of officers in the service of any country."

Fact #209. Co. H, assigned to Benteen's battalion, consisted of two officers and 45 enlisted men.

Fact #210. James Calhoun (1st Lt., Co. C, 30 at LBH) was married to Margaret Emma Custer, sister of George and Thomas Custer. KIA.

Fact #211. Seventh Cavalry soldier Henry Barton enlisted as Albert Pilcher (Pvt., Co. F).

Fact #212. Theodore Goldin, quoted in *Troopers With Custer* by E.A. Brininstool, said, of the water carriers' foray to the river and back with water for the wounded, "We all made the rush to safety, save little Campbell [5'5½] of G troop, who went down with a ball in the shoulder, just a few feet from the shelter of the ravine. One or two of the men halted and turned back to his assistance, but he pluckily called out, 'Go on, boys; I can make it back some way.'" And he did, living until 1906, but he was not among the recipients of the Medal of Honor awarded to those who participated in the water carriers' effort.

Fact #213. Richard P. Hanley (Sgt., Co. C, 32 at LBH) was born in Boston (MA) and signed his fifth enlistment in 1873 in Cincinnati (OH).

Fact #214. Pvt. William M. Harris (Co. D) was one of a number of volunteers who earned a Medal of Honor for fetching water for the wounded at the Reno-Benteen site by going down Water Carriers' Ravine to the Little Big Horn River on June 26, 1876.

Fact #215. Patrick McDonnell (Pvt., Co. D, 24 at LBH), a laborer, born in Ireland, enlisted November 1872 in Pittsburgh (PA). WIA.

Lieutenant George Wallace

USAMHI

Fact #216. Seventh Cavalry soldier George W. Glease enlisted as George W. Glenn (Pvt., Co. H).

Fact #217. Otto Durselew (Pvt., Co. A) was also listed as Derslow, Derslew, Dinnlen, Durselow, Dunselen, Denslow, Dressles.

Fact #218. Lt. Charles DeRudio (Co. A), who was considered by Custer to be "the inferior of every first lieutenant in this Regt.," had fought in Garibaldi's rebellion in Italy and was a self-confessed assassin.

Fact #219. Soon after "Officers' Call" on June 22, Lt. George Wallace, "who was inclined to be superstitious," told Lts. Godfrey and McIntosh, ". . .Custer is going to be killed on this trip. ...He acts, talks, and looks like it, and mark my words, he will be killed." (Published account of Lt. W.S. Edgerly, Co. D, shortly after the battle)

Fact #220. Henry James Nowland (Nolan, Nowlan), 1st Lt., Regimental Quartermaster, 7th Cavalry, Dakota Column, was born in Corfu (Ionian Islands).

Fact #221. Seventh Cavalry soldier John Hiley enlisted as John Stuart Stuart Forbes (Pvt., Co. E).

Fact #222. 1st Lt. Charles Braden, Co. L, 7th Cavalry, was absent on June 25, 1876; sick leave.

Fact #223. Company H, 7th Cavalry, assigned to Benteen's battalion on June 25, 1876, was commanded by Capt. Frederick Benteen and 1st Lt. Francis M. Gibson.

Fact #224. Anthony Assadaly (Pvt., Co. L, 34 at LBH) was born in Prussia. KIA.

Fact #225. Henry Cody (Cpl., Co. M, 24 at LBH), a painter, was born in New Hampshire. KIA.

Fact #226. Seventh Cavalry soldier Roman Ruttenauer enlisted as Roman Rutten (Pvt., Co. M).

Fact #227. Pvt. James Pym (Co. B) was one of the volunteers who earned a Medal of Honor for fetching water for the wounded at the Reno-Benteen site by going down Water Carriers' Ravine to the Little Big Horn River on June 26, 1876.

Fact #228. Henry Holden (Pvt., Co. D, 37 [or 40] at LBH) was born in London, England.

Fact #229. William Teeman (Cpl., Co. F, 29 at LBH), a laborer, born in Denmark, enlisted September 1867 in Pittsburgh (PA). KIA.

Fact #230. Seventh Cavalry soldier Louis Braun enlisted as Aloys Bohner (Trumpeter, Co. D).

Fact #231. White Man Runs Him (Pvt., Detachment of Indian Scouts, about 18 at LBH) was also named Crow Who Talks Gros Ventre.

Fact #232. William Van Wyck Reily (22 at LBH), 2d Lt., Co. E, 7th Cavalry (temporarily assigned Co. F, 7th Cavalry), Dakota Column, was assigned to the 7th Cavalry January 1876. KIA.

Fact #233. 1st Lt. William Thomas Craycroft, Co. B, 7th Cavalry, was absent on June 25, 1876, serving as a Member of the Board for purchasing horses, April-September 1876.

Fact #234. Co. M, assigned to Reno's battalion, consisted of one officer and 57 enlisted men.

Fact #235. Seventh Cavalry soldier Frank Howard enlisted as Morris H. Thompson (Pvt., Co. E).

Fact #236. Co. C, assigned to Custer's battalion, consisted of two officers and 50 enlisted men. All with Custer perished in the battle.

Fact #237. David Cooney (Pvt., Co. I, 28 at LBH), a laborer, born in Ireland, enlisted December 1872 in Boston (MA), was wounded at the Reno-Benteen site June 26 and died of wounds at Fort Abraham Lincoln.

Fact #238. Francis Marion Gibson (1st Lt., Co. H, 28 at LBH) was born in Philadelphia (PA).

Fact #239. Seventh Cavalry soldier Felix Villiet enlisted as Felix Vinatieri (Chief Musician, Staff).

Fact #240. Jacob Horner (Pvt., Co. K), who was on detached service at the Yellowstone Depot from June 15, 1876, was the last surviving member of the 7th Cavalry regiment who participated in the Sioux Expedition of 1876 from May 17, 1876, when Gen. Alfred Terry's column marched out of Fort Abraham Lincoln (D.T.). Horner died in Bismarck (ND) in 1951.

Fact #241. Alexander McPeake (Pvt., Co. L, 26 at LBH), a teamster, was born in Pennsylvania, the youngest of seven brothers and two sisters.

Captain George W. Yates

USAMHI

Fact #242. Col. Samuel D. Sturgis became the second commanding officer of the 7th U.S. Cavalry Regiment in 1869, succeeding Col. Andrew J. Smith, the original commander in 1866. Active command of the regiment from the outset was the duty and responsibility of Lt. Col. George A. Custer.

Fact #243. Seventh Cavalry soldier Heinrich (or Henry) Klein enlisted as Gustav Klein (Pvt., Co. F).

Fact #244. Capt. George W. Yates (33 at LBH) was born in New York. He commanded Co. F and was killed June 25, 1876, with the Custer column.

Fact #245. The 7th Cavalry had fewer foreign immigrants than many of the frontier regiments. Most of the officers were seasoned Civil War soldiers, though the rank and file had little or no combat experience. For many of them, their first battle would be their last battle.

Fact #246. The 7th Cavalry at LBH had two soldiers each from Hungary, Norway, Poland, Saxony, Silesia, and Sweden.

Fact #247. 2d Lt. Charles William Larned, Co. F, 7th Cavalry, was absent on June 25, 1876; on detached service at West Point.

Fact #248. Seventh Cavalry soldier Charles Chesterwood enlisted as John C. Creighton (Pvt., Co. K).

Fact #249. James Butler was the 1st Sgt. of L Co., assigned to Custer's battalion.

Fact #250. William White, who was with Gibbon's Montana Column which discovered the bodies of Custer and his men on June 27, 1876, began offering a "guide service" at Custer Battlefield in 1937.

Fact #251. Thomas P. Eagan (Cpl., Co. E, 23 at LBH), a laborer, was born in Ireland. KIA.

Fact #252. William George (Pvt., Co. H, 29 at LBH), a laborer, was born in Kentucky and signed his second enlistment May 1875 in New Orleans (LA); wounded at the Reno-Benteen position and died of the wounds aboard the steamer *Far West*.

Fact #253. Seventh Cavalry soldier Francesco Lombardy enlisted as Frank K. Lombard (Pvt., Band).

Fact #254. Pvt. Thos. W. Stivers (Co. D) was one of a number of volunteers who earned a Medal of Honor for fetching water for the wounded at the Reno-Benteen site by going down Water Carriers' Ravine to the Little Big Horn River on June 26, 1876.

Fact #255. Fearing discovery by two Indian horse hunters on the east side of the divide between the Rosebud and the Little Big Horn, Chief of Scouts Charles Varnum, with interpreter Mitch Boyer, scout Charley Reynolds, and two Crows "started off dismounted to [kill the Indians]. After, perhaps, a half mile of hard work through very broken country, where we could see nothing I heard a call like a crow cawing from the hill and we halted," he wrote historian Walter Camp in 1909, recalling the events. "Our two Crows repeated the immitation [sic] but you could easily see they were talking or signaling and we started back. I asked Boyer what was the matter but he did not know. On our return we learned that the Sioux had changed their course away from the pass but soon after our return they changed again and crossed the ridge."

Fact #256. Civilian correspondent Mark Kellogg sent his last published dispatch to the *New York Herald*: "A new campaign is to be organized...and tomorrow, June 22, General Custer with twelve cavalry companies, will scout from its mouth [south] up the valley of the Rosebud until he reaches the fresh trail discovered by Major Reno...move on that trail with all rapidity...in order to overhaul the Indians, whom it has been ascertained are hunting buffalo and making daily and leisurely short marches. In the meantime, General Terry will move on the steamer [*Far West*] to the mouth of the Big Horn River... This part of the command marches [south] up the Big Horn valley to intercept the Indians if they should attempt to escape from General Custer down that avenue."

Fact #257. George H. King (Cpl., Co. A, 27 at LBH) served with Reno; died of wounds aboard the *Far West*; not listed on monument.

Fact #258. Seventh Cavalry soldier William Irvine enlisted as William McClurg (Pvt., Co. A).

Fact #259. John Meadwell (Pvt., Co. D, age 21), born in Pennsylvania, was on detached service on June 25, 1876.

Fact #260. Only one soldier from Australia fought with the 7th Cavalry at LBH: Pvt. Morris Farmer (Co. C) straggled from the Custer battalions and fought at the Reno-Benteen position.

Fact #261. The officers of Co. A, 7th Cavalry, in June 1876 included Capt. Myles Moylan, commanding; 1st Lt. A.E. Smith, killed while commanding Co. E; 2d Lt. C.A. Varnum, commanding Detachment of Indian Scouts. Replacements: 1st Lt. A.H. Nave; 2d Lt. E.B. Fuller.

Fact #262. The commander of the 7th U.S. Cavalry in 1876 was Col. Samuel Sturgis, but he was assigned to "detached duty" in St. Louis (MO) and did not serve on the frontier. The field commander, in charge at Fort Abraham Lincoln (D.T.), was Lt. Col. (Bvt. Maj. Gen.) George Armstrong Custer.

Fact #263. Seventh Cavalry soldier Fred Streing enlisted as Fred Stressinger (Cpl., Co. M).

Fact #264. Edward Settle Godfrey (32 at LBH) enlisted as a private during the Civil War, attended the U.S. Military Academy 1863-1867 (appointed from Ohio), and was posted to the 7th U.S. Cavalry where he was 1st Lt. of Co. K, Dakota Column, at the time of the battle June 25, 1876.

Fact #265. The largest contingent of immigrant soldiers in the 7th Cavalry on June 25, 1876, was from Ireland (136). Germany was second with 98, but if you add in Bavaria (14), Prussia (8), Saxony and Silesia (2 each), all of which are part of Germany today, the total of Deutschland soldiers is 124. England was third with 41. Only Canada (20) and Scotland (11), of the English-speaking nations, also reached double-digits, as did Switzerland (12).

Fact #266. Lewis Merrill, Maj., 7th Cavalry, was absent on June 25, 1876; on detached service in Philadelphia (PA).

Fact #267. Capt. Frederick W. Benteen, at LBH, was placed in command of a three-company battalion consisting of Cos. D, H, and K, after Custer divided the entire regimental command on June 25, 1876.

Fact #268. Seventh Cavalry soldier Erastus Grover Brown enlisted as Hiram Erastus Brown (Pvt., Co. F).

Fact #269. Co. F, assigned to Custer's battalion, consisted of two officers and 51 enlisted men. All with Custer perished in the battle.

Fact #270. John Dolan (Pvt., Co. M, 33 at LBH), a machinist, was born in Ireland. His account of the Little Big Horn River fight was published July 23, 1876, in the *New York Herald*.

Fact #271. Charles L. Haack (Pvt., Co. I, 54 on June 25, 1876), born in Germany, enlisted in the 7th Cavalry Band 1874 and was sick in the hospital at Fort Abraham Lincoln (D.T.) from May 17, 1876.

Fact #272. "We were not very well entrenched," Pvt. William C. Slaper (Co. M) wrote after the battle, "as I recall that I used my butcher knife to cut the earth loose and throw a mound of it in front of me upon which to rest my carbine. . .a bullet struck the corner of this mound, throwing so much dirt in my eyes that I could scarcely see for an hour or more. . .while lying face down on the ground, a bullet tore off the heel of my left boot as effectively as though it had been sawed off." Pvt. Slaper was in Capt. Thomas French's company at the Reno-Benteen site, at the south salient on the second day, June 26.

Fact #273. Seventh Cavalry soldier Thomas Hagan enlisted as Thomas P. Eagan (Cpl., Co. E).

Fact #274. Fearing discovery by a couple of small bands of Sioux in the vicinity of Custer's column as it resumed the march on the morning of June 25, Custer's Chief of Scouts Charles Varnum (2d Lt., Co. A) rode down to report to the oncoming column. As he wrote historian Walter Camp in 1909, "The command came in vision about this time and we watched it approach the gap where it halted. I rode down towards the column & soon met the Genl. He said, 'Well, you've had a night of it.' I said yes, but I was still able to sit up & notice things. [Capt.] Tom Custer and [Lt. James] Calhoun then came up to us & Custer was angry at their leaving the column & ordered them back. I told the Genl. all I had seen [about the scouting parties], as we rode back towards the Crow['s] nest hill and we climbed the hill together. Custer listened to Boyer while he gazed long and hard at the valley."

Fact #275. Daniel Alexander Kanipe (Sgt., Co. C, 23 at LBH), a farmer, was born in North Carolina (his family name was Knipe).

Fact #276. During a 26 year career with the 7th Cavalry, Capt. Myles Moylan (Co. A) saw service in Kansas, Kentucky, Dakota and Montana Territories, and Oklahoma. He retired on his own application after 35 years of service to the Army.

Fact #277. Frank Tolan (Pvt., Co. D, 22 at LBH), a farmer, enlisted August 1875 in Boston (MA).

Fact #278. Seventh Cavalry soldier Thomas Morton enlisted as Thomas E. Rush (Sgt., Co. D).

Fact #279. The officers of Co. C, 7th Cavalry, in June 1876 included Capt. T.W. Custer, killed; 1st Lt. J. Calhoun, killed while commanding Co. L; 2d Lt. H.M. Harington, killed. Replacements: Capt. H. Jackson; 1st Lt. C.A. Varnum; 2d Lt. G.O. Eaton, transferred; 2d Lt. H.G. Sickel.

Fact #280. Luther Rector Hare (24 at LBH) was appointed to the U.S. Military Academy from Texas (although born in Indiana); posted to the 7th Cavalry in 1874; 2d Lt., Co. K, Dakota Column, at the Little Big Horn.

Fact #281. One hundred and five of the 378 immigrant soldiers and civilians in the 7th Cavalry on June 25, 1876, were killed at LBH. Two more died as the result of wounds from the Battle, a 28.8% mortality rate.

Fact #282. Andrew Humes Nave, 2d Lt., Co. I, 7th Cavalry, was absent on June 25, 1876; sick leave since July 1874.

Fact #283. Seventh Cavalry soldier Christopher Pandtle enlisted as Christopher Pendle (Pvt., Co. E).

Fact #284. John M. Ryan was the 1st Sgt. of Co. M, assigned to Reno's battalion.

Fact #285. Co. L, assigned to Custer's battalion, consisted of two officers and 57 enlisted men. All with Custer perished in battle.

Fact #286. James Butler (1st Sgt., Co. L, 34 at LBH) was born in New York; rode with the Custer column and was killed up the ravine from Minneconjou Ford.

Fact #287. David E. Dawsey (Pvt., Co. D, 24 at LBH), a farmer, was born in Belleville (OH).

Fact #288. Seventh Cavalry soldier Edward Dellienhousen enlisted as Edward Housen (Pvt., Co. D).

Fact #289. George W. Hammon (Pvt., Co. F, 23 at LBH), a farmer, enlisted September 1873 in Cincinnati (OH). KIA.

Fact #290. Alfred Howe Terry, a lawyer, began his military career in May 1861 as Colonel of the 2d Connecticut Infantry, and decided to stay in service after the Civil War; he was granted a brigadier general's star. The Sioux Expedition of 1876 was the only noteworthy event in his post-Civil War career. As the commander of the Dakota Column and the entire expedition, his was the ultimate responsibility for the Army's disaster at the Little Big Horn.

Fact #291. The largest contingent of the 487 American soldiers and civilians in the 7th Cavalry on June 25, 1876, was from New York (98) with Pennsylvania (80) second and Ohio (61) third.

Fact #292. Robert H. Hughes (Sgt., Co. K, 35 at LBH), born in Ireland, carried Custer's battle flag and was killed on Custer Hill June 25, 1876.

Fact #293. Seventh Cavalry soldier Archibald McEllarge enlisted as Archibald McIlhargey (Pvt., Co. I).

Fact #294. James J. Tanner (Pvt., Co. M, 26 at LBH) enlisted September 1875 in Chicago (IL), wounded at the Reno-Benteen position, and died in the field hospital June 26.

Fact #295. The officers of Co. E, 7th Cavalry, in June 1876, included Capt. C.S. Ilsley, detached service; 1st Lt. C.C. DeRudio with Co. A; 2d Lt. W.V.W. Reily, killed with Co. F.

Fact #296. Only 22 of the 487 "American" soldiers serving in or with the 7th Cavalry at LBH were from states in the Old Confederacy: Georgia (2), Louisiana (2), North Carolina (3), South Carolina (3), Tennessee (2), Texas (1), and Virginia (9). Adding soldiers from the Civil War "border states"—Kentucky (20), Maryland (15), Missouri (13), and West Virginia (2)—you get another 50 potential Johnny Rebs, just 72 out of 487.

Fact #297. Minton (Mitch) Bouyer (Boyer), interpreter; born 1837, place of birth unknown; half-blood Crow attached to 7th Cavalry from 2d Cavalry on June 22, 1876; with Lt. Varnum on trip to Crow's Nest; killed June 25, 1876, at age 39.

This view looks east, with the Little Big Horn river in the foreground. Marcus Reno's command retreated from the floor of the valley over the rough terrain to the series of ridges beyond. *USAMHI*

Fact #298. Seventh Cavalry soldier Eugene L. Cooper enlisted as George C. Morris (Cpl., Co. I).

Fact #299. Only one soldier from California served with the 7th Cavalry on June 25, 1876: Pvt. Jesse Kuehl (or Kuchl) (Co. D), on detached service from June 16, 1876, at Yellowstone Depot (M.T.).

Fact #300. Company C, 7th Cavalry, assigned to Custer's battalion, was commanded by Capt. Thomas W. Custer and 2d Lt. Henry Harington.

Fact #301. James H. Alberts, aka James M. Albert (Pvt., Co. D, 28 at LBH), was a farmer and enlisted in the 7th Cavalry in September 1875 in St. Louis (MO).

Fact #302. Dr. James M. DeWolf (Acting Asst. Surgeon, HQs) was assigned to 7th U.S. Cavalry June 21, 1876, and was killed on the bluffs during the retreat from the valley fight, June 25, 1876, with one gunshot wound through the abdomen and six wounds in the head and face.

Fact #303. Seventh Cavalry soldier J.R. Meadville enlisted as John Meadwell (Pvt., Co. D); killed in Nez Perce War in 1877.

Fact #304. Edward Davern (Pvt., Co. F) was Maj. Reno's orderly on June 25, 1876. Lt. Godfrey (Co. K) later reported that "During the retreat [to the bluffs], Private Dalvern [sic] troop 'F' had a hand-to-hand conflict with an Indian, his horse was killed; he then shot the Indian, caught the indian's pony, and rode to the command." According to Walter Camp's letter of October 26, 1908, to John Ryan, Davern denied the story.

Fact #305. James Flanagan (Sgt., Co. D, 37 at LBH) was born in Ireland.

Fact #306. Marcus Henry Kellogg (civilian correspondent, attached to Co. C, 43 at LBH), was a reporter for the *Bismarck [D.T.] Tribune* who accompanied Custer's column despite Gen. Philip Sheridan's directive against journalists. He was killed down near the river from Custer Hill.

Fact #307. Elijah T. Strode (Pvt., Co. A, 25 at LBH), a farmer, was born in Kentucky and enlisted there in October 1872. WIA.

Fact #308. Seventh Cavalryman George P. Weldon enlisted as George P. Walker (Pvt., Co. E).

Fact #309. The officers of Co. K, 7th Cavalry, in June 1876, included Capt. Owen Hale, detached service; 1st Lt. E.S. Godfrey, commanding; 2d Lt. L.R. Hare, with detachment of Indian Scouts. Replacements: 1st Lt. C. Braden; 2d Lt. E.P. Andrus, transferred; 2d Lt. J.W. Biddle.

Fact #310. Benjamin Hubert Hodgson, 2d Lt., Co. B, 7th Cavalry, battalion adjutant to Maj. Reno at LBH; graduated from the U.S. Military Academy at West Point in 1870, having been appointed from Pennsylvania; killed June 25, 1876, while crossing Little Big Horn River during the Reno retreat, five days before his 28th birthday.

Fact #311. Boston Custer, brother to George and Tom Custer, was hired by the 7th Cavalry Quartermaster on the order of the regimental commander as a civilian guide for the Sioux expedition. He was with the pack train but joined the Custer column near Little Big Horn River and was killed June 25, 1876, at age 27.

Fact #312. Of the 487 American soldiers and civilians at LBH, 155 of them died in action, and another four died soon thereafter from wounds suffered in the Battle, a 31.8% mortality rate. (The 15 "birthplace unknowns" are assumed to be Americans, white or Indian. . .)

Fact #313. Seventh Cavalry soldier John Burke enlisted as Oscar F. Pardee (Pvt., Co. L).

Fact #314. Frank Braun (Pvt., Co. M, 28 at LBH), a laborer, was born in Switzerland; enlisted in September 1875 in Louisville (KY). WIA.

Fact #315. Mary Hannah Ross married Marcus A. Reno in 1863; he later was assigned to the 7th U.S. Cavalry and commanded two battalions during LBH.

Fact #316. Tom Custer, George's brother, served most of the Civil War as an enlisted man. He was killed at LBH on Last Stand Hill.

Fact #317. Max Mielke (Pvt., Co. K, 30 at LBH) was born in Germany. WIA.

Fact #318. Seventh Cavalry soldier Giovanni Martini enlisted as John Martin (Trumpeter, Co. H).

Colonel John Gibbon

Generals in Blue

Fact #319. The officers of Co. G, 7th Cavalry, in June 1876, included Capt. J. Tourtellotte, detached service; 1st Lt. D. McIntosh, killed; 2d Lt. G.D. Wallace. Replacements: 1st Lt. E.A. Garlington; 2d Lt. J.W. Wilkinson.

Fact #320. "The conduct of this gallant veteran [Col. John Gibbon, commander of the Montana Column] during the [1876] Sioux campaign would prove strangely unaggressive—and at times simply enigmatic." (Sarf, *The Little Bighorn Campaign*)

Fact #321. James Ezekiel Porter (1st Lt., Co. I, 29 at LBH) was appointed to U.S. Military Academy at West Point from Maine and graduated 1869. KIA.

Fact #322. Dr. James Madison DeWolf, acting assistant surgeon, was a contract surgeon holding no military rank. KIA.

Fact #323. Seventh Cavalry soldier Maurice Cain enlisted as Morris Cain (Pvt., Co. M).

Fact #324. Joseph Greene Tilford, Maj., 7th Cavalry, was on leave of absence on June 25, 1876.

Fact #325. James Montgomery Bell, 1st Lt., Co. D, 7th Cavalry, on June 25, 1876, was absent on six months' leave since March 1876.

Fact #326. Co. D, 7th Cavalry, assigned to Benteen's battalion, was commanded by Capt. Thomas B. Weir and 2d Lt. Winfield Scott Edgerly.

Fact #327. Ferdinand A. Culbertson (Sgt., Co. A, 30 at LBH), a clerk, was born in Pittsburgh (PA).

Fact #328. Theodore Goldin (Golden) was awarded the Medal of Honor, upon his own application, for valor in bringing water to the wounded at the Reno-Benteen site. He wrote extensively in later years on his participation at the Battle of the Little Big Horn.

Fact #329. Seventh Cavalry soldier Charles Hughes enlisted as Thomas Hughes (Pvt., Co. H).

Fact #330. Describing the counterattack he led on the morning of June 26, 1876, to defend the southeasternmost tip of the defensive line, Capt. Frederick Benteen later wrote: ". . .when the throttles of the 'H sters' were given full play, and we dashed into the unsuspecting savages. . .they somersaulted and vaulted as so many trained acrobats, having no order in getting down those ravines, but quickly letting the de'il take the hindmost."

Fact #331. The first field expedition of the 7th Cavalry Regiment, after its establishment at Fort Riley (KS) in July 1866, was aimed at clearing the central and southern areas of the Western plains of marauding Indians. Gen. Winfield Scott Hancock, known as "Hancock the Superb" from his service at the Battle of Gettysburg, came from department headquarters in St. Louis (MO) to head up the expedition.

Fact #332. Algernon Emory Smith (1st Lt., Co. A, 33 at LBH) commanded Co. E at LBH and was killed June 25, 1876, with the Custer column.

Fact #333. The 7th Cavalry Headquarters/Staff personnel in June 1876 included: Col. Samuel D. Sturgis, detached duty at St. Louis (MO); Lt. Col. G.A. Custer, killed while commanding in the field, replaced by Lt. Col. Elmer Otis; Maj. J.G. Tilford, leave of absence; Maj. Lewis Merrill, detached service; Maj. M.A. Reno, commanding Cos. A, G, and M; 1st Lt. W.W. Cooke, Adjutant, killed, replaced by Lt. G.D. Wallace; 1st Lt. H.G. Nowland, Quartermaster, on detached service with expedition; Mr. C.A. Stein, Veterinary Surgeon, detached service at Yellowstone Depot (M.T.).

Fact #334. Seventh Cavalry soldier Francis Johnson enlisted as Francis Johnson Kennedy (Pvt., Co. I).

Fact #335. Marcus Albert Reno, Maj. (Bvt. Brig. Gen. [Volunteers]), 7th Cavalry, Dakota Column, was appointed to the U.S. Military Academy from Illinois, graduated 1857; served with distinction in the Civil War.

Fact #336. Only one soldier from Delaware fought with the 7th Cavalry at the Little Big Horn: Cpl. George C. Morris (or Eugene L. Cooper) (Co. I) died with Custer's command.

Captain Thomas M. McDougall

Fact #337. Co. L, 7th Cavalry, assigned to Custer's battalion, was commanded by 1st Lt. James Calhoun and 2d Lt. John Crittenden.

Fact #338. Patrick M. Golden (Pvt., Co. D, 26 at LBH), a slater, was born in Ireland and enlisted January 1872 in Boston (MA). KIA.

Fact #339. Seventh Cavalry soldier John Vickory enlisted as John Groesbeck (Sgt., Co. F).

Fact #340. Thomas Mower McDougall, the son of Bvt. Brig. Gen. Charles McDougall of the Medical Corps, on the march to the Little Big Horn commanded Co. B, the pack train escort, and was engaged in the fighting at the Reno-Benteen position.

Fact #341. James Severs (Pvt., Co. M, 25 at LBH), a teamster, was born in New York and enlisted November 1872 in Chicago (IL).

Fact #342. Charles White (Sgt., Co. M, 29 at LBH), a farmer, was born in Saxony (Germany).

Fact #343. Casualties during Reno's retreat to the bluffs following his late morning attack on the village on June 25 included three officers and 29 enlisted men and scouts killed, seven enlisted men wounded, and one officer, one interpreter, and 14 enlisted men and scouts missing.

Fact #344. Seventh Cavalry soldier Charles Answorth enlisted as Thomas Sherborne (Pvt., Band).

Fact #345. As Maj. Reno remounted in the trees, and ordered the retreat back across the stream, Lt. Charles C. DeRudio (Co. E) lost his horse. With Indians all around him, DeRudio darted into the trees where he was joined by quartermaster Frederick Girard, Indian scout William Jackson, and Pvt. Thomas O'Neill (Co. G). They had several narrow escapes but finally rejoined the troops at the Reno-Benteen position on the morning of June 27.

Fact #346. Frederick [Frederic] F. Gerard [Girard] was a civilian interpreter for the Arikara and Sioux Indian scouts.

Fact #347. Edwin Philip Eckerson, 2d Lt., Co. L, 7th Cavalry, was absent on June 25, 1876; appointed May 2, 1876, had not yet reported.

Fact #348. Owen Hale, Capt., Co. K, 7th Cavalry, was absent on June 25, 1876; detached service at St. Louis (MO).

Fact #349. Company F, 7th Cavalry, assigned to Custer's battalion, was commanded by Capt. George W. Yates and 2d Lt. William V.W. Reily.

Fact #350. Seventh Cavalry soldier John Gorham enlisted as John E. Quinn (Pvt., Co. D).

Fact #351. Michael Martin was the 1st Sgt. of D Co., assigned to Benteen's battalion.

Fact #352. Fred Hohmeyer was the 1st Sgt. of E Co., assigned to Custer's battalion.

Fact #353. Capt. Frederick Benteen (Commanding, Co. H) had Indian Wars experience with the 7th Cavalry prior to the Little Big Horn at the Saline River (KS) August 1868, the Washita River fight, November 1868. He was wounded in the right thumb and contracted malarious dysentery at LBH.

Fact #354. Boston Custer, brother of George and Tom Custer, received a $100 monthly compensation as a civilian guide for the Sioux expedition.

Fact #355. John Frett (packer, age unknown) was employed by the 7th Cavalry Quartermaster in St. Paul (MN) as a civilian packer on the Sioux expedition.

Fact #356. Seventh Cavalry soldier John Sullivan enlisted as Cornelius Cowley (Pvt., Co. A).

Fact #357. Pvt. Frank Tolan (Co. D) was one of the volunteers who earned a Medal of Honor for fetching water for the wounded at the Reno-Benteen site by going down Water Carriers' Ravine to the Little Big Horn River on June 26, 1876.

Fact #358. Jacob Hetler (Pvt., Co. D, 23 at LBH), a carpenter, was born in Ohio and enlisted February 1872 in Chicago (IL). WIA.

Fact #359. Michael Martin (1st Sgt., Co. D, 41 at LBH) enlisted for his second hitch December 1872 in Alabama.

Fact #360. James Ezekiel Porter (1st Lt., Co. I, 29 at LBH) was born in Maine. He was presumed killed with Custer's column on June 25, 1876, although his remains were never identified.

Fact #361. Seventh Cavalry soldier William Evans enlisted as James Frank Barsantee (Pvt., Co. B).

Fact #362. James Henry Russell (Pvt., Co. C, 24 at LBH), was the son of a former Confederate major who was later a Florida state legislator. KIA.

Fact #363. Charles Windolph (Pvt., Co. H, 24 at LBH), a shoemaker, was born in Bergen (Germany). WIA.

Fact #364. During the ordeal of Lt. Charles DeRudio (Co. E), trapped in the timber following the valley fight on June 25, he and several companions observed a scalp dance around the dead body of Lt. Donald McIntosh (Co. G), which could also be seen and heard from the Reno-Benteen position.

Fact #365. Charles Albert Varnum, 2d Lt., Co. A, 7th Cavalry, Dakota Column, commanded the Arikara Indian Scouts Detachment at LBH.

Fact #366. Only one soldier from New Mexico fought with the 7th Cavalry at LBH: 2d Lt. James Garland Sturgis (Co. M, assigned to Co. E in the Battle), the son of Col. Samuel D. Sturgis, the commanding officer of the 7th Cavalry in June 1876, who was serving in the Army in Albuquerque when his son was born in January 1854.

Scout Charley Reynolds

USAMHI

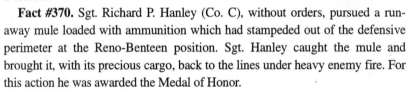

Fact #367. Seventh Cavalry soldier Frank Rankin enlisted as Edward Clyde (Cpl., Co. F).

Fact #368. Charles Stillman Ilsley, Capt., Co. E, 7th Cavalry, was absent on June 25, 1876; aide-de-camp to Gen. Pope since 1868.

Fact #369. Company A, 7th Cavalry, assigned to Reno's battalion on June 25, 1876, was commanded by Capt. Myles Moylan and Lt. Charles C. DeRudio.

Fact #370. Sgt. Richard P. Hanley (Co. C), without orders, pursued a runaway mule loaded with ammunition which had stampeded out of the defensive perimeter at the Reno-Benteen position. Sgt. Hanley caught the mule and brought it, with its precious cargo, back to the lines under heavy enemy fire. For this action he was awarded the Medal of Honor.

Fact #371. George Loyd (Cpl., Co. G, 33 at LBH) was born in Ireland.

Fact #372. Pvt. Neil Bancroft (Co. A) was one of the volunteers who earned a Medal of Honor for fetching water for the wounded at the Reno-Benteen site by going down Water Carriers' Ravine to the Little Big Horn River on June 26, 1876.

Fact #373. Seventh Cavalry soldier Charles White enlisted as Henry Charles Weihe (Sgt., Co. M).

Fact #374. Henry Moore Harington (2d Lt., Co. C, 27 at LBH), born in New York, entered the U.S. Military Academy in 1868 on appointment from Michigan and was the 2,429th graduate of the Academy; missing from the Custer battalion on June 25, 1876, and presumed dead.

Fact #375. Sgt. Stanislaus Roy (Co. A) was one of the volunteers who earned a Medal of Honor for fetching water for the wounded at the Reno-Benteen site by going down Water Carriers' Ravine to the Little Big Horn River on June 26, 1876.

Fact #376. Edward H. Pickard (Pvt., Co. F, 22 at LBH), a clerk, was born in Massachusetts.

Fact #377. Scout Charley Reynolds, riding with the Reno battalion for $100 a month, was shot through the heart in the valley fight as he stopped near Dr. Henry Porter, who was treating a wounded soldier.

Fact #378. Seventh Cavalryman Patrick C. White enlisted as Patrick Connelly (Sgt., Co. H).

Fact #379. George Daniel Wallace (2d Lt., Co. G, four days short of his 27th birthday at LBH) was born in South Carolina.

Fact #380. As Reno's battalion prepared for its attack on the (southern) lower end of the village along the banks of the Little Big Horn, Col. John Gibbon, commander of the Montana Column, lay on board the steamer *Far West*, stricken with illness. Gen. Alfred H. Terry, commander of the Dakota Column and of the entire Sioux Expedition, marched on with the Montana Column toward the confluence of the Big Horn and the Little Big Horn rivers, where they were to meet Custer's 7th Cavalry.

Fact #381. When riding in Custer's column up the bluffs to the east of the river, two of the soldiers assigned to the "four" group of Pvt. Peter Thompson (Co. C), Pvt. John Brennan and Blacksmith John Fitzgerald, also of Co. C, "turned their horses toward the rear, when they had gone two miles beyond the lone tepee," about two miles from the Indian village ahead. The column at this time consisted of companies C, E, F, I and L, probably with F in the lead.

Fact #382. Lt. W.S. Edgerly (Co. D) observed: "When McDougall came up [to the Reno-Benteen position on June 25] with the packs we commenced utilizing them for breastworks. When the first box of hard bread was put down on Benteen's line a man threw himself down behind it very eagerly. He had hardly gotten his head against the box when a bullet came tearing through it, killing the man instantly. Strange as it may sound here, nearly every man who saw this laughed."

Fact #383. Only one soldier from Texas fought with the 7th Cavalry at the Little Big Horn: Pvt. James Henry Russell (Co. C), who died with Custer.

Fact #384. Seventh Cavalryman William J. Woolslayer enlisted as William J. Randall (Pvt., Co. D).

Fact #385. Otto Voit (Saddler, Co. H) was awarded the Medal of Honor October 1878 for bravery in action as a sharpshooter for the water party.

Fact #386. Henry Jackson, 1st Lt., Co. F, 7th Cavalry, was absent on June 25, 1876; on detached service in Washington (DC).

Fact #387. The Indian Scouts Detachment of the 7th Cavalry Regiment, commanded by Lt. Col. George A. Custer, consisted of 2d Lt. Charles A.

Varnum, 2d Lt. Luther R. Hare, two interpreters, five guides (quartermaster employees), and 35 enlisted Indian scouts.

Fact #388. William Heyn was the 1st Sgt. of A Co., assigned to Reno's battalion.

Fact #389. William Slaper in *Troopers With Custer* by E.A. Brininstool noted that "Isaiah Dorman, a negro scout and interpreter, was found with many arrows shot in his body and head, and badly cut and slashed. . ." His body was found about 30 feet from the body of scout Charley Reynolds.

Fact #390. Seventh Cavalry soldier John Desmond enlisted as Michael Reagan (Pvt., Co. K).

Fact #391. The sharpshooters at Water Carriers' Ravine were positioned at the edge of the river bluff, above the mouth of the ravine, and fired their carbines to pin down some of the Indians and draw fire away from the volunteers who were risking their lives to fetch water for the wounded at the Reno-Benteen site on the morning of June 26; they were Sgt. George H. Geiger (Co. H), Pvt. Charles Windolph (Co. H), Saddler Otto Voit (Co. H), and Blacksmith Henry Mechlin (Co. H).

Fact #392. George Lell (Cpl., Co. H, 28 at LBH), a gasfitter, was born in Ohio. KIA.

Fact #393. Private Frank Neely (Co. M) inscribed "F. Neely, Co. M, 7th Cav" on May 28, 1876, on a rock near the camp on Davis Creek while on the Sioux Expedition of 1876.

Fact #394. Arikara Indian scouts referred to Maj. Marcus A. Reno, commanding Cos. A, G, and M on June 25, 1876, as "the man with the dark face," apparently in reference to his dark complexion.

Fact #395. When Pvt. Patrick Golden (Co. D), who had distinguished himself in the first day's fighting at the Reno-Benteen position, asked his sergeant that night if the Indians would be back in the morning, the sergeant said they would probably return around daylight. Golden cried out, "Tom, if they come back, they will kill me," and could not be consoled. When the firing began the next morning, Golden was among the first to be killed.

Fact #396. Seventh Cavalry soldier Michael J. Miller enlisted as James J. Galvan (Pvt., Co. L).

Fact #397. Frederick William Benteen, Capt., Commanding Co. H, 7th U.S. Cavalry, Dakota Column, joined the 7th Cavalry in 1866.

Fact #398. Mark Kellogg, civilian correspondent who was killed with Custer, was born in Brighton, Ontario, Canada.

Fact #399. Following the peace council at Fort Larned (KS) in April 1875, Gen. Winfield Scott Hancock, commanding the expedition which included four companies of the 7th Cavalry under the field command of Lt. Col. George A.

Custer, attempted to meet with various chiefs and leaders, including Tall Bear, Gray Beard, Medicine Wolf, and Roman Nose, all Cheyenne, and Pawnee Killer, a Sioux. These efforts were unsuccessful, due to unfulfilled promises by the Indians.

Fact #400. Following the 7th Cavalry's departure from the Rosebud encampment on June 22, Gen. Terry and Col. Gibbon boarded the river steamer *Far West* and proceeded to overtake Gibbon's Montana Column which had started marching up the banks of the Yellowstone River the preceding day.

Fact #401. William Henry Nelson, 1st Lt., Co. H, 7th Cavalry, was absent on June 25, 1876; sick at Fort Shaw (M.T.).

Fact #402. Michael Vincent Sheridan, Capt., Co. I, 7th Cavalry, was absent on June 25, 1876, on detached service as aide-de-camp to Gen. Philip Sheridan (his brother) since 1871.

Fact #403. Seventh Cavalryman James Wilber enlisted as James Darcy (Pvt., Co. M).

Fact #404. A soldier from Co. M was walking from one part of the line to another at the Reno-Benteen position when a bullet hit his carbine, splintering the stock. Without breaking stride, he looked towards the Indians and shouted, "Damn you! You will have to shoot better than that to get me!" (Lt. W.S. Edgerly's narrative written after the battle)

Fact #405. Frank C. Mann (packer, date and place of birth unknown) was employed as a civilian packer April 1876 by 7th Cavalry Quartermaster; killed at Reno-Benteen position June 25, 1876.

Fact #406. John Eaton Tourtellotte, Capt., Co. G, 7th Cavalry, was absent on June 25, 1876, on detached service as aide-de-camp to Gen. William T. Sherman since 1870.

Fact #407. William Winer Cooke (30 at LBH), 1st Lt., Adj., 7th Cavalry, Dakota Column, was born in Canada. KIA.

Fact #408. Seventh Cavalryman Edward Wilson enlisted as Edward Grayson (Pvt., Co. G).

Custer

Fact #409. George A. Custer was born in New Rumley, Harrison County (OH), December 5, 1839, the son of Emanuel and Maria Ward Fitzpatrick Custer.

Fact #410. "On the plains in his Indian campaigns, [Custer] wore a suit of fringed buckskin with a broad-brimmed hat, and his hair, close cropped when in cities or in garrison, was allowed to grow freely in the field. The Indians named him Long Hair. But the dashing Boy General was now a mature and studious officer. His deep-set blue eyes often sparkled in boyish fun but his face was grave, and he had become a student not only of general military matters but also of Indian characteristics and language." (Bates, *New York Times*, June 20, 1926)

Fact #411. Gen. Winfield Scott Hancock, in 1867, left department headquarters in St. Louis (MO) and headed West, assuming command of six companies of infantry and a battery of artillery at Fort Leavenworth (KS), bringing them on to Fort Riley (KS). Here he added to his expedition strength with another company of infantry and four companies of the 2d Cavalry, plus the 7th Cavalry, under the field command of Lt. Col. George A. Custer. Two more companies of cavalry joined the expedition at Fort Harker (KS) a few days later. The march was then resumed with Fort Larned (KS) as the destination.

Fact #412. Custer held Officers' Call at the base of the Crow's Nest in the Wolf Mountains about 10-15 miles from the village on the Little Big Horn, and told his officers that he had been told by the scouts that they could see a village, ponies, tepees, and smoke. He then said he had looked through his glasses and could see no evidence of the camp. But he pressed on in the sincere belief that if it were a Sioux camp, they would scatter as soon as they realized the 7th Cavalry was near.

Fact #413. "General Terry was a splendid soldier but his orders left much to the discretion of Custer, and the conditions which confronted Custer made it impracticable for him to carry out Terry's suggestions." (Lt. W.S. Edgerly, Co. D, writing shortly after the battle)

Fact #414. The first field movement of the new 7th U.S. Cavalry Regiment occurred in April 1867. The commanding officer, Col. Andrew J. Smith was on detached duty, so the second-in-command, Lt. Col. George A. Custer took the active field command of the regiment, headquartered at Fort Riley (KS).

Fact #415. Custer was the oldest (36) of the 7th Cavalry officers who died at the Little Big Horn.

Fact #416. After Custer received his orders from Gen. Alfred Terry on June 22, he wrote his wife Elizabeth (Libbie) as follows: "MY DARLING—I have but a few moments to write as we start at twelve, and I have my hands full of preparations for the scout. Do not be anxious about me. ...Your devoted boy AUTIE."

Fact #417. Gen. George B. McClellan, commander of the Army of the Potomac, wrote to President Lincoln: "Soon after reaching the Chickahominy [River], I took as one of my Aides, Lt. G.A. Custer, as a reward for an act of daring gallantry [at Bull Run]. ...In those days, Custer was simply, a reckless, gallant boy, undeterred by fatigue, unconscious of fear; but his head was always clear in danger and he always brought me clear and intelligible reports of what he saw under the heaviest fire. I became much attached to him."

Fact #418. The Dakota Column of the 1876 Sioux Wars campaign was composed of the entire 7th U.S. Cavalry, commanded by Lt. Col. (Bvt. Maj. Gen.) George Armstrong Custer.

Fact #419. "As has been stated, it was the general belief that when the Indians saw us approaching their village they would break away and Custer meant to go when they went. When he saw that they were not leaving the village, he sent the order to Benteen by Colonel [sic] Cooke, and at that time I believe he fully intended charging in the rear of and in support of Reno but when he saw how formidable the stream was and what little resistance Reno was making, he determined to move down the stream to the village, then in plain view, strike it in the flank and he undoubtedly expected to meet the victorious Reno in the middle of the village. This doesn't appear to me to be bad tactics, and if his orders to Reno had been carried out and there had not been more than eight hundred Indians, the plan might have worked." (Lt. W.S. Edgerly, Co. D)

Fact #420. The 7th Cavalry, Lt. Col. George A. Custer commanding, left the mouth of the Rosebud on June 22, 1876, striking a two-day-old Indian trail on June 23, which they followed "as rapidly as the animals could be urged." (Lt. Francis Gibson, Co. H)

Fact #421. When young George Custer graduated from McNeely Normal School in Hopedale (OH) in July 1856, he got a job teaching school at nearby Cadiz (OH), the home of Republican Congressman John A. Bingham.

Fact #422. Arriving on April 7, 1867, at Fort Larned (KS) for an April 10 peace council, the Hancock Expedition, commanded by Gen. Winfield Scott Hancock and including four companies of the 7th Cavalry, Lt. Col. George A. Custer, commanding, went into camp. A snowstorm blew in on April 9, delaying the arrival of the Indians for several days. The Army therefore marched northwest from Fort Larned up Walnut Creek toward the large Sioux and Cheyenne camps.

Fact #423. Custer was not a good cadet at the Military Academy, his many boyish pranks and escapades resulted in demerits that brought his rating near the bottom of his class. He was the class "goat" when he graduated 34th in his class of 34 in June 1861. He was commissioned as a 2d Lt. in the 2d U.S. Cavalry and immediately went to war.

Fact #424. During the Civil War, George Custer received six brevet promotions for gallant and meritorious service, at the Battles of Gettysburg, Yellow Tavern, Winchester, and Fisher's Hill. His final brevet, to Maj. Gen., was awarded when he was 25 years old, making him one of the youngest major generals in the volunteer army.

Fact #425. When he first entered the Regular Army, George Custer was just over 21 years of age, ". . .but there was an indefinable something about his vivacious personality that attracted the attention of his superiors. His conspicuous courage and zeal brought him many coveted honors and rewards." (Luce)

Fact #426. Custer spent much of his early life with his half-sister, Lydia Reed, at her home in Monroe (MI) where he attended school.

Fact #427. Custer had originally been slated for command of the Sioux Expedition of 1876, but he offended President Ulysses S. Grant with his testimony before a Congressional committee in Washington (DC) which implicated Grant's brother in a graft situation. Grant relieved Custer of his command, but, after both Gens. Sherman and Sheridan intervened, he was allowed to command his regiment, the 7th Cavalry.

Fact #428. While at Fort Wallace (KS) in 1867, men of the 7th Cavalry erected a monument in memory of 10 members of the regiment, and the 3d Infantry, who had died in battle.

Fact #429. Custer's published writings and the publicity given his activities made him a "beau ideal" among Indian fighters.

Fact #430. Serving with the 7th U.S. Cavalry from 1866 on, Lt. Col. Custer, who never achieved higher rank, spent the early months of his association with the regiment in the field against hostile Indian bands in Kansas, Nebraska, and the Indian Territory.

Fact #431. George Armstrong Custer was killed in battle June 25, 1876, at the Little Big Horn (M.T.), age 36; buried at the U.S. Military Academy at West Point.

Fact #432. "Custer, when asked. . .why he wore so unusual a uniform [when he was a 23-year-old Union general], said that as a boy, only a short time out of West Point, he was in command of a brigade in which were men old enough to be his father. He felt young and insignificant, and wished his men to recognize him in any part of the field. He not only caught their attention but captured their imagination as well." (Bates, *New York Times*, June 20, 1926)

Fact #433. On the trail of Cheyenne Indians who had "escaped" from a "surrounded" camp northwest of Fort Larned (KS), Custer and the 7th Cavalry reached Fort Hays (KS) on May 3, 1867, where they went into camp. The rest of the Hancock Expedition, under the command of Gen. Winfield Scott Hancock, consisting of infantry and artillery units, arrived a few days later. Gen. Hancock proceeded on to Fort Leavenworth (KS) to urge the forwarding of supplies.

Fact #434. "Custer's Civil War record proved his ability as a soldier. In the six months preceding Lee's surrender at Appomattox, his cavalry division took

111 guns, 65 battle flags, and more than 10,000 prisoners of war without losing a flag or a gun, and without a failure to capture whatever it set out for." (Bates, *New York Times*, June 20, 1926)

Fact #435. Following the Sioux attempt to stampede Custer's pony herd from his camp near Fort McPherson (NE) in the early summer of 1867, Custer and the Sioux chief parleyed unsuccessfully. The soldiers then chased the Indians, killing two; no soldiers became casualties.

Fact #436. The famous Brady photograph of 1865 shows Maj. Gen. (Volunteers) George A. Custer, 25, in an outfit which included a wide-brimmed hat, a sailor's shirt, and a red cravat, designed by Custer.

Fact #437. Having received information in June 1856 from Ohio Congressman John A. Bingham on the qualifications for admission to the U.S. Military Academy, young George Custer sent his second letter to Rep. Bingham immediately: "Dear Sir: Yours of the fourth was duly received and I feel myself compelled to write again to express my sincere thanks for your prompt attention, explicit information as to qualifications, etc. I will also add that in all the points specified I would come under the requirements set forth in your communication, being about seventeen years of age, above the medium height and of remarkably strong constitution and vigorous frame. If that young man from Jeff. County of whom you spoke does not push the matter, or if you hear of any other vacancy, I should be glad to hear from you. Yours with great respect, G.A. Custer."

Fact #438. Fort Hays, located on the southern edge of Hays (KS), at the present-day intersection of US 183 and US 40, was one of the guardians of the Smoky Hill Trail. The fort supported Gen. W.S. Hancock's 1867 campaign, which involved Custer and the 7th Cavalry on its first Indian-fighting foray. It also served as the temporary headquarters in 1868-1869 for Gen. Philip Sheridan. Captives from the Battle of the Washita, in western Oklahoma Territory, which pitted Custer's 7th Cavalry against a Cheyenne village headed by Chief Black Kettle, were imprisoned in a stockade next to the Fort Hays guardhouse. Custer and his regiment headquartered at the fort for several summers late in the 1860s and camped nearby.

Fact #439. "Custer obeyed the letter and the spirit of [Terry's] instructions by hugging the 'warm' Indian trail. If he had done otherwise, he could not have got back until the 28th of June, which would have left Terry and Gibbon with about 350 men to face all the Sioux alone." (Bates, June 20, 1926, *New York Times*)

Fact #440. At the age of 15, in Monroe (MI), George Custer met Elizabeth Bacon, daughter of a local judge; less than 10 years later they were married.

Fact #441. Some have written that George A. Custer, commissioned a brigadier general of volunteers at the age of 23 and a major general only two years later, was the youngest brigadier general and major general in the history of the

U.S. Army; but, in fact, one Galusha Pennypacker was the youngest brigadier general, at 20, and was commissioned major general one month before Custer, when he was 21.

Fact #442. After most of the Union Army was disbanded following the Civil War, the regular army was increased by several regiments. Custer, who had reverted to his permanent rank of captain, was assigned to the newly-organized 7th U.S. Cavalry as its lieutenant-colonel.

Fact #443. Custer's first and only major victory in the Indian Wars was at Washita River in northwestern Oklahoma, November 27, 1868, where he and his 7th Cavalry defeated Black Kettle's band of Cheyenne Indians. (*Custer Battlefield* handbook, Luce)

Fact #444. George Custer, as a recent graduate of the U.S. Military Academy at West Point, went to his new assignment with the 2d U.S. Cavalry in time to take part with his company at the First Battle of Bull Run.

Fact #445. Despite Custer's activities as a nominal Democrat, the teen-aged Custer was able to secure his West Point appointment in 1857, with the unsolicited assistance of the father of his girl friend who thought Custer was not a good match for daughter Mary. (Cadets were not allowed to marry while enrolled at the military academy.)

Fact #446. Custer wrote in his last dispatch to the *New York Herald* on June 22, 1876: "Yesterday, Terry, Gibbon, and Custer got together, and, with unanimity of opinion, decided that Custer should start with his whole command [south] up the Rosebud valley to the point where Reno abandoned the trail, take up the latter and follow the Indians as long and as far as horse flesh and human endurance could carry his command. Custer takes no wagons or tents with his command, but proposes to live and travel like Indians; in this manner the command will be able to go wherever the Indians can."

Fact #447. The Washita Battlefield, the site of Custer's most successful engagement with Indians, is located northwest of Cheyenne (OK) and is a recent addition to the National Park Service.

Fact #448. Five days after Custer's graduation from the U.S. Military Academy, last in his class, with excessive demerits, he was court martialed for allowing two plebes to fight while he was Officer of the Guard. The new 2d Lt. pled guilty to the charge. On July 6, 1861, a week after the court martial, the court reprimanded Custer "for conduct unbecoming an officer and a gentleman. The court is thus lenient in the sentence owing to the peculiar situation Cadet Custer represented in his defense, and in consideration of his general good conduct as testified to by Lieutenant Hazen, his immediate commander." The "peculiar situation" was intercession by Custer's old Ohio friend, Cong. John A. Bingham, who had secured his appointment to West Point in 1857, and was now a powerhouse in the Republican Party. Because of Bingham, Gen. Scott chose Custer to carry dispatches to Gen. McDowell at the Battle of Bull Run.

Fact #449. The Rev. Dr. T.T. Monger, the clergyman who preached Gen. Terry's funeral sermon (1890), said: "Custer's fatal movement was in direct violation of verbal and written orders. When his rashness and disobedience ended in the total destruction of his command, General Terry withheld the fact of the disobeyed orders and suffered an imputation hurtful to his military reputation to rest upon himself, rather than subject a brave but indiscreet subordinate to a charge of disobedience."

Fact #450. During the winter of 1872, the Grand Duke Alexis of Russia visited the United States on a goodwill tour. In plans for the official welcome, Lt. Col. Custer was chosen to escort the Duke about the West and to participate in a buffalo hunt. Duke Alexis was delighted not only with the hunt but with Custer, whom he saw for the first time in the picturesque buckskin hunting attire which he always wore on the plains.

Fact #451. When military duties did not demand his attention, George Custer spent his time reading, writing, hunting and mounting the trophies of the chase, or participating in social affairs with his wife, family, and friends.

Fact #452. While Custer's rapid promotions during the Civil War caused some jealousy and resentment, his most loyal followers were the men of the Michigan Volunteer Cavalry Brigade, whom he had led at the Battle of Gettysburg.

Fact #453. George Custer received a brevet (temporary) promotion to major general of volunteers for outstanding services during the campaign ending in the surrender of the Confederate Army of Northern Virginia at Appomattox.

Fact #454. In June 1857, George A. Custer, 17, entered the United States Military Academy at West Point.

Fact #455. The unit referred to as Custer's battalion in the histories of LBH was commanded by Lt. Col. George A. Custer and consisted of Cos. C, E, F, I, and L.

Fact #456. After the 7th Cavalry rode out on June 22 from the main column at the Powder River Camp, Gen. Alfred Terry, commander of the 1876 Sioux Expedition, said, "Custer is happy now, off with a roving command for 15 days."

Fact #457. George Custer believed that the 1860 West Point graduating class "was the finest for producing officers." (Custer graduated in the second class of 1861.)

Fact #458. After the surrounded Cheyenne village was found to be empty of inhabitants on the morning of April 14, 1867, Custer, whose 7th Cavalry soldiers were part of the larger Hancock Expedition, commanded by Gen. Winfield

Scott Hancock, wrote later: "It was then decided that with eight troops of cavalry I should start in pursuit of the Indians at early dawn on the following morning April 15." The trail led the cavalry column northward.

Fact #459. George A. Custer was the 1,966th graduate of the U.S. Military Academy.

Fact #460. During the Southern Cheyenne campaign of 1867, Custer was court-martialed on several counts, including absenting himself from his command and ordering deserters shot without trial; convicted, he was suspended from rank and command without pay for one year.

Fact #461. In 1863, President Abraham Lincoln told Republican Congressman John A. Bingham of Ohio, Custer's patron, "Phil Kearney was my brigadier. Now that he's gone, I look for someone to fill his boots." Kearney was killed at Chantilly (VA) in 1862. Rep. Bingham told Lincoln, "That someone is Captain Custer [now 23], Mr. President," and Lincoln replied, "Then he's my Brigadier." Shortly after, Brig. Gen. George A. Custer of the Michigan Brigade repelled Jeb Stuart's Confederate horsemen at East Cavalry Field outside of Gettysburg.

Fact #462. After being convicted by an 1867 court-martial and suspended from rank and command without pay for one year, Custer was recalled to again command the 7th Cavalry by Gen. Philip Sheridan for the 1868 winter campaign against the Southern Cheyenne.

Fact #463. At Appomattox (VA), in early April of 1865, Maj. Gen. Custer was the officer who received the flag of truce from the Confederate Army of Northern Virginia.

Fact #464. Charles Francis Bates described Custer as "a man of commanding presence. Nearly six feet in height, of magnificent physique, quick and lithe in his movements, he had a personality that dominated every one around him." (June 20, 1926, *New York Times*)

Fact #465. When young George Custer first wrote Ohio Congressman John A. Bingham in May 1856 regarding an appointment to West Point, Rep. Bingham replied that he had committed to appointments for the first and second semesters upcoming.

Fact #466. "In the Civil War, as a boy general of 23, he prescribed his own uniform of black velvet jacket with gold lace, tight black velvet breeches, top boots and a broad white hat. With his long yellow curls covered by the big sombrero, a crimson necktie flying out over his shoulders, a pistol in his boot, long spurs on his heels and a heavy saber swinging at his side, he rode forth to battle, like a veritable Prince Rupert." (Bates, June 20, 1926, *New York Times*)

Fact #467. By mid-May 1867, when additional supplies arrived from Fort Leavenworth (KS) for the Hancock Expedition encamped at Fort Hays (KS),

Custer and his cavalrymen were ordered to scout the territory between Fort Hays and Fort McPherson on the Platte River in Nebraska. They found Indian sign at the Republican River, and upon arriving at Fort McPherson, they were told that Pawnee Killer's band of Sioux were camped about a dozen miles from the post. Custer held a council with Pawnee Killer and other chiefs, presenting gifts such as sugar, coffee, etc., but made no significant progress in extracting promises from the Indians to settle down near the post.

Fact #468. Ohio Congressman John A. Bingham described Custer shortly after the Battle of First Bull Run as "beautiful as Absalom with his yellow curls." (*The Custer Story*, a compilation of letters between George and Elizabeth Custer edited by Marguerite Merington)

Fact #469. Shortly after his graduation from West Point, Custer was charged for failing to separate two brawling cadets while he was Officer of the Day. His classmate, Morris Shaff, commented: "Meanwhile the Officer in charge appeared and Custer was put under arrest and charges were filed against him. Fortunately for the Country, they were not pressed, and he got away in time to reach the field before the Battle of Bull Run."

Fact #470. Custer's 7th Cavalry, part of the 1867 Hancock Expedition, arrived at Fort Wallace in central Kansas in July to find the garrison under strength and in bad need of supplies. Custer proceeded to Fort Harker (KS) to arrange for supplies to be sent to Fort Wallace, then traveled on to Fort Riley (KS), headquarters for the regiment and home for his wife. This unauthorized journey resulted in his court martial and suspension from duties for over a year.

Fact #471. "Not since the horn of Roland sounded out his call for help through the Valley of the Pyrenees had a more moving call for aid gone forth. But Custer's appeal, like the call of Roland, had fallen on ears that either could not or would not hear." (Bates, *New York Times*, 1926)

Fact #472. "Lieut.-Col. G.A. Custer of the Seventh Cavalry, was at first assigned to the command of this force [the 1876 Sioux Expedition]; but under subsequent instructions I [Terry] assumed the command in person, Lieutenant-Colonel Custer being assigned to the command of his regiment." ("Official Report," Gen. Alfred H. Terry on the 1876 Sioux Expedition)

Fact #473. Gen. Philip Sheridan's favorite officer was George Armstrong Custer, "a man who wept with his wife at sentimental drama but who could ride whooping with his troopers over an Indian village full of women and children." (*The American Heritage History of The Great West*, Lavender)

Fact #474. In 1864, when Brig. Gen. (Bvt. Vols.) George Custer was transferred to command of the 3d Cavalry Division, many Michigan men sought, through petition, to join Custer in his new command.

Fact #475. Custer's soldiers sometimes referred to him as "Hardass."

Fact #476. In May 1856, young George A. Custer wrote Ohio Congressman John A. Bingham: "Sir: Wishing to learn something in relation to the matter of appointment of cadets to the West Point Military Academy, I have taken the liberty of addressing you on the subject. My only apology for thus intruding on your notice is, that I cannot obtain such information here [Hopedale (OH)]. And as the matter is to be firmly settled in Washington [DC], I have thought better to make application at headquarters from the beginning. If in the multiplicity of your duties, which I know you must have on hand, you can find time to inform me as to the necessary qualifications for admission, and if our Congressional district is unrepresented there or not, or at least when there will be a vacancy, you will confer a great favor on me."

Fact #477. After failing to make contact with the leading Indian chiefs following the Fort Larned (KS) peace council in April 1867, Gen. Winfield Scott Hancock, commanding the Hancock Expedition, ordered an attack on a Cheyenne camp, with the object of capturing the whole body of Indians. Custer's cavalry was ordered to surround the camp.

Fact #478. Custer was "usually the spearhead of Sheridan's [Civil War] attacks with the Army of the Potomac, and after Lee's surrender Sheridan gave him, as a present for Mrs. Custer, the table on which Grant had written the conditions of surrender." (Bates, *New York Times*, June 20, 1926)

Fact #479. Accepting the fact that the Sioux Expedition was going to have to go in search of the elusive Sitting Bull and his Sioux tribesmen, Custer wrote on May 30, 1876, "Considering the advanced stage of the season, the fine and plentiful growth of grass everywhere available on the plains, Sitting Bull cannot only keep himself thoroughly informed as to our movements but is in condition and free to act as may be most to his advantage. He can fight or run away or by a combination of both annoy us greatly without suffering severely in return. At the same time the coils are tightening about him; he has not only one enemy or two to watch, but three powerful columns. . . Now Sitting Bull may dodge one or two of these columns, but in dodging one does he not run the risk of placing himself in the path of the other two?"

Fact #480. George A. Custer, then 16 years old, wrote the Hon. John A. Bingham of Ohio, about seeking an appointment to West Point. He concluded his letter: "I am desirous of going to West Point, and I think my age and tastes would be in accordance with its requirements. But I must forebear on that point for the present. I am now in attendance at the McNeely Normal School in Hopedale [OH], and could obtain from the principal, if necessary, testimonials of moral character. I would also say that I have the consent of my parents in the course which I now have in view. Wishing to hear from you as soon as convenient, I remain, Yours respectfully, G.A. Custer."

Fact #481. Custer and his companies of cavalry surrounded a Cheyenne village northwest of Fort Larned (KS) during the night of April 13-14, 1867, at the order of Gen. Winfield Scott Hancock, commander of the Hancock Expedition. At daylight the next morning, the camp was still there, but all the Cheyenne were gone.

Fact #482. Custer owned a dog named Lucy Stone. Mrs. Custer reported that she was embarrassed by the name, but says in *Boots and Saddles* that the dog's name was bestowed by a previous owner, and the dog would answer to no other.

Fact #483. Custer reached the "Crow['s] nest" hill shortly after dawn on June 25, 1876. Custer listened to the report of possible discovery by at least two small Sioux scouting parties, while looking in the direction of the village on the Little Big Horn River, 10-15 miles away. "He then said, 'Well I've got about as good eyes as anybody & I can't see any village Indians or anything else,' or words to that effect. Boyer said, 'Well, General, if you don't find more Indians in that valley than you ever saw together you can hang me.' Custer sprang to his feet saying, 'It would do a damned sight of good to hang you, wouldn't it?' and he & I went down the hill together." (Chief of Scouts Charles Varnum in a letter to historian Walter Camp in 1909)

Fact #484. Bugler Joseph Fought, who served with Custer through most of the Civil War, had kind remarks about young 2d Lt. Custer immediately after Bull Run. "Custer never let up, never slackened control. Then, when Arlington [VA] was reached and his Company assigned to its camp, he snatched a few hours sleep between a tree. . ."

Fact #485. Custer returned to duty from a one year suspension to take part in Gen. Philip Sheridan's 1868 winter campaign against the Cheyenne. In that campaign his command destroyed the village of Black Kettle along the Washita River in Indian Territory. This attack and the months of campaigning that followed effectively put an end to the raiding and killing in western Kansas.

Fact #486. Lt. James Bradley, 7th Inf., Chief of Scouts for the Montana Column under Col. John Gibbon, wrote in his journal, just before LBH: "Though it is General Terry's expectation that we will arrive in the neighborhood of the Sioux village the same time and assist each other in the attack, it is understood that if Custer arrives first he is at liberty to attack if he deems prudent."

Fact #487. Describing the scene on the hills above the west bank of the Little Big Horn on the morning of June 27, 1876, Lt. James H. Bradley, 7th Infantry, Montana Column, told the *Helena Herald* in a July 15, 1876, interview, "Custer fell upon the highest point of the field; and around him, within a space of five rods square, lay forty-two men and thirty-one horses. The dead soldiers all lay within a circle embracing only a few hundred yards."

Fact #488. Following the successful Washita campaign in the winter of 1868, Gen. Sheridan wrote Lt. Col. Custer: "I am very much rejoiced at the success of your expedition, and feel very proud of our winter operations, and of the Officers and Men who bore privations so manfully. The energy and rapidity shown during one of the heaviest snow storms known to this section of the Country, with temperatures below freezing, the gallantry and bravery displayed, resulting in such signal success, reflects credit on the 7th Cavalry. . .and the Major-General Commanding expresses his thanks to the Officers and men engaged in the Battle of the Washita, and his special congratulations to their distinguished Commander Brevet Major General George A. Custer for the efficient and gallant service opening the campaign against hostile Indians north of the Arkansas [River]."

Fact #489. In a *New York Herald* article, June 27, 1876, Custer's written comments from May 30 were quoted: "The Whereabouts of Sitting Bull is now as much of a conundrum to the military as is the hiding place of Boss Tweed to the New York Police. Rumor—that busy but not always reliable dame—now places Sitting Bull on the Powder River. . .distant from this point about 100 miles, be the same more or less. The troops, will, probably, find it more. It was expected, partly hoped, I believe, that Sitting Bull would make good his boasts and actually attack the troops, thereby bringing matters to a speedy issue and putting an end to what must be to Uncle Sam a very expensive undertaking."

Fact #490. In his last dispatch to the *New York Herald*, sent on June 22, 1876, Custer wrote: "Gibbon's command has started for the mouth of the Big Horn. Terry on the *Far West* starts for the same point today, when, with Gibbon's force, and the *Far West* loaded with thirty days' supplies, he will push up the Big Horn as far as the navigation of that stream will permit, probably as far as old Fort C.F. Smith (M.T.), at which point Custer will reform the expedition after completing his present scout. Custer's command takes with it, on pack animals, rations for fifteen days. Custer advised his subordinate officers, however, in regard to rations, that it would be well to carry an extra supply of salt, because if at the end of fifteen days the command should be pursuing a trail, he did not propose to turn back for lack of rations, but would subsist his men on. . . game, if the country provided it; pack mules if nothing better."

Fact #491. The 7th United States Cavalry Regiment was established in July 1866, with Col. Andrew J. Smith as its commanding officer. The unit was headquartered at Fort Riley (KS). George Armstrong Custer, whose rank had reverted to Captain after the Civil War had ended and the reorganization of the Army had occurred, was promoted Lt. Col., joining the regiment in October.

Fact #492. Gen. William T. Sherman, the commanding general of the U.S. Army, visited Custer's camp near Fort McPherson (NE) in mid-June 1867, shortly after Custer's parley with Pawnee Killer and other Sioux chiefs. Gen. Sherman, convinced that Indian promises were worthless, told Custer that force was the only means to be used in controlling the nomadic tribes.

Fact #493. From 1866, when the regiment was formed, until 1876 and LBH, Lt. Col. George A. Custer was its field commander. During that time elements of the regiment fought 33 separate engagements and skirmishes against Indian enemies, most of them small affairs. (Sarf, *The Little Bighorn Campaign*)

Fact #494. Fort Harker, at Kanopolis (KS), was the starting point and major base of Maj. Gen. Winfield Scott Hancock's 1,400 man expedition of 1867 that sought to intimidate the Cheyenne and other Kansas tribes, but inflamed them instead and aroused the ire of eastern humanitarians. No major engagement occurred, but the belligerent Hancock burned villages and pursued the Indians relentlessly. During the campaign, Lt. Col. George A. Custer assembled troops and replenished supplies at Fort Harker.

Fact #495. The animosity of Capt. Frederick W. Benteen toward his commander, Lt. Col. George A. Custer, stemmed from the Battle of the Washita; Benteen believed Custer had abandoned, without just cause, a detachment under Maj. Joel Elliott which was subsequently wiped out.

Fact #496. Pursuing the fleeing inhabitants of a Cheyenne village that had been surrounded on the night of April 13-14, 1867, during the Hancock Expedition, 7th Cav. soldiers commanded by Lt. Col. George A. Custer discovered that the Indians, who had just disappeared from the surrounded camp during the night, had burned a stage station about 15 miles from Fort Hays (KS) and killed all the employees. The troops reached Fort Hays without further sign of the Indians.

Fact #497. Neither Col. Andrew J. Smith, the original commanding officer of the 7th U.S. Cavalry, founded in 1866, nor his successor in 1869, Col. Samuel D. Sturgis, ever led the 7th Cavalry in any campaign until after LBH.

Fact #498. The Battle of the Washita (O.T., November 1868) was the major engagement in Gen. Philip Sheridan's winter campaign of 1868-1869 against the southern Plains tribes. It involved "a lamentable loss of Indian life" and "also incited controversy between humanitarians and frontiersmen." Custer led the 7th Cavalry regiment in a dawn attack through deep snow against a Cheyenne village suspected of harboring marauders responsible for raids along the Smoky Hill Trail in western Kansas. The regimental band played "Garry Owen" as the cavalry charge began. (*Soldier and Brave*, NPS book about Indian Wars sites)

Fact #499. Fort Riley, located northeast of Junction City on present-day Kansas Highway 18, was activated at the junction of the Smoky Hill and Republican forks of the Kansas River in 1853. At the fort in 1866, the 7th U.S.

Cavalry Regiment was organized, with George A. Custer as its lieutenant colonel, and, for the next 10 years, field commander. The Custer home is still open for visits.

Fact #500. Fort Wallace was located northeast of Wallace (KS). It was established in 1865 and was often besieged by marauding Indians. When Custer's 7th Cavalry, participating in the 1867 Hancock expedition, arrived at Fort Wallace in July, they found the slender garrison exhausted, its supplies low, and travel over the Smoky Hill Trail at a standstill.

Fact #501. Picking their way across the Custer battle site on June 27, 1876, two days after Custer's entire command was slain on the banks of the Little Big Horn, a detail under Capt. Frederick Benteen (Co. H) looked for the bodies of Custer and his dead officers. "The [dead] men, with the exception of General Custer, were stripped, scalped and horribly mutilated. Some had an arm cut off; others were decapitated, while many other bodies were lacking feet which the Indians had hurriedly cut off in order to get boots later. . . As I walked over the field I saw many unfortunate dead who had been propped into a sitting position and used as targets by bowmen who had proceeded to stick them full of steel-headed arrows." (Pvt. Jacob Adams, Co. H) (Since steel-headed arrows weren't all that plentiful, Pvt. Adams' statement is curious.)

Fact #502. Custer was "[b]rash, outspoken, and flamboyant. . .not an individual who produced a mild reaction in anyone he met. Undisciplined himself, he could nevertheless be a brutal disciplinarian to those serving under him." (*Encyclopedia of American Indian Wars*)

Fact #503. At the Battle of the Washita in November 1868, large numbers of Cheyenne, Arapaho, Kiowa, Kiowa-Apache, and Comanche began to assemble on the hills around Black Kettle's Cheyenne camp, which was part of a lengthy winter encampment stretching for 10 miles along the Washita River. Custer's troops had routed the Cheyenne, burned the village, and destroyed the pony herd. In the face of mounting enemy strength, Custer made a feint as night fell, then withdrew his forces, leaving Maj. Joel H. Elliot and his 16-man detachment unaccounted for. This perceived "desertion" of his men, who were later found dead and butchered, caused morale problems in the 7th Cavalry officer corps for years.

Fact #504. As the 7th Cavalry column (A, C, E, F, G, I, L, M companies) rode into the valley of Sundance Creek (later known as Reno Creek or Reno's Creek), they stopped in a "deep depression of the valley." Pvt. Peter Thompson, writing many years after the battle, recalled, "Custer rode some distance ahead of us and then turning to the right ascended to the highest point of the hills where he must have been able to see a long distance. He was not long in returning; and then the bugle was blown for the first time in a number of days. It was a call for the officers and they soon gathered around their chief. [Scout] Frank Gerard so far forgot himself as to go and sit down near the place where the officers were gathered. General Custer looked at him and said, 'Go where you belong, and stay there.' He did not wait for a second bidding. It was Custer's desire to keep everyone in his proper place."

Fact #505. George Armstrong Custer was just under six feet tall, weighed about 170 pounds, had blonde hair and mustache, and blue eyes.

Fact #506. On June 24, the day before the battle, the 7th Cavalry column marched 28 miles, the Indians' trail becoming fresher and fresher as the cavalrymen ascended the valley (south). Deserted camps were passed, and frequent signal smokes seemed to indicate that the Indians were monitoring the column's progress, easily seen by enormous clouds of dust raised by the cavalry horses.

Fact #507. Lt. Col. George A. Custer, field commander of the 7th U.S. Cavalry in the fall of 1868, initiated a program designed to improve the marksmanship of his soldiers. The men were given firing practice twice a day and the 40 best shots were put in an elite company of sharpshooters, excused from picket and guard duty.

Fact #508. "Custer was mounted on his sorrel horse and it being a very hot day he was in his shirt sleeves; his buckskin pants tucked into his boots; his buckskin shirt fastened to the rear of his saddle; and a broad brimmed cream colored hat on his head, the brim of which was turned up on the right side and fastened by a small hook and eye to its crown. This gave him opportunity to sight his rifle while riding. His rifle lay horizontally in front of him; when riding he leaned slightly forward." (Peter Thompson, Pvt., Co. C)

Fact #509. By June 24, Custer had "very accurate knowledge as to the location of the big Indian camp. He could generally be seen during the march about a mile in advance, taking advantage of every rise in the ground, on top of every hill, eagerly straining his experienced and untiring eyes through his trusty and well-used field glasses to satisfy himself as to what was in front. . ." (1st Lt. Francis Gibson, Co. H)

Environment

Fact #510. Many, if not most, of the rivers relevant to the 1876 Sioux Expedition flowed north, rather than flowing south as the great majority of American rivers do. Therefore, when a movement was made "upriver," the troops were moving south. "Downriver" meant north. The rivers (and creeks) so affected, in the context of the Expedition, were the Yellowstone, the Rosebud, the Powder, the Big Horn, the Little Big Horn, Reno Creek, and others.

Fact #511. In the winter of 1875, 7th Cavalry troops at Fort Abraham Lincoln (D.T.) and Fort Rice (D.T.) were experiencing a climate aptly described as "nine months winter and three months late in the fall," when the mercury often registered 50 degrees below zero. (Lt. Gibson, Co. H)

Fact #512. Since the Black Hills lay within the Great Sioux Reservation, the Federal government was bound by treaty stipulation to prevent the migration of its citizens to the area. The Army tried without success to stem the tide.

Fact #513. The Dakota Column, after leaving Fort Abraham Lincoln (D.T.) on May 17, made its way slowly to the mouth of the Powder River on the Yellowstone, near the present site of Terry (MT), arriving in early June.

Fact #514. After leaving Reno to attack the (southern) upper end of the Indian village on the banks of the Little Big Horn, Custer's column (C, E, F, I, L companies) rode up the hill to the bluffs overlooking the river. The cavalry column "soon gained the top of the bluffs where a view of the surrounding country was obtained. The detail of Company F which was sent to investigate the ['lone'] tepee now passed by us on their way to the front with the report that it [the tepee] contained a dead Indian and such articles as were deemed necessary for him on his journey to the 'Happy Hunting Ground.'" (Peter Thompson)

Fact #515. Co. E, assigned to Custer's battalion, consisted of two officers and 61 enlisted men. All with Custer perished in the battle.

Fact #516. The plan for the Sioux Expedition of 1876 was to march into "hostile" Indian territory with three separate expeditions from different directions. (*Custer Battlefield* handbook, Luce)

Fact #517. The night of June 25, some of the men at the Reno-Benteen position were "smoking their pipes and talking over the events of the day and the probabilities for tomorrow, and some [were] sleeping as soundly and snoring as loudly as if they were in their bunks in garrison." (Lt. Edgerly, Co. D)

Fact #518. When Gen. Alfred Terry's Dakota Column arrived at the battlefield, immediate action was taken to care properly for the wounded men in Maj. Marcus Reno's command. They were transferred before the day ended from the Reno-Benteen position on the hills to the valley where Gen. Terry's and Col. Gibbon's columns had set up camp, and the men began work making litters on which to transport them.

Fact #519. Viewing Reno's charge in mid-afternoon of June 25, 1876, on the Indian village from a vantage point along the ridge north of "Weir Point," where he had ridden with Custer's column (C, E, F, I, L companies), Pvt. Peter Thompson (Co. E) recalled that the charge was "grand" and the Indians were in "great commotion when they beheld the bold front presented by the cavalry. But alas! How deceptive are appearances. The cavalry dashed into the village where one of the non-commissioned officers halted and struck up the company's guidon alongside of a teepee before he was shot from his horse. The halt was but for a moment, for the Indians came rushing towards them in great numbers."

Fact #520. Custer's column carried 15 days' rations from the Yellowstone, and the "general belief was that when the Indians found that the whole 7th Cavalry (12 companies) was coming, they would run, and then the hard stern chase would begin." (Lt. W.S. Edgerly, Co. D)

Fact #521. After dividing his command into four battalions (Reno, Benteen, Keogh, and Yates, commanding), Custer ordered Capt. Benteen, with companies D, H, and K, to move off to the left (Custer indicating an angle of about 35 or 40 degrees from the direction of the village), "attack any Indians you come across, and you will be supported," reported Lt. W.S. Edgerly (Co. D). Most modern historians, in error, refer to "three battalions," under Reno, Benteen, and Keogh, with Custer accompanying the latter column.

Fact #522. Writing to historian Walter Camp in 1909, after his retirement following more than 50 years of Army service, Charles A. Varnum, Custer's Chief of Scouts on the Sioux Expedition, expressed disbelief that an important Indian trail some 10 miles earlier had escaped his notice. "After discussion [with Custer], Lieut. Hare was ordered to report to me as an assistant and I changed horses and went back the ten miles with some of my Rees and found where quite a party had gone up a stream. . .to find a suitable crossing. . .and then resumed my place in advance Hare taking the right front and I the left. We made about ten miles more and went into camp. Custer came over to the Sioux camp and had a long talk with the Crows. (Half Yellow Face was still out to the front somewhere so there were only five Crows present.)"

Fact #523. The retreat from Weir Point to the Reno-Benteen position was timely, ". . .for Reno was in an excellent position for defense and it wasn't made a moment too soon, for the men had but just been dismounted and placed in position on the crests of the hills which formed what we called our corral, when a very heavy fire opened on us which continued for about three hours, our command losing in that time eighteen men killed and forty-six wounded." (Lt. W.S. Edgerly, Co. D)

Fact #524. Col. John Gibbon, with a force of cavalry from Fort Ellis (M.T.) and infantry from Fort Shaw (M.T.) started in April and moved slowly east down the Yellowstone River to join with Gen. Terry and the Dakota Column as part of the 1876 Sioux Expedition.

Fact #525. During the Black Hills Expedition of 1874, rumors of gold in the hills were confirmed by prospectors who accompanied the 7th Cavalry military force led by Custer. This area, which the Sioux had taken from the Crow, had been guaranteed to the Indians in the Fort Laramie Treaty of 1868, as part of The Great Sioux Reservation.

Fact #526. The trail down Reno Creek from the cavalry column's halt at the "divide" to its mouth on the Little Big Horn River measures about 12 miles, rolling country divided by deep ravines.

Fact #527. After receiving Trumpeter Martin's message from Custer, many in Benteen's command believed "it would all be over before we could get near enough to see it and certainly before we could take an active part in it." (Lt. W.S. Edgerly, Co. D)

Fact #528. As Maj. Marcus Reno's command attacked the Indian village on the afternoon of June 25, 1876, and was faced with a growing number of counterattacking Indians, he ordered a skirmish line. Pvt. Peter Thompson (Co. C) was on the ridge across the Little Big Horn River from the village and observed these actions. Writing nearly 40 years after the battle, Thompson noted, "Major Reno dismounted his men in the usual manner; number 4 remaining on horseback to hold the horses of the others. A skirmish line was formed, which advanced to the edge of the timber, to await the enemy which soon appeared in great numbers."

Fact #529. Eleven cavalry men were mustered by Capt. Frederick Benteen on the morning of June 26, 1876, to drive out a large party of Indians who had secured a position in the ravine on the western arc of the Reno-Benteen perimeter. One of these men was Pvt. Peter Thompson (Co. C) who later wrote: Benteen exhorted the men to "Charge down there and drive them out," and then, "with a cheer away they dashed, their revolvers in one hand and their carbines in the other. Benteen turned around and walked away to the extreme left, seemingly tireless and unconscious of the hail of led that was flying around him." Other reports say Benteen rounded up at least 15 or 16 soldiers (including Thompson) and a few civilian packers. The Indians were scattered. According to Benteen's account, he went with the soldiers.

Fact #530. At the meeting on the steamer *Far West* on June 21, Gen. Terry outlined the plan to be followed by the Montana Column: Col. Gibbon's troops were to go back (south) up the Yellowstone, cross to its south side, and march (south) up the Big Horn River, then (south) up the Little Big Horn River. The *Far West* would follow these streams as far as it could go.

Fact #531. Fort Abraham Lincoln (D.T.) was the headquarters of the famed 7th U.S. Cavalry in the winter and spring of 1876. Built on the site of a former Indian village, the Fort was one of the most colorful and important posts on the western frontier.

Fact #532. Early on the morning of June 25, scouts reported to Custer that, from a high point on the divide (the Crow's Nest), they had spied the smoke of a large Indian village, but by the time he reached the vantage point a haze, caused by the brilliance of the sun, obscured the view.

Fact #533. The 7th Cavalry was considered one of the better Indian-fighting units on the Plains, and yet, at the Reno Court of Inquiry in 1879, Lt. George D. Wallace (Co. G, part of Reno's attack force in the valley fight), said, "Many of the men had never been on a horse until that campaign, and they lost control of their horses when galloping into line."

Fact #534. While Custer and his staff were examining a scalp-bedecked medicine lodge on June 24, Sgt. Robert Hughes (Co. K), who carried Custer's battle flag, stuck the staff in the ground and left it standing there. In a short time, the flag fell over, pointed back toward the Yellowstone River. After the battle, Lt. W.S. Edgerly (Co. D) reported that the superstitious Lt. G.D. Wallace (Co. G) remarked that the fallen guidon boded ill for Custer.

Fact #535. The 7th Cavalry soldiers were amazed when they found "the largest Indian village ever seen on the plains." The "winter roamers," reinforced by refugees from the reservations, in the still-growing village on the banks of the Little Big Horn included some 10,000 Sioux and Cheyenne, with 1,500 to 2,000 warriors. (Hedren, *The Great Sioux War*)

Fact #536. From the viewpoint of the whites, the frontier warfare with Indians was caused by the hostility of certain Indians who made raids on white settlements and refused to live on the government-ordered reservations.

Fact #537. Captain Benteen's column, sent off to the left when Custer divided his command into three columns, arrived on Reno-Benteen Hill at 4:20 p.m., by Lt. Godfrey's watch.

Fact #538. In his July 20, 1926, column commemorating the 50th anniversary of LBH, Charles Francis Bates wrote, "Reno arrived on the bluffs about 2:30 p.m.; heavy firing had thereafter been heard down the river where Custer had gone and officers and men were growing uneasy at the failure to make any effort to join Custer. There was no fighting going on at that time on Reno Hill, nearly all the Indians having withdrawn in Custer's direction. Finally Captain Weir and Lt. Edgerly without authority started with one troop to make their way to where they knew Custer was fighting."

Fact #539. The first afternoon out from the Yellowstone (June 21, 1876), the 7th Cavalry column made about 12 miles, encamping on the banks of a stream. (Lt. W.S. Edgerly, Co. D)

Fact #540. Told by Custer the evening of June 24 that Crow scouts had said the Sioux village was probably along the Little Big Horn and could be seen at dawn from a high promontory the Crows used for spying ("a Crow['s] nest"), Chief of Scouts Charles Varnum (2d Lt., Co. A) volunteered to go with the Crow scouts to the Crow's Nest and try to spy out the distant village at dawn on June 25. In a 1909 letter to historian Walter Camp, Varnum wrote: "[Custer] told me to do so and to start about 9 o'clock [p.m.] and he would move with the command at 11 [p.m.] and in the morning he would be bivouaced [sic] under the base of the hill I was on and he would expect to get word from me there. I left as directed taking [Mitch] Boyer, Charley Reynolds, five Crows. . .and eight or ten Rees. The Crows were our guides."

Fact #541. Lt. W. S. Edgerly, Co. D: "The general belief shared by Generals Terry, Gibbon, and Custer was that the hostile Indians could not assemble more than eight hundred warriors, with the probabilities in favor of a lesser number."

Fact #542. The smallest column in the Sioux Expedition of 1876 was the Montana Column, commanded by Col. John Gibbon, consisting of four companies of cavalry, six companies of infantry, and about a dozen civilians hired as packers and guides, a total of about 460 men. (*Henry Bostwick*)

Fact #543. The 7th Cavalry column broke camp at 11 p.m. on June 24, planning to cross the divide between the Rosebud watershed and the Little Big Horn watershed before daylight.

Fact #544. At the beginning of the 1876 Campaign against the Sioux, the larger part of the 7th U.S. Cavalry was stationed at Fort Abraham Lincoln (D.T.) and Fort Rice (D.T.), both posts being situated on the west bank of the Missouri River.

Fact #545. Straining his eyes to see the Little Big Horn village from the "Crow['s] nest" at dawn on June 25, Chief of Scouts Charles Varnum had to tell his Crow scouts that he couldn't discern the pony herd they were seeing, even with the aid of the "cheap spy glass" they gave him. "My eyes were somewhat inflamed from the loss of sleep & hard riding in dust & hot sun & were not in the best of condition, but I had excellent eyesight and tried hard to see but failed. About 5 o'clock [a.m.] I sent the Rees [Arikara scouts] back with a note to Custer telling him what the Crows reported, vis a tremendous village on the Little Big Horn. I do not remember the wording but I was told when the command arrived that Custer got it." (Walter Camp)

Fact #546. Gen. George Crook, commander of the Dept. of the Platte, had been ordered ". . .to move during the inclement season [mid-winter 1876] by forced marches, carrying, by pack animals, the most urgent supplies, secretly and expeditiously surprise the hostile bands and if possible chastise them before spring fairly opened, and they could receive as they always do in the summer, reinforcements from the reservations." ("Official Report," May 1876)

Fact #547. The Indian attack at the Reno-Benteen position reached its peak at mid-morning of June 26. Capt. Benteen led a charge to drive the Indians away from his part of the line, "and then came over near where Reno was, and from the high point where he stood he could see Indians crawling up on our left." (Lt. Edgerly, Co. D)

Fact #548. Students of the battle need only to walk over the battlefield today and observe the terrain to understand how well the Indian warriors could hide themselves from the fire of the soldiers.

Fact #549. Capt. Frederick Benteen's troops, sighting the "immense Sioux village" from the bluffs above the Little Big Horn River just after midday on June 25, were "uncertain for a moment which way to turn; no soldiers were in sight." (Lt. Francis Gibson, Co. H)

Fact #550. Indian warriors swarmed into open view as Reno and his men rode (north) down the valley. At Reno's command, the men dismounted and formed a skirmish line to fight on foot. After almost half an hour, an increasing number of Indians forced the soldiers into a timber thicket.

Fact #551. Meeting on the supply steamer *Far West* at the Yellowstone River on June 21, Gen. Terry, commanding Dakota Column, and Col. Gibbon, commanding Montana Column, decided that Lt. Col. Custer and the 7th U.S. Cavalry would follow an Indian trail (south) up the Rosebud and seek an encounter with the "hostiles." (Camp, *Custer In 76*)

Fact #552. About two-thirds of Reno's command made it from the valley to the bluffs, where they entrenched. Few of the Indians followed them beyond the river, although some commenced sniping at the new position.

Fact #553. When Capt. Frederick Benteen's three-company "scouting party" returned after midday June 25 to the vicinity of the main column's trail, about three miles east of the south end of the village, a messenger brought a note from the Adjutant of the Regiment: "Benteen, come on, big village, be quick, bring packs. W.W. Cooke. P.S. Bring pacs [sic]," reported Lt. Francis Gibson, Benteen's second-in-command of Co. H.

Fact #554. "If Reno had charged through the village [instead of halting his charge], Custer would have joined him in a very short time, and Benteen later, and we might have had an expensive victory." (Lt. W.S. Edgerly, Co. D)

Fact #555. The demand for water at the Reno-Benteen position became so frequent and so distressing that several soldiers volunteered to climb down the bluffs to the Little Big Horn River and bring back water for the wounded. Two men lost their lives, another lost a leg.

Fact #556. Given the actual and potential values of the sacred Paha Sapa (the Black Hills), the Sioux inhabitants could be expected to deal harshly with white or red intruders into the lands set aside by treaty for exclusive use by the Indians.

Fact #557. Upon receiving Custer's written order to "bring packs," Capt. Frederick Benteen pressed on with his three companies, arriving at the top of "very high bluffs on the east side of the Little Big Horn River, and from this point our eyes rested on the immense Sioux village." (Lt. Francis Gibson, Co. H)

Fact #558. On June 24, the day before the battle, Custer's column came to a recently-built Sioux medicine lodge, the center pole of which was adorned with two scalps of whites; the command was halted for Custer to examine the lodge. (Lt. W.S. Edgerly, Co. D, in Benteen's command)

Fact #559. The 7th Cavalry column marched 33 miles on June 23, two days before the battle, striking the hostile trail and passing through deserted camps.

Fact #560. Reno's command, scrambling to escape from the woods on the west (left) bank of the Little Big Horn River to the bluffs high above on the east (right) bank, "by the luckiest accident found after they had gone a few yards from the right bank that they were perfectly screened from their pursuer's fire, a turn in the ravine leaving a spur of the bluff between the two parties." (Lt. W.S. Edgerly, Co. D)

Fact #561. At sunset on June 24, the evening before the battle, the 7th Cavalry column went into camp. The officers were summoned to Custer's tent about 9:30 p.m. and told the march would resume at 11 p.m., Crow scouts having brought word "that the Indian village had been located in the valley of the Little Big Horn." (Lt. Edgerly, Co. D)

Fact #562. Capt. Thomas M. McDougall's B Company was detailed as rear guard when Custer divided his command, on the morning of June 25, 1876, and ordered to bring up the pack train under the immediate charge of Lt. Edward Mathey.

Fact #563. The steamer, *Far West*, loaded with supplies was at the mouth of Rosebud Creek on June 21. Gen. Terry had used the boat as his headquarters, and as a means of keeping contact with the Dakota and Montana Columns.

Fact #564. After Reno's command crossed the river to attack the village in the late morning of June 25, a horse of M Company became excited during the charge and dashed to the front carrying the rider into the village, where the soldier was killed. (Lt. Edgerly, Co. D)

Fact #565. Spying Indians crawling up on the left of the Reno-Benteen position on the morning of June 26, Capt. Benteen called out to Maj. Reno "that if the Indians were not driven away from our flank they would gather us in. (Reno couldn't see them as he was lying down in a rifle pit like the rest of us.) Benteen led another charge. 'All right. Get ready men! Now charge! Give 'em hell!' The Indians 'fled incontinently,' Benteen said." (Lt. Edgerly, Co. D)

Fact #566. Lt. Francis Gibson (Co. H): "We bivouaced on the night of [June] 24th about 8 o'clock on one of the unnamed streams flowing from the Wolf Mts. Here we expected to be undisturbed for the night and I gladly accepted

Col. Keogh's invitation to take some beans soon, at his mess, a couple of hours later. But that supper was never served—poor Keogh had eaten his last one. . ."

Fact #567. The surviving wounded from LBH included 42 soldiers, two officers, and two Indian scouts. (Sarf, *The Little Big Horn Campaign*)

Fact #568. After receiving Custer's urgent message about bringing the "packs" (including ammunition), Capt. Benteen "believed that if Custer needed him at all it would be quickly, so sending word to McDougall to hurry up with the packs, he pressed on towards the village. . ." (Lt. W.S. Edgerly, Co. D)

Fact #569. As the attack against Reno's troops, now entrenching atop the bluffs, eased off, the mass of Indians, possibly up to 5,000 warriors, started after the Custer column, consisting of 225 officers, men, scouts, and civilians. (Luce, *Custer Battlefield*)

Fact #570. About a third of Reno's command, retreating from the valley to the bluffs, dropped out, having either been killed, wounded, or forced to seek cover in the brush.

Fact #571. Writing to historian Walter Camp in 1909, Custer's Chief of Scouts Charles A. Varnum (2d Lt., Co. A) told of discovering two Sioux Indians riding near the 7th Cavalry column, and trying to head them off. "We could see them as they went down the trail [still on the Rosebud side of the divide] and could then see a long trail of dust showing Custer was moving but we could not see the column. Before it came in sight the Sioux stopped suddenly, got together & then as suddenly disappeared, one to the right & one to the left, so we knew that the Sioux had discovered our approach." During this same time period, several more Sioux "rode single file along the crest of a ridge forming a divide of the stream running into the Rosebud and in the direction of that stream. That they would soon discover Custer's command we knew, and watched them accordingly.".

Fact #572. The firing at the Reno-Benteen position ceased about 9 p.m. June 25, and the troops were moved and extended to close up the intervals; the horse holders were relieved by tying the horses to picket lines, and the men began digging rifle pits.

Fact #573. Col. Gibbon's Montana Column, under Gen. Terry's instructions, had proceeded down the Yellowstone River as far as the Tongue River, where Miles City (MT) is located today, but had returned to camp at the mouth of the Rosebud Creek, now Rosebud (MT), awaiting the approach of Terry's column from the east.

Fact #574. A few hundred yards from Custer's final line of battle was another, lower, ridge, the far slope of which was not commanded by his line. It was from here that the Indians, some believe, moved on Custer from the lower (northern) part of the village, cutting off all access to the river and the village.

Gall and his warriors, it is believed, were the first to meet Custer's immediate command. (*Custer Battlefield*, Luce)

Fact #575. The general belief among the beleaguered troops at the Reno-Benteen position was that, "having gone so far from the main body of troops, [Custer] was cut off and could not return to us. We imagined him sheltered in the timber about six miles west." (Lt. Francis Gibson)

Fact #576. After the first division of Custer's command on the morning of June 25, Capt. Benteen's battalion (Cos. D, H, K) was ordered to proceed across the big hills to the south some five or six miles to ascertain if the Indians were trying to escape [south] up the valley of the Little Big Horn; and if so, the orders were to intercept them and drive them [north] down towards the location of the village. If no Indians were seen, Benteen was to "hurry back and re-form the command as soon as possible." (Lt. Francis Gibson, Co. H)

Fact #577. About the time Reno started to recross the river (about 4 p.m. according to John Gray in *Custer's Last Campaign*), Custer's approach was discovered. "Reno's retreat encouraged [the Indians] greatly as it convinced them that their medicine was good, and the mounted warriors who had started for Reno turned at once towards Custer," according to Lt. W.S. Edgerly (Co. D) in his narrative.

Fact #578. Lt. W.S. Edgerly (Co. D): "Probably about two thousand warriors rushed upon the less than two hundred and fifty soldiers [in Custer's command], poured over them like an avalanche, and in about twenty minutes, not one was left to tell the tale."

Fact #579. Custer descended from the Crow's Nest on the morning of June 25, 1876, where the large Indian village 15 miles away on the banks of the Little Big Horn had been pointed out to him by his Indian scouts, and had the bugler sound Officers' Call. "In a short time, the [officers'] council broke up and as these signs increased in numbers, Bloody Knife, one of the chiefs of the Red Indians [actually just a scout with the Arikara—or Ree—contingent] became greatly excited, and his followers partook of his spirit and became excited also." (Pvt. Peter Thompson, Co. C)

Fact #580. "During this fight [at the Reno-Benteen position] I saw a great many deeds of gallantry and only saw three men who appeared nervous. I came out of the fight with perfect confidence in the bravery and reliability of the American soldier and my subsequent experience has fully confirmed it." (Lt. Edgerly, Co. D)

Fact #581. The chain of command for the 1876 Sioux Expedition ran from President U.S. Grant, through Secretary of War William Belknap, to Gen. W.T. Sherman, Chief of Staff of the Army, to Gen. Philip Sheridan, Commanding General of the Army's Missouri Division. Gen. Sheridan appointed two field commanders, Brig. Gen. Alfred Terry, commander of the Dakota Dept., and Brig. Gen. George Crook, commander of the Platte Dept.

Fact #582. About a dozen men had been left behind when Reno's command retreated from the village at midday June 25 to form a position high above the river on prominent bluffs. (*Custer Battlefield,* Luce)

Fact #583. When Custer's column (12 companies of the 7th Cavalry) moved (south) up Rosebud Creek on June 22, they moved cautiously along the creek, crossing it several times as they sought the most advantageous marching and camping ground. (Luce, *Custer Battlefield*)

Fact #584. ". . .at this time General Sheridan knew that Sitting Bull's campaign had been reinforced by eighteen hundred lodges, but they did not join him by the trail we were following, and we have received no intimation of it, and this is the principal reason for the disaster. We were marching to attack from twenty-five hundred to three thousand men, believing we had less than one-third of that number to fight." (Lt. Edgerly, Co. D)

Fact #585. Arriving on the hilltops high above the east bank of the Little Big Horn River, Benteen's command heard "irregular and very scattered firing, quite a distance due north of us but there was no evidence of a general engagement in any direction." (Lt. Francis Gibson)

Fact #586. Discussing Custer's strategy after the battle, Lt. W.S. Edgerly (Co. D): "The universal opinion seemed to be that we must keep them within feeling distance and strike them at the first good opportunity, being careful not to let them get out of reach before that opportunity should occur."

Fact #587. The objective of the Montana Column and the Dakota Column, as outlined at the June 21 meeting on the steamer *Far West* by Gen. Terry, was "to get the Indians between the two forces and compel them to fight, should they be inclined to run away from a pitched battle, as Indians were reputed to do."

Fact #588. In 1874, Lt. Col. George A. Custer, field commander of the 7th U.S. Cavalry, had led his men into the Black Hills, as escorts for a scientific expedition, "to explore the area and to secure military information." (Luce, *Custer Battlefield*)

Fact #589. "Officers' Call" was sounded about 8 p.m., June 23, the second evening out of the Yellowstone encampment; their commanding officer explained "that there was no doubt of the presence of a considerable number of Indians within striking distance, that in all probability it would take hard riding to catch them, that he believed they could be overtaken and whipped, that if any troops could accomplish these objects the 7th Cavalry could, and that he hoped we would be successful, and soon be marching back to Fort A. Lincoln (D.T.)." (Lt. Edgerly, Co. D)

Fact #590. The immediate effect of the circulation of gold discoveries in the Black Hills by the 7th Cavalry's 1874 "scientific expedition" was the invasion by hordes of miners into the region which had been set aside as The Great Sioux Reservation, for the exclusive use of the Indians under the Fort Laramie Treaty of 1868. The Army was unable to check this illegal exploitation of Sioux lands.

Fact #591. Soon after Benteen's command came in sight of the Little Big Horn River, they "saw Reno's command fly across it and up the bluffs. In about 10 minutes from this time we were being warmly received by our comrades on top of 'Reno's Hill' where we had been led by the Crow scout, Half Yellow Face." (Lt. Edgerly, Co. D)

Fact #592. The day was hot and dry with a thin layer of clouds in the sky along the Little Big Horn River in southeastern Montana Territory on June 25, 1876. The Greasy Grass River, as the Indians called it, meandered along the east side of a valley, timber-lined in places, overlooked by steep bluffs in others. The day was quiet in the village until mid-afternoon.

Fact #593. White adventurers in 1874 were more than ready to brave the dangers of a Dakota winter in an isolated wilderness inhabited by semi-hostile Indians, and the possibility of military eviction, in their quest for gold.

Fact #594. On the morning of June 26, at the Reno-Benteen position, Capt. Benteen led two successful charges against attacking Indians. After the second repulse, "the firing suddenly and almost entirely ceased, and a great many Indians went to the village." (Lt. Edgerly, Co. D)

Fact #595. The immediate cause of the Sioux Campaign of 1876 was the government's December 3, 1875, order directing that all Sioux be notified "that unless they shall remove within the boundaries of their reservation before the 31st of January next, they shall be deemed hostile and treated accordingly by the military force."

Fact #596. Two Indian scouts saw Benteen's command arriving on the high ridge above the Little Big Horn River and pointed out to Benteen the remnants of Reno's command "climbing the broken hills retreating out of the river bottom." Benteen moved to join Reno, making a total of six companies, seven when the pack train showed up. (Lt. Francis Gibson, Co. H)

Fact #597. After joining Reno's command on "Reno's Hill," one of Benteen's company commanders, Capt. Thomas Weir (Co. D), dismounted and formed a skirmish line to drive away the few Indians who were, at that time, atop the bluffs, Lt. W.S. Edgerly (Co. D) later wrote.

Fact #598. In the spring of 1876, the Sioux Expedition began, with a military force under the command of Brig. Gen. George Crook moving northwest from Fort Fetterman (W.T.). Brig. Gen. Alfred H. Terry, Commander, Dept. of Da-

kota, and in charge of operations to the north, organized two separate columns, one under his command, the other commanded by Col. John Gibbon.

Captain Thomas B. Weir

USAMHI

Fact #599. Blackfeet Sioux chief Kill Eagle's account of his recent activities with Sitting Bull at the Little Big Horn, contained in a September letter from the Standing Rock Reservation (D.T.), commenced "with the date at which he left the agency, last spring, with twenty-six lodges, for the purpose of hunting buffalo and trading with hostile Indians." (Graham, *The Custer Myth*)

Fact #600. Shortly after Benteen's command had returned to the main trail, a courier from Custer arrived, Sgt. Daniel Kanipe, Co. C, with a message for Capt. McDougall to hurry up the pack train.

Fact #601. In 1876, the 12 companies in each cavalry regiment were identified by letter, skipping "J," because of the chances for misunderstanding in verbal or written orders (A, G, I). If "J" were used, it was for the "John" or recruit company.

Fact #602. Gen. Terry and the Dakota Column started from Fort Abraham Lincoln (D.T.) on May 17, 1876, with two companies of the 17th U.S. Infantry, one company of the 6th U.S. Infantry, the 20th U.S. Infantry Gatling Gun Battery, and the entire 7th U.S. Cavalry, numbering in all about 925 men. (Luce)

Fact #603. From the Reno-Benteen position, heavy firing could be heard downriver; it was thought to be Custer's command. Capt. Thomas Weir (Co. D) decided to "go out to a high point that overlooked the valley and see what was going on there." (Lt. Edgerly, Co. D)

Fact #604. Early on June 21, Gen. Terry ordered Col. Gibbon's column to begin the march up the Yellowstone again, while Gibbon remained behind for a conference with the other officers.

Fact #605. When Capt. Thomas B. Weir (Co. D) rode out from the Reno-Benteen position, seeking a better vantage point to view the scene of the heavy firing which they had heard at the Reno-Benteen position, Lt. W.S. Edgerly (Co.

D) thought Weir had received permission to advance toward the sound of the firing, and ordered D Company to follow Weir, and the remaining companies prepared to follow. (Luce, *Custer Battlefield*)

Fact #606. When the 7th Cavalry scouts, on June 24, found that the Indians' trail they had been following had veered to the west, away from the Rosebud and toward the Little Big Horn River, they were just eight miles from where the Indians had defeated Crook's force on June 17.

Fact #607. The skirmishers from the Reno-Benteen position remained in the vicinity of Weir Point "about two hours, according to my recollection, doing considerable shooting but I imagine very little hitting," said Lt. W.S. Edgerly (Co. D) in his after-battle narrative. Soon after, all three companies (D, K, M) withdrew on orders from Maj. Reno.

Fact #608. "Owing to the broken character of the country, Reno's command could not retreat in order and it looked to us like utter confusion, but we afterwards found them cool and level-headed and as a rule with their wits about them. There had been no way to get out of this bottom except in disorder as we afterwards found on investigating the ground." (Lt. Gibson, Co. H)

Fact #609. The Dakota Column of the Sioux Expedition of 1876 left from Fort Abraham Lincoln (D.T.) in May of that year. In 1876, the two states of North and South Dakota were part of the Dakota Territory, which had been formed by the U.S. Government in 1861. The Territory was split in two to form the states, which were admitted to the Union in 1889.

Fact #610. On the morning of June 22, the 7th Cavalry prepared to depart the Rosebud encampment. The pack mules were laden with boxes of ammunition and food rations for 15 days, principally hard bread, coffee, sugar, salt, and bacon. (*Custer Battlefield*, Luce)

Fact #611. The Dakota Column, commanded by Gen. Alfred Terry, commander of the Department of Dakota, and also commander of the Sioux Expedition of 1876, included all 12 companies of the 7th Cavalry Regiment, six companies of infantry, and 45 scouts and packers, a total of 1,040 men, who left Fort Abraham Lincoln (D.T.) on May 17, 1876, heading west. (Bostwick)

Fact #612. Indians from the Custer engagement noticed Capt. Thomas B. Weir and Lt. W.S. Edgerly leading D Company toward a high point on the ridge, and a large number of warriors started in the direction of the soldiers, by which time Capt. Thomas French with M Company and Lt. E.S. Godfrey with K Company had joined the advance. (Lt. W.S. Edgerly)

Fact #613. As the 7th Cavalry prepared to move out from the Rosebud encampment on June 22, each man was supplied with 100 rounds of carbine ammunition and 24 rounds of pistol ammunition to be carried on his person and in his saddlebags. He also was to carry on his horse 12 pounds of oats. (Luce, *Custer Battlefield*)

Fact #614. The Crook column of the 1876 Sioux Expedition left Fort Fetterman (W.T.) on May 29. Plans to join forces with the Dakota Column and the Montana Column went awry, when Crook's column was stymied at the Battle of the Rosebud (M.T.) and withdrew back south to Goose Creek (W.T.), near the present-day town of Sheridan (WY).

Fact #615. During the night of June 25, 1876, soldiers at the Reno-Benteen position augmented their makeshift breastworks with horse and mule carcasses, which were dragged from the center of the position to the perimeter. By the next day, the stench from all the dead animals added to the great discomfort of the troops.

Fact #616. During the two days of fighting, Reno's and Benteen's commands lost 32 men killed and 44 wounded. (Luce, *Custer Battlefield*)

Fact #617. After the battle, transporting the wounded from Reno's command by hand litters proved so unsatisfactory that mule litters were constructed and used with more ease.

Fact #618. On the afternoon of the third day of moving (south) up the Rosebud, June 24, 1876, Custer's scouts reported that the Indian trail they had been following turned abruptly to the right and went westward toward the Little Big Horn River.

Fact #619. As Custer's column (C, E, F, I, L companies) passed Weir Point in the late afternoon of June 25, 1876, Pvt. Peter Thompson (Co. C), who rode with his company which was probably the second in line of march, wrote: "It was all in commotion. One party of Indians were dashing [north] down the river; others were rushing toward the [southern] upper end of the village. The cause of this commotion was Major Reno with three companies of men [A, G, M] about a mile distant from the [southern] upper end of the village, dashing along in a gallop towards them. The officers were riding in order, a little in advance of their respective companies."

Fact #620. Because Gen. Crook had not communicated with the Dakota Column about his setback on Rosebud Creek on June 17, Custer's 7th Cavalry had no idea they were riding close on the trail of a much larger enemy force than had been expected.

Fact #621. After darkness set in on the evening of June 24, and the men and horses had rested, Custer broke camp and continued to follow the trail for several miles, finally halting to await daylight so that a more careful reconnaissance could be made.

Fact #622. When Maj. Reno and his battalion crossed the Little Big Horn River to the west side and advanced (north) down the valley to attack the southern end of the village, it became evident that there were a great many more tepees and Indians in the valley than had been observed from the hills prior to his separation from Custer. Bluffs and the foliage of tall cottonwoods had hidden the camps from their view.

Fact #623. The weather on June 25 and 26 was sunny and oppressively hot, and the lack of water at the Reno-Benteen position caused terrible suffering among the wounded. (Lt. Francis M. Gibson, Co. H)

Fact #624. Writing to Walter Camp in 1909, Charles Varnum, Custer's Chief of Scouts at LBH, retired after 50 years of Army service, recalled being ordered to take scouts and an interpreter to the "Crow['s] nest." The party left the column about "9 o'clock" Varnum wrote. "Except that we stopped two or three times in the dense undergrowth along a stream to let the Crows smoke cigarettes we were on the go till about 2:30 or 3 a.m. on the 25th, and as day light broke I found myself in a peculiar hollow like old Crow Nest at West Point, near the summit of a high ridge in the divide between the Rosebud and the Little Big Horn. This latter stream was in plain sight about ten miles off. A timbered tributary led down to the Rosebud and up which we had evidently come during the night."

Fact #625. The men of Co. H, Capt. Frederick Benteen's company, were not ordered to dig in when the troops began fortifying the Reno-Benteen position in the early evening of June 25, 1876. This part of the defensive line was on top of a long, high, narrow ridge, the highest point in the perimeter. Co. H, in the ensuing action, that evening and the next day, suffered the greatest casualties of any of the seven companies (A, B, D, G, H, K, M).

Fact #626. Walter Camp's field notes: "It is amusing to read the accounts of some writers, who, ignorant of the facts, have sought to show how Custer, when he ordered Reno forward, intended to support Reno by striking the village in the center, and have Benteen swing around to the left and come into the valley behind Reno." Camp didn't believe either of these theories.

Fact #627. Reno's men made a defensive stand in the timber until they were ordered to mount again and retreat to the bluffs. This retreat became a panicky flight, with every man for himself, while the Indians continued their attack as the troops crossed the river.

Fact #628. "Much has been written about the Custer phase of the Battle of the Little Big Horn, but very few facts can definitely be stated," except for casualty figures. (Luce, *Custer Battlefield*)

Fact #629. Capt. Benteen, now in charge of the three companies at Weir Point (D, H, K), had the troops dismount and throw out skirmish lines, to make a stand here along with the rest of the troops at the Reno-Benteen position.

Fact #630. Custer's route after sending Reno to attack in the valley is a matter of much debate: did the column stay atop what is now known as Nye-Cartwright ridge all the way to Last Stand Hill, did they try to cross the Little Big Horn at Medicine Tail Coulee, etc., etc.? Some, but not all, of the questions were answered by the 1984 and 1985 archaeological surveys.

Fact #631. Many of the horses which had brought the men of Custer's command almost 1,000 miles were shot to make breastworks against the deadly bullets and arrows from the Sioux and Cheyenne warriors.

Fact #632. It is thought that not long after the Indians began to show a strong force in Custer's front, he turned his column to the left, toward the river, and advanced in the direction of the Indian village to the junction of two ravines just below a spring.

Fact #633. Early on the morning of June 26, 1876, the defenders at the Reno-Benteen position were awakened by heavy rifle fire from the Indians. Pvt. Peter Thompson (Co. C), in his 1913 memoir, reported that he had slept through the opening volleys: "The Indians had been pouring in volleys upon us long before I had been awakened and they were still at it. Under cover of darkness, they had gained a foothold in some of the numerous ravines that surrounded us. Some of them were so close that their fire was very effective. The ping of bullets and the groaning and struggling of the wounded horses was oppressive. But my duty was plain. The way that I had to go to my post was up a short hill towards the edge of the bluff. ...I could not see how I could possibly get there alive for the bullets of the Indians were ploughing up the sand and gravel in every direction; but it was my duty to go."

Fact #634. At the junction of two ravines, just below a spring, some believe that Custer dismounted two companies under the command of Keogh and Calhoun (I and C) to fight on foot; it is possible that these companies advanced to a knoll, near Crittenden's marker, while the remaining three mounted companies (E, F, L) continued along the ridge to Custer Hill. (Luce, *Custer Battlefield*)

Fact #635. Trumpeter Martin's comments to Benteen that Reno was "driving everything before him" caused consternation for some, making "the hearts of some of the younger men who had not won their spurs to sink as they had looked forward to what we all thought would probably be the last great Indian fight of any consequence in this country. . ." (Lt. W.S. Edgerly, Co. D)

Fact #636. In the Kill Eagle account published in the September 24, 1876, *New York Herald*, about his involvement at LBH, the Blackfeet Sioux tribal chief spoke of "having heard reports that troops were going out to punish the hostiles but thought he would have time to do his hunting and trading and get out of the way before a battle occurred." (Graham, *The Custer Myth*)

Fact #637. Gen. Terry wrote, in his "Official Report" after LBH, that his plan for the disposition of his forces on June 21 "was founded on the belief that at some point on the Little Big Horn, a body of hostile Sioux would be found; and that although it was impossible to make movements in perfect concert, as might have been done had there been a known fixed objective point to be reached, yet by the judicious use of the excellent guides and scouts which we possessed, the two columns might be brought within cooperating distance of each other, so that either of them [Gibbon or Custer] which should be first engaged might be a waiting fight—give time for the other to come up."

Fact #638. The account of Lt. Francis Gibson (Co. H), who rode with Benteen's column, reported that Maj. Marcus A. Reno, commanding three companies (A, G, M) opened the battle, "with, as his officers say, an assurance of support from Custer," by attacking the southern end of the village.

Fact #639. After the Civil War, when Custer was campaigning against the Indians, "he became indignant at the corrupt management of Indian affairs by the Department of the Interior. The Indians on the reservations were, by agreement, to be fed and clothed by the Government. But much of the food issued was of inferior quality, and frauds were perpetrated on the Indians by civilian employees. Besides this, guns and ammunition of better quality than those with which the soldiers were equipped were sold to the Indians by civilian traders. Against this state of affairs, Custer protested vehemently at Washington [DC], but without effect." (Bates, *New York Times*, June 20, 1926)

Fact #640. The line occupied by Custer's battalion in the late afternoon of June 25, 1876, near Last Stand Ridge, was the first "considerable" ridge back of the river. His front was extended about three-quarters of a mile. Most of the village was in view. (Luce)

Fact #641. Some of the men left behind in the trees along the river after Reno's retreat following the midday attack on the south end of the village June 25 were able to gain the bluffs on the night of the 25th, but others were trapped until the night of June 26, after the Indians had moved off. All the survivors returned to the command.

Fact #642. At the Reno-Benteen position many of the combatants on both sides were on foot, and doing much of their fighting from a prone position on the ground. On June 25-26, the warriors outnumbered the troops by as many as 20-1. Hordes of Indians were wriggling along gullies and hiding behind knolls on all sides of the troops.

Fact #643. Privates Peter Thompson and James Watson (Co. C) dropped out of Custer's column (C, E, F, I, L) as it rode along the ridges across the Little Big Horn River from the Indian village on June 25, 1876, due to the exhaustion of their horses. After dodging Indians, they made their way back toward the trail they had ridden over. Writing about it nearly 40 years later, Thompson said, "We were becoming so tired that the presence of Indians was no longer a terror to us. The hill we were climbing seemed very long, so much so to me that I fell down and lay there without any inclination to move again, until Watson called my attention to the head of the columns of cavalry which now came into plain view. So with renewed energy we made our way up amid showers of lead [from sniping Indians]. The savages seemed loathe to let us go."

Fact #644. After first arriving at the blufftop position, Reno's command present for duty consisted of 112 men, 20 or more Arikara scouts, three or four Crow scouts, three white scouts, and one Negro listed as an interpreter. (*Custer Battlefield*, Luce) [Actually, the Negro interpreter, Isaiah Dorman, had been killed in the valley fight.]

Fact #645. "It was thought that a double attack [by Custer and Gibbon] would very much diminish the chances of a successful retreat by the Sioux, should they be disinclined to fight. It was believed to be impracticable to join Colonel Gibbon's column to Lieutenant-Colonel Custer's force; for more than one-half of Colonel Gibbon's troops were infantry, who would be unable to keep up with cavalry in a rapid movement; while to detach Gibbon's mounted men and add them to the Seventh Cavalry would leave his force too small to act as an independent body." ("Official Report" of Gen. Terry published after the Battle)

Fact #646. By midday on June 25, Capt. Benteen's three-company battalion (H, D, K) had seen no action, for he had swung to the left to scout the country as ordered. Finding that the bluffs were almost impassable and that his horses were fast wearing out, he swung back to the main trail taken by Custer and Reno.

Fact #647. Pvt. Francis J. Kennedy (Co. I): "The surviving [mules and] horses were arranged in a semi-circle with their saddles and bridles on, the wounded being in the valley, between the horses."

Fact #648. Trumpeter John Martin, bearer of the "last message" from Custer to Benteen, reported to Benteen that he had been fired upon during his ride, and his horse was wounded. But he was also elated, telling Benteen that the Indians were "skedaddling" and that Custer was charging the village.

Fact #649. The troops of Gen. Alfred Terry and Col. John Gibbon, numbering about 450 men, left the mouth of Rosebud Creek on June 21, proceeded up (south and west) the Yellowstone River, and crossed to its south side just above the mouth of Tullock Creek.

Fact #650. ". . .dismounting from my horse, which had carried me so many miles, I dashed down the ravine toward the bushes; but the sudden flight of a flock of birds from that point caused me to turn aside and I made a bee line for the pillar of rocks above me." Peter Thompson, Co. C, had ridden up on the

This view looks west from Reno Hill toward the Indian village and the Little Big Horn valley. Seventh Cavalry troopers with Reno held this position until the morning of June 27, 1876. *USAMHI*

ridges above the Little Big Horn River in Custer's advance on the afternoon of June 25, 1876. Abandoning his exhausted mount, Thompson decided to make his way on foot. "After arriving [at the pillar of rocks] I took inventory of my ammunition. My pistol contained five cartridges, my belt contained seventeen cartridges for my carbine, a very slim magazine as a means of defense. I. . .left nearly a hundred rounds in my saddle bags, but. . .was unable to carry more with me."

Fact #651. Hearing the sound of firing from (north) down river, and seeing D Company ride out behind Capt. Thomas B. Weir and Lt. W.S. Edgerly, Capt. Benteen and the other two companies of his battalion followed Weir, and soon the remaining men prepared to follow. (*Custer Battlefield*, Luce)

Fact #652. When Capt. McDougall arrived at the Reno-Benteen position on the bluffs, over an hour after Custer's message, "Be quick—Bring Packs!", had been delivered by Trumpeter Martin, the officers conferred on what action to take.

Fact #653. As Reno's battalion was attacking the south end of the Indian village, Custer's five companies (C, E, F, I, L) moved along the high ridge of the east bank, with the intention, it is supposed, of making a flank movement and thereby placing the Indians between his and Reno's command. (Lt. Francis Gibson, Co. H)

Fact #654. When the 7th Cavalry column rode out on June 22, 1876, to seek out and destroy the Indians in their village, the famed band (which played as the cavalry attacked the Cheyenne village at the Washita River in 1868) and Custer's hounds were left behind.

Fact #655. Having joined Reno's command as it rode forward from Reno Hill about 6 p.m., June 25, 1876, to provide support for Capt. Thomas Weir's advance party from Co. D, Pvt. Peter Thompson (Co. C) was questioned about his separation from the Custer column (C, E, F, I, L), and the status of that detachment. Thompson wrote "The Experience of a Private Soldier in the Custer Massacre" nearly 40 years after LBH, telling about the Reno command's subsequent withdrawal back to the Reno-Benteen position. "We did not retreat very far, for that was impossible. Our retreat was covered by Company D commanded by Capt. [Thomas] Weir. He was the only captain who wished to go to the relief of Custer. He had begged in vain to have Reno advance to Custer's relief. That being denied him, he asked permission to take his company and ascertain Custer's positions; but he was refused that privilege."

Fact #656. The *Reader's Encyclopedia of the American West* notes that Gen. Alfred H. Terry, commanding the 1876 Sioux Expedition, sent Maj. Marcus Reno with six companies of the 7th Cavalry to scout (south) up to the forks of the Powder River, in search of Indians. They were to search the tributaries of both streams, then move west to the Tongue River and (north) down to the confluence with the Yellowstone. But, in what the contributing editor referred to as a "technical violation of his orders," Reno went on to the Rosebud Creek, where they found the remains of a large Indian village, with the Indians moving (south) up that stream. He then returned to the Yellowstone rendezvous point.

Fact #657. When the group of officers at the Reno-Benteen position considered what action to take after the pack train arrived, considering the orders to both McDougall and Benteen from Custer to "bring packs," the fact that Reno's retreat had damaged the morale of his command, combined with the fact that Benteen's men, having so far faced no action, were naturally more confident, caused indecision.

Fact #658. After hearing heavy and continuous firing from the north, evidently the Custer engagement, troops at the Reno-Benteen position believed that Custer and his five companies might be in need of assistance. (Luce, *Custer Battlefield*)

Fact #659. Co. A, assigned to Reno's battalion, consisted of two officers and 48 enlisted men.

Fact #660. After receiving reports at the base of the Crow's Nest in the Wolf Mountains from scout George Herendeen and Capt. Tom Custer that the column had been spotted by Indians, Custer ordered Officers' Call blown by trumpeter

Sgt. John Martin (Giovanni Martini). Years later, Martin would recall this order as unusual since he had been told that to insure the command was not discovered, there would be no bugle calls. Martin said this made him think that Custer was no longer worried about being discovered by the Indians. (Robert Church, 1991 CBH&MA Symposium)

Fact #661. The Fetterman Fight of 1866 and the Custer Fight of 1876 are analogous, in that the immediate commands of both leaders were killed with no survivors to tell the story.

Fact #662. Peter Thompson (Pvt., Co. C), nearly 40 years after the battle, recalled watching Reno's attack, withdrawal, and retreat. Thompson rode that afternoon, June 25, 1876, with Custer's column (C, E, F, I, L) along the ridges across the Little Big Horn River from the Indian village, and reported in his memoir, "After Major Reno gained the top of the hill [at what is now known as the Reno-Benteen position], he was joined by Captain Benteen and his three companies [D, H, K]; likewise by Capt. [Thomas] McDougall [Co. B] with the pack train making seven companies [including Reno's A, G, M] besides twenty men of the right wing who had been detailed to attend to the pack mules of the right wing." The "right wing" was not further identified, but each company had supposedly sent one non-commissioned officer and six enlisted men to look after that company's mules.

Fact #663. Each company of the 7th U.S. Cavalry normally consisted of two officers and 40-50 enlisted men. The regulation strength of cavalry companies, however, was 100 men. (Scott and Fox, *Archaeological Insights Into the Custer Battle*)

Fact #664. The area around the Reno-Benteen position was covered by sagebrush and long grass, providing excellent cover for advancing Indian attackers. The surface soil was dry and powdery for the first inch or two, then extremely hard. There was no gravel. The shortage of digging implements plus the hard soil made entrenching impracticable, so the defenders relied mostly on breastworks constructed of hardtack boxes, packs, and saddles, especially across the eastern, open end of the horseshoe-shaped position.

Fact #665. The largest column in the Sioux Expedition of 1876 was the column from the Department of the Platte, commanded by Maj. Gen. George Crook. He left Fort Fetterman (W.T.) with 15 companies of cavalry, five companies of infantry, and 270 Indian scouts, a total of 1,320 men, on May 29, 1876, headed in a northerly direction. (Bostwick)

Fact #666. Charles Francis Bates, *New York Times*, June 20, 1926: "The discovery of gold in the Black Hills of Dakota became another source of friction between the Indians and the whites. This area had been solemnly pledged to the Indians in the Treaty of 1868. When it was learned that gold had been found in these hills, called 'the haunted Sinais of the Sioux,' an exploring party was sent in with a guard of troops under Custer. The presence of gold was confirmed by the expedition and the Government permitted the white men to take the hills. This aroused keen resentment among the Indians."

Fact #667. Pvt. Peter Thompson (Co. C) wrote that about a half mile past where George and Tom Custer had "reviewed" the companies as they crested the hill atop the bluffs, "we came in sight of the Indian village and it was truly an imposing sight to anyone who had not seen anything like it before. For about three miles on the left [west] bank of the river the tepees were stretched, the white canvas gleaming in the sunlight. Beyond the village was a black mass of ponies grazing on the short green grass."

Fact #668. Upon seeing Capt. Weir (Co. D) mount up and ride from the Reno-Benteen position toward the sound of heavy firing, Lt. W.S. Edgerly (Co. D) ordered his company to mount and follow, riding along the bluffs where Custer was last seen alive by Reno's men. (Lt. Edgerly)

Fact #669. Fort Abraham Lincoln (D.T.) was described by author James Horan in *The Great American West* as "one of the most impressive on the frontier," with a V-shaped palisade guarded by blockhouses at the corners and a steep bank on the third side, encompassing officers' quarters, barracks, a hospital, a laundry, and stables for the cavalry horses.

Fact #670. In his unsuccessful effort to strike the (downstream) north end of the Indian village on the morning of June 25, 1876, Custer "took his five troops too far" from the rest of his divided regiment, and men under Reno and Benteen had too few numbers to fight their way to Custer, according to Lt. Francis Gibson (Co. H). Many later historians strongly disagreed with Gibson's assessment, while many others agreed.

Fact #671. Gen. Alfred Terry provided Custer with written orders on the morning of June 22: "COLONEL—The Brigadier-General Commanding directs that as soon as your regiment can be made ready for the march you proceed up the Rosebud in pursuit of the Indians whose trail was discovered by Major Reno a few days since. It is, of course, impossible to give any definite instructions in regard to this movement, and were it not impossible to do so, the Department Commander places too much confidence in your zeal, energy, and ability to wish to impose upon you precise orders which might hamper your action when nearly in contact with the enemy. He will, however, indicate to you his own views of what your actions should be, and he desires you should conform to them unless you shall see sufficient reason for departing from them." Many consider these orders a "blank check" for Custer to do as he saw fit.

Fact #672. Custer's "last message" to Benteen meant "that Custer recognized he was fighting against heavy odds and that he needed every man and every cartridge available. Benteen did not send any hurry-up order to the pack train, nor do anything to assist its commander, although he knew that a number of mules were stuck in the mud at a water-hole. He said he did not return for the pack train because he deemed it to be perfectly safe where it was. He moved on down the trail and joined Major Reno and his men on the bluffs. Reno, then, as senior officer, was in command, and Benteen turned over to him the order he had received from Custer." (Bates, *New York Times,* June 20, 1926)

Fact #673. The Sioux Expedition of 1876 was Brig. Gen. Alfred Terry's first campaign in 11 years, and his first against Indian foes.

Fact #674. In "The Experience of a Private Soldier in the Custer Massacre," Pvt. Peter Thompson (Co. C) told of his experiences riding with the Custer column (C, E, F, I, L) along the ridges across the Little Big Horn River from the Indian village. Writing nearly 40 years after the battle, Thompson said: "While I was making calculations as to leaving my ['practically useless'] horse and trying my luck on foot, I thought I was seeing something familiar in [the] appearance [of some approaching Indians]. On coming close, I saw they were our Ree scouts and two Crow Indians, one of whom was Half Yellow Face or Two Bloody Hands. He had received this latter name from the fact that on the back of his buckskin shirt the print of two human hands was visible, either put there by red ink or blood." Thompson must have mistaken another Crow for Half Yellow Face, or the shirt decoration was not unique; Half Yellow Face was with Reno.

Fact #675. Kill Eagle's tribal band of 26 Blackfeet Sioux lodges was "obliged to hunt, as they were starving at the [Standing Rock Reservation, D.T.], and from his account they were very successful, killing twenty or thirty buffalo some days, and in one herd they killed all but two." (*New York Herald,* September 24, 1876, about Kill Eagle's involvement in the June 25 battle)

Fact #676. The field notes of noted LBH historian Walter Camp include this observation by Camp: "The remark of [scout Mitch] Bouyer to [Crow scout] Curley, that Custer was seeking a high point to await the arrival of the other troops; and Bouyer's remark that he did not think they would come, having probably been 'scared out', shows that Custer had probably been waiting for Benteen and watching the result of Reno's battle."

Fact #677. Capt. Benteen's decision to make a stand with the Reno-Benteen forces at Weir Point proved impracticable: it was impossible to bring up the wounded and the pack mules had been scattered.

Fact #678. In 1876, standard time zones had not yet been established, so the watches in Custer's column were set, generally, on what was known as "Chicago [IL] time," making "dawn" on June 25 come around 3 a.m.

Fact #679. Capt. Frederick Benteen either sent or led a charge of nearly two dozen soldiers and packers against a build-up of Sioux in the ravine just west of the Reno-Benteen defense perimeter, leading down to the river. The Indians were scattered, and several casualties were suffered by the attackers: Pvt. Thomas Meador (Co. H) was killed and Pvt. James Tanner was mortally wounded. At least one, and maybe two, were wounded.

Fact #680. The 7th Cavalry's record under the field command of George Custer well illustrates the important part played by the U.S. Army in the advance of frontier settlements. Stationed at remote army posts and isolated cantonments they were called on to guard emigrants and freighters, mail stages, and telegraph lines. Sometimes they undertook exploring expeditions into little-known regions, and sometimes they protected scientific expeditions into new territory. They shielded surveyors laying out the route for railroads, and the construction crews who built the roads. Sometimes they evicted white trespassers from Indian reservations, and sometimes they risked their lives in campaigns against the Indians.

Fact #681. In February 1876, Gen. Alfred E. Terry, Commander of the Department of Dakota, sent a letter to Col. John Gibbon, commander of the Montana Division: "Plan a campaign down the Yellowstone on the theory that Crook is coming up from the south and that you and Custer must prevent the Sioux from getting away northward and then, in turn, help Crook give them a whipping."

Fact #682. Considering the advantages of the Reno-Benteen position over the potential position at Weir Point, orders were given to re-consolidate the forces back at the Reno-Benteen position, about a mile and a half to the south. The cavalry companies in the forward position, under the command of Capt. Benteen (H, D, K), then withdrew back to the comparative safety of the Reno-Benteen position, followed by increasing numbers of attacking Indians.

Fact #683. Each cavalry regiment in the frontier army was theoretically divisible into three battalions of four companies each, the battalion being commanded by a major, and numbered. Sometimes these divided units were referred to as squadrons rather than battalions, and the subsets were called companies or troops. In writings on LBH, the terms "companies" and "troops" are used fairly interchangeably, although the unit designation as "troop" was not instituted until 1882.

Fact #684. As the cavalry forces withdrew from Weir Point back to the earlier position at Reno-Benteen to complete their entrenchment, Indians swarmed the position from every direction. Lines were thrown out for defense and the heavy firing continued until dark, when the warriors withdrew to the valley.

Fact #685. "Maj. M.A. Reno, Seventh Cavalry, with six companies of his regiment and one Gatling gun, was directed to reconnoiter the valley of the

Powder as far as the forks of the river, then to cross to Mizpah Creek, to descend that creek to near its mouth, thence to cross to Tongue River and descend to its mouth. He was provided with rations for ten days, carried on pack saddles." ("Official Report," June 10, of Gen. Alfred H. Terry, commander of the Dakota Column and the 1876 Sioux Expedition)

Fact #686. During the night of June 25, at the Reno-Benteen position, efforts were made to prepare for the return of the Indians at the next dawn. Only three or four spades and shovels were available to dig rifle pits and trenches. Some waited their turn for the shovels, while others used knives, tin cups, or mess kits to dig protection for themselves.

Fact #687. Custer's column, including Cos. A, C, E, F, G, I, L, M, came upon an Indian camping place on the late morning of June 25, 1876. Pvt. Peter Thompson (Co. C), writing many years later, recalled: "Here we came to a halt for the purpose of noting the extent of the camp, and by this means to approximate the number of Indians in the party. After wandering around we found that but a small party had made this their camping-place, but from all appearances they must have had a high time. They had placed in the ground four upright posts upon which they had made a small platform of limbs of trees. On this they had placed the heads of several buffalo and from the appearance of the ground they must have had what is called a buffalo dance."

Fact #688. Two officers were wounded during LBH: 2d Lt. Charles Varnum (Co. A, commanding the Detachment of Indian Scouts), wounded in both legs, and Capt. Frederick Benteen (Co. H, commanding the Benteen battalion), wounded, very slightly, in the right thumb.

Fact #689. According to Army regulations adopted in 1861, each company was to consist of a minimum of "One captain, one first lieutenant, one second lieutenant, one first sergeant, one company quartermaster-sergeant, four sergeants, eight corporals, two musicians, two farriers, one saddler, one wagoner, 56 privates; aggregate, 79. Maximum: 72 privates; aggregate, 95."

Fact #690. The troops entrenching at the Reno-Benteen position on the night of June 25, used ammunition cases and hardtack boxes for barricades. Occasionally, the men would wander to the packs for hardtack or bacon to allay their hunger.

Fact #691. Spying a comrade in Custer's column (C, E, F, I, L companies) whose horse had fallen and was struggling to regain its footing, Pvt. Peter Thompson (Co. C) noted, "Beside [my comrade Watson (Pvt. James Watson, Co. C)], I saw Sargeant [sic] [George August Finckle] Finkle of our company [C] sitting calmly on his horse looking on and making no effort to help Watson in his difficulty. But finally [Watson's] poor animal gained his feet with a groan, and Finkle passed on with a rush to overtake our company." Finckle died with Custer.

Fact #692. As Custer rode toward his last battle, he was supported by a regiment not at its best, whose ranks were filled with men who were headed toward their first battle. Indeed, 30-40% of the enlisted men were in their first enlistment. Sgt. Ferdinand Culbertson (Co. A) later testified: "[The new men] had very little training. They were poor horsemen, and would fire at random. They were brave enough, but they had not the time nor the opportunity to make soldiers. Some of them were not fit to take into action."

Fact #693. While Maj. Reno was attacking the village, and Custer was riding along the ridgeline high above the Little Big Horn River, Capt. Benteen, "having found no Indians in the country he had been sent to scout, returned to the main trail. He reached this trail at a point just ahead of the slow-moving train of pack mules, which carried all of the reserve ammunition. As he proceeded along the trail, Trumpeter Martin arrived with a brief message from Custer, which was at once a peremptory order and an S.O.S." (Bates, *New York Times*, June 20, 1926)

Fact #694. Fort Ellis (M.T.) is located about three miles east of present-day Bozeman (MT). Established in 1867, it was the base at which Col. John Gibbon, operating out of Fort Shaw (M.T.), acquired additional troops in the spring of 1876 before proceeding eastward in the ill-fated operation that ended in LBH.

Fact #695. "At dawn on June 26, the Indians returned from their village and the battle was renewed. Most of the soldiers were suffering from thirst, and the wounded especially were in great need of water. Dr. Henry Porter, the surviving surgeon, asked that water be obtained at any cost." (*Custer Battlefield*, Luce)

Fact #696. About dusk on June 26, hostile action around the Reno-Benteen position ceased, and the Indian bands began moving their camp around sunset, seeming to be "gradually melting away as they marched off with their many belongings, pack animals, and loose ponies." (Lt. Francis Gibson, Co. H)

Fact #697. Camp kettles and canteens were gathered together in response to Dr. Porter's plea for water "at any cost" to relieve the suffering of the wounded at the Reno-Benteen position atop the bluffs, and a group of volunteers crept down a deep ravine to the Little Big Horn River on the morning of June 26, despite fire from the surrounding Sioux and Cheyenne warriors.

Fact #698. In May 1861, the Army officially defined a cavalry battalion as having a minimum of "316 company officers and enlisted men; one major, one battalion adjutant (lieutenant), one battalion quartermaster and commissary (lieutenant), one sergeant-major, one quartermaster-sergeant, one commissary-sergeant, one hospital steward, one saddler-sergeant, one veterinary-sergeant;

aggregate, 325. Maximum: 380 company officers and enlisted men; aggregate, 389." The 7th Cavalry at LBH was markedly under-strength.

Fact #699. As the volunteers from the Reno-Benteen position went down the ravine for water on the morning of June 26, 1876, ". . .four Army sharpshooters stood on a high point to draw the Indians' fire and also to protect the water carriers with their own fire." (Luce, *Custer Battlefield*) Water was desperately needed, not only for the wounded, but for the rest of the command.

Fact #700. On the morning of June 25, 1876, Pvt. Peter Thompson (Co. C) rode with the main column on the way to the Little Big Horn. In his memoirs, he recalled: "Our gait was a lively walk. Having had a few hours sleep the men began to be talkative and speculation ran high on how soon the campaign would end. One old soldier said that it would end just as soon as we could catch old Sitting Bull. Another said, 'If that is all, the campaign will soon be over, and Custer will take us with him to the Centennial.' 'Of course,' said a wag, 'We will take Sitting Bull with us.' This created a roar of laughter among those who heard him."

Fact #701. When the 7th Cavalry moved out from the Yellowstone in search of the Indians, it was common knowledge among the soldiers that "a large and fresh Indian trail" had been found by Maj. Reno's scout [south] up the Rosebud, and it was believed that "nothing but the rapid flight of the Indians could save them from fight or surrender." (Lt. Edgerly, Co. D)

Fact #702. The men at the Reno-Benteen position moved with great caution after the apparent departure of all the Indians, to avoid possible ambush by concealed warriors.

Fact #703. The basic organizational unit for cavalry in the U.S. Army of the 1870s was the regiment, to consist of "975 battalion officers and enlisted men; one colonel, one lieutenant-colonel, one regimental adjutant (lieutenant), one regimental quartermaster and commissary (lieutenant), two chief buglers, 16 musicians for band; aggregate, 997. Maximum: 1,167 officers and enlisted men; aggregate, 1,189."

Fact #704. Some of the words to "Garry Owen," the regimental song of the 7th U.S. Cavalry, were: "Let Bacchus' sons be not dismayed, But join with me each jovial blade; Come booze and sing, and lend your aid, to help me with the chorus. Instead of spa we'll drink down ale, And pay for the reck'ning on the nail; No man for debt shall go to gaol, From Garry Owen in glory."

Fact #705. After having trouble with his horse as he rode along the high ground east of the Little Big Horn River with Custer's column on June 25, 1876, Pvt. Peter Thompson (Co. C) watched his riding companion turn his horse to the rear. Thompson recalled: "I finished putting on my spurs, mounted my [failing] horse again, and rode on after my company, but my progress was very slow. My spurs having been poorly fastened came off, and seeing a pair lying on the trail, I got off my horse to secure them. Hearing an oath behind me, I looked back and saw my comrade [Pvt. James] Watson [Co. C] trying to get his horse on its feet. The poor brute had fallen and was struggling to gain an upright condition." Several of Custer's soldiers had trouble with their horses, and, as a result, straggled back to Reno's command.

Fact #706. At the Reno-Benteen position on the evening of June 26, realization that the Indians had gone allowed the men to water the horses and mules for the first time since before the battle started. A few men made fires for coffee, and the position on the bluff was moved slightly and strengthened.

Fact #707. 7th Cavalry soldiers at Fort Abraham Lincoln (D.T.) suffered through hordes of mosquitos from the Heart and Missouri rivers in the summer, and bone-numbing cold in the severe Dakota winter. The only relief was provided at "The Point," a settlement of saloons, gambling halls, etc., across the Heart River from the fort. A ferry connected the fort and The Point, and in the winter, soldiers walked across the icy, frozen river. Visitation was interrupted by spring thaw, when the rushing torrent was impassable.

Fact #708. Custer sent three different messages to Benteen, asking for reinforcements and supplies. "It is fair to assume that [Custer] sent some messages to Reno, although Reno denied that he received any. We have the statements of two men, one a soldier and the other an Indian scout, that they delivered messages from Custer to Reno." (Bates, *New York Times*, June 20, 1926)

Fact #709. On the night of June 24, the combined Terry-Gibbon columns camped on the lower Tullock Creek. June 25, the day of Custer's battle, they traversed the arid hills along the Big Horn River in an effort to get to the mouth of the Little Big Horn River.

Fact #710. Charles Francis Bates, *New York Times*, June 20, 1926, outlined the strategy decided upon by Gen. Terry, Col. Gibbon, and Lt. Col. Custer at their meeting on June 21 on the steamer *Far West*: "As Custer moved to intercept the Indians from the south, Terry and Gibbon were to make a wide detour along the north, and the Indians were to be caught between the two columns. Terry and Gibbon planned to be at the mouth of the Little Big Horn on the 26th. Custer's regiment had rations for fifteen days in case they found it necessary to go far in pursuit of the Indians. Six hundred strong, it started up the Rosebud on the 22d, reaching the river's headwaters on the evening of the 24th. Through his scouts Custer learned that the Indians were not far away. Their main trail was discovered leading toward the Little Big Horn River."

Fact #711. Camp Supply (I.T.), one mile east of Fort Supply in western Oklahoma, was established by Lt. Col. Alfred Sully and Lt. Col. George A. Custer in November 1868, near the junction of Wolf Creek with the North

Canadian River. From here Custer and the 7th Cavalry moved south to the Battle of the Washita, and to this place the column returned with captives but without Maj. Joel Elliott and 16 of his men who had been left behind and were later found slaughtered by the Cheyenne whose village had been attacked in a snowy dawn.

Fact #712. Custer's attempt to trap the Indians between Reno's command, attacking the south (upper) end of the village, and his own command, striking, he thought, the northern end, failed because of the size of the village. Custer and his command attacked about "midway" along a "three-mile long" village, and "the enemy proved too strong for the plan to work." (Lt. Francis Gibson, Co. H)

Fact #713. The 7th Cavalry fought at the Little Big Horn with 17 officers missing out of an authorized complement of 48.

Fact #714. "At a conference which took place on [June] 21st between Colonel Gibbon, Lieutenant-Colonel Custer, and myself, I communicated to them the plan of operations which I had decided to adopt," Gen. Alfred H. Terry, commander of the Dakota Column and the 1876 Sioux Expedition, wrote in his "Official Report" on the Expedition. "It was that Colonel Gibbon's column should cross the Yellowstone near the mouth of the Big Horn, and thence up that stream, with the expectation that it would arrive at the last-named point by the 26th; that Lieutenant-Colonel Custer with the whole of the Seventh Cavalry should proceed up the Rosebud until he should ascertain the direction in which the trail discovered by Major Reno led; that if it led to the Little Big Horn it should not be followed; but that Lieutenant-Colonel Custer should keep still farther south before turning toward the river. . ."

Fact #715. In practice, cavalry regiments and battalions were widely dispersed in and along the frontier areas during the Indian Wars era; frequently frontier forts were manned by just one company.

Fact #716. Pvt. Peter Thompson (Co. C) recalled his life-saving reunion with Reno's command after he and Pvt. James Watson (Co. C) had become separated from Custer's column (C, E, F, I, L) due to the exhaustion of their horses. "When we stepped out into the trail at the head of the advancing column, it was about five o'clock in the afternoon [probably closer to 6 p.m., when Reno and Benteen rode out to support Weir at Weir Point]. The first man we recognized was Sargeant [sic] [Daniel] Kanipe of our company. He had been sent back by Custer to hurry up the ammunition. . . .There is no doubt they needed it very badly."

Fact #717. A *New York Herald* newspaper article on September 24, 1876, told of the intensity of the firing as swarms of Indians overwhelmed the Custer command. "Then the [fire] gradually slackened and gradually grew more feeble.

A few scattering shakes, like rain on a window pane, and then the movement ceased as the last of Custer's band of heroes went down with the setting sun."

Fact #718. Charles Varnum, 2d Lt., Co. A, commanded the Detachment of Indian Scouts on June 25, 1876. He was the last surviving officer of Custer's command.

Fact #719. Fort Keogh (M.T.) was located at present-day Miles City (MT) on US 10. Situated on the south bank of the Yellowstone River, and originally known as the Tongue River Cantonment, it was relocated and renamed in honor of Capt. Myles Keogh (Co. I, 7th Cavalry), who died at LBH.

Fact #720. An eyewitness to Reno's charge and subsequent retreat to the bluffs, Pvt. Peter Thompson (Co. C): ". . .Major Reno led the retreat toward the river and across it and up to the top of the bluff. In crossing the river there was great confusion; each man seemed to be for himself. Here Lieu. [sic] [1st Lt. Donald McIntosh] MacIntosh [Co. G] with a number of others was shot from his horse."

Fact #721. After the spirited but brief fight on and around Battle Ridge and Last Stand Hill, the Sioux and Cheyenne warriors turned their attention to the seven companies under Reno and Benteen on the bluffs high above the Little Big Horn. "The fight continued hard and furious until night fell, and then, after about five hours respite, reopened with renewed vigor very early in the morning . . .before daybreak." (Lt. Francis Gibson, Co. H)

Fact #722. Battle historian Walter Camp, in his field notes, disagreed with the theory that Custer planned to support Reno "by striking the village in the center": "When Custer ordered Reno forward, neither he nor Reno nor Benteen were aware of the existence of a village. No one in the command had as yet seen a single tepee other than the lone one where they now were, which gave Custer the impression that the Sioux had pulled off the village, until he came out on the bluffs over the river, and even then he did not see it all."

Fact #723. "We had no protection. . .we were being surrounded. . .I think Reno did the only thing possible under the circumstances. If we had remained in the timber all would have been killed." (2d Lt. G.D. Wallace, Co. G, speaking of the valley fight on the morning of June 25)

Fact #724. Commenting on the potential success of the Sioux Expedition of 1876, Gen. Philip Sheridan, Division of Missouri Commander who had ordered out the three columns of the expedition, said, "Unless they [the "hostile" Indians] can be caught before early spring, they cannot be caught at all." The elusiveness of these "roamer" bands had been proven over and over during the past decade.

Fact #725. Custer's plan of attack (as recalled by Pvt. Peter Thompson) was based on the column's knowledge, at mid-morning on June 25, 1876, ". . .that a large band of Indians were in camp a short distance down the river. The plan marked out was to attack the Indians in the following manner: Major Reno was to cross the river to its left bank and proceed down until Custer had time to pass down the right bank and cross over and attack them in the rear." However, Custer had advised Reno, through adjutant W.W. Cooke, that he, Reno, would be supported by the whole outfit, and Reno assumed this meant that Custer's command would follow him down the valley to the (southern) upper end of the village.

Fact #726. After the destruction of the Powder River Indian village on March 17, 1876, by Gen. George Crook's force commanded by Col. J.J. Reynolds, it would be two months before Crook could refit his forces for another offensive, barely in time to join the Sioux Expedition. His independent Army command, thanks to Col. Reynolds, had failed in a winter attack against a weakened foe. (Panzieri, *Little Big Horn 1876: Custer's Last Stand*)

Fact #727. Capt. Frederick Benteen reported after the battle that on the night of June 25, 1876, the sentinels at the Reno-Benteen position were so exhausted they could not be kept awake, even through kicking them.

Fact #728. Although Gen. Crook, after the Battle of the Rosebud on June 17, 1876, withdrew his forces, over 1,000 men, to a base camp near present-day Sheridan (WY), he did not inform Gen. Terry that he would no longer be an active force in the Sioux Expedition.

Fact #729. In a report to Gen. Terry on June 19, Maj. Marcus Reno, commanding a scouting party, said: "I can tell where the Indians are not, and much more information when I see you in the morning."

Fact #730. Harry H. Anderson, an assistant secretary of the South Dakota Historical Society, wrote in 1960 that it "would not be unreasonable to believe the Cheyenne camp [at the Little Big Horn River June 25, 1876] contained about seventy lodges at the time of the attack by the 7th Cavalry."

Fact #731. "[The Indians] fought and yelled like devils all day long on the 26th, and their unerring showers of 'lead' inflicted severe loss in killed and wounded, thus lessening our effective force," Lt. Francis Gibson (Co. H) reported, after the battle, about the fight at the Reno-Benteen position.

Fact #732. "The Montana column felt disappointed when they learned that they were not to be present at the final capture of the great village, but General Terry's reasons for according the honor of the attack to General Custer were good ones.* * * [sic] So it was decided that Custer's men, were as usual, to have the post of honor, and the officers and men of the Montana column cheered them and bid them God-speed." (One of General Terry's officers, writing in the *New York Herald* in 1876, as reported in "Lost and Won: Custer's Last Battle" by Charles Francis Bates, published in 1926.)

Fact #733. General Terry said "that if he were in Custer's place and the Indian trail turned, as it did, to the Little Big Horn, he would scout on south to the headwaters of the Tongue, but whether to do so or not was left to Custer's discretion." (Bates, June 20, 1926, *New York Times*)

Fact #734. In 1866, four additional regiments of cavalry were authorized and recruited to take charge of the growing Indian problem on the frontier. One of these was the 7th U.S. Cavalry.

Fact #735. "To soldiers full of stories and even some direct observation of torture, mutilation, and atrocity. . .it was easy to believe that the only good Indian was a dead Indian." (*Indian, Soldier, and Settler*, Utley)

Fact #736. When the position on Reno-Benteen hill came under furious assault around noon on June 26, Capt. Benteen decided to make a "charge," which resulted in "marked success, for the Indians met with considerable loss while we had not a man killed." (Lt. Francis Gibson, Co. H)

Fact #737. Fort Shaw (M.T.) was located near the present-day town of Fort Shaw (MT) on state highway 20. Founded in 1867 to protect settlers and the road between Fort Benton (M.T.) and Helena (M.T.), the fort served as the headquarters for Col. John Gibbon, who commanded units of the 2d Cavalry and 7th Infantry in the Montana Column, one of three converging columns in the 1876 Sioux Expedition.

Fact #738. The soldiers at the Reno-Benteen position may have heard the old frontier saying about Indians not fighting after dark. But the saying was wrong. Pvt. Peter Thompson (Co. C), in his 1913 memoir about "the Custer Massacre," wrote: "By the time we had everything arranged [establishing the defensive position], the sun was going down. We all knew that the Indians never fought after night fall. We thought we would have time enough to fortify ourselves before the light of another day appeared. ...We saw that our horses and mules were beginning to drop quite fast, for they were in a more exposed position. This is very trying to a cavalry man. . ."

Fact #739. Gen. Terry's plan of action on June 21, 1876, as outlined in his "Official Report" written after LBH, intended that the 7th Cavalry column not follow the Indian trail to the Little Big Horn, "but, if it led in that direction, to instead keep farther to the south before turning toward that river, in order to intercept the Indians should they attempt to pass around his left, and in order, by a longer march, to give time for Colonel Gibbon's column to come up."

Fact #740. When Custer left the mouth of the Rosebud on June 22, he left behind the band, the recruits whose mounts were unfit, and the wagon train, taking only a pack train of mules loaded with rations and ammunition. His 12 companies, 660 officers and men, were expected to be more than a match for the anticipated 800-1,000 warriors they were chasing.

Fact #741. On June 10, 1876, Gen. Alfred Terry, commanding the 1876 Sioux Expedition, wrote in his private diary: "Issued orders for Reno to make a scout [south] up the Powder to go to the forks of the Powder thence to go to the head of Mizpah & then by Pumpkin Creek to Tongue River. Reno moved at 5 p.m." On Monday, June 19, he wrote: ". . .received despatches from Major Reno informing me that he had been to Mouth of Rosebud. ...Sent Hughes to meet Reno. Hughes returned at ———— [sic]. Reno gave him no reason for his disobedience of Orders."

Fact #742. After Custer divided his column a second time near midday on June 25, 1876, sending Reno with A, G, and M companies to cross the Little Big Horn again and attack the (southern) upper end of the Indian village, Custer's immediate command (C, E, F, I, L companies) "now left the valley in which we had been traveling and commenced to climb the bluffs overlooking the river and surrounding country. At this time our horses were in a trot. At our right, and on a slight elevation, sat Gen. Custer and his brother Tom reviewing the companies as they passed by. This was the last review General Custer ever held." (Peter Thompson, Pvt., Co. C)

Fact #743. Unable to keep white trespassers out of the Black Hills, as called for in the Treaty of 1868, or to purchase the lands from the Sioux (who had, just a few generations earlier, taken them from the Crow), Indian Bureau Inspector Erwin C. Watkins filed a report in November 1875, with this recommendation: "In my judgement, one thousand men, under the command of an experienced officer, sent into their [Sioux] country in the winter, when the Indians are nearly always in camp, and at which season of the year they are most helpless, would be amply sufficient for their capture or punishment. The Government has done everything that can be done, peacefully to get control of these Indians, or to induce them to respect its authority. They are still as wild and untamable, as uncivilized and savage, as when Lewis and Clark first passed through their country." ("Senate Executive Document," 9 November 1875)

Fact #744. Pvt. Peter Thompson (Co. C) wrote that he fell farther and farther behind as Custer's column (C, E, F, I, L) advanced, due to the exhaustion of his horse. "All urging on my part [to keep the horse moving] was useless. Getting vexed I dismounted and began to fasten on my spurs, when I heard my name called and, on looking up I saw [Pvt. John] Brennan [Co. C] near me on horseback. He asked, 'What is the matter?' I told him that I was afraid my horse was entirely played out. 'Well,' said he, 'Let us keep together.' I straightened myself up and said, 'I will tell you what I will do. I will trade horses with you if you will.' He gave me a strange look and turned his horse around and rode toward the rear, leaving me to shift for myself. 'Well,' I thought, 'I will get along anyway.'"

Fact #745. Sitting Bull and others attempted to "induce Kill Eagle and his band to join in the contemplated movements and hostilities," according to Kill Eagle's account published September 24, 1876, *New York Herald*. He claimed "they were desirous of getting back to the protecting arms of the [Standing Rock Reservation D.T.], but were unable to escape from the meshes of the wily Sitting Bull."

Fact #746. After advancing 45 miles (south) up the Rosebud in three days, the 7th Cavalry took its noon stop at the deserted sun dance camp; the halt was extended for four hours while Custer interpreted "the variation" in the Indian trail signs, according to *The Dust Rose Like Smoke*, by James O. Gump. The well-defined trail they had been following had now broken; Custer feared the Indians were scattering. A more reasonable explanation is that the original Indian column was being joined along the trail by other bands. Scout George Herendeen wrote in 1878, "Custer said he did not want to lose any of the lodges, and if any of them left the main trail he wanted to know."

Fact #747. Entrenchments, including rifle pits, were the number one priority of those surrounded on top of the bluffs at the Reno-Benteen position on July 25-26. Lt. E.S. Godfrey (Co. K in Benteen's battalion) wrote later: ". . .settled down to the work of digging rifle pits. The men worked in pairs, in threes and fours. The ground was hard and dry. There were only three or four spades and shovels in the whole command; axes, hatchets, knives, table forks, tin cups, and halves of canteens were brought into use. However, everybody worked hard, and some were still digging when the enemy opened fire at early dawn [on June 26]."

Fact #748. After Custer, Lt. Varnum and the Crow and Arikara scouts returned to the column on the morning of June 25 from the Crow's Nest, quartermaster of scouts George Herendeen told Custer that the camp had been discovered by two Indians. Then Capt. Tom Custer, Custer's brother, rode up and reported "Some troops from company F had had a run in with some Indians on the back trail."

Captain Tom Custer

National Archives

Fact #749. Noted author Stanley Vestal in his *American Heritage* article, "The Man Who Killed Custer," noted, "Nobody who knows Plains Indians can doubt that the man who killed Custer, if living, would be named to lead that Indian column" at the 50th anniversary of Custer's Last Stand. Sioux Chief White Bull led the column; he told Vestal six years later that he had killed Custer toward the end of the battle in hand-to-hand combat.

Fact #750. The overall plan for the Sioux Expedition had been laid out in final concept on May 29, 1876, when Gen. Philip Sheridan, commander of the Division of the Missouri, wrote to Gen. William T. Sherman, "As no very accurate information can be obtained as to the location of the hostile Indians, and as there would be no telling how long they would stay in one place, if it was known, I have given no instructions to Generals Crook or Terry, preferring that they should do the best they can under the circumstances. . .as I think it would be unwise to make any combination in such a country as they will have to operate in, as hostile Indians in any great numbers, cannot keep the field as a body for more than a week, or at most ten days. I therefore consider—and so do Terry and Crook—that each column should be able to take care of itself, and to chastise the Indians should it have the opportunity. . ."

Fact #751. Lt. Francis M. Gibson (Co. H) noted that, after the Indian village started melting away (about sunset on June 26), the troops "had no tidings of Custer, but no one for a moment dreamed of the terrible fate that had overtaken his command."

Fact #752. Writing to Gen. William T. Sherman, Chief of Staff of the U.S. Army, in late May 1876, Gen. Philip Sheridan, commanding general of the Division of Missouri, outlined his thoughts on the Sioux Expedition then in progress: "I presume the following will occur: General Terry will drive the Indians towards the Big Horn valley and General Crook will drive them back towards Terry; Colonel Gibbon moving down on the north side of the Yellowstone, to intercept if possible such as may want to go north of the Missouri to the Milk River. The result of the movement of these three columns may force many of the hostile Indians back to the agencies on the Missouri River and to Red Cloud and Spotted Tail Agencies."

Fact #753. When Reno returned from his scout toward the Powder and Tongue Rivers on June 18, Col. John Gibbon, commander of the Montana Column, wrote Gen. Alfred Terry, commander of the Sioux Expedition: "Col. Reno made his appearance at the mouth of Rosebud today & I have communicated with him by signal & by scouts swimming the river. He has seen no Indians but I gather from the conversations which the scouts had with Mitch Bouyer that they found signs of camps on Tongue & Rosebud & trails leading up Rosebud. I presume the only remaining chance of finding Indians now is in the direction of the headwaters of Rosebud or Little Big Horn. I have been anxiously looking for the boat [*Far West*] & shall be glad to meet you again or to hear of your future plans."

Fact #754. The soldiers of the Montana Column, led by Gen. Alfred Terry and Col. John Gibbon, reached the outskirts of the abandoned village on the bank of the Little Big Horn on the morning of June 27. The earth was scorched and smoking from fires left by the departing Indians. Soldiers broke ranks, despite orders not to enter the funeral lodges and found five dead warriors in one, three dead warriors in the other, all dressed in their best finery and resting on scaffolds. Articles of clothing belonging to 7th Cavalry officers were discovered. A number of white bodies were discovered, white men, beheaded, so mutilated they were unidentifiable. The heads of three of the men were found hanging from a lodgepole, tied together with wire. The shocking realization broke over the column that Custer and the 7th Cavalry had lost the Battle of the Little Big Horn. (Wiltsey, *Brave Warriors*)

Fact #755. Having been ordered by Custer on June 24, 1876, to go "take a look" at Tulloch's Fork with another white scout, Charley Reynolds, white scout George Herendeen "told the General it was not time yet, as we were then traveling in the direction of the head of the Tulloch, and I could only follow his trail. I called [Mitch] Bouyer [half-Sioux scout for the 7th Cavalry], who was a little ahead, back and asked him if I was not correct in my statement to the General, and he said, 'Yes, further [south] up on Rosebud [Creek] we would come opposite a gap, and then we could cut across and strike the Tulloch in about 15 miles ride.' Custer said, 'All right, I could wait.'"

Fact #756. Col. John Gibbon's Montana Column was ordered to patrol out of Fort Shaw (M.T.), north of the Yellowstone River, to try and prevent any Indians from crossing to the north, and to scout south for any signs of Indians, moving down the Yellowstone until they connected with Gen. Alfred Terry's Dakota Column coming from Fort Abraham Lincoln (D.T.).

Fact #757. A "great peace council" had been arranged for Fort Larned (KS) on April 10, 1867. The "Hancock Expedition," commanded by Civil War hero Gen. Winfield Scott Hancock, and including four companies of the 7th Cavalry under the field command of Lt. Col. George A. Custer, arrived on April 7.

Fact #758. On Sunday afternoon, June 25, 1876, fair-goers at the Centennial Exhibition grounds in Philadelphia (PA) contemplated the giant forearm of a statue, "Liberty Enlightening the World," a Centennial gift from France. Cavalry soldiers in far-off Montana began the most famous and storied fight in Indian Wars history.

Fact #759. The march of the Dakota Column from Fort Abraham Lincoln (D.T.) in May 1876 was "attended by very disagreeable weather, snow and rain interfered with our wagon transportation, impeded the progress of the troops, and delayed our arrival at the Yellowstone River some 10 days." (Lt. Francis Gibson, Co. H)

Fact #760. Pvt. Theodore Goldin (Co. G) wrote after LBH that he had been sent as a courier from Custer's column to Reno, to advise Reno of Custer's plan to move (north) downstream before attacking the village. The Crow scout Curly told a similar story. Reno denied getting any messages from Custer.

Fact #761. Peter Thompson (Pvt. Co. C) told of seeing Reno's charge from the ridgetop east of the Little Big Horn River, where Thompson had ridden with Custer's column. As the attack slowed, the village caught on fire, and squaws fought the fire, trying to save the teepees from destruction. "Major [Marcus] Reno, seeing that he was outnumbered ordered an immediate retreat to a grove of cottonwood trees, which stood on the bank of the river about a mile from the [southern] upper end of the village, where they found shelter for their horses and protection for themselves."

Fact #762. In response to Sioux depredations at the Red Cloud and Spotted Tail Indian agencies in the winter of 1873-74, Gen. William T. Sherman, commanding general of the U.S. Army wrote Gen. Philip Sheridan, commander of the Division of the Missouri, that "many people even [Interior Secretary Columbus] Delano, would be happy if the troops should kill a goodly proportion of those Sioux, but they want to keep the record to prove they didn't do it. We can afford to be frank and honest, for sooner or later these Sioux have to be wiped out or made to stay just where they are put." (Dr. Paul Hutton, *Phil Sheridan and His Army*)

Fact #763. Following Maj. Marcus Reno's discovery of a large Indian village on the banks of Rosebud Creek, Lt. Col. George Custer was ordered to take the 12 companies of the 7th Cavalry and follow the trail of the Indians who had moved (south) up that watercourse. "[Custer] was not to hasten his march, and if the trail was found to lead west across the Little Wolf Mountains into the Little Big Horn valley, he was not to follow." (*Reader's Encyclopedia of the American West*)

Fact #764. The following message was sent by Gen. Alfred Terry, commander of the Sioux Expedition, to Gen. Philip Sheridan, commander of the Division of the Missouri, on June 21, 1876, less than a week before LBH: "No Indians met with as yet but traces of a large and recent camp discovered some twenty to thirty miles [south] up the Rosebud. Gibbon's column moved this morning to the north side of the Yellowstone for the mouth of the Big Horn where it will be ferried across by the supply steamer [*Far West*] and whence it will proceed to the mouth of the Little Horn and so on. Custer will go up the Rosebud tomorrow with his whole regiment and thence to the headwaters of the

Little Horn and thence [north] down the Little Horn. I hope that one of the two columns will find the Indians. I go personally with Gibbon's."

Fact #765. Pvt. Peter Thompson (Co. C) described how he found himself abandoned and on foot: ". . .I was perusing my way along the trail on foot leading my horse for I was afraid he would fall down under me, so stumbling and staggering was his gait. After the disappearance of Custer and his men [who had ridden on ahead], I felt that I was in a terrible predicament to be left practically alone in an enemy's country, leading a horse practically useless."

Fact #766. The concerted plan of action agreed to by Gen. Alfred Terry, commander of the Dakota Column and the Sioux Expedition, Col. John Gibbon, commander of the Montana Column, and Lt. Col. George A. Custer, commander of the 7th Cavalry, called for the Montana Column (infantry and cavalry) to move up the Yellowstone River, to the Big Horn River, and thence to the Little Big Horn, while Custer's cavalry column (12 companies and a pack train) was to move farther south before turning west (to give Gibbon's slower infantry time to get into position), and then to move north in what has been called a "hammer and anvil" operation. Gen. Terry accompanied Col. Gibbon's column.

Fact #767. Pvt. Peter Thompson (Co. C) was shot through the right hand and arm as he hurried to the ravine coming up from the river on the western arc of the Reno-Benteen defense perimeter on the morning of June 26, 1876. Capt. Frederick Benteen had tapped Thompson for a sortie party to drive Indians from the ravine. He reported on this action in his 1913 memoir: "A short distance below I saw several cavalry men who were soon joined by others, eleven in all; a slim force indeed to clean out the ravine held by so many Indians, but they were resolute men. Capt. Benteen soon joined them and made a short speech. He said, 'This is our only weak and unprotected point and should the Indians succeed in passing this in any force they would soon end the matter as far as we are concerned.' And now, he asked, 'Are you ready?' They answered, 'Yes.' 'Then,' said he, 'Charge down there and drive them out.'"

Fact #768. On the morning of June 25, after the division of Custer's command into four battalions, Capt. Benteen's battalion (Cos. H, K, M) moved "off to the left," as ordered. As the horsemen approached some high and steep hills, Lt. Gibson was ordered to ride to the top of them and scout for Indians. Gibson's report was negative. (Lt. W.S. Edgerly, Co. D)

Fact #769. The 12 companies and pack train of the 7th Cavalry column were camped near the summit on the eastern slope of the Little Wolf Mountains on the morning of June 25, 1876. "Scouts sent ahead reported a large Indian village in the valley below. Custer professed not to believe this, but on learning that the presence of his command had been discovered and fearing that the village, if indeed there, would begin to scatter, he decided to move forward and to do something almost without precedent in Indian warfare: attack in the middle of the day." (In Indian warfare it was almost standard procedure to attack at dawn.) (*Reader's Encyclopedia of the American West*)

Fact #770. Army fatalities at LBH numbered 268, five of whom died later from their wounds. (*The Little Big Horn Campaign*, Sarf)

Fact #771. The original plan for June 25 was for the cavalry column, having crossed the Rosebud/Little Big Horn divide before daylight, to remain concealed during the day, and attack the village at daybreak on June 26. (Lt. W.S. Edgerly, Co. D)

Fact #772. On the morning after the Custer battle, at daybreak, "Indians came swarming out of the valley like bees from a hive, and took up positions which nearly surrounded us [at the Reno-Benteen position]," said Lt. W.S. Edgerly (Co. D). "The firing was kept up with great persistence, the Indians frequently firing volleys, by word of command, until about 9:30 a.m., when it was discovered that they were making a desperate attempt to rout us."

Fact #773. The 7th U.S. Cavalry rode into Fort Abraham Lincoln (D.T.) in 1873, making the installation the headquarters for nine companies of cavalry and attached infantry units. From this installation, the 7th rode out in May 1876 on the Sioux Expedition from which more than 260 of its men did not return.

Fact #774. The Montana Column of the 1876 Sioux Expedition left Fort Ellis (M.T.) in April of that year. Montana Territory was formed by the U.S. Government in 1864, and the state was admitted to the Union in 1889.

Fact #775. The Wyoming Territory was formed by the U.S. Government in 1869, and the state was admitted to the Union in 1890.

Fact #776. The Battle of the Washita, fought by the 7th Cavalry under Custer's command against the Cheyenne village of Black Kettle, occurred in what later became known as Indian Territory, but, in 1868, was unorganized land, referred to as the Indian Nations.

Fact #777. Shortly after coming across a small Indian camp on the late morning of June 25, 1876, the 7th Cavalry column spied a gruesome sight. ". . . one of the members of Company C found two scalps dangling from a short willow which had been stuck in the ground. From the appearance of the hair one scalp belonged to a man and the other to a woman. The hair on both scalps was light in color." (Pvt. Peter Thompson, Co. C)

Fact #778. Of Custer's five companies (C, E, F, I, L), a total of 61 men—14 from C, nine from E, 15 from F, 10 from I, and 13 from L —ended up at the Reno-Benteen position rather than on the killed-in-action-with-Custer list. Twenty-six men, because their horses were exhausted, because they were assigned to the pack train, because they made a personal decision to, or for other reasons unknown at this juncture, showed up in Reno's command after the battle.

Fact #779. At daybreak on June 26 (between 2:30 and 3:00 a.m., by their timepieces—Chicago [IL] time), the men at the Reno-Benteen position "heard the crack of two rifles, which was the signal for a tremendously heavy fire which officers who had served through the War of the Rebellion said they had never seen equalled." (Lt. W.S. Edgerly, Co. D)

Fact #780. In theory, seven men—one non-commissioned officer and six enlisted men—from each company (A, C, E, F, G, I, L, M) were assigned to the pack train on Custer's orders (according to Peter Thompson's narrative). In reality, 49 men with the pack train, plus 61 men of Custer's companies who ended up in Reno's command during LBH, made a total of at least 110 soldiers who could or should have been assigned to their normal company duties, Thompson asserts. He claims that over 25% of the regiment, counting those on detached duty, leave, pack train escort, etc., etc., were not available for service with Custer's doomed command. Would they have made a difference or would they have been wiped out too? Who knows?

Fact #781. As the column drew closer to the Indian village on the morning of June 25, Maj. Reno's instructions from Custer were to take his battalion (companies A, G, M) and "Move directly on the village, attack anything you come to and you will be supported." (Lt. W.S. Edgerly, Co. D)

Fact #782. Pvt. Peter Thompson (Co. C) told of riding with the Custer column atop the bluffs for a short distance. "When the companies came in sight of the village, they gave the regular charging yell and urged their horses into a gallop. At this time a detail of five men from Company F was sent ahead to reconnoiter and from this point I was gradually left behind in spite of all I could do to keep up with my company. There were others also in the same fix."

Fact #783. After delivering a note from Lt. W.W. Cooke to Capt. Benteen's command, telling Benteen "Come. . .quick. . .Bring packs," trumpeter John Martin said Reno had surprised the village, "that some of the Indians were asleep in their tepees when Reno struck them, that he was driving everything before him and killing men, women, and children." (Lt. W.S. Edgerly, Co. D)

Fact #784. After detailing the progress and incidents of each march from the Standing Rock Reservation (D.T.) in his account published in the September 24, 1876, *New York Herald* article, Blackfeet Sioux chief Kill Eagle said that on the seventh day after leaving the reservation, "they arrived at Sitting Bull's village, where a feast and numerous presents of ponies and robes were given to them."

Fact #785. Pvt. Peter Thompson (Co. C) recalled riding with Custer's column along the ridges overlooking the Little Big Horn, and, finally, being able to look down on Reno's charge in the valley on the (southern) upper end of the village. "It was a grand sight to see those men charging down upon the village of their enemies, who outnumbered them many times. The well-trained horses were kept well in hand. There was no straggling; they went together, neck and neck, their tails streaming in the wind, and the riders' arms gleaming in the sunlight. It was no wonder that the Indians were in great commotion."

Fact #786. After dividing the command, Custer rode off with Myles Keogh's and George Yates' battalions, following a course described by Lt. W.S. Edgerly (Co. D) as ". . .to the right of and nearly parallel with Reno's command ready to move in any direction."

Fact #787. After Capt. Frederick Benteen's three-company command had scoured the southern hills, searching unsuccessfully for "escaping" Indians, its steps were retraced and the command found itself "considerably to the rear" of the rest of the column. The force then began to consolidate with Maj. Reno's three-company command. "The whereabouts of Custer's five companies were not known." (Lt. Francis Gibson, Co. H)

Fact #788. Lt. James E. Wilson of the Army Corps of Engineers was on board the steamer *Far West* on the Yellowstone River on June 25, 1876, continuing his practice of recording the daily range of temperatures. He recorded a low of 63 degrees on that day, and a high of 91, but he was some 30 miles north of the high, dry ridges east of the Little Big Horn River, where the temperatures were probably several degrees warmer.

Fact #789. Minneconjou Ford (known today as Medicine Tail Ford), at the mouth of Medicine Tail Coulee, is the only ford in close proximity to the Indian village, about three-quarters of a mile below the bluffs along which most of Custer's column rode. Most of the Indians crossed from the village across Minneconjou Ford to attack Custer's five companies.

Fact #790. Separated from Custer's column, having abandoned his horse, surrounded by hostiles, 22-year-old Pvt. Peter Thompson (Co. C) was in dire straits on the afternoon of June 25, 1876. Thompson observed, "After completing my inventory, I sat down and began to reflect on my chances for my life, if I remained where I was. I knew that if the cavalry drove the savages from their village, they would scatter in all directions, and if any of the struggling devils came across such an unfortunate as myself, I would stand a poor show. I looked back toward the trail where I had left my horse; he was still in the same place with an Indian riding toward him." Thompson's horse was returned to him later, saddlebags untouched.

Fact #791. When Maj. Reno ordered men to "Mount and get to the bluffs," after the late morning attack on the village had stalled, most of the command followed Reno out of the trees and down to the river, jumping over a cut bank about four feet high into the river, wrote Lt. W.S. Edgerly (Co. D), who was with Benteen's battalion at this time.

Fact #792. At the time Custer divided his command into four battalions "... it was expected that the Indians would break away as soon as they caught sight of the troops, the only fear being that they would scatter and disappear. . ." (Lt. W.S. Edgerly, Co. D)

Fact #793. The Reno-Benteen position was in a dish-shaped depression on the bluff, about 225 feet above the Little Big Horn River, with the interior center 35-40 feet lower than the outside perimeter. The defensive line resembled a huge horseshoe, with the open end facing east. The left side and curve of the horseshoe were along the bluff which sloped away to the river, the right side, longer than the left, bending away to the south. The center was the site of the field hospital.

Fact #794. In the opinion of 2d Lt. W.S. Edgerly (Co. D), ". . .Custer was evidently holding his five troops in hand to put them where they could do the most good," after the division of the command into four battalions.

Fact #795. Capt. (Bvt. Col.) Frederick Benteen could have gone forward to Custer, bringing the pack train, if he had so desired, argues Daniel Magnussen, author of *Peter Thompson's Narrative of the Little Bighorn Campaign 1876.*

Fact #796. "Suddenly we heard above all other sounds, the call of a bugle." Pvt. Peter Thompson (Co. C) in his "The Experience of a Private Soldier in the Custer Massacre," told of the harrowing night of June 25, 1876, when the remnants of Reno's three companies (A, G, M), joined by Benteen's battalion (companies D, H, K), Co. B, the pack train escort, and the pack train, lay besieged at the Reno-Benteen position more than 200 feet above the Little Big Horn River across from the Indian village. "The sound came from the direction of the village, and immediately following was the sound of two others. The officers hearing those bugles ordered our buglers to sound certain calls and waited to see if they would be answered. The only answer was a long wailing blast; it was not what was expected." Survivors of Reno's command hiding in the timber along the river also heard these bugles.

Fact #797. "Instead of charging through the village as I believe [Reno] could have done if he had pushed forward vigorously, he had dismounted to fight on foot, and when only a few of his command had been hit, he gave the. . .order. . . 'Mount and get to the bluffs.'" (Lt. W.S. Edgerly, Co. D)

Fact #798. In his memoir about "the Custer Massacre," Pvt. Peter Thompson (Co. C) described the setting up of the defensive perimeter at the Reno-Benteen position. "Major Reno moved to the left of the trail and went into a flat-bottomed ravine. By this time the Indians were pouring a shower of lead into us that was galling in the extreme. Our horses and mules were huddled together in one confused mass. The poor brutes were tired and hungry. Where we made our stand there was nothing but sand, gravel, and a little sagebrush. Our means of defense were very poor. There were numerous ravines leading into the one which we occupied. This gave the savages a good opportunity to close in on us and they were not long in doing so. Some of us unloaded the mules of the hard tack they were carrying and used the boxes for a breastwork."

Equipment

Fact #799. History records that Custer declined the offer of two Gatling guns as he separated his 7th Cavalry from the main Dakota Column under Gen. Terry.

Fact #800. During the 1876 Sioux Campaign, the columns from Dakota Territory and Montana Territory relied on two steamboats: the *Far West* and the *Josephine*.

Fact #801. Much has been written about the condition of the 7th Cavalry's horses when the column arrived at what is now known as Reno Creek. Gen. W.H. Carter, who served as a 2d Lt. in the 6th Cavalry from 1874, wrote, in 1895, *Horses, Saddles and Bridles*, in which he discussed the endurance of horses: "When not in the actual presence of the enemy, where troopers are liable to be detached at a moment's notice, it would increase efficiency and be vastly more economical to attach light wagons to every cavalry command to relieve the saddle animals of all extra weight. This would save the horses until the theater of operations is entered, at which moment every strap should be in place, for the 'eyes and ears' of the army would be untrue to its traditions if it failed to be ready to gain contact with the enemy, whom once encountered, should never be lost sight of until success is achieved."

Fact #802. "Custer carried a Remington Sporting rifle, octagonal barrel; two Bulldog self-cocking, English white-handled pistols, with a ring in the butt for a lanyard; a hunting knife, in a beaded fringed scabbard; and a canvas cartridge belt." (Gen. E.S. Godfrey, a 1st Lt. commanding Co. K in Benteen's battalion at the Battle of the Little Big Horn)

Fact #803. At the Reno Court of Inquiry in 1879, the question was asked of Lt. Charles Varnum (Reno's Chief of Scouts), "Was the range of the Indian rifles greater or less than the soldier's carbines?" Lt. Varnum replied: "I believe the longest range guns the Indians had were those they took from General Custer's command, with one or two exceptions. There were one or two parties in particular (who) had very long range guns." Then Lt. Varnum was asked, "Is the range of the Winchester rifle the same as the Army carbine?" Lt. Varnum answered: "No sir, I think it is much less."

Fact #804. Custer's men were armed with single-shot carbines while many of the Indians were armed with repeating rifles, probably Henrys. (James Wyckoff, *Famous Guns That Won The West*)

Fact #805. The more than 250 slain soldiers at the Little Big Horn yielded their Springfield carbines and Colt revolvers to the victors, nearly 600 carbines and pistols in all.

Fact #806. The first Springfield Model '65 carbines were .58 caliber, but later models used a .45 caliber bullet, with 70 grains of powder in each rifle cartridge. This weapon was to be the standard long arm for infantry, and was made as a carbine for the cavalry.

Fact #807. Custer's 7th Cavalry soldiers were issued 100 rounds each for the carbine and 24 for the pistol. Fifty carbine cartridges were carried on their person and 50 more in their saddle bags. The pistols were fully loaded with six rounds and the remainder were carried in their bullet pouches or cartridge belts. (*Custer Battle Guns*, John du Mont)

Fact #808. "The condition of the animals of the Indian scouts was pitiful. They had not only made the distances that the regiment had covered, but they had ranged far and wide in advance, and on the flank, day and night, until they covered many more miles than any troop horse." (Col. Elwood Nye, 1941 article, *Veterinary Bulletin*)

Fact #809. Custer declined the use of two Gatling guns because he feared they would slow down his cavalry column, yet the Montana Column, augmented by all of Gen. Terry's Dakota Column except the 7th Cavalry, averaged more miles per day than did Custer. (*The Terry Diary: Yellowstone Expedition 1876*, published in 1970, Old Army Press)

Fact #810. "Remounts for cavalry must have certain qualifications, the most important of which are the possession of sufficient mobility to execute tactical maneuvers at varying degrees of speed and the ability to stand hard service while carrying great weight. It should be constantly borne in mind that cavalry horses are required to carry loads on their backs averaging about one-fourth their own weight." (Carter, *Horses, Saddles and Bridles*, 1895)

Fact #811. The Model 1874 McClellan saddle, used by the 7th Cavalry at LBH, was made of black leather without a saddle skirt, with a 7½" girth and a heart-shaped safe.

Fact #812. Custer's men at the Little Big Horn were armed with 1873 Springfield .45-55 carbines, a single-shot, breech-loading weapon, which, when used repeatedly over a short time, were known to heat up and jam.

Fact #813. When Maj. Reno led his men on a scout up the Powder River and across to the Rosebud (June 10-19, 1876) he had Lt. W. H. Lowe (20th Inf.) along with a battery of Gatling guns. Lt. W.S. Edgerly (Co. D) told Walter

Camp that "when Custer advised against taking [the Gatling guns] along [with the 7th Cavalry column], Lowe. . .almost cried."

Fact #814. The Colt Single Action Army revolver has become known as "the gun that won the West." It was manufactured at the Colt Patent Firearms Manufacturing Co. in Hartford (CT), and first issued to the Army in 1873. All of Custer's soldiers were armed with the Colt SA with a 7½" barrel length, .45 caliber, and walnut grips. According to *Saga of the Colt Six-Shooter* by George Virgines, it is possible that any U.S. Colt .45 stamped up to the serial number 22000 may have been issued to the 7th Cavalry. Only a small fraction of these revolvers were actually issued to Custer and his men, and no serial numbers of the issue itself has ever been found.

Fact #815. 7th Cavalry officers' and soldiers' sabers were boxed for shipment aboard the steamer *Far West* at the confluence of the Powder and the Yellowstone Rivers, when the 7th was prepared for "light marching order" prior to their scout down the Rosebud.

Fact #816. Reports indicate that 38,030 rounds of ammunition for the Springfield carbine and 2,954 cartridges for the Colt pistols (single-action six-shooters) were expended or lost during the two days of fighting at the Reno-Benteen position.

Fact #817. The ponies of the Indian scouts with Custer were, in many instances, too exhausted to proceed with the attack on the village. Some dropped out completely. Col. Elwood L. Nye wrote in a 1941 article for the *Veterinary Bulletin*, "Others tried to lash their faltering mounts forward but in several instances horse flesh had given all it could. There was no reserve remaining. Most of the scouts whose ponies retained sufficient strength to go on, fought with Reno, and their mounts shared in degree the hardship and fate of that sore-beset command."

Fact #818. The 1873 Springfield carbine caused serious extraction problems for its users in the removal of the .45 caliber cartridge from the breech-loading mechanism. Sometimes the soldiers had to literally dig out the brass cartridge with a knife or other tool. The few Army carbines found on the battlefield after the battle had clogged breeches.

Fact #819. The .45 caliber cartridge used in the soldiers' 1873 model Springfield carbines used 55 grains of powder in each cartridge, which caused considerable recoil and muzzle blast. The soldiers' aim was definitely affected by the recoil and resultant sore shoulders. The battlefield visibility was definitely affected by the cloud of smoke emitted from the muzzle after each round was fired.

Fact #820. Many sources state that "no sabers" were taken to the Little Big Horn. However, Lt. Edward G. Mathey with the pack train detachment had secured his personal sword inside a pack; there is no evidence that it was removed from its hiding place during the battle. (*Custer Battle Guns*, du Mont)

Fact #821. Commenting on the ordnance of his command, Co. H, at Fort Rice (D.T.), in March 1874, Capt. Frederick Benteen said of the pistols: "The Remington pistol (Revolver) is a tolerable pistol for years ago; the revolving springs get out of order very easily—and a company of cavalry is supplied with no tools to repair arms. In my opinion, the purchase of ammunition for the pistols for the use of cavalry should be confined wholly to metallic cartridges, all paper cartridges being wasted by being jolted to pieces in the pouch. I have now requisitions in for Springfield Carbines and Colt improved Army pistols to equip my Co. Very respectfully, Yr. obdt. Sevt., F.W Benteen, 7th Cav."

Fact #822. When firing from a skirmish line, as at the Reno-Benteen position, a soldier normally took a handful of cartridges from his belt and laid them on the ground on his right side, for ease of loading. An order to move frequently resulted in the loose ammunition being left behind, causing in some instances considerable loss of ammunition.

Fact #823. Due to government parsimony as far as ammunition was concerned, few soldiers had much target, or even firing, practice with live ammunition. The War Department's "General Order 103," August 5, 1874, authorized the issuance of 10 rounds of .45 caliber ammunition per month; officers were to be held strictly accountable. On September 23, 1875, this was increased, by "General Order 83," to 15 rounds per man per month, and applied only to cavalry companies.

Fact #824. The issue carbine of the 7th Cavalry at LBH was the 1873 model Springfield .45 caliber "Trapdoor," single-shot, breech-loading carbine.

Fact #825. Pvt. Charles Windolph (Co. H), the subject of *I Fought With Custer* by Frazier and Robert Hunt, claimed to be accurate with the Springfield 1873 carbine at 600 yards. The rifle weighed seven pounds, and had a firing rate of 12-13 times per minute. It had an adjustable rear sight for long range firing, but no windage adjustment.

Fact #826. The pack train, commanded by 1st Lt. Edward Mathey, and escorted by Co. B under Capt. Thomas Mower McDougall, arrived at the Reno-Benteen position about 4:30 in the afternoon of June 25, 1876. Without the arrival of those mules, carrying heavy loads including extra ammunition, the men with Reno and Benteen "must have shared very quickly the fate of those with Custer." (Nye, "Marching With Custer," 1941, *Veterinary Bulletin*)

Fact #827. The 1873 Springfield rifles fired a .45 caliber bullet (meaning its size was 45/100ths of an inch in diameter), propelled by 70 grains of black powder, hence the designation .45-70. The lead bullet weighed 611 grains. The cartridge was modified in the 1874 model to .55 caliber, with the same 70 grains of powder (.55-70) to cut down the jamming, recoil, and barrel fouling problems which plagued the weapon's user under rapid fire conditions.

Fact #828. In *Horses, Saddles and Bridles*, published in 1895, we learn from Gen. William Harding Carter that "there are four natural gaits" for a horse, "the walk, amble, trot, and gallop. . . Marches, drills, and maneuvers are performed at varying degrees of speed, but the only authorized and desirable gaits are the walk, trot, and gallop. Especially should officers' horses be trained to perform those gaits at the regulation rate of speed per mile. Nothing is so trying to the temper, or so productive of discomfort to the men in ranks, as an officer leading the columns on a horse with a running walk instead of a square walk, or a single foot instead of a trot." Gen. Walker wrote his basic cavalry horse manual from his years of experience in the U.S. Cavalry, dating from 1874 when he entered the 6th U.S. Cavalry as a 2d Lt.

Fact #829. Capt. Frederick Benteen, commanding Co. H, then at Fort Rice (D.T.), wrote the Adjutant of Cavalry on March 12, 1874, "Sir: In answer to communications just received from Regimental Headquarters, relative to the number and kind of arms my company is supplied with, and their relative merits: I have the honor to state, that I have sixty-seven Sharp's improved Carbines, Cal. 50/100 and fifty-three Remington Army Pistols, Cal. 44. I have no other kinds of Carbines or Pistols. The Carbines are very good, if some of the parts were of stronger make—such as the muzzle sight & the hind sight & sliding scale and the swivl [sic] attachment. In my opinion, the barrel of the carbine is altogether too short for accurate shooting at long ranges."

Fact #830. Both Gen. Alfred Terry and Maj. Marcus Reno served on the 1873 Board on Breech-Loading Small Arms, examining 100 arms of American or foreign invention or manufacture. Although questions were raised about the 1873 Springfield's performance values, the board insisted that it be produced and issued to troops in the field.

Fact #831. The 1874 expedition to the Black Hills was delayed by Lt. Col. Custer pending receipt of the new 1873 Springfield carbines.

Fact #832. The .45-55 cartridge used by the 1873 Springfield carbine was copper cased, with thin casings, and initial tests proved that in rapid-fire situations, cases had a tendency to swell and stick in the breech mechanism. This was caused by dirt, black powder residue, heat, the heavy powder load, and sometimes verdigris on the copper casings. Jamming caused by the extractor mechanism tearing the head off the casing, or coming over the rim, left the soldier with an inoperable weapon.

Fact #833. Soldiers at the Little Big Horn had trouble with the ejection of shells by the "extractor" of their 1873 model Springfield carbine. Instructions on dealing with this hazard were contained in "Description and Rules for the Management of the Springfield Rifle, Carbine and Army Revolvers, Calibre .45," published by the National Armory in Springfield (MA). "VII [cont]. Should the head of a cartridge come off in the act of firing, the best mode of extracting a shell is to take out a ball from a cartridge and reduce it with a knife by rolling so that it can be inserted into the muzzle of the barrel. Ram the ball hard with the ramrod when the breech is closed; this will upset the ball and fill the headless shell. Open the breech block and the ball and shell can be easily pushed out with the ram rod."

Fact #834. "An Indian scout who was with that portion of the Regt which Custer took into battle, in relating what he saw in that part of the battle, says that from his hiding place he could see the men sitting down under fire & working at their guns—a story that finds confirmation in the fact that officers, who afterwards examined the battlefield, as they were burying the dead, found knives with broken blades, lying near the dead bodies—" (*Custer Battle Guns*)

Fact #835. "General Order 13" was issued by the War Department on February 16, 1876: "Empty metallic cartridge shells for the Springfield carbine and musket (rifle) can, after being fired, be used an indefinite number of times by refilling and capping. Great care should be exercised by all officers to prevent Indians from procuring empty shells thrown away by troops after firing, either in action or at target practice." Army carbines captured at the Rosebud battle on June 17, 1876, were undoubtedly used against the Army on June 25, 1876, with "refilled" Army cartridges being fired from them.

Fact #836. Gen. William Harding Carter in his 1895 book, *Horses, Saddles and Bridles*, outlined the "qualifications" for a good cavalry horse. "Good points in a horse are not mere matters of beauty, but shapes which, on mechanical principles, are likely to answer the required ends. However, shapes which may be objectionable for one class of work, are not necessarily so for another. Thus small 'chunky' or pony-built horses are better for work in the mountains, than larger and longer-coupled horses." The horses of Custer's column, of average size for cavalry horses, were required to do a lot of rough climbing in the advance to the Little Big Horn.

Fact #837. Jammed breeches on the 1873 Springfield carbine plagued soldiers throughout the frontier cavalry. The Army's solution was to provide one wooden cleaning rod to each 10 carbines, thereby requiring soldiers in a fire fight to "wait their turn" if their carbine jammed. It has been recorded that most soldiers bought pocket knives or even butcher knives from post sutlers to use for prying stuck cartridge casings from their carbines. (*Custer Battle Guns*)

Fact #838. The pack train which accompanied the 7th Cavalry column to the Little Big Horn lightened the loads of the cavalry horses considerably. H.W. Daly, chief packer for the Quartermasters' Dept., U.S. Army, wrote, in 1908, a

Manual of Pack Transportation, based on his experience which began as a packer for Gen. George Crook in the Sioux Expedition of 1876. He commented on the capability of the mules used in Indian Wars campaign pack trains: "The mules carried loads averaging 250 pounds; the average day's march was 30 miles, except when climbing mountains, when about 15 miles per day was the rule. The mules subsisted entirely on the grasses found in the country, and when the campaign was over were returned to their posts in good condition." Except for those killed in action, as at the Reno-Benteen position on June 25-26, 1876.

Fact #839. "The ponies [of the Indian scouts] were so exhausted [in the early afternoon of June 25, 1876] toward the end that when Custer ordered some of the scouts forward in pursuit of fleeing Sioux as the regiment approached the Little Big Horn, they refused to go because of the condition of their animals. Some of the scouts dropped out completely during the last few miles of the approach, saying their horses were too poor (meaning in too poor condition) to go on." (Col. Elwood L. Nye, *Veterinary Bulletin*, 1941)

Fact #840. An army may travel on its stomach, but the 7th Cavalry going to the Little Big Horn traveled on its horses. In an 1895 book entitled *Horses, Saddles and Bridles*, Gen. W.H. Carter wrote about the criteria for choosing cavalry horses: ". . .conformation and soundness are the things to which attention is mainly directed, but there are some other requisites, however, which are absolute essentials in a saddle horse worthy of the name. The most important of these are a gentle disposition; a good mouth; regular and easy gaits, without stumbling, interfering or over-reaching; courage and ambition, without being nervous or fidgety; of proper size to carry the weight, which for cavalry service requires a horse about fifteen to fifteen and three-fourths hands high, and weighing from 950 to 1100 pounds."

Fact #841. Four cavalry horses involved in Reno's charge against the (southern) upper end of the village on the mid-afternoon of June 25, 1876, ran away with their riders. Two of the soldiers—Pvts. George E. Smith and Henry Turley of Co. M—were carried into the mass of counterattacking Indians and presumed dead, although their bodies were never found. Two others—Pvts. J.H. Meier and Roman Rutten of Co. M—managed to return to Reno's command despite being wounded. Custer's horses were untested in warfare for the most part, nor were they used to being forced to a two-mile gallop, and so some became unmanageable.

Fact #842. Breech jamming was the biggest problem 7th Cavalry soldiers had with the 1873 Springfield carbine. In "Description and Rules for the Management of the Springfield Rifle, Carbine and Army Revolvers, Calibre .45," published by the National Armory in Springfield (MA) in 1874, the following suggestions for dealing with this problem are found: "VII. It should be borne in mind that the ejector, cam latch and firing springs are convenient rather than essential; and that the break of one or all of them does not necessarily unfit the piece for further service. The extractor alone will loosen the shell so that it can be easily removed by the forefinger, or it will fall to the ground if the muzzle be elevated when the breech is open."

Fact #843. As Custer's soldiers approached the Little Big Horn River on June 25, 1876, several of the mounts were increasingly slowed by fatigue, the column having been on the march since May. Gen. W.H. Carter in his 1895 book *Horses, Saddles and Bridles* warned against the overwork and lack of training of cavalry horses. "For the few brief charges upon the field of battle, into which the excitement of the moment may carry the sick and the lame, there must be months and years of patient and laborious work in reconnaissance, patrol, advance and rear guard, outpost duty, and route marches with horses loaded down with heavy and unwieldy packs. Few men upon first entering the service can realize how accurate a balance is required for the large amount of baggage and kit to be placed upon the horse." Many of Custer's soldiers lacked experience as cavalrymen.

Events

Fact #844. Capt. Frederick Benteen, Maj. Reno's second-in-command at the Reno-Benteen battlesite, led a group to Last Stand Hill on June 27, 1876, for the first official survey of the field.

Fact #845. *Little Big Horn 1876: Custer's Last Stand*'s "real-time" hypothesis for June 25: 1710—As increasing numbers of warriors gather to oppose the cavalry soldiers, they begin to envelop both wings of Custer's column.

Fact #846. The men of Co. A fought on the east side of the circular trench line surrounding the swale where the field hospital and the horses and mules were protected. The entrenchments were a makeshift barricade of pack saddles, hardtack boxes, sides of bacon, dead horses and mules, and anything else that might possibly turn a bullet. The remains of one soldier were discovered in 1958 in this saucer-shaped depression, where many horses and mules were also killed.

Fact #847. On June 25, 1876, four battalions of the 7th U.S. Cavalry engaged an Indian village on the banks of the Little Big Horn River in south central Montana, resulting in the loss of the commander Lt. Col. (Bvt. Brig. General) George Armstrong Custer, and the five companies under his command.

Fact #848. *Little Big Horn 1876: Custer's Last Stand*'s "real-time" hypothesis for June 25: 0300—Custer halts the 7th Cavalry at Davis Creek.

Fact #849. The "Dakota Column," Gen. Alfred Terry, commanding, which included Custer's 7th Cav., was only one of three cavalry columns dispatched by the War Department to deal with "hostiles" in the spring of 1876. The others were the "Montana Column," Col. John Gibbon, commanding, and "Crook's column," coming from the south, under the command of Gen. George Crook, which encountered the Indians at the Battle of the Rosebud on June 17.

Fact #850. Custer and his two-hundred-odd soldiers on a barren, windswept hill in southeastern Montana fought one of the bloodiest battles with Indians in the annals of American military history.

Fact #851. *Little Big Horn 1876: Custer's Last Stand*'s "real-time" hypothesis for June 25: 1620—Benteen reaches Reno Hill (the Reno-Benteen site).

Fact #852. Some historians believe Custer probably underestimated the strength of the Indian camp, and believed it safe to divide his regiment into four battalions. By attacking immediately, he might have hoped to prevent the Indians from escaping. (1978 "Custer Battlefield" brochure)

Fact #853. W.W. Cooke [Custer's adjutant] added the postscript ("P.S. Bring pacs [sic].") for emphasis to the famed "last message" to Benteen, to indicate how urgently Custer wanted his reserve supplies.

Fact #854. *Little Big Horn 1876: Custer's Last Stand*'s "real-time" hypothesis for June 25: 1730—Co. E attempts a break-out from Custer Hill toward Deep Ravine, but is overwhelmed by increasing numbers of warriors attracted by its efforts at escape.

Fact #855. The blame for the LBH disaster rested squarely on Maj. Reno. "But Reno did not come. Terry and Gibbon were more than a day's march away, and Custer and his men had to meet alone the overwhelming numbers of the Indians. In previous Indian fights, when white soldiers had called for help, every available man had been hurled to their relief no matter what the odds." (Bates, *New York Times*, June 1926)

Fact #856. *Little Big Horn 1876: Custer's Last Stand*'s "real-time" hypothesis for June 25: 1605—Custer's right wing (Cos. C, I, L) advances along Luce Ridge, after Custer splits his battalion into two "wings."

Fact #857. When Custer and his command (including Reno's column) neared the Little Big Horn, Custer turned north toward the lower end of the Indian encampment, sending Reno across the river to attack the southern end of the village. (1978 "Custer Battlefield" brochure)

Fact #858. On June 17, 1876, just over a week before LBH, the forces of Gen. George Crook, over 1,000 men, were attacked by "hundreds of Indians" along the Rosebud Creek in southern Montana Territory, but managed to fight the attackers to a tactical draw. The Indians withdrew to their encampment along the Little Big Horn. Crook withdrew to his camp along Goose Creek (near present-day Sheridan [WY]) and effectively removed his forces from the Sioux Expedition.

Fact #859. *Little Big Horn 1876: Custer's Last Stand*'s "real-time" hypothesis for June 25: 0845—Custer column resumes advance after the halt at Davis Creek.

Fact #860. Reno's command, having retreated from the head of the village to the bluffs east of the village, was joined by Capt. Benteen's battalion of three companies, and, shortly thereafter, by the pack train with its B Company escort. All seven companies faced increasing pressure from attacking Indians as the day wore on.

Fact #861. With his position at the Reno-Benteen site under heavy crossfire on the morning of June 26, 1876, Capt. Frederick Benteen realized that the Indians were threatening to break the defense perimeter. Benteen requested reinforcements from Co. M and led a counterattack from his position on the southeast end of the defenders' line. The charge, launched about 9 a.m., surprised the attackers and drove them back into the ravine.

Fact #862. *Little Big Horn 1876: Custer's Last Stand*'s "real-time" hypothesis for June 25: 1610—Co. E reconnoiters Miniconjou Ford (also called Deep Coulee Ford) while Co. F supports; this is Custer's "left wing."

Fact #863. The men under Maj. Reno and Capt. Benteen entrenched and held their defenses throughout June 25 and most of the next day, returning Indian fire and fighting off attempts to take their position. The siege ended when the Indians broke their great encampment and withdrew upon the approach of columns under Gen. Terry and Col. Gibbon.

Fact #864. *Little Big Horn 1876: Custer's Last Stand*'s "real-time" hypothesis for June 25: 1610—Stragglers reach Reno-Benteen site.

Fact #865. Charging within sight of the Hunkpapa village, the largest and southernmost tribal circle in the Indian encampment along the banks of the Little Big Horn River, Maj. Marcus Reno ordered a halt. His men were perhaps 150 yards away from the river, out on the flat. As the troops dismounted, at least one cavalry horse bolted, carrying his rider into the clouds of dust which masked mounted warriors. He was never seen again.

Fact #866. *Little Big Horn 1876: Custer's Last Stand*'s "real-time" hypothesis for June 25: 1730—Indian warriors overrun the last survivors at Custer Hill and a small group attempting to flee toward Deep Ravine.

Fact #867. As Custer's column (Cos. C, E, F, I, L) and Reno's column (Cos. A, G, M) parted company, Reno to attack the southern (upper) end of the village and Custer to proceed (north) downstream to attack the village in flank, Custer gave permission to both Lt. Charles Varnum (commanding the Detachment of Indian Scouts) and Lt. G.W. Wallace (who as acting topographical officer was riding with Custer) to join Reno's column which would open the attack. Both officers survived the battle.

Fact #868. Reno reported that, as he and his men charged the southern (upper) end of the village in the afternoon of June 25, he "soon saw that I was being drawn into some trap as they certainly would fight harder as we were nearing their village which was still standing. Besides, I could not see Custer or any other support." (Lt. Edgerly, Co. D)

Fact #869. *Little Big Horn 1876: Custer's Last Stand*'s "real-time" hypothesis for June 25: 1620—Facing minimal resistance at Miniconjou Ford (also known as Deep Coulee Ford), Custer's left wing (Cos. E and F) moves to link up with the rest of Custer's battalion (Cos. C, I, L), the "right wing."

Fact #870. In 1874, gold was discovered in the Black Hills (D.T.), the heart of the huge Indian reservation established by the Fort Laramie (W.T.) treaty of 1868. Thousands of goldseekers swarmed into the region, in violation of that treaty, which promised to protect the Indians "against the commission of all depredations by people of the United States."

Fact #871. *Little Big Horn 1876: Custer's Last Stand*'s "real-time" hypothesis for June 25: 1212—Custer divides the 7th Cavalry into three battalions (Reno's, Benteen's, Keogh's), and orders the advance.

Fact #872. At the Battle of the Rosebud, Gen. Crook learned of the Sioux strength and will to fight, but word of the battle never reached Custer, who still estimated Indian strength at 800 warriors. (1978 "Custer Battlefield" brochure)

Fact #873. Terry's entire command began its movement (north) down the Little Big Horn Valley on the night of June 28, heading for the site where the steamer *Far West* was moored to the river bank.

Fact #874. *Little Big Horn 1876: Custer's Last Stand*'s "real-time" hypothesis for June 25: 1630—Custer's five companies (C, E, F, I, L) link up at Calhoun Hill.

Fact #875. "Before reaching the village, Major Reno decided that the Indians were too strong for him and abandoned the charge. After fighting on the defensive for a time, he issued several contradictory orders. These confused his men. Finally he led them in a wild retreat to the bluffs on the side of the river from which he had come. The Indians came up in increasing numbers under the leadership of Gall as they saw their foes retreating, and shot down the fleeing cavalrymen as if they were running buffalo. On this retreat Reno lost nearly half his command in killed, wounded and abandoned." (Bates, *New York Times*, June 20, 1926)

Fact #876. *Little Big Horn 1876: Custer's Last Stand*'s "real-time" hypothesis for June 25: 1635—Custer's left wing (Cos. E and F) continues north and west from Calhoun Hill seeking other sites over which the column might ford the Little Big Horn River.

Fact #877. Upon receiving a report that an Indian had been seen on the cavalry column's back trail on the morning of June 25, trying to break open a lost box of hardtack, the officers were assembled; and "Genl. Custer said that of course all possibility of surprising the Indians was now gone and that the only way to catch them was to move on them at once." (Lt. Edgerly, Co. D)

Fact #878. Brig. Gen. Alfred Terry, Dakota Department Commander, and his staff reached Fort Abraham Lincoln (D.T.) in mid-May 1876, a few days before the expedition was to begin. Gen. Terry took command of the Dakota Column and the overall operation.

Fact #879. *Little Big Horn 1876: Custer's Last Stand*'s "real-time" hypothesis for June 25: 1725—Survivors of Custer's column fort up near Custer Hill, but surrounded and under intense fire, their tactical cohesion begins to disintegrate.

Fact #880. The Fort Laramie (D.T.) peace agreement of 1868 collapsed when goldseekers invaded and despoiled the Black Hills, sacred to the Indians, and supposedly "protected" by the treaty. (1978 "Custer Battlefield" brochure)

Fact #881. At the last Officers' Call on the morning of June 25, Custer announced to the officers that the column had been discovered by the Indians, and that the village had been sighted about 15 miles distant. Companies were ordered to resume the march in the order they were ready. Co. H led out. (Lt. Francis Gibson, Co. H)

Fact #882. *Little Big Horn 1876: Custer's Last Stand*'s "real-time" hypothesis for June 25: 1410—Custer's cavalry column sees Cheyenne Indians fleeing from the "Lone Tepee."

Fact #883. On the evening of June 24, after the 7th Cavalry had bivouaced for the night, "boots and saddles" was sounded about 10 p.m. (not by the usual bugle, but by whispers), and a silent march was begun. (Lt. Francis Gibson, Co. H)

Fact #884. *Little Big Horn 1876: Custer's Last Stand*'s "real-time" hypothesis for June 25: 1715—Pack train, escorted by Co. B, reaches the Reno-Benteen position on the bluffs.

Fact #885. "Custer, forced to retreat, did so in such a way as to compel the Indians to spread out with their rear exposed to the hoped-for advance of Reno and Benteen. At this time, the combined command on Reno Hill, at a smart trot or gallop, could have reached in fifteen or twenty minutes the rear of the Indians who were fighting Custer. This estimate was made by General [Nelson] Miles, the noted Indian fighter, who in going over the battlefield a year later, had one of his cavalry horses cover the distance. They would have met with no opposition at this time, for the Indians were all fighting Custer." (July 20, 1926, Bates)

Fact #886. At dawn "of the fatal 25th of June," Custer's column resumed its ride, pushing on until around 10 a.m., when Officers' Call was bugled, breaking the long advance from the Crow's Nest. The column consisted of all 12 companies (A, B, C, D, E, F, G, H, I, K, L, M). (Lt. Francis Gibson, Co. H)

Fact #887. *Little Big Horn 1876: Custer's Last Stand*'s "real-time" hypothesis for June 25: 1650—Weir departs the Reno-Benteen position with Co. D.

Fact #888. Attacking the southern (upper) end of the Indian village spreading along the Little Big Horn River, Maj. Reno's command was quickly outnumbered by counterattacking Indians and broke off the attack, withdrawing, first into the trees, and then to the bluffs across the river. (Lt. Francis Gibson, Co. H, with Benteen's column, who estimated the length of the village at three miles)

Fact #889. *Little Big Horn 1876: Custer's Last Stand*'s "real-time" hypothesis for June 25: 1725—Custer's left wing (Cos. E and F) join with the few survivors of the right wing (Cos. C, I, L) around Custer Hill, coalescing around the headquarters command.

Fact #890. About an hour after Capt. Benteen and his command had joined forces with Maj. Reno's command on top of the bluffs overlooking the Little Big Horn River, Capt. McDougall came up with his company (B) and the train of pack mules.

Fact #891. *Little Big Horn 1876: Custer's Last Stand*'s "real-time" hypothesis for June 25: 1640—Sioux warriors led by Hunkpapa chief Gall engage the troops on Calhoun Hill from Henryville Draw.

Fact #892. 2d Lt. G.D. Wallace (Co. G), the official "itinerist" of the march of Custer's column, said, in his report, "June 24, 1876—The column moved at 5 A.M. this morning. After we had been on the march about an hour, our Crow scouts came in and reported fresh signs of Indians, but in no great numbers."

Fact #893. "I had been sent ahead of the column with my scouts when my attention was called to some Indians ahead. [F]rom the top of a little knoll I saw 40 to 50 Indians on a rise between us and the Little Bighorn. They evidently discovered us for they disappeared right away." (2d Lt. Luther Hare, Detachment of Scouts)

Fact #894. As Reno's attacking battalion slowed its charge, ". . .over the middle of the ridge came riding a dense swarm of Dakotas in one mass toward [Arikara scout] Bob Tailed Bull. ...The Dakota attack doubled up the [soldiers'] line from the left and pushed this line back. . . They all retreated back across the river lower down about two miles. . .across the flat and up the bluff. . .which was hard climbing." (*The Arikara Narrative*)

Fact #895. Hearing firing from the north, Capt. Thomas Weir, followed by Cos. D, H, K, and M, reached a high point (a place now referred to as Weir point), about a mile and a half to the northeast of the Reno-Benteen position, from which he saw a field of action several miles beyond, farther north on the west bank of the Little Big Horn River.

Fact #896. *Little Big Horn 1876: Custer's Last Stand*'s "real-time" hypothesis for June 25: 1640—Indian riflemen fire at Calhoun Hill from Greasy Grass Ridge.

Fact #897. On the morning of June 25, 1876, a sergeant from Capt. McDougall's pack train, who had been back on the trail a few miles to find some hard bread lost from a pack mule, saw an Indian trying to break open the box of bread, leading the soldiers to believe that the element of surprise was lost.

Fact #898. *Little Big Horn 1876: Custer's Last Stand*'s "real-time" hypothesis for June 25: 1415—Custer gives Reno's battalion the order to pursue the fleeing Cheyenne and attack the village.

Fact #899. The second phase of LBH, fought more than four miles from the Reno action, in the vicinity of what is now the battlefield visitors' center, involved five badly-outnumbered cavalry companies (C, E, F, I, L) under the personal command of Lt. Col. George A. Custer, which were overwhelmed by the savage fury of the attacking Indians.

Fact #900. *Little Big Horn 1876: Custer's Last Stand*'s "real-time" hypothesis for June 25: 1712—Benteen departs the Reno-Benteen position with H, K, and M companies, to join Weir and Co. D at "Weir Point."

Fact #901. As the column advanced rapidly from the Crow's Nest on the morning of June 25, Custer decided to divide the command into four battalions, giving one each to Maj. Marcus Reno (Cos. A, G, M), Capt. Frederick Benteen (Cos. D, H, K), Capt. Myles Keogh (Cos. C, I, L), and Capt. G.W. Yates (Cos. E & F); Co. B, under Capt. Thomas McDougall, escorted the pack train. Custer rode with Keogh's and Yates' battalions.

Fact #902. *Little Big Horn 1876: Custer's Last Stand*'s "real-time" hypothesis for June 25: 1722—Survivors of Custer's right wing (Cos. C, I, L) flee from the Calhoun Hill position and are overrun as they try to reach Custer and the left wing (Cos. E and F) near Custer Hill.

Fact #903. As Reno's initial charge toward the village halted, the men dismounted and horse-holders (every fourth man) took charge of the horses. After Sgt. John Ryan and about 10 men from Co. M scouted the timber and underbrush along the river, the mounts were led to the protection of the tree line, with the 90 or so men remaining to form a skirmish line.

Fact #904. *Little Big Horn 1876: Custer's Last Stand*'s "real-time" hypothesis for June 25: 1608—Co. F is detailed to scout the right flank of the right wing advance, over to Henryville Draw.

Fact #905. When the Custers' younger brother Boston, who had joined the expedition as a civilian packer, came to Benteen's column on the way to join his brothers that morning of June 25, he gave a "cheery salutation, as he passed, and then, with a smile on his face, rode to his death, dying as he, although not a soldier, would have chosen to die, fighting gallantly by the side of his brothers." (Lt. Edgerly, Co. D)

Fact #906. *Little Big Horn 1876: Custer's Last Stand*'s "real-time" hypothesis for June 25: 1430—Benteen's battalion, having been sent to the left to scout for Indians, rejoins the main column's trail at what is now known as Reno Creek.

Fact #907. When Reno's command was within about four and one half miles from the village, Custer, still following a nearly parallel course, ". . .sent [Adj. W.W.] Cooke to Reno with orders 'To move forward at as rapid a gait as I thought prudent and to charge afterwards, and that the whole outfit would support me' (Reno's Report)." (Lt. W.S. Edgerly, Co. D)

Fact #908. *Little Big Horn 1876: Custer's Last Stand*'s "real-time" hypothesis for June 25: 1625—Custer's right wing (Cos. C, I, L) advances along Nye-Cartwright Ridge, firing on small groups of warriors.

Fact #909. After receiving Custer's order on the morning of June 25 to "move forward. . .and to charge," Reno ordered the trot "and soon reached an excellent ford of the Little Big Horn River which he crossed in a column of fours." (Lt. Edgerly, Co. D)

Fact #910. *Little Big Horn 1876: Custer's Last Stand*'s "real-time" hypothesis for June 25: 1715—Custer's right wing (C, I, L companies) collapses.

Fact #911. The 7th Cavalry, under the field command of Lt. Col. George Custer, continued (south) up the Yellowstone from the mouth of the Powder River to the mouth of Rosebud Creek, arriving there around noon June 21, 1876. (Luce, *Custer Battlefield*)

Fact #912. Reno's men were deployed as skirmishers after they crossed the Little Big Horn River in the late morning of July 25, with the scouts on the left (away from the river) and charged (north) down the valley for about two and a half miles, "driving the Indians with ease." (Lt. W.S. Edgerly, Co. D)

Fact #913. *Little Big Horn 1876: Custer's Last Stand*'s "real-time" hypothesis for June 25: 1722—Capt. Myles Keogh and Co. I, on the back slope of Calhoun Hill, are overwhelmed from three sides by Hunkpapa and Oglala warriors, and wiped out to a man.

Fact #914. Forces of Gen. George Crook, the Commander of the Department of the Platte, marched north from Fort Fetterman (W.T.) into Montana Territory, and attacked Old Bear's camp of over 100 Sioux and Cheyenne lodges and about 250 warriors including Little Wolf, Two Moon, and He Dog, on March 17, 1876.

Fact #915. *Little Big Horn 1876: Custer's Last Stand*'s "real-time" hypothesis for June 25: 1650—The Oglala war leader Crazy Horse and his followers cross Battle Ridge while Custer's left wing (Cos. E and F) are reconnoitering toward the North Ford; the Sioux warriors advance toward Calhoun Hill up Crazy Horse Ravine.

Fact #916. Fearing a trap, Maj. Reno halted his charge as he neared the village on the afternoon of June 25, "till the arrival of the mounted warriors, soon after which event he beat his hasty retreat across the river, which in his report he calls a charge." (Lt. W. S. Edgerly, Co. D)

Fact #917. *Little Big Horn 1876: Custer's Last Stand*'s "real-time" hypothesis for June 25: 1440—Benteen's battalion waters the horses at "the morass."

Fact #918. Long after the battle, Lt. W.S. Edgerly (Co. D) stated that he believed the Reno "retreat" from the village on the afternoon of June 25, "was a grave error, that there was little excuse for making it, and none for the manner in which it was executed."

Fact #919. The only order Reno gave for his "charge" (retreat) from the southern (upper) end of the Indian village on the afternoon of June 25, was "Mount and get to the bluffs," and this order was only heard by a few people in his immediate vicinity. (Lt. W.S. Edgerly, Co. D)

Fact #920. *Little Big Horn 1876: Custer's Last Stand*'s "real-time" hypothesis for June 25: 1600—Scattered warriors west of Luce Ridge withdraw as Custer's left wing (Cos. E and F) advances north toward the river.

Fact #921. As the cloud of warriors came toward the cavalry troops at Weir Point, about a mile and a half northeast of the Reno-Benteen position, the soldiers were forced to dismount and prepare to fight on foot.

Fact #922. The Battle of the Little Big Horn River on June 25-26, 1876, was one of the last major instances of violent resistance by the American Indians to the advance of white settlement, earning its place in history.

Fact #923. *Little Big Horn 1876: Custer's Last Stand*'s "real-time" hypothesis for June 25: 1722—Crazy Horse and his Oglala warriors attack survivors from Calhoun Hill as they flee from Gall's attack into Keogh's position.

Fact #924. The "Custer fight," as it was referred to in Army circles for many years, was the largest engagement in the war which led to the Northern Cheyenne and several tribes of the Sioux, described as "hostile," being subdued.

Fact #925. After Reno ordered a halt to the initial attack on the village within sight of the Hunkpapa circle at the (southern) upper end of the encampment, the troops dismounted on the prairie, with every fourth man serving as a horse-holder. The line faced north, curving slightly to the left, away from the river, as the soldiers continued to advance on foot.

Fact #926. *Little Big Horn 1876: Custer's Last Stand*'s "real-time" hypothesis for June 25: 1455—Custer turns north onto the high ground, separating from Reno's battalion.

Fact #927. The Battle of the Little Big Horn opened shortly before noon when three companies of cavalry under the command of Maj. Marcus A. Reno (A, G, M) attacked the southern end of the Indian village along the river and met with stubborn resistance, causing a retreat back across the river to high bluffs where the troops entrenched and were later joined by another three companies (D, H, K) under Capt. Frederick Benteen, as well as the column's pack train, escorted by Capt. Thomas McDougall's Co. B. (*Custer Battlefield*, Luce)

Fact #928. Reno's command crossed the Little Big Horn River at what is known today as Reno Ford, Lt. W.S. Edgerly (Co. D) wrote, and halted his men, "ten minutes more or less, to gather the battalion. . ."

Fact #929. *Little Big Horn 1876: Custer's Last Stand*'s "real-time" hypothesis for June 25: 1650—Co. D, following Capt. Weir, leaves Reno-Benteen position heading toward the highest point on the battlefield, later named Weir Point.

Fact #930. A base of supply was established by the Dakota Column at the mouth of the Powder River on the Yellowstone (M.T.), and left under the guard of infantry troops and some cavalry troops. All wagons were abandoned and from there supplies were carried by pack mule.

Fact #931. Shortly after arriving on the bluffs, the men of Reno's command could hear heavy gunfire from the north and Capt. Thomas B. Weir, later followed by his Company (D), attempted a scout, marching downstream to a high hill, from which the Custer battle site was barely visible. When the rest of the command arrived on the hill, it was attacked by a large force of Indians and Reno ordered a withdrawal to the original position on bluffs overlooking the Little Big Horn River and the southern head of the village.

Fact #932. *Little Big Horn 1876: Custer's Last Stand*'s "real-time" hypothesis for June 25: 1630—As the elements of Custer's battalion re-gather at Calhoun Hill, the left wing (Cos. E and F) continues north along Battle Ridge.

Fact #933. Custer divided his command on June 25, sending one battalion of three companies under Capt. Frederick W. Benteen to scout the bluffs to the south (on Custer's left). At the same time, a column of three companies under Maj. Marcus A. Reno and two battalions of three and two companies respectively under Custer marched along the opposite banks of a small creek to attack the Indian village in the valley of the Little Big Horn. (1978 "Custer Battlefield" brochure)

Fact #934. The first 1876 clash between Indian warriors and soldiers was on March 17. About half of Gen. Crook's forces, under Col. J.J. Reynolds, attacked a Northern Cheyenne camp on the Powder River near what is now Moorhead (MT). The Indians fled while the soldiers burned the vacated tepees. (Luce, *Custer Battlefield*)

Fact #935. *Little Big Horn 1876: Custer's Last Stand*'s "real-time" hypothesis for June 25: 1720—Hunkpapa war chief Gall and his warriors rush the southern slopes of Calhoun Hill, firing furiously at the surviving soldiers.

Fact #936. Sgt. Daniel Kanipe, Co. C, arrived at Benteen's command shortly after it returned to the main trail. The sergeant was smiling; as he passed Benteen's men on his way to the pack train with his message to Capt. McDougall, he called out, "We've got 'em, boys!"

Fact #937. At the Crow's Nest, Custer could not see the Indian village 15 miles away at the Little Big Horn River, although his scouts assured him they could see it. (James O. Gump, *The Dust Rose Like Smoke*)

Fact #938. *Little Big Horn 1876: Custer's Last Stand*'s "real-time" hypothesis for June 25: 1503—Benteen leaves "the morass" as the pack train arrives.

Fact #939. "About 4:30 p.m. [on July 25, 1876] Captain MacDougal[l] arrived with the pack train. [McDougall] reported to Reno that he had heard the firing of two volleys from the quarter where he supposed Custer to be. Half an hour later, Reno, influenced by the growls of his officers and men, and by [Thomas B.] Weir's and [W.S.] Edgerly's courageous example, moved some of his companies down the trail taken by Capt. Weir [and Co. D]. But by this time it was too late to be of any assistance to Custer, as the Indians had begun to return in force." (Bates, June 20, 1926, *New York Times*)

Fact #940. *Little Big Horn 1876: Custer's Last Stand*'s "real-time" hypothesis for June 25: 1730—Custer's position collapses.

Fact #941. Reno's dismounted skirmish line on the prairie west of the Little Big Horn River and within sight of the Hunkpapa circle at the (southern) upper end of the village was faced by a growing number of Indians on horseback, some 700-900 yards away, firing steadily.

Fact #942. *Little Big Horn 1876: Custer's Last Stand*'s "real-time" hypothesis for June 25: 1545—Custer reaches the top of Medicine Tail Coulee.

Fact #943. In the valley of the Little Big Horn River on June 25 and 26, 1876, more than 260 soldiers and attached personnel of the U.S. Army met defeat and death at the hands of hundreds, if not thousands, of Sioux and Cheyenne warriors. Among the dead were Lt. Col. George Armstrong Custer and every member of his immediate command.

Fact #944. *Little Big Horn 1876: Custer's Last Stand*'s "real-time" hypothesis for June 25: 1555—Reno orders a retreat toward the river.

Fact #945. The U.S. Army's campaign against "hostile" Indians on the Northern Plains, which resulted in LBH, called for three columns (Terry's, Gibbon's, and Crook's) to converge on the main body of Indians, concentrated in southeastern Montana under the leadership of Sitting Bull, Crazy Horse, and other war chiefs of the Sioux and Cheyenne.

Fact #946. *Little Big Horn 1876: Custer's Last Stand*'s "real-time" hypothesis for June 25: 1605—First of fleeing stragglers reach the Reno-Benteen site (Reno Hill).

Fact #947. At LBH, the 7th Cavalry lost the five companies (C, E, F, I, L) that were under Custer's direct command, about 225 men. Of the other six companies of the regiment, under Reno and Benteen, 47 men were killed and 52 wounded. (1978 "Custer Battlefield" brochure)

Fact #948. *Little Big Horn 1876: Custer's Last Stand*'s "real-time" hypothesis for June 25: 1610—Less than a dozen warriors snipe at Co. E's attempt to reconnoiter Miniconjou Ford (also called Deep Coulee Ford).

Fact #949. During his attack on the southern end of the Indian village at the Little Big Horn River, Maj. Marcus Reno and his men were outflanked by attacking Indians, and retreated in disorder to the river, finally taking up a defensive position on the bluffs beyond the river.

Fact #950. *Little Big Horn 1876: Custer's Last Stand*'s "real-time" hypothesis for June 25: 1455—Reno and his battalion (Cos. A, G, M) ford the Little Big Horn River and prepare to attack the village.

Fact #951. By about 11 a.m. on June 25, Benteen's command had progressed back toward the main trail, when they were overtaken by Boston Custer, George and Tom Custer's younger brother, hurrying to join Custer's immediate command. (Lt. W.S. Edgerly, Co. D)

Fact #952. *Little Big Horn 1876: Custer's Last Stand*'s "real-time" hypothesis for June 25: 1515—Custer sees Reno's charge on the village from the vantage point of the bluffs at Weir Point.

Fact #953. When the Army was called upon in the early winter of 1875 to enforce the order of the Commissioner of Indian Affairs and return to their reservations the Indians who had fled in protest and fear, a campaign was planned (notes the 1978 "Custer Battlefield" brochure) involving three converging columns, from Wyoming Territory, Dakota Territory, and Montana Territory.

Fact #954. *Little Big Horn 1876: Custer's Last Stand*'s "real-time" hypothesis for June 25: 1700—Custer's left wing (Cos. E and F) deploys in skirmish line above the North Ford on The Flats.

Fact #955. Scouting "off to the left" on the morning of June 25, Benteen's battalion discovered no Indians, but continued "skirting the hills looking for a chance to break through the chain without giving the horses and men too grueling a climb." (Lt. W.S. Edgerly, Co. D)

Fact #956. *Little Big Horn 1876: Custer's Last Stand*'s "real-time" hypothesis for June 25: 1655—Custer's left wing (Cos. E and F) reverses course and heads back toward the remainder of the column, to wait for Benteen and the pack train.

Fact #957. The morning of June 25, Gen. Custer decided that the Indians, having been warned of the cavalry's approach, would probably take flight, so he abandoned the original plans to delay the attack for 24 hours, and ordered his companies on the move, as each officer reported them ready; Capt. Benteen's Company (H) took the lead. (Lt. W.S. Edgerly, Co. D)

Fact #958. *Little Big Horn 1876: Custer's Last Stand*'s "real-time" hypothesis for June 25: 1650—Custer's left wing (Cos. E and F) locates the North Ford, espies non-combatants in hiding, does not advance.

Fact #959. At noon on June 22, 1876, the 7th U.S. Cavalry, commanded by Lt. Col. George A. Custer, set out from the Yellowstone in search of "hostile" Indians, passing in review before Gen. Alfred Terry, commander, Dakota Column; Col. John Gibbon, commander, Montana Column; and Lt. Col. Custer.

Fact #960. *Little Big Horn 1876: Custer's Last Stand*'s "real-time" hypothesis for June 25: 1640—Crazy Horse and his warriors cross the Little Big Horn River north of the village at the Deep Ravine, and advance in back of Battle Ridge toward Calhoun Hill.

Fact #961. *Little Big Horn 1876: Custer's Last Stand*'s "real-time" hypothesis for June 25: 1530—Reno withdraws his battalion to the tree line along the Little Big Horn River.

Fact #962. When 300 soldiers from Crook's column, commanded by Col. J.J. Reynolds, attacked the Sioux and Cheyenne camp along the Powder River valley (M.T.), the Indians fled to nearby bluffs and offered a determined resistance. The troops burned the camp, destroying all Indian stores, and then withdrew, suffering four dead, and six wounded during the engagement, and abandoning one of the wounded. The warriors followed and managed to recapture most of their pony herd. Reynolds was disgraced.

Fact #963. *Little Big Horn 1876: Custer's Last Stand*'s "real-time" hypothesis for June 25: 1715—Co. C launches an attack from Calhoun Hill to clear Calhoun Coulee, but intense fire from Greasy Grass Ridge drives them back.

Fact #964. "When Reno and his men galloped toward the upper [sic] end of the village there was almost no opposition, according to all the Indian accounts. His attack caused so much consternation that Sitting Bull took alarm and galloped away, forgetting one of his twin children in the melee, until he was overtaken fourteen miles from the battlefield. He explained his flight by saying that he had to go into the hills to make medicine to propitiate the evil spirits." (Bates, *New York Times*, June 20, 1926)

Fact #965. *Little Big Horn 1876: Custer's Last Stand*'s "real-time" hypothesis for June 25: 1640—Custer's right wing deploys on Calhoun Hill, Co. L in skirmish line and Cos. C and I in reserve.

Fact #966. "Lt. [W.S.] Godfrey [Co. K], now a Brigadier General, retired, in the way he covered the retirement of the advanced troops, showed the value of organized resistance. Reno's command [returning from Weir Point] resumed its former position on the hill [Reno-Benteen site], where about 6 p.m. it was heavily attacked." (Bates, *New York Times,* June 20, 1926)

Fact #967. *Little Big Horn 1876: Custer's Last Stand*'s "real-time" hypothesis for June 25: 1600—The north end of the village is virtually empty of warriors, most of whom are fending off the Reno attack.

Fact #968. Thirteen men left behind by Reno in his retreat from the valley rejoined his command without seeing more than five Indians. (Bates, *New York Times*, July 20, 1926)

Fact #969. *Little Big Horn 1876: Custer's Last Stand*'s "real-time" hypothesis for June 25: 1520—Custer sends trumpeter to find Benteen and deliver the "Last Message"—Come on. . .bring packs.

Fact #970. In *The Dust Rose Like Smoke*, James O. Gump refers to the events which preceded the Little Big Horn as occurring "in the context of late nineteenth century global economic expansion. . . ," and compares them to the events which preceded the notable defeat of Queen Victoria's forces at Isandhlwana by Zulu forces.

Fact #971. *Little Big Horn 1876: Custer's Last Stand*'s "real-time" hypothesis for June 25: 1720—Lame White Man, a Southern Cheyenne war chief visiting his Northern Cheyenne cousins, leads mounted warriors from Greasy Grass Ridge to pursue C Co. which is retreating toward Calhoun Hill after a sortie toward Calhoun Coulee.

Fact #972. After halting his initial charge in the valley fight, Reno directed his men into the timber, where he seemed uncertain as to his next move. A Sioux-Arikara scout, Bloody Knife, who was standing next to Reno, was hit in the head by a bullet, spraying Reno's face with blood and brains. According to Scout George Herendeen, in the confusion Reno ordered his troops to mount, then dismount, then mount again and "charge" toward the river to seek the high ground beyond.

Fact #973. *Little Big Horn 1876: Custer's Last Stand*'s "real-time" hypothesis for June 25: 1620—As Custer's left wing (Cos. E and F) leaves Miniconjou

Ford (also known as Deep Coulee Ford), Hunkpapa war chief Gall and other warriors advance northeast across the ford.

Fact #974. The soldiers at the Reno-Benteen site had been without water for many hours by the morning of June 26. Lt. E.S. Godfrey (commanding, Co. K) wrote: "The excitement and heat made our thirst almost maddening. The men were forbidden to use tobacco. They put pebbles in their mouths to excite the glands, some ate grass roots, but did not find relief; some tried to eat hard bread, but after chewing it awhile would blow it out of their mouths like so much flour."

Fact #975. *Little Big Horn 1876: Custer's Last Stand*'s "real-time" hypothesis for June 25: 1830—Reno's command re-assembles at the Reno-Benteen position.

Fact #976. As the soldiers retired after charging in counterattack from the southeast end of the Reno-Benteen position line on the morning of June 26, 1876, Pvt. Thomas Meador (Co. H) was killed, and Pvt. James J. Tanner (Co. M) was mortally wounded.

Fact #977. Lt. Francis Gibson (Co. H): "On the second day [June 26]. . .H company had three men killed and twenty-one wounded. We occupied the most exposed position and the Indians had a clear fire at us from four sides, and my only wonder is that every one of us wasn't killed."

Fact #978. *Little Big Horn 1876: Custer's Last Stand*'s "real-time" hypothesis for June 25: 1720—Custer's Calhoun Hill position collapses as soldiers and warriors engage in severe hand-to-hand fighting.

Fact #979. On the evening of June 26, the Indians broke camp, moving off to the south toward the Big Horn Mountains. The men at the Reno-Benteen position were relieved, but hesitant to let down their guard; many suspected a trick, so they spent another miserable night on the bluffs. Early the next morning, the nearly exhausted soldiers spied a large dust cloud in the valley to the north; Terry was marching (south) upriver.

Fact #980. *Little Big Horn 1876: Custer's Last Stand*'s "real-time" hypothesis for June 25: 1800—Retreat of all troops from Weir Point begins in the face of increasing Indian pressure.

Fact #981. At the time Custer's column witnessed Reno's charge from high atop the ridge, around 3:15 p.m., Custer released his Crow Scouts, most of whom went back to join Reno when he returned to the top of the bluffs, leaving there to make contact with Col. Gibbon's column on June 26, 1876.

Fact #982. As the two columns (Custer's and Reno's), riding together on the north bank of Reno Creek, halted at "the Lone Tipi," about four miles south of the Indian village, rising dust was seen four or five miles (north) down the valley. Interpreter Fred Girard from a nearby knoll waved his hat and shouted to Custer: "Here are your Indians, General, running like devils!"

Fact #983. *Little Big Horn 1876: Custer's Last Stand*'s "real-time" hypothesis for June 25: 1515—Reno halts his charge, dismounts and forms a skirmish line out in the open.

Fact #984. The battle at the Little Big Horn River, June 25-26, 1876, consisted of two entirely separate actions: one under the leadership of Maj. Marcus A. Reno, in the valley and atop the bluffs; the other, over four miles away, under the leadership of Lt. Col. George A. Custer, on the hills and ridges overlooking the river.

Fact #985. *Little Big Horn 1876: Custer's Last Stand*'s "real-time" hypothesis for June 25: 1720—Co. L, on Calhoun Hill, attempts to cover the retreat of Co. C from its attempted assault on Calhoun Coulee.

Fact #986. Reno's attack on the (southern) upper end of the village in the early afternoon of June 25, 1876, was conducted in line, with Co. A and Co. M in the line and Co. G in reserve. Co. G later was moved up onto the line. Reno rode in the center of the line, about 20 yards in front, with the Indian scouts, led by Lt. Charles Varnum and Lt. Luther Hare, on the left of the line, away from the river, 50-75 yards in advance of the line. The battalion's right wing was anchored near the twisting river with its timber and underbrush along the banks.

Fact #987. The Dakota Column, from Fort Abraham Lincoln (D.T.), commanded by Brig. Gen. Alfred Terry, joined with the Montana Column from Fort Shaw (M.T.), commanded by Col. John Gibbon, at the Yellowstone River; and the two commanders met together with Lt. Col. Custer, on June 21, 1876, on the supply steamer *Far West*, to plan the next phase of the 1876 Sioux Campaign. (Lt. Francis Gibson, Co. H)

Fact #988. *Little Big Horn 1876: Custer's Last Stand*'s "real-time" hypothesis for June 25: 1750—Reno follows Benteen to Weir Point with A, B, and G companies.

Fact #989. While many believe Custer's defeat at the Little Big Horn was the worst whipping inflicted by Indians on the frontier army, the St. Clair "massacre" of 1791 was much worse. A column under Gen. Arthur St. Clair ("sinclair") left Fort Washington (Cincinnati [NW.T.]) in August 1791 to build a series of outposts in the Northwest Territory from which Indian activities could be monitored and controlled. St. Clair started with 2,300 men, plus 200 women and children, but by November the column was much diminished and dispirited. A powerful force of Wyandots, Iroquois, Shawnees, Miami, Delawares, Ojibwas, and Potawatomis, were led by chief Little Turtle and two white renegades—a turncoat taken into the Iroquois, Blue Jacket, and frontiersman Simon

Girty. The defeat was the worst in the Army's Indian Wars history: 623 killed, 258 wounded, plus the nearly 200 women and children lost. St. Clair escaped.

Fact #990. *Little Big Horn 1876: Custer's Last Stand*'s "real-time" hypothesis for June 25: 1505—Reno advances on the south end of the village, then attacks in a charge.

Fact #991. Toward the end of Reno's valley fight just after 3 o'clock on June 25, 1876, civilian scout George Herendeen witnessed the death of two other civilians, Charles (Lonesome Charley) Reynolds, and Isaiah (Teat) Dorman, the only black man with the Reno battalion. Herendeen's horse was shot from under him on the retreat from the timber, and he hurried back to the cover. "I saw Reynolds come out of timber and said, 'Charley, don't try to ride out. We can't get away from this timber.' Reynolds was then trying to mount his horse. He finally mounted and got about 150 yds. when he was shot, and Isaiah fell near him, and while I was in the timber, I saw Indians shooting at Isaiah and squaws pounding him with stone hammers. His legs below the knees were shot full of bullets only an inch or two apart. Most of the men with me in the timber were a badly scared lot of fellows, and they were already as good as whipped."

Fact #992. Describing the Officers' Call held after Custer was shown the large village 15 miles away on the banks of the Little Big Horn by his Arikara scouts, Peter Thompson, Pvt., Co. C, wrote: "From the manner of the conversation it would seem as though Custer had discovered something that was of great importance. We [C Co., which was resting "quite close to the place where the officers sat in council"] could not hear the conversation but paid great attention while Custer and the more experienced officers were seeking to solve some difficult problem."

Fact #993. *Little Big Horn 1876: Custer's Last Stand*'s "real-time" hypothesis for June 25: 1700—As Indian numbers continue to increase, warriors encircle and infiltrate on Custer's left wing (Cos. E and F) as it returns from the North Ford.

Chief Sitting Bull

USAMHI

Chapter 3

Facts About the Indians

Individuals

Fact #994. Fanny Kelly, a white captive, who lived nearly half a year with Sitting Bull and his family, described him later: "a true nobleman, and great man. He was uniformly gentle, and kind to his wife and children and courteous and considerate in his intercourse w. [sic] others."

Fact #995. Crazy Horse always stuck close to his rifle, according to his lifelong friend He Dog, an Oglala war chief. "He always tried to kill as many as possible of the enemy without losing his own men. He never spoke in council and attended very few. There was no special reason for this; it was just his nature. He was a very quiet man except when there was fighting."

Fact #996. Hunkpapa war chief Gall, who led one strong segment of the Sioux force at LBH, gave an account of the battle to noted Western photographer D.F. Barry a decade after the battle: "We first noticed several companies of soldiers about two miles east of our camp, marching along the bluffs in the direction of the lower end of our village. These soldiers kicked up a lot of dust and they came in sight the second time about two hours after noon. They were mounted on white horses and it was a nice sight to see this parade across the river to the east. We watched these soldiers and were rounding up our pony herd so we could fight if the soldiers attacked us." This portion of Gall's account is counter to most other Indian reports, which state that the village was completely surprised.

Fact #997. "And now came Crazy Horse on his yellow pinto; the hailstone markings on his body, the lightning streak on his face, and the red-backed hawk that was his medicine on his head. 'Hoppo!' he called as he came up. 'Let us

Hunkpapa war chief Gall

USAMHI

go!' So, following our Strange Man, we drove the soldiers away from the Hunkpapa camp and back into the woods along a cutbank where once, long before, the river had flowed. Here they rallied and made a stand." (Charging Bear, a young Sioux warrior, remembering Crazy Horse's leadership early in the valley fight, June 25, 1876, against Reno's soldiers.)

Fact #998. Two Moon, a chief of the Northern Cheyenne, said of the battle: ". . .the shooting was quick, quick. Pop-pop-pop very fast. Some of the soldiers were down on their knees, some standing. . . The smoke was like a great cloud, and everywhere the Sioux went the dust rose like smoke. We circled all around him—swirling like water 'round a stone. We shoot, we ride fast, we shoot again. Soldiers drop, and horses fall on them."

Fact #999. The war chief who rallied the beleaguered Indians after Maj. Reno's attack on the south end of the village was 36-year-old Pizi, or Gall. The young Hunkpapa had distinguished himself as a hunter and a warrior, and Sitting Bull had adopted him as a younger brother. (*Bury My Heart At Wounded Knee*, Dee Brown)

Fact #1000. A 13-year-old Oglala boy, Black Elk, was swimming with friends in the Little Big Horn River the morning of the battle, when he heard a crier shouting at the Hunkpapa camp, "The chargers are coming! They are charging! The chargers are coming!" The cry was repeated up the river from the south end of the camp; first by the Oglala crier, then others north to the Cheyenne camp.

Fact #1001. A chief, High Elk, was killed in front of the Reno-Benteen position. (Blackfeet chief Kill Eagle, September 24, 1876, *New York Herald*)

Fact #1002. The half-Sioux, half-Arikara Bloody Knife, "Custer's favorite scout," told Custer that there were "enough Sioux to keep fighting for two-three days" in the village discovered 12-15 miles away from the column on the early morning of June 25. (*Custer: The Life of General George Armstrong Custer*, Monaghan)

Fact #1003. It was about 2:30 p.m., Sunday, June 25, 1876, when Crow King and Crazy Horse broke off their resistance to the Reno attack on the (southern) upper end of the Indian village at the Little Big Horn. "Crow King shot from the South [into Custer's column] and Crazy Horse from the North. The soldiers were trying to get back up the hill, but Crazy Horse and his warriors were behind the top of the hill shooting. Soldiers were falling all around; they were on foot and their horses were in the upper [eastern] end of the ravine where Crazy Horse was." (Chief Gall of the Hunkpapa, in "Indian Notes on the Custer Battle")

Fact #1004. When Maj. Reno's battalion charged the south end of the village, cavalry rifle bullets killed several women and children, including most of the family of Hunkpapa war chief Gall. "It made my heart bad. After that I killed all my enemies with the hatchet." (Dee Brown's *Bury My Heart At Wounded Knee*)

Fact #1005. Leaders of the Oglala Sioux at LBH included Crazy Horse, Low Dog, and Big Road.

Fact #1006. Sitting Bull, the Hunkpapa "medicine man" (shaman), while not a fighting man at the time of LBH, exercised a strong influence over the Indians. (Luce, *Custer Battlefield*)

Fact #1007. After either killing or running over the last cluster of soldiers east of Custer's group, they "went on down to where the last soldiers were. They were fighting good. The men were loading and firing, but they could not hit the warriors in the gulley and the ravine. The dust and smoke was black as evening. Once in a while we could see the soldiers through the dust and finally we charged through them with our ponies. When we had done this, right here on this ground, just a few rods South of us, the fight was over." (Gall to D.F. Barry)

Fact #1008. Crazy Horse and He Dog "went together on a war trip to the other side of the mountains," shortly after they had both been made "shirt-wearers" of the Oglala people. "When we came back, the people came out of the camp to meet us and escorted us back and at a big ceremony presented us with two spears, the gift of the whole tribe, which was met together. These spears were each three or four hundred years old and were given by the older generation to those in the younger generation who had best lived the life of a warrior." (He Dog to Eleanor Hinman, July 1930)

Fact #1009. The *Yankton [D.T.] Dakotaian* advanced the theory that Sitting Bull had "studied the campaigns of Napoleon," and W. Fletcher Johnson's *Red Record of the Sioux* (1891) stated, "Sitting Bull has read French history carefully, and he is especially enamored of the career of Napoleon, and endeavors to model his campaigns after those of the 'Man of Destiny'." Both claims are obviously spurious.

Fact #1010. Bloody Knife, an Arikara scout for the Army since 1873, was described on his 1874 discharge papers as "a Private of excellent and reliable character." He signed up again in March 1876 as a guide with "the Sioux expedition."

Fact #1011. Bob Tail Bull was an Arikara scout in the valley fight with Reno's command. He reenlisted with the 7th Cavalry April 26, 1876, for six months, and was the first leader of the Arikara scouts enlisted at Fort Abraham Lincoln (D.T.). Known as Hocus-ta-nix (or Hocus-ta-ris), Bob Tail Bull was the leader of the rescue party for Good Elk during the march of the expedition to the Powder River. He was the leader of the first scouting party on June 22, was on the June 24 scouting party, and with Custer at the Crow's Nest on the early morning of June 25. One of 13 Indian scouts participating in the valley fight, he was killed on the left of the skirmish line.

Fact #1012. Half-white, half-Crow interpreter Minton (Mitch) Bouyer was also known as Ka-Pesh, Ca Pay, Kar-paysh, Man-Wearing-Calfskin-Vest, and Mitchel Bouyer, Bouer, Boyer. KIA.

Fact #1013. "Crow King turned to the right before he got to the North end [of the village] and got in a deep gulley and those soldiers (Custer's) could not see the warriors. Ride down there and you will see that this gulley is so deep that no one can see you from there. This gulley, the upper part, brought Crow King very close to the soldiers. Crazy Horse went to the extreme north end of the camp and then turned to his right and went up another very deep ravine, and by following it, which he did, he came very close to the soldiers on their north side. Crow King was on their South side." (Gall in "Indian Notes on the Custer Battle")

Fact #1014. "Crazy Horse came riding like the wind on a fresh war horse and shouting: 'Oglalas! Follow me! It is time to end this fight!' So we were off, through the choking dust, across the river and around the end of the ridge where the soldiers fought. Up a ravine and over the top of a hill, Crazy Horse led us—and down upon the soldiers below. Hoh, but they were brave—those trapped white men! When their long guns jammed from too much shooting, they fired their many-shots short guns, and when they too were empty, they used them as clubs. For just a little while they fought strongly—and then there were no more of them left to kill. Long Hair and his men were all dead—their pale, bloody faces staring up at the sky." (Charging Bear, a young Sioux riding with Crazy Horse's warriors at LBH)

Fact #1015. Sitting Bull's age at LBH has been estimated at 42 and 45.

Fact #1016. Commenting after LBH on Reno's charge in the early afternoon of June 25, 1876, the wife of Sioux warrior Spotted Bull said: "The man who led those troops must have been drunk or crazy. He had the camp at his mercy, and could have killed us all or driven us away naked on the prairie."

Fact #1017. Of the six Crow scouts with Reno, only White Swan was wounded, in the valley fight as he crossed the river in retreat to the bluffs.

Fact #1018. A Southern Cheyenne warrior leader named Lame White Man was visiting his Northern Cheyenne cousins when the encampment along the Little Big Horn River was attacked; he joined the battle and led warriors against the troops on Calhoun Hill, losing his life in the furious fighting there.

Fact #1019. The civilian interpreter Frank Grouard, an adopted son of Sitting Bull, said "the name Sitting Bull was a 'tipi word' for all that was generous and great. The bucks admired him, the squaws respected him highly, and the children loved him." (Stanley Vestal in his biography of Sitting Bull)

Fact #1020. Leaders of the Northern Cheyenne at LBH included Two Moon, Lame White Man, and Dirty Moccasins.

Fact #1021. After Joseph Reynolds' attack at the Powder River Indian camp in March 1876, the Indians moved to join with the tribal camps under Sitting Bull, along the Yellowstone River. Their attitude toward running from the soldiers had changed. As Low Dog, an Oglala chief, remembered it later: ". . . When it began to be plain that we would have to yield or fight, we had a great many councils. I said, why should I be kept as a humble man, when I am a brave warrior and on my own lands? The game is mine, and the hills, and the valleys, and the white man has no right to say where I shall go or what I shall do. If any white man tries to destroy my property, or take my lands, I will take my gun, get on my horse, and go punish him."

Fact #1022. Crazy Horse was married three times. The first time was to No Water's wife, but she only stayed with him a few days. Shortly after that he married Red Feather's sister, Black Shawl. By her he had one child, a little girl who died when she was about two years old. A long while after, when he had surrendered at Fort Robinson (NE), he married a young half-breed girl. He did not have any children by her. (told to Eleanor Hinman, July 1930, by He Dog)

Fact #1023. Sitting Bull dispatched the Hunkpapa warrior Gall to Fort Rice (D.T.) in 1868 as his emissary to the peace commission. He spoke to the commissioners, rifle over his arm, and demanded that the Missouri River forts be removed declaring that "when they would take away all the soldiers and would burn Forts Rice [D.T.], Buford [D.T.], and Kearny [W.T.], and he could walk through the ashes, then he would sign the treaty."

Fact #1024. After capturing a slain soldier's rifle during the melee in the timber following Reno's charge, young Sioux warrior Charging Bear later recalled, "Suddenly the soldiers jumped back on their horses and ran away to the river, trying to reach the hills beyond. The little soldier-chief—the one called Reno—galloped ahead of all the others, spurring his horse like a crazy man to get away. We rode right into the water after them, knocking them off their horses with war clubs as they tried to get out the other side of the river."

Fact #1025. The Indian scout Bloody Knife, born of a Hunkpapa Sioux father and an Arikara mother in a Hunkpapa camp in Dakota Territory, returned with his mother to her people as he approached manhood. KIA.

Fact #1026. Iron Hail, a young Minneconjou warrior who fought at LBH and again at Wounded Knee (SD), was also known as Dewey Beard.

Fact #1027. Crow scout Goes Ahead was married to a Crow woman named Pretty Shield.

Fact #1028. Crow scout White Man Runs Him was also known as Crow Who Talks Gros Ventre and White Buffalo That Turns Around.

Fact #1029. Hunkpapa chief Sitting Bull, the Medicine Chief of the Little Big Horn encampment, was described by Gen. Nelson A. Miles, a contemporary of Custer's and later General of the Army, as ". . .the great organizer and controlling spirit of the hostile element. None of the other Indians possessed the power of drawing and molding the hearts of his people to one purpose."

Fact #1030. The principal wife of Oglala warrior and leader Crazy Horse was Black Shawl.

Fact #1031. According to author D.S. Benson, the westward movement of the northern Sioux caused conflict with Arikaree, Cheyenne, Crow, and Kiowa Indians. The Cheyenne grew to be allies, the Crow grew to be bitter enemies. The scope of Sioux migration found their tribes spread from the Mississippi River to the Big Horn mountains.

Fact #1032. Hunkpapa chief Gall, years after the battle, claimed that all of Custer's men were dead by the time soldiers from Reno's command atop the bluffs reached the point named for Capt. Thomas Weir (Co. D).

Fact #1033. Army interpreter Mitch Boyer (Bouyer), a French-Santee Sioux, was known as Two Bodies to the Crow Indians he interpreted for, presumably because of his mixed heritage.

Fact #1034. Curly, a Crow Indian serving as a private with the Detachment of Indian Scouts, was about 18-20 at LBH.

Fact #1035. One soldier with Custer's command, "with three yellow marks on his sleeve [probably 1st Sgt. James Butler, Co. H] ran up on a little hill and fought us all alone until he died full of bullets. He was a brave warrior—the soldier of Long Hair's." (Charging Bear)

Fact #1036. "The soldiers we were watching [after noon on June 25, 1876] were headed for the camp of the Cheyenne [northeast of Minneconjou Ford at the lower (north) end of the village]. While we were thus watching them, some boys who were out Southeast of the camp ran into the Blackfoot [sic] camp and told them soldiers were coming from the Southeast and had shot at them. Very soon we heard a great amount of shooting in that direction [Reno's attack]. Crazy Horse rushed through our camp headed in the direction of the shooting and his men followed; I started that way too, and so did Crow King. We paid no attention to the soldiers marching toward the North end. About two thousand warriors finally gathered down where the shooting was [Reno's command]." (Gall in "Indian Notes on the Custer Battle" by D.F. Barry)

Fact #1037. Goes Ahead, a Crow Indian Scout, served as a private in the Detachment of Scouts at LBH; 25 at LBH.

Fact #1038. Pretty Shield, a Crow woman married to Indian scout private Goes Ahead, died 25 years after her husband, in 1944, at the age of 92; she was interred with her husband, who had died in 1919, at CBNC.

Fact #1039. Hairy Moccasin, a Crow Indian scout, enlisted in the 7th Cavalry April 1876 for six months' service.

Fact #1040. Hunkpapa warrior Gall, acting as Sitting Bull's emissary to the 1868 peace commission at Fort Rice (D.T.), declared that "whites had ruined the country" and showed his wounds inflicted by soldiers. Then he told the commissioners, "This is our land and our home. We have no exact boundaries, but the graves of the Sioux nation mark our possessions. Wherever they are found, the land is ours." Yet, the next day he signed (with an "X") the treaty in return for piles of food and other presents.

Fact #1041. Black Elk, a young Sioux warrior at LBH, said later, "Several of us boys watched our horses together until the sun was straight above and it was getting very hot. Then we thought we would go swimming and my cousin said he would stay with our horses till we got back. When I was greasing myself I did not feel well; I felt queer. It seemed that something terrible was going to happen. But I went with the boys anyway."

Fact #1042. Crazy Horse was in his early 30s at the time of LBH.

Fact #1043. Indian riflemen occupied all the ridges to the east and southeast of the Reno-Benteen site and tightened the siege, using carbines and ammunition taken from the Custer dead.

Fact #1044. During the night of June 25, 1876, a large number of warriors crawled up the ravines leading to the Reno-Benteen position's southwest salient, from the river. When the firing resumed the next morning, the Indians were near enough to throw clods of dirt into Co. H's position. A young Sans Arc Sioux, Long Road, rushed the soldiers but was killed at the bottom of the slope, just a few yards from Capt. Benteen's line.

Fact #1045. Chief Gall of the Hunkpapa Sioux was the leading Indian war chief at LBH.

Fact #1046. "As soon as we chased these soldiers out (Reno's force), we did not fight them again right away. Crow King and Crazy Horse were afraid the soldiers that we had seen march in the direction of the north end of the camp might kill our women and children. They went back the way they had come; their ponies were racing." (Gall, "Indian Notes on the Custer Battle," D.F. Barry)

Fact #1047. At about mid-day on June 26, 1876, soldiers spotted the Minneconjou warrior, Dog's Backbone, about 200 yards northeast of the southeastern defense line. Just as he uttered a warning for his tribesmen to be careful, Dog's Backbone was shot through the forehead.

Fact #1048. Crazy Horse was unmarried when he was made a "shirt-wearer," an "honor" chief of the band, chosen for prowess in war and in peace. "A few years after [being made a chief], he began to pay attention to the wife of a man named No Water. No Water did not want to let the woman go [Black Buffalo Woman]. . . .Crazy Horse started off on a. . .war expedition and No Water's wife went along with him. No Water followed them and came to the tipi of Bad Heart Bull [He Dog's brother] and asked to borrow a certain good revolver. . . Crazy Horse and the woman were sitting by the fire in a tipi belonging to some of their friends. No Water entered the tipi. . .and shot [Crazy Horse] through the face. The bullet entered just below the left nostril. That is how Crazy Horse got his scar. No Water took his wife back." (He Dog, in an interview with Eleanor Hinman, 1930)

Fact #1049. Mrs. C. Weldon, a missionary to the Hunkpapa Sioux, reported that Sitting Bull "distrusted the innovations sought to be forced upon the Indians" by white civilization, which, with its hypocrisy and avarice, "did not impress him." She said, "He never signed a treaty to sell any portion of his people's inheritance, and he refused to acknowledge the right of other Indians to sell his undivided share of tribal lands." (T.A. Bland, *Brief History of the Late Military Invasion of the Home of the Sioux*, 1891)

Fact #1050. Charging Bear, a Sioux warrior, remembered the action immediately following Reno's attack on the southern (upper) end of the immense Indian village on the afternoon of June 25, 1876: "Gall led a charge straight at the soldiers, and the Wasichus (white men) stopped and huddled together. The soldiers got off their horses to fight on foot. Hoh, what a bad mistake that was! Our hearts sang when we saw the soldiers do this foolish thing, for then we knew that our helpless ones were safe from pursuit, and we could fight hard without fearing for them."

Fact #1051. When the 7th Cavalry left Fort Abraham Lincoln (D.T.) on May 17, 1876, the Ree (Arikara) scout Bloody Knife, half-Hunkpapa Sioux, rode with the column. He accompanied Custer to the Crow's Nest in the early morning of June 25, and when the command was divided that morning, he was assigned to the Reno battalion. He rode with Maj. Reno into the valley fight, and was killed in the timber before the retreat to the bluffs.

Fact #1052. Crazy Horse lost his status as a "shirt-wearer" honor chief because of an adulterous relationship he had with Black Buffalo Woman, the wife of No Water. (historian Eleanor Hinman)

Fact #1053. After most of Reno's command escaped the valley fight by retreating across the river and up to the bluffs, the young Sioux warrior Charging Bear recalled: "Now a messenger came racing his lathered horse and crying out, 'Brothers, come! More soldiers are coming to kill our helpless ones! Come quickly!' We could see them—a double line of soldiers this time, riding along the ridge on the other side of the river opposite the lower [northern] camps. The bone war whistles shrilled as Crazy Horse and Gall and Knife Chief called the warriors together. 'Remember the helpless ones! This is a good day to die!' cried Crazy Horse. And we Oglalas cried back, 'It is a good day to die! Hoka hey!'"

Fact #1054. Gall, the Hunkpapa war chief, was named Pizi, for the gall bladder of an animal, by his mother who observed him as a child eating that organ.

Fact #1055. Crazy Horse, who received his father's name as an adult name following a glory-filled battle with the Arapaho, was one of three children, according to He Dog in his 1930 interview with Eleanor Hinman. "The oldest was a sister, the next was Crazy Horse, and the third was a brother. All are dead now [in 1930]."

Fact #1056. Hairy Moccasin, one of the Crow scouts with Lt. Charles Varnum (Co. A) at the Crow's Nest, said he could see clearly the signs of the large Indian village on the banks of the Little Big Horn River some 10-15 miles away, but Varnum was unable to see them, as was Custer when he arrived at the high promontory in the Wolf Mountains.

Fact #1057. "There was one force of Arikara scouts with this band of soldiers [Reno's battalion] and they were on our right as we sped in that direction. We charged them first because it made us mad to see Indians fighting us. They ran first and we never saw them again. We turned toward our left to fight the soldiers. They were hard to drive out because they were on foot and in the brush and grass. We could not shoot them, so we charged them and soon we were successful, they ran almost straight east and crossed the river and got up on a high hill [Reno Hill]. We killed many while they were fighting with their horses, and we killed many more while they were running as our ponies were more speedy. . ." (Gall in "Indian Notes on the Custer Battle")

Fact #1058. The name of Crazy Horse's encampment band at the Little Big Horn was Hunkpatila (End-of-Circle) because when the group was encamped together, it occupied one end of the tribal crescent of the village.

Fact #1059. Col. John Gibbon, commanding the Montana Column, wrote of Mitch Bouyer, a half-French, half-Crow: "He was the protege and pupil of Jim Bridger; was the best guide in this section of the country, and the only half--breed I ever met who could give the distances to be passed over with any accuracy in miles."

Fact #1060. Aged Sioux warrior, Charging Bear, remembering his youth at LBH, told of riding with Crazy Horse and watching Custer's advance to Minne-conjou Ford turned back by "nine Stronghearts."

Fact #1061. According to the Oglala war chief He Dog, a childhood and manhood friend of Crazy Horse, "Crazy Horse always lead his men himself when they went into battle, and he kept well in front of them."

Fact #1062. Gall, the Hunkpapa war chief, gave an account of LBH to U.L. Burdick, who edited a pamphlet, "Indian Notes on the Custer Battle," by D.F. Barry, a well-known photographer of the West, over 10 years after the battle: "On the morning of [June] 25th away to the East we saw soldiers marching down the divide in our direction. They passed out of sight behind the rough land several miles from the river. Just how these soldiers were divided, I do not know. We never saw the pack train (McDougall's command) until it joined Reno on the hill." Gall was probably referring to scouts sighting the approaching column rather than himself personally.

Fact #1063. At LBH, June 25, 1876, Hunkpapa war chief Gall had led warriors in opposition to Reno's original attack, and cornered the three compa-nies (A, G, M) on the bluffs above the river, when he realized that Crow King and Crazy Horse were fighting another band of soldiers across the river from the north end of the village. "I saw what was going on and I left. . .Reno Hill and ran for the battle. I struck the train the soldiers had made as they had marched down to the North end [of the village] and soon came up to some of them to the east of where the rest were [meaning, east of Custer]. We either killed or ran over these and went on down to where the last soldiers were." (Gall to Barry, "Indian Notes on the Custer Battle")

Fact #1064. Kate Bighead was a Cheyenne woman whose story was re-corded in a booklet by historian Dr. Thomas B. Marquis, *She Watched Custer's Last Battle*. She stated that as a result of the initial attack by Reno's soldiers, a number of lodges were taken down in preparation for flight. After Custer's immediate command had been annihilated and the immediate threat to the camp was over, some of the lodges were put up again, but not in the same locations. Other families did not bother to re-erect their lodges, and instead spent the night in temporary shelters, or wicki-ups. Her story casts doubt on those who "count lodges and wicki-ups" to estimate the total number of Indians in the Little Big Horn encampment.

Fact #1065. The six Crow scouts who joined the Dakota Column at the Yellowstone Depot were transferred from Col. John Gibbon's Montana Column. They were Paints-Half-His-Face-Yellow (Half Yellow Face), Goes Ahead, Hairy Moccasin, White Swan, White Man Runs Him, and Curley. Half Yellow Face was their leader.

Custer

Fact #1066. Dr. Thomas Marquis, a noted authority on the Indian side of LBH, stated in *Which Indian Killed Custer?* that although no one really knew who had slain the cavalry commander, many of the Indians had finally settled on Brave Bear as an "exemplification of poetic justice." Brave Bear, a Cheyenne, had been with Black Kettle on the Washita River when Custer destroyed that village in 1868, had passed the peace pipe to Custer at Stone Calf's village in Texas in 1869, and was present at LBH. The consensus chose Brave Bear, Dr. Marquis said, because "the avenging warrior must have been one who had been in personal touch with both the first and last phases of Custer's perfidy."

Fact #1067. Custer, on May 30, 1876, lamented the fact that Sitting Bull was so elusive. "Now as Sitting Bull has failed to answer the hopes and expectations of his enemies by butting his head and those of his people against one of the best organized and equipped expeditions ever sent by the Great Father to effect his destruction, since the mountain will not come to Mohammed, Mohammed must go to the mountain. In other words, this expedition must move in search of the apparently ubiquitous Sitting Bull. The latter may be caught napping, but such an occurrence is exceedingly improbable."

Fact #1068. "If I were an Indian, I often think that I would prefer to cast my lot among those of my people who adhered to the free open plains, rather than submit to the confined limits of a reservation there to be the recipient of the blessed benefits of civilization, with its vices thrown in without stint or measure." (Custer, *My Life on the Plains*, 1874)

Fact #1069. Failure to engage the Sioux was Custer's only concern. (Gump, *The Dust Rose Like Smoke*)

Fact #1070. While a cadet at the Academy at West Point in the late 1850s, George A. Custer penned an essay on "The Redman": "When we first beheld the Redman, we beheld him in his home, the home of peace and plenty, the home of nature. His manly limbs were not weakened by being forced to sleep in dreary caves and deep morasses, fireless, comfortless and coverless, through fear of the hunter's deadly rifle. His heart did not quake with terror at every gust of wind that sighed through the trees, but on the contrary. They were the favored sons of nature, and she like a doting mother, had bestowed all her gifts on them. They stood in their native strength and beauty, stamped with the proud majesty of free born men, whose soul never knew fear, or whose eyes never quailed beneath the fierce glance of man."

Fact #1071. The legend about Custer having an Indian son by a Cheyenne woman named Monahseetah was an item of Indian gossip which seems to have entered Custer historiography through the writings of Capt. Frederick Benteen in 1896. The facts, according to *The Western Hero in History and Legend*, argue "against an affair with an Indian. Nevertheless, the Custer Monahseetah legend lives on in books and newspaper articles."

Fact #1072. Although Custer was not convinced as to the location of the Indian village, because haze obscured his vision from the Crow's Nest, the reports that the column's presence had been discovered by the Indians caused him to advance his timetable, and attack on June 25 instead of waiting till dawn on June 26.

Fact #1073. Custer was known to his family and friends as one who admired and respected Indians and their way of life. Long after her husband's death at LBH, widow Elizabeth Custer in 1927 wrote: "I well remember how the great chiefs of the Sioux came frequently to General Custer's quarters at Fort Abraham Lincoln (D.T.) and held long conferences with him about the Black Hills. They urged that the white man must not go into the Hills, that it was dangerous and would bring war. The Indians deeply cherished the Black Hills. . .These Indian conferences were always given complete right of way by the General and the greatest respect and deference was shown to the chiefs. . . .He recognized a true nobility in the Indian character, and respected their feelings of attachment to the land."

Fact #1074. As Custer approached the Little Big Horn River down Medicine Tail Coulee to Minneconjou Ford, he may have "seen Reno's retreat to the bluffs. At this moment the main body of Indians, who had been watching Custer's approach, swarmed up like bees to defend their village. The Cheyennes [sic] under Crazy Horse galloped across the river at the lower ford, and attacked Custer on [his] right. Gall, with the Indians released by Reno's retreat to the bluffs, crossed at a higher ford and attacked [Custer's] left. Indians on foot waded through the river at many points, crept up the ravines and fired from ambush." (Bates, July 20, 1926, *New York Times*)

Sioux warrior Rain-In-The-Face. One of the many lingering—albeit erroneous—accounts of the Little Big Horn fight credits him with cutting out Tom Custer's heart—and eating it. *National Archives*

Fact #1075. Indian nominees in the "Who killed Custer?" contest include White Bull, Rain-in-the-Face, Appearing Elk, Brave Bear, and about a dozen others. But, "None of the Indians knew who killed Custer. None of them knew until long afterward that he was there." (*Which Indian Killed Custer?*, Marquis)

Fact #1076. George Custer, as a cadet at West Point, wrote an essay on "The Redman," in which he spoke of the majesty of their past. "But," he asked, "what are they now, those monarchs of the west? They are like the withered leaves of their own native forest, scattered in every direction by the fury of the tempest. The Redman is alone in his misery. The earth is one vast desert to him. Once it had its charms to lull his mind to repose, but now the home of his youth, the familiar forests. . .are swept away by the axe of the woodman. The hunting grounds have vanished from his sight and. . .he beholds the hand of desolation. We behold him now on the verge of extinction, standing on his last foothold, clutching his blood stained rifle, resolved to die amidst the horrors of slaughter, and soon he will be talked of as a noble race who once existed but have now passed away."

Fact #1077. According to Pretty Shield, wife of the Crow Scout Goes Ahead, Custer died at Minneconjou Ford, where Medicine Tail Coulee emerges onto the Little Big Horn River's east bank.

Fact #1078. Dee Brown's *Bury My Heart At Wounded Knee* (1970) and Mari Sandoz' *Battle of the Little Big Horn* (1966), both presented as non-fiction, are based on the Indian view of history. Brown's book, a Pulitzer Prize-winner, covers the whole scope of America's Indian Wars history, while Sandoz focuses on the Little Big Horn, and stresses the theory that Custer had political ambitions and that his "reckless" attack at the battle can be attributed to his desire to gain the presidential nomination of the Democratic Party, meeting that summer in St. Louis (MO). Another book from the Indian viewpoint is *Custer's Fall: The Indian Side of the Story* by David Humphreys Miller (1957), which proposes that Custer was killed trying to cross at Minneconjou Ford. All are worth reading to broaden your viewpoint.

Fact #1079. "It took about thirty-five minutes to wipe out this bunch of soldiers (Custer's), and I never saw any men fight harder. They were right down on their knees firing and loading until the last man fell. I never saw any soldier offer to surrender." (Gall, quoted by D.F. Barry)

Fact #1080. Five percent of Custer's command were scouts (36) while 20% of Gen. George Crook's Wyoming Column were scouts (86 Shoshone and 176 Crow). Custer used his scouts to guide him through unknown territory and did not expect them to fight, while Crook was dependent upon his scouts, would not move without them, and expected them to fight. (Robert Church, 1991 CBH&MA Symposium)

Environment

Fact #1081. On the Great Plains of the United States, a unique culture had sprung up among the horse nomads, a culture like a three-legged stool: the Indians, the horse, and the buffalo each making a vital contribution to the culture. Abandoning their life in the traditional wooded surroundings, the Lakota Sioux began living in highly-mobile "tepee" camps. (D.S. Benson)

Fact #1082. In his NPS booklet, *Indian, Soldier, and Settler*, Robert M. Utley described the appearance of the Plains Indians, saying they were "clad in dressed skins ornamented with bead- and quill-work of enduring artistic merit; weapons and braided, jet-black hair fluttering with eagle feathers; skilled horsemen and bowmen; masters of war and hunt."

Fact #1083. During the 19th century, the northern Sioux came to number about 14 subdivisions: those of the four Santee Dakota (the Meda Wakanton, Wahpekuta, Sisseton, and Wahpeton), those of the three Yanktee (Yanktonais) Nakota (the Yankton, Yanktonay, and Assiniboine), and those of the seven Teton Lakota (the Hunkpapa, Sihapsa [Blackfeet Sioux], Itazipcho [Sans Arc], Ohenonpa [Two Kettle], Minneconjou, Sichangou [Brulé], and Oglala). (*The Black Hills War 1876-1877*, Benson)

Fact #1084. Discussing the tradition of Sioux face painting at the Sun Dance ceremony, one of which was held shortly before LBH, a 1918 bulletin of the Bureau of American Ethnology noted that the first warrior who had killed an enemy in a battle was entitled to black face paint, although the man might paint his entire body if he so desired.

Fact #1085. According to the oral tradition of the Dakota or Sioux people, the largest group of Siouan-speaking Indians, the Lakota (or "prairie dwellers") were the westernmost of the original seven Dakota divisions or "council fires." The number seven is sacred to the Lakota, signifying the ideal number of classifications in Siouan society. The Lakota, in turn, divided themselves into seven sub-bands: Oglalas, Brulé, Minneconjous, Hunkpapas, Sans Arc, Two Kettles, and Blackfeet Sioux (Sihasapas).

Fact #1086. The "sun dance lodge" where a sacred Indian ceremony of great importance was held about June 5, 1876, was passed by Custer's column prior to LBH, but the soldiers at the time did not realize its significance in Indian life.

Fact #1087. Bands of wandering Indian tribes sometimes drifted together during the spring of 1876, but in doing so found the encampment became so large that difficulties were experienced in obtaining a sufficient supply of food. (Luce, *Custer Battlefield*)

Fact #1088. Reno's men, abandoning their charge, dismounting on the flat ground west of the river, then taking cover in the timber, rallied and made a stand. Then, ". . .the fighting became all mixed up, with warriors charging the soldiers in twos and threes to count coups, and take scalps and guns. I wanted one of those guns, so I rode my pony right up to a big soldier with red hair all over his face and shot him with an arrow. He fell to the ground with the arrow sticking in his throat." (Sioux warrior Charging Bear)

Fact #1089. By 1835 the Teton Lakota Sioux had moved westward to lands all across the southern part of what is now South Dakota, while the Yankton Nakota Sioux and the Santee Dakota Sioux remained in Minnesota and western Wisconsin. The Black Hills, at this time, were occupied by the Crow tribe, another Siouan-speaking nation, while Arikara Indians occupied the northern part of what is now South Dakota. Keep in mind all these tribes were nomadic.

Fact #1090. While Custer, Varnum, and the Indian scouts were ascending The Crow's Nest on the morning of June 25, six Indians were observed spying on the column; they escaped in the direction of the village.

Fact #1091. The largest group of Indians in the village along the banks of the Little Big Horn River in June 1876 were Lakota or Teton Sioux. The Lakota were the largest division of the Sioux people, who were, in turn, the largest of the Siouan-speaking Indian groups. Lakota is a dialect of the Dakota language and Teton means "prairie dwellers."

Fact #1092. Four weeks after the battle, seven Sioux warriors who had been at LBH told the Commanding Officer of the Standing Rock Reservation (D.T.) about the Custer battle's aftermath: "After the battle the squaws entered the field to plunder and mutilate the dead. A general rejoicing was indulged in, and a distribution of arms and ammunition was hurriedly made. Then, the attack on Major Reno was vigorously renewed."

Fact #1093. The Oglala warriors from Red Cloud's tribe were led in battle at the Little Big Horn by chief American Horse, and war chiefs Low Dog, and He Dog. (*Little Big Horn 1876: Custer's Last Stand*, Panzieri)

Fact #1094. As the brunt of the massive Indian attack bore on Custer's immediate command, the Indians pushed the cavalrymen from their original route of march to the positions now indicated by the silent white markers that dot Custer Hill.

Fact #1095. Crow King, a Sioux warrior who was in the Hunkpapa camp near the south end of the village, said after the battle that Reno's "pony soldiers" had opened fire on the village from about 400 yards distance.

Fact #1096. "Teton Sioux Music," an article in a bulletin from the American Bureau of Ethnology in 1918, discussed the traditions of the Sun Dance, a ceremony which was held near the Little Big Horn village by Sitting Bull shortly before the Battle. In the Sioux Sun Dance, the "dancers were painted by the men whom they had selected for that purpose. A few of the sources for this article stated that the bodies of the dancers were painted white on the first day of the ceremony, the colors being added on the morning of the second day, but others. . .stated positively that the painting in colors was done before the opening of the dance."

Fact #1097. The Northern Cheyenne and Arapaho, Algonquian-speaking Plains Indians who had experienced a great migration of their own, became close allies of the Sioux. (*Black Hills War 1876-1877*, Benson)

Fact #1098. There has long been confusion between the designation Blackfoot and Blackfeet. These are two distinct tribal and language groups, the Blackfoot being an Algonquian-speaking tribe, roaming Northern Montana and up into Canada. The Blackfeet (Sioux) are a sub-set of the Eastern Sioux, Siouan-speaking and ranging from Minnesota to Montana. The two tribes were traditional enemies.

Fact #1099. The stampede of some of Custer's horses on "Last Stand Hill" was followed quickly by a concerted attack by the Indians, according to many accounts. This final attack was so swiftly carried out and was so successful that none of the soldiers survived. (Luce, *Custer Battlefield*)

Fact #1100. The Indians were really surprised at Reno's first attack "although they knew that troops were only about 15 miles from them at 9 or 10 o'clock that morning. They said afterwards that they supposed of course we would attack as soldiers usually did, i.e., at daybreak." (Lt. W.S. Edgerly, Co. D)

Fact #1101. The continued expansion of the white men west of the Mississippi River forced the Plains Indians on to restricted reservations. The Fort Laramie Treaty (1868) set aside "The Great Sioux Reservation" for the exclusive use of the Northern Plains Indians. This area included the sacred Black Hills.

Fact #1102. The Indian scouts, Crow and Arikara, reached "the Lone Tipi" ahead of the two columns (Custer's and Reno's) riding on the north bank of the creek later known as Reno Creek. As the columns approached, they began to prepare themselves, cosmetically and sartorially, for battle.

Fact #1103. Other Indians sometimes referred to the northern Sioux as "Cut Throats," from the sign used on the Plains to refer to them. (D.S. Benson)

Fact #1104. The battle at the Reno-Benteen position continued throughout the morning of June 26 and into the early afternoon, when the warriors began to withdraw, leaving only a small group to keep up occasional firing.

Fact #1105. Reports from Sioux Indians who came in to the Standing Rock Reservation (D.T.) on July 21, 1876, coincided with the soldiers' accounts of Reno's attack on the south end of the village: ". . .how he was quickly confronted, surrounded; how he dismounted, rallied in the timber, remounted and cut his way back over the ford and up the bluffs, with considerable loss. . ." (Letter from the Commanding Officer at Standing Rock, July 1876)

Fact #1106. Gen. Philip Sheridan, commander of the Department of the Missouri, had written in 1869, seven years before LBH, that the "Indian is a lazy, idle vagabond; he never labors and has no profession except that of arms, to which he is raised from a child; a scalp is constantly dangled before his eyes, and the highest honor he can aspire to is to possess one taken by himself. It is not to be wondered at, therefore, if he aims for this honor when he grows up; especially if there is no punishment to follow the barbarous act. The Government has always been very liberal to Indians, especially whenever they have settled on reservations; the lands allotted to them have been of the very best character, making them perhaps by far the richest communities in the country." (Philip Sheridan Papers in the Library of Congress)

Fact #1107. The Dakota Sioux originally inhabited the central Ohio Valley region, but by the time of French contact in the mid-17th century, they had moved to the forests of central Minnesota. White pressure continued to force the tribes westward.

Fact #1108. The Santee Sioux at the Little Big Horn had 10 lodges in the Hunkpapa "circle" and 25 lodges, under Kill Eagle, in the "Santee Circle." (Panzieri, *Little Big Horn 1876: Custer's Last Stand*)

Fact #1109. It was, practically, impossible for the Indian tribes to comply with the Army's December 3, 1875, order compelling the "roaming" tribes to return to the reservation or be considered "hostile," due to the limited time allowed and the extreme winter weather.

Fact #1110. "The soldiers looked on their Indian foes with an ambivalence uncharacteristic of the civilian population in the West. On the one hand, with the civilians, they subscribed to that tired old saying, already a cliche in the 1870s, about the only good Indian. A cavalry recruit at an Indian agency on the upper Missouri overheard it in an exchange between a young officer and the regimental commander, the same [Samuel] Sturgis who two decades earlier had led [a] memorable charge [against a Mescalero Apache raiding party]. 'There are many good Indians here, Colonel,' observed the lieutenant. 'The *good Indians*,' replied Sturgis, pointing to a hillside cemetery where Sioux dead, according to custom, lay on elevated platforms, 'are up there on those poles'. . . .Sturgis had just lost a son at the Little Big Horn." (Utley, *Indian, Soldier, and Settler*)

Fact #1111. "The fight with Reno commenced about noon, the Indians all rushing to oppose his advance, until the approach of Custer from the lower end of the village was announced, when the wildest confusion prevailed throughout the camp." (Kill Eagle, *New York Herald*, September 24, 1876)

Fact #1112. The Little Big Horn village that Custer attacked included families and warriors from the sub-groups of the Teton Sioux: Hunkpapas, Oglalas, Miniconjou, Sans Arc, Blackfeet, and Brulé. (Peter Panzieri)

Fact #1113. Gen. Fry had estimated from 8,000-10,000 Indians were in Sitting Bull's camp, and, Fry said, "I believe they had more than fifteen thousand ponies. The unridden ponies were being headed past us, covered a space more than two miles long and a mile wide, and when they first started out they looked like an immense brown carpet being dragged over the ground." (Lt. W.S. Edgerly, Co. D)

Fact #1114. The Indians assaulted the Reno-Benteen position beginning around 3 a.m. June 26 (daybreak), and by 10 a.m. a desperate attack was hurled "against that portion of the line held by Troops H and M, one Indian coming so close to Colonel Benteen's line that he touched a soldier with his coup stick." (Lt. W.S. Edgerly, Co. D)

Fact #1115. "Rarely, unless absolutely certain of victory, did the Plains Indian stand and fight; usually he faded into the hills and easily eluded his slow-moving pursuers." (1978 "Custer Battlefield" brochure)

Fact #1116. Author D.S. Benson says that the word "Sioux" seems to have been derived from French frontiersmen, who heard Chippewa Indians describe the Dakota tribes as "little snakes" (naduwesiug), their symbol for hostility. This was transcribed in French as "nadouessioux" and shortened to "Sioux."

Fact #1117. According to most Indian accounts, there was no "final charge on horseback" as has often been represented in writings, paintings, and movies. The only semblance to such a culminating action was a "charge" by the mounted Indian youths and old men in a rush to seize plunder from the dead bodies of Custer's men. (Luce, *Custer Battlefield*)

Fact #1118. The Santee Sioux, one of the smaller bands in the village at the Little Big Horn, were led into battle by both Indpaduta (Red-on-Top) and Walks-Under-the-Ground. (Luce, *Custer Battlefield*)

Fact #1119. Fifty-one "friendly" Indians served in the 1876 Sioux Expedition's Detachment of Indian Scouts, under the command of 2d Lt. Charles A. Varnum (Co. A). There were six Crow Indians, four Dakota Sioux, two Pikuni Blackfoot, 38 Arikara (Ree), and one Teton Sioux.

Fact #1120. One of the main causes of Indian discontent on the reservations was that rations issued did not always seem sufficient to meet their wants; in fact, some reservation agents profited from the rations system.

Fact #1121. Because of the Indians' failure to comply with the Army edict of December 3, 1875, ordering the "roaming" tribes to return to the reservations or be deemed "hostile," on February 7, 1876, the Secretary of the Interior and the

General of the Army gave Lt. Gen. Philip Sheridan authority to commence operations against the "hostile" Indians.

Fact #1122. "Fourteen [dead warriors] had fallen in front of Reno, thirty-nine went down with Custer and fourteen were dead in camp." (Kill Eagle, September 24, 1876, *New York Herald*)

Fact #1123. Groups which became known as Teton Lakota Sioux reached the Missouri River in about 1775, forced to move westward by increasing pressure on all the Siouan-speaking tribes, who left the lands they originally occupied in the Ohio and Mississippi valleys. There they encountered the Cheyenne tribes, and the horse (tashunka). (D.S. Benson)

Fact #1124. The information on which the Army based its 1876 campaign against the "hostile" tribes was that the "roamers" totaled about 800 warriors. That number may have been correct in the winter of 1875-76, but with the arrival of spring, more and more Indians slipped away to the western hunting grounds. (1978 "Custer Battlefield" brochure)

Fact #1125. Stanley Vestal, in his biography of Sitting Bull, wrote about the first reaction to Reno's attack on the upper (southern) end of the village: "Old men were yelling advice, young men dashing away to catch their horses, women and children rushing off afoot and on horseback to the north end of that three-mile camp, fleeing from the soldiers. They left their tents standing, grabbed their babies, called their older children and hurried away, frightened girls shrinking under their shawls, matrons puffing for breath, hobbling old women, wrinkled and peering, with their sticks, making off as best they could, crying children, lost children, dogs getting in everybody's way and being kicked for their pains, nervous horses resisting the tug of the reins, and over all the sound of shooting."

Fact #1126. "A red hand painted on a warrior's blanket denotes that he has been wounded by the enemy, and a black one that he has been unfortunate in some way." (*Belden, the White Chief, or Twelve Years among the Wild Indians of the Plains*, George P. Belden, 1870)

Fact #1127. With the coming of warm weather, in the spring of 1876, more and more "agency" Indians left the reservations and joined the "hostile" roamers. (Luce, *Custer Battlefield*)

Fact #1128. "It was dusk as the successful combatants returned to camp littered with their dead and wounded. It had not been to them [the Indians] a bloodless victory." (Kill Eagle, September 24, 1876)

Fact #1129. As a result of the miners' invasion of the Black Hills, in violation of the Fort Laramie Treaty (1868), "Large numbers of Indians left the reservations to join the hostile Indians who had never submitted to the Government. Sitting Bull was the best-known chief of the hostiles, but the leading war chiefs were Gall and Crazy Horse. Sitting Bull was dominant in peace councils, but he was primarily a medicine man. Gall, sometimes referred to as the Sioux Napoleon, was regarded by Buffalo Bill as the greatest of the Indian chiefs. He had been for years welding into a unit the Sioux and Cheyennes. Crazy Horse, pining for revenge for the destruction of his village, was known as the Red Stonewall Jackson. . .a steed driven mad." (Bates, *New York Times*, 1926)

Fact #1130. When the Teton Sioux reached the Missouri River late in the 18th century, they encountered the Cheyenne tribe, and the "plains culture" associated with a strange (to them), new animal, the horse. Pushing farther west, they drove the Crow tribes from the Black Hills, and by 1830, the Teton Sioux had reached the Powder River. (D.S. Benson, *The Black Hills War 1876-1877*)

Fact #1131. The village that Custer attacked along the banks of the Little Big Horn River was "one of the largest in the history of the Great Plains," according to noted historian Robert M. Utley.

Fact #1132. In addition to the Teton Sioux at LBH, there were also Northern Cheyenne, a handful of warriors from tribes of Eastern Sioux, and a few Arapaho. (1978 "Custer Battlefield" brochure)

Fact #1133. Secure in their unaccustomed strength, the Sioux and Cheyenne moving up Rosebud Creek in mid-June 1876 wasted little thought on the news that soldiers had been seen beyond the head of Rosebud Creek. (1978 "Custer Battlefield" brochure)

Fact #1134. Reporting on accounts by seven Sioux participants in LBH, who had come in to the Standing Rock Reservation (D.T.) on July 21, 1876, the Reservation's Commanding Officer noted that the Indians said, "[Custer] crossed the river, but only succeeded in reaching the edge of the Indian camp. After [Custer] was driven to the bluffs, the fight lasted perhaps an hour."

Fact #1135. The Indians along the Little Big Horn were clustered around six tribal circles, and altogether they numbered perhaps 10,000 to 12,000 people, mustering a fighting force of between 2,500 and 4,000 men. (1978 "Custer Battlefield" brochure)

Fact #1136. Crazy Horse had 100 lodges from his band of Oglala Sioux at the Little Big Horn encampment in mid-June of 1876. (Panzieri, *Little Big Horn 1876: Custer's Last Stand*)

Fact #1137. Custer "was steadily forced back and surrounded until all were swept from the field by the repeated charges of the Indians as if they had been carried into eternity by the irresistible." (Kill Eagle, *New York Herald*, September 24, 1876)

Fact #1138. When the great gathering of Indians crossed the Wolf Mountains and came to rest on a tributary of the Little Big Horn later named Reno Creek, they heard more reports of soldiers descending the Rosebud (going north), and more than 1,000 warriors rode over the mountains to contest the advance toward their village. The two groups collided June 17 in the Battle of the Rosebud, from which Gen. Crook was forced to retire to Goose Creek. (1978 "Custer Battle-field" brochure)

Fact #1139. The "horse culture" adopted by the Teton Sioux tribes in the late 1700s gave them a whole new lifestyle. Open plains hunting and conical dwell-ings (tepees that could be assembled, disassembled, and transported easily) formed the basis for this lifestyle. (Benson, *The Black Hills War 1876-1877*)

Fact #1140. The concentration of Indians in the villages along the Little Big Horn on June 25, 1876, may have included between 12,000 and 15,000 Indians, probably as many as 5,000 being warriors. (Luce, *Custer Battlefield*)

Fact #1141. Of the 51 "friendly" Indians serving in the 1876 Sioux Expedi-tion's Detachment of Indian Scouts, just two died, both Arikara (Ree) scouts.

Fact #1142. Kill Eagle (*New York Herald*, September 24, 1876) placed the number of wounded Indians in the June 17 Battle of the Rosebud "at as high as 400, and says they had 180 horses killed, besides those that were captured."

Fact #1143. One hundred twenty lodges made up the combined Blackfeet, Brulé, and Two Kettle Sioux "circle" at the Little Big Horn encampment. (Panzieri, *Little Big Horn 1876: Custer's Last Stand*)

Fact #1144. Indian warriors who were triumphant at the Battle of the Rose-bud on June 17 returned to their tepees along Reno Creek to celebrate, then crossed the Little Big Horn and laid out a new camp, lining the west bank of the river for three miles, sprawling in places all the way across the mile-wide valley. This was the encampment attacked by Custer on June 25. (1978 "Custer Battle-field" brochure)

Fact #1145. When the Indians learned of a "great body of troops" advancing (south) up the river, they decided to abandon the camp. "Lodges having been previously prepared for a move, a retreat, in a southerly direction, followed, towards and along the base of the Rosebud Mountains." (Graham, *The Custer Myth*)

Fact #1146. Lt. James Bradley of the Montana Column, who arrived at the battle scene with the Montana Column on June 27, later wrote: "The number of Indians who participated in the battle was variously estimated at 1,000 to 1,500. They afterward admitted at Fort Peck [M.T.] that it was the combined force of three camps under the leadership of the famous Sitting Bull."

Fact #1147. As Custer's command was overwhelmed by hordes of Indian warriors swarming across the Little Big Horn River from the village, "the firing at this point [was] simply terrific. . ." Blackfeet Sioux chief Kill Eagle illustrated the force of the firing "by clapping his hands together with great rapidity and regularity." Then, "there came a lull in the fearful storm of iron hail and his hands were still again." (Graham, *The Custer Myth*)

Fact #1148. In the book, *Little Big Horn 1876: Custer's Last Stand*, author Peter Panzieri estimated the size of the Hunkpapa Sioux "circle" at the Little Big Horn encampment at 260, including 25 lodges of Yanktonais and Santee Sioux.

Fact #1149. Except for the acquisition of large horse herds, the horse nomads of the northern Plains, the Teton Lakota Sioux, were unlike the nomads of Central Asia. The Sioux had no domesticated cattle or sheep; only domesticated dogs were available for both food and work animals. (*The Black Hills War 1876-1877*)

Fact #1150. The Blackfeet Sioux chief Kill Eagle, who, with his band of 26 lodges, left the Standing Rock Reservation (D.T.) in late May 1876 on a hunting trip, claimed (September 24, 1876, *New York Herald*) to have been "an unwilling spectator rather than as a participant, who, during [the] progress [of LBH] remained quietly in his lodge in the middle of the Indian village." Nonetheless, he provided many details on the tragic battle.

Fact #1151. One of the major groups of Sioux-speaking people, whose dialect derives from a common language family called "Siouan," is the Crow group, who lived in the Plains and comprised the bands of the Minnetaree, Minneseparee, and Absaroka. (*The Black Hills War 1876-1877*, Benson)

Fact #1152. Records reflect about half of Lt. Varnum's 41-man Arikara scout detachment "disappeared during the battle," but rejoined the command on June 28, 1876. (Graham, *The Custer Myth*)

Fact #1153. From the viewpoint of the Indians, the frontier warfare with whites was due to the repeated encroachments upon their lands by whites, often in violation of treaty stipulations.

Fact #1154. War chiefs among the Miniconjou Sioux included Touch The Clouds, Hump, and Lame Deer. Other chiefs included Red Horse, the principal chief, Fast Bull, and High Backbone. (*Little Big Horn 1876: Custer's Last Stand*)

Fact #1155. The Indian village along the Little Big Horn was six miles long and one mile wide, "and the Indians swarmed there as thick as maggots on a carcass, so numerous were they." (Kill Eagle, September 24, 1876, *New York Herald*)

Fact #1156. Ten lodges of Oglala Sioux, under Kicking Bear, Jack Red Cloud, Big Road, and Walking Blanket Woman, were present at the Little Big Horn at the time of the battle. (Panzieri, *Little Big Horn 1876: Custer's Last Stand*)

Fact #1157. During the spring of 1876, a number of Indian tribes moved about in the region south of the Yellowstone River, and between the Powder River and Rosebud Creek. (Luce, *Custer Battlefield*)

Fact #1158. The *New York Herald* reported on September 24 that a letter had been received from Standing Rock Reservation (D.T.) with "quite a lengthy account of Sitting Bull's forces the past season," written by Blackfeet Sioux Chief Kill Eagle, who had led his band of 26 lodges to the Little Big Horn and participated in the battle on June 25, 1876.

Fact #1159. "As I think back upon those days, it seems that no people in the world were ever any richer than we were." Wooden Leg, a Northern Cheyenne warrior whose tribe roamed with the Sioux, and who fought at LBH, was quoted by Robert M. Utley in *Indian, Soldier, and Settler*. Utley went on to say that this was a life "they loved while they lived it and mourned when they lost it."

Fact #1160. The "horse culture" of America's northern Plains never developed the dietary component of horse milk for sustenance, as had happened among the central Asia horse nomads. (D.S. Benson)

Fact #1161. The Cheyenne had named Custer Hi-es-tzie (Long Hair); they probably would not have recognized him at the Little Big Horn, because he had cut his hair before leaving on the Sioux Expedition.

Fact #1162. Most Indians, whether living on the reservations or not, were angered by the invasion of their reservations by white gold seekers, who, in defiance of government orders and despite the eviction of some of their number by the military, persisted in going into the "protected" Black Hills.

Fact #1163. "The Indians say that many of them were unable to fire a shot, their own men being in such a compact mass about them that all they could do was to whip the ponies in front of them and drive them over the soldiers." (Lt. W.S. Edgerly, Co. D)

Fact #1164. The village along the Little Big Horn River extended about three miles along the west bank, immediately south and west of the current visitors' center location, in the direction of the current town of Garryowen, according to E.S Luce. Later research has estimated the length of the village at about one to two miles when the soldiers attacked.

Fact #1165. The only accounts of the Custer phase of the Little Big Horn battle have come from Indian participants; no whites survived. Because of circumstances, much of what happened may never be solved conclusively.

Fact #1166. Each Sioux camp was governed by its own council of "elder men," and policed by its own paramilitary group. Each camp had half a dozen or more militia groups or soldier brotherhoods, known as "akicitas."

Fact #1167. The attacking Indians managed to startle some of the horses of Custer's command into a stampede and many horses were reportedly caught by the women in the valley. Some of these horses had extra ammunition in their saddlebags, which may have seriously affected the battle in its later stages. (Luce, *Custer Battlefield*)

Fact #1168. When men were chosen to paint Indian braves who were to participate in the Sun Dance ceremony, each man had a special color "associated with his dream" and "he used this color first in the paintings." ("Teton Sioux Music," 1918 bulletin of the Bureau of American Ethnology)

Fact #1169. Even though he claimed to have been 40 to 50 miles away from the Battle of the Rosebud, having "succeeded in escaping temporarily from the hostiles," Blackfeet Sioux tribal chief Kill Eagle, in the *New York Herald* account published September 24, 1876, related "many of the details and incidents which he was able subsequently to gather from participants," placing the loss of Indians at the Rosebud fight at "four dead, left on the field, and twelve [dead] that were brought to camp."

Fact #1170. The Indian tribes of the Mandan, Winnebago, Iowa, Oto, and Missouree belong to the Chiwery Sioux-speaking group, one of five major groups whose languages are part of the language family known as "Siouan." (*The Black Hills War 1876-1877*, Benson)

Fact #1171. Jumping Bear was the war chief for the Blackfeet Sioux at LBH. (Panzieri, *Little Big Horn 1876: Custer's Last Stand*)

Fact #1172. At Reno's early afternoon attack on June 25, a few Indians seized their rifles and went unmounted to meet Reno and hold him in check if possible, but the great majority rushed for the pony herd, more than a mile away, ". . . a Plains Indian considering himself only half a warrior without his pony." (Lt. W.S. Edgerly, Co. D)

Fact #1173. While the 7th Cavalrymen, along with packers, guides, and scouts, worked to dig entrenchments at the Reno-Benteen position, a "wild celebration" was in progress at the Indian encampment. Fires lighted the sky, and the "weird sounds of Indian chants" penetrated the still of the night. (*Custer Battlefield*, Luce)

Fact #1174. South of the Chiwery Sioux-speaking group, who lived between the Missouri and Mississippi rivers, were the Theygia Sioux-speaking peoples, another major group in the language family called "Siouan." The Theygia Sioux-speakers were the Ponca, Omaha, Kansa (Kaw), Osage, and Arkansa (Quapaw) tribes. (*The Black Hills War 1876-1877*, Benson)

Fact #1175. At the Little Big Horn encampment, just opposite Medicine Tail Coulee, the Miniconjou Sioux "circle" consisted of 150 lodges, with Red Horse as the principal chief. (Panzieri, *Little Big Horn 1876: Custer's Last Stand*)

Fact #1176. The official government documents pertaining to the Sioux Expedition of 1876 indicated that about 800 warrior Indians could be expected, but from sign, scouting reports, and, finally, visual confirmation, it was generally known among the officers, at least, that many more Indians could be expected than originally reported.

Fact #1177. 2d Lt. Charles Albert Varnum, Co. A, 7th Cavalry, commanded the Arikara Indian Scouts detachment, which was enlisted specifically for the 1876 Sioux expedition. Varnum's detachment numbered 41 Arikaras, of whom 39 were enlisted at Fort Abraham Lincoln (D.T.), and two more added the day of the battle. (*The Custer Myth*, Graham)

Fact #1178. The Siouan-speaking group most popularly identified as "Sioux-speakers" are the groups of the Sioux Nation inhabiting the Northern Plains. Their dialect divisions are the Dakota, the Nakota, and the Lakota. (*The Black Hills War 1876-1877*, Benson)

Fact #1179. Late on the afternoon of June 26, the Indians fired the grass in the valley, and when the cloud of smoke lifted, the troops at the Reno-Benteen position high above the river watched with relief the departure of the entire Indian encampment, a long procession of ponies and tepee pole travois slowly trailing off south toward the Big Horn Mountains. Before dark the last of the Indians had disappeared from sight. (*Custer Battlefield*, Luce)

Fact #1180. Two Arikara scouts were not part of Lt. Charles Varnum's Detachment of Indian Scouts, although they were nominally under his command. Both Bloody Knife, "Custer's favorite scout," and Bob Tail Bull were killed in the valley fight with Reno's command. (*The Custer Myth*, Graham)

Fact #1181. Sitting Bull was not personally engaged in the Battle of the Little Big Horn. He remained in the council tent directing operations, reported Sioux warriors who participated in the battle. (Graham, *The Custer Myth*)

Fact #1182. Crazy Horse of the Oglalas and Black Moon and Gall of the Hunkpapa were the principal war leaders on June 25, even though Crazy Horse did not have the formal status of "shirt-wearer honor chief."

Fact #1183. It is generally difficult to establish exact numbers of Indians involved in frontier engagements; estimates of the number at the Little Big Horn, an unusually large concentration, possibly the largest in history, vary greatly. (*Custer Battlefield*, Luce)

Fact #1184. Kill Eagle was a Blackfeet Sioux chief, who left the Standing Rock Reservation (D.T.) toward the end of May 1876 with 20 lodges [or more]. He was prominently engaged in LBH, and "afterwards upbraided Sitting Bull for not taking an active personal part in the engagement." (Graham, *The Custer Myth*)

Fact #1185. To the Plains Indians, the buffalo was the source of all good things physical and spiritual. The flesh was food, the hide was for clothing, blankets, and tepee coverings, the sinews were for weapons and cord, the horns and hooves were for implements and decorations. What their immense herds of domestic cattle and sheep were to the Asiatic horse nomads, the buffalo was to the American Plains Indians.

Fact #1186. In the combined "circle" of various Sioux tribal groups at the Little Big Horn, the Brulé Sioux had 68 lodges under Brave Bird, Coffee, Crazy Bull, Elk Thunder, Grass Rope, High Bald Eagle, and Hollow Horn Eagle. (*Little Big Horn 1876: Custer's Last Stand*, Panzieri)

Fact #1187. During the spring of 1876, small groups of "hostile" Indians kept in touch with their assigned reservations, obtaining what supplies they could from the reservation Indians. (*Custer Battlefield*, Luce)

Fact #1188. Kill Eagle's band found there was "no escape" for them from Sitting Bull's camp, which they had joined after a lengthy buffalo hunt following their departure from the Standing Rock Reservation (D.T.) "as they were starving at the agency." Their horses were shot or stolen, and "wounds and insults were showered upon them from every side." (Kill Eagle, September 24, 1876, *New York Herald*)

Fact #1189. The impact of the Powder River fight in March 1876 which resulted in the destruction of the Cheyenne village had an adverse effect on the Army's plan to bludgeon the Indians into submission. Instead, ". . .it had driven them into combinations to provide for more effective defense. As the summer came on, the Army would have greater problems to deal with than it had originally anticipated." (Benson, *The Black Hills War 1876-1877*)

Fact #1190. The religion of the Plains Indians was grounded in the fact that they "lived close to the land, venerated it mystically as 'Mother Earth,' and utterly failed to understand how it could be sold. They practiced a religion ordered by the wonders of nature and that rewarded each communicant with a highly personal brand of 'power' to carry him along the pathways of life. They cherished individual freedom and independence and embraced a democracy that bordered on anarchy." (Utley, *Indian, Soldier, and Settler*)

Fact #1191. The few Indian warriors who opposed Reno's initial charge into the village on June 25 "were so demoralized that they offered but a feeble resistance thus causing him to believe he was being drawn into ambush and to halt near the village." (Lt. W.S. Edgerly, Co. D)

Fact #1192. The Indians fighting Reno's command on the bluffs, following the repulse of his attack in the valley on the south end of the village, "had not. . . the slightest intimation of fighting at any other point," until runners came from down river with news of another attack, according to seven Sioux Indians who came in to Standing Rock Reservation (D.T.) on July 21, 1876, after participating in the LBH.

Fact #1193. Soon after Kill Eagle's band came to Sitting Bull's camp and discovered there was "no escape" from cavalry forces from the south under Gen. Crook, the Blackfeet Sioux chief and his people "succeeded in escaping temporarily from the hostiles." Kill Eagle claimed "to have been distant some forty to fifty miles at the time of the Rosebud fight. . ." (September 24, 1876, *New York Herald*)

Fact #1194. Oglala chief American Horse led 37 lodges at the Little Big Horn camp. (Panzieri, *Little Big Horn 1876: Custer's Last Stand*)

Fact #1195. When Reno's approach on the south end of the village around noon on June 25 was announced, a great many warriors were in their tepees and the pony herd was more than a mile away. (Lt. W.S. Edgerly, Co. D)

Fact #1196. "The [Indians] were celebrating their greatest of religious festivals—the sun dance—when runners brought news of the approach of cavalry. The dance was suspended and a general rush—mistaken by Custer, perhaps, for a retreat—for horses, equipment and arms followed. Major Reno first attacked the village at the south end and across the Little Big Horn." (Graham, *The Custer Myth*)

Fact #1197. As the word spread of Custer's advance on the midpoint of the sprawling Indian village along the banks of the Little Big Horn River on June 25, 1876, "Lodges were struck and preparations made for instant flight." (Graham, *The Custer Myth*)

Fact #1198. "Vast numbers of Indians left Reno's front and hastened to the assistance of their red brethren engaged with Custer." (Kill Eagle, September 24, 1876, *New York Herald*)

Fact #1199. Indian witnesses of the LBH who talked with the Commanding Officer of Standing Rock Reservation (D.T.) on July 21, 1876, said that when the warriors fighting Reno heard of another attack downriver, "A force large enough to prevent Reno from assuming the offensive was left and the surplus available force flew to the other end of the camp, where, finding the Indians there successfully driving Custer before them, instead of uniting with them, they separated into two parties and moved around the flanks of his [Custer's] cavalry." (*The Custer Myth*, Graham)

Fact #1200. On the evening of June 25, 1876, "Horses and travois were laden with [Indian] wounded on every hand and in countless numbers." (*New York Herald*, Kill Eagle) Kill Eagle said 67 warriors had been killed on the first day of the battle.

Fact #1201. The Sun Dance ceremony allowed individuals in the tribe to demonstrate personal heroism in the interests of tribal unity, bringing the Sioux together to seek favor from Wakan Tanka, the "Principal Deity" of the Sioux "religion." (Gump, *The Dust Rose Like Smoke*)

Fact #1202. Following a morning of intense fighting on June 26 at the Reno-Benteen position, the Indians withdrew back across the river to the village, a few coming back around 2 p.m. to resume light firing for about an hour, when they, too, withdrew. (Lt. W.S. Edgerly, Co. D)

Fact #1203. The winter count kept by White Bull, a Minneconjou Sioux and nephew of Sitting Bull, reflects skirmishes with white interlopers only twice between 1854 and 1876, with conflicts between the Sioux and Assiniboines and Crows 15 out of the 22 years. Military conflicts with other indigenous but enemy tribes were a significant part of Indian life.

Fact #1204. Sitting Bull came into prominence as an uncompromising protector of Sioux territory after the treaty of 1868. A deeply religious man, Sitting Bull believed that contact with white civilization would weaken and destroy Teton Lakota culture. Those who shared his concerns regarded Sitting Bull as the head chief of all the Lakota, and this reputation spread to the whites. (Gump, *The Dust Rose Like Smoke*)

Fact #1205. ". . .it seems as if everyone was wounded," and Kill Eagle placed the number of wounded "as high as 600." One "Ogalalla" band alone, he said, "had twenty-seven wounded on travois and thirty-eight thrown across horses." (September 24, 1876, newspaper article)

Fact #1206. The Hunkpapa warriors at the Little Big Horn were led by their principal war chief Pizi (Gall), and war chiefs Crow King, Rain-in-the-Face, and Four Horns, plus Deeds, Brown Back, and Black Moon. (Panzieri, *Little Big Horn 1876: Custer's Last Stand*)

Fact #1207. On the extreme southern rim of the Indian camp at the Little Big Horn were the Hunkpapa Sioux, and at the opposite end were the Northern Cheyenne. (*Custer Battlefield*, Luce)

Fact #1208. Sitting Bull was "about five feet ten inches [tall]; he is very heavy and muscular and big around in the breast; he has a very large head; his hair is not long, it only comes down to his shoulders. . .he has light hair [but] he is not a white man." (Kill Eagle, *New York Herald*, September 24, 1876)

Fact #1209. All of the Indians were not engaged at any one time in the fight at the Reno-Benteen position. "Heavy reserves were held to repair losses and renew attacks successively. The fight continued until the third day when runners, kept purposely on the lookout, hurried in to camp and reported a great body of troops (Gen. Terry's column) advancing [south] up the river." (*The Custer Myth*, Graham)

Fact #1210. Sioux chief Red Horse was "one of the head council men" at the Indian encampment along the banks of the Little Big Horn River. In a statement given to Col. W.H. Wood, commandant of the Cheyenne Agency in February 1877, he said his "lodge was situated in the center of the camp. The Uncpapas (Hunkpapas), Yanktonais and Santees were camped northeast of us, on the right, facing the battlefield. The Minneconjous, Sans Arc, Two Kettles and Brulé formed the center. On the left to the west were the Ogalallas and Cheyennes."

Fact #1211. Before the white man came, Indian life, as they remembered, was "rich and satisfying. The plains had teemed with deer, antelope, elk, and buffalo." (Utley, *Indian, Soldier, and Settler*)

Fact #1212. Kill Eagle was "very positive. . .that no [white] prisoners were taken. There were no white men in the fight [on the side of the Indians] or on the field. . . .The bugle calls so often spoken of were sounded by an Indian." (*New York Herald,* September 24, 1876)

Fact #1213. In the combined "circle" of 120 Sioux lodges at the Little Big Horn, the Blackfeet Sioux had 34 lodges. (*Little Big Horn 1876: Custer's Last Stand*, Panzieri)

Fact #1214. During his Sun Dance experience, Sitting Bull, who bore many scars from past sun dances, offered 100 pieces of flesh, cut from his arms by his adopted brother, Jumping Bull, to Wakan Tanka. Then, streaming blood, he danced for 18 hours suspended from a 20-foot pole by a rawhide rope attached with a skewer through his breast muscles. He then fell into a trance and had a vision dream about "soldiers falling into camp," a prophecy of victory.

Fact #1215. "Hostile" Indians who had remained in their camps rather than submit to the Army's January 1876 deadline to return to the reservations, had moved in early April to the Tongue River and conducted raids on Gibbon's Montana Column, advancing from the west, throughout May.

Fact #1216. Dr. George Bird Grinnell and Dr. Thomas B. Marquis, two veteran observers of Cheyenne history, wrote in the 1930s and the 1950s, that at the time of the LBH, the Cheyenne circle numbered 200 lodges, and Marquis even said it contained some 1,600 people. Each received his information from extensive first-hand contact with the Cheyenne people over an extended period of time.

Fact #1217. Two noted Indian authorities, George E. Hyde, a distinguished historian on a number of the Plains tribes, and Dr. Charles Eastman, a half-blood Sioux, offered the conclusion that the Cheyenne tribal circle along the Little Big Horn River on June 25, 1876, numbered 50-55 lodges.

Fact #1218. The Plains Indians who fought Custer were "a handsome, proud, and strong people. . .and they might have provided the stereotypical image evoked today by the word 'Indian'; tall, lithe, sinewy, bronze-skinned; with high cheek bones, aquiline nose, low forehead, thick, wide mouth, dark, expressive eyes. . ." (Utley, *Indian, Soldier, and Settler*)

Fact #1219. No ceremony held more significance in the Sioux "religion" than the Sun Dance; the observance of this tradition prior to the LBH would have caused a significant impact on the morale of the Indian warriors. Anthropologist Clark Wissler, in a 1911 letter to Dr. James Walker at the Pine Ridge agency, called the Sun Dance "the one great unifying ceremony of the Plains

Indians toward which all other ceremonial activities converged." (Gump, *The Dust Rose Like Smoke*)

Fact #1220. During the night of June 25, 1876, the besieged soldiers at the Reno-Benteen position were assaulted with the sounds of Indian celebration and/or mourning rites for the dead warriors. "I wandered to the edge of the bluff overlooking the village. By this time it was dark; I could plainly see several fires which the Indians had built. There was a noise in the village that increased as night advanced. The deep voices of the braves, the howling of the squaws, the shrill piping of the children, and the barking of the dogs made the night hideous; but they appeared to enjoy it amazingly." (Pvt. Peter Thompson, Co. C)

Fact #1221. Capt. J.S. Poland of the Standing Rock Reservation (D.T.), after talking with seven Sioux warriors on July 21, 1876, who claimed to have been in the Little Big Horn fight, said, "The general outline of this Indian report coincides with published reports. The first attack of Reno's began well on in the day, say the Indians. They report about 300 whites killed. They do not say how many Indians were killed. A report from another source says the Indians obtained from Custer's command 592 carbines and revolvers." (Graham in *The Custer Myth*)

Fact #1222. In *The Sixth Grandfather*, edited by Raymond DeMallie, the life force of the universe in the Sioux religion "was called Wakan Tanka, Great Incomprehensibility, the whole of all that was mysterious, powerful, sacred, holy." It was to this life force that the Sioux prayed and sacrificed during the significant Sun Dance ceremony, like the one which immediately preceded LBH.

Fact #1223. The Arikara scout Red Star, in *The Arikara Narrative of the Campaign Against the Hostile Dakotas, June 1876*, had carefully studied the site of the abandoned sun dance camp, discovered on June 24 by the 7th Cavalry column. "Here there was evidence of the Dakotas having made medicine, the sand had been arranged and smoothed, and pictures had been drawn. The Dakota scouts in Custer's army said that this meant the enemy knew the Army was coming. In one of the sweat lodges was a long heap or ridge of sand. On this one Red Bear, Red Star, and Soldier saw figures drawn indicating by hoof prints Custer's men on one side and the Dakota on the other. Between them dead men were drawn lying with their heads toward the Dakotas. . . .All the Arikara knew what this meant, namely, that the Dakotas were sure of winning."

Fact #1224. Mitch Bouyer, a half-blood Sioux scout for Col. Gibbon's Montana Column, was ordered to join Custer's 7th Cavalry column. On the eve of LBH, Boyer told Lt. W.S. Godfrey (commander, Co. K) that the Cavalry was in for "a damned big fight."

Fact #1225. Following his participation in the Sun Dance ceremony prior to the Battles of the Rosebud (June 17, 1876) and the Little Big Horn (June 25, 1876), Sitting Bull, the Hunkpapa chieftain and shaman, had a vision dream in which he saw "many soldiers falling into camp." The Rosebud victory did not fulfill the prophecy because the soldiers were nowhere near the Indian camp, but the Little Big Horn victory did.

Fact #1226. Indian warriors reporting on the battle to the Commanding Officer at the Standing Rock Reservation (D.T.) four weeks afterward said the Indians' "most serious loss" occurred when the attack on the Reno-Benteen position was renewed after Custer's command was wiped out. (*The Custer Myth*, Graham)

Fact #1227. The large gathering of Indians in the encampment along the Little Big Horn River in June 1876 was due to good fortune far more than good planning. After the Powder River fight in March of that year, the Cheyenne and Oglala took refuge in the camp of Sitting Bull. They were joined by Lame Deer and his Minneconjou band, as well as Sans Arc and Blackfeet Sioux to complete the six principal circles in the village. Other bands of Cheyenne and small numbers of Wahpeton, Yanktonai, and Brulé Sioux, as well as Assiniboine and Arapaho bands, also joined the camp, as small groups of "roamers" did every summer. That year of 1876, huge herds of buffalo and antelope made it possible for the unusually large assembly to find food and stay together for at least 26 days, maybe more than a month. (*The Book of the American West*, Monaghan)

Fact #1228. "Sioux-speakers" can be used to identify any people speaking dialects derived from a certain common language family called "Siouan." Linguists have classified Siouan-speaking people into five major groups, one in the Carolinas, but most Siouan-speaking peoples were found in the West. (*The Black Hills War 1876-1877*, Benson)

Fact #1229. The Oglala Sioux, Red Cloud's group, had 240 lodges at the Little Big Horn. (*Little Big Horn 1876: Custer's Last Stand*, Panzieri)

Fact #1230. Warriors occupied virtually all of the hilltops and many of the ravines south and east of the Reno-Benteen site. Sharpshooters' Ridge, a long ridge about 1,000 yards due north, was the principal position from which Indians fired on the troops entrenched along the bluff and into the swale.

Fact #1231. "There was a high ridge on the right. . .and one Indian in particular I must give credit for being a good shot. While we were lying in the line he fired a shot and killed the fourth man on my right. Soon afterward he fired again and shot the third man. His third shot wounded the man on my right, who jumped back from the line, and down among the rest of the wounded. I jumped up with Captain [Thomas] French [Co. M] and some half a dozen members of my company, and, instead of firing straight to the front, as we had been doing. . .we wheeled to our right and put an end to that Indian, as there were no more killed at that particular spot." (1st Sgt. John Ryan [Co. M] referring to the deadly firing on the southwestern salient of the Reno-Benteen defense line)

Fact #1232. The northern "Sioux" nation consisted of the Santee Sioux (Dakota) in the east, the Yanktee (Yanktonais) Sioux (Nakota) in the middle section, and the Teton Sioux (Lakota) in the westernmost area of northern Sioux territory. (*The Black Hills War 1876-1877*)

Fact #1233. The death of the Sioux nation began when the many divisions of the Siouan speaking groups moved out onto the plains from their ancestral home in the vicinity of Mille Lacs (MN). "Gradually the bonds of the Seven Council Fires were weakened. Then the bonds that tied the seven bands of the Teton together began to disintegrate." (Milligan, *Dakota Twilight*)

Fact #1234. Dewey Beard called the Battle of the Little Big Horn ". . .a turmoil of dust and warriors and soldiers, with bullets whining and arrows hissing all around. Sometimes a bugle would sound and the shouting would get louder. Some of the soldiers were firing pistols at close range. Our knives and war clubs flashed in the sun. I could hear bullets whiz past my ears. But I keep going and shouting, It's a good day to die so that everyone who heard would know that I was not afraid of being killed in battle."

Fact #1235. There were generally eight soldier brotherhoods (akichita osh-paye) in each Sioux camp: the Brave Hearts (Chante Tinza), the Badgers (Ihoka), the Foxlings (Tokala), the All Crows (Kangy Yuha), the All Smooth (Sotka Yuha), the White Things (Wichy Ska), the Mandans (Mawatany) and the Omaha, the latter two adopted from two neighboring tribes for which they were named. (D.S. Benson)

Fact #1236. The "Crow Agency" referred to in many of the writings about the LBH was located about 40 miles east of present-day Billings (MT). Established in 1874, it was in existence about five years. The "Crow Agency" just four miles from LBBNM was established much later, and was not there at the time of the battle.

Fact #1237. The winter counts of the Oglala Sioux show an emphasis on conflicts with their indigenous neighbors/enemies, far in excess of conflicts with white soldiers or settlers prior to the 1870s.

Fact #1238. The Dakota are the largest group of Siouan-speaking people. They became popularly known as "Sioux" in the 17th century because of the French pronunciation of a Chippewa word meaning little snakes or adders. In recent history the term "Sioux" has become most closely identified with the Teton or Lakota division of the Dakota.

Fact #1239. Reporting on accounts by seven Sioux who said they had been at LBH and then came in to the Standing Rock Reservation (D.T.) on July 21, 1876, the Reservation's Commanding Officer said the Indians told him: "a small number of cavalry broke through the line of Indians in their rear and escaped, but was overtaken, within a distance of five or six miles, and killed. I infer from this that this body of retreating cavalry was led by the missing officers, and that they tried to escape only after Custer fell."

Fact #1240. "The Plains [Indian] 'war complex' produced magnificent warriors. But it did not produce soldiers. Emphasis on individual distinction discouraged strategic and even tactical thinking." (Sarf, *The Little Bighorn Campaign*)

Fact #1241. Lt. William P. Clark wrote that Indian warriors, accustomed ". . . from their earliest youth to take advantage of every knoll, rock, tree, tuft of grass and every aid the topography of the country affords to secure game, become adept in their way of fighting, needing no orders to promptly seize, push and hold any opportunity for success, or in retreating protect themselves from harm."

Fact #1242. Wooden Leg, recounting his recollections of the LBH years after the battle, recalled the confusion: "We ran to our camp and to our home lodge. Everybody there was excited. Women were hurriedly making up little packs for flight. Some were going off northward or across the river without any packs. Children were hunting for their mothers. Mothers were anxiously trying to find their children. I got my lariat and my sixshooter. I hastened on down toward where had been our horse herd. I came upon three of our herder boys. One of them was catching grasshoppers. The other two were cooking fish. I told them what was going on and asked them where were the horses. They jumped on their picketed ponies and dashed for the camp, without answering me."

Fact #1243. During Reno's original attack on the (southern) upper end of the Indian village in the early afternoon of June 25, 1876, a group of Arikara scouts riding to the left of the advancing cavalry line surprised a group of Sioux women who were away from the camp and killed them, then seized some Sioux ponies before warriors from the camp rallied and forced the scouts back.

Fact #1244. The Oglala and Brulé Sioux, the most populous of the seven Lakota bands, ventured into the plains southwest of the Missouri River in the early 19th century, migrating into the region from the Black Hills in western South Dakota to the headwaters of the Niobrara and White rivers in northwestern Nebraska to the Laramie plains in eastern Wyoming.

Fact #1245. As the buffalo herds were disrupted by the tens of thousands of overland trail emigrants in the mid 1800s, the Great Plains tribes faced greater competition for food, horses, and hunting grounds. This caused the Teton Sioux to form a more-or-less permanent alliance with the Cheyenne and Arapaho in

1825, and to wage war on the Arikara, Crow, Hidatsa, Kiowa, Mandan, and Pawnee tribes. The Sioux-Cheyenne-Arapaho alliance would dominate the north and central plains for the next half century. (Richard White, "The Winning of the West," September 1978 *Journal of American History*)

Fact #1246. The Pawnee Indians numbered about 12,000 in the early 1830s. After years of bloody warfare with the Sioux, culminating in an 1873 Lakota attack on a Pawnee village which left over 100 Pawnee dead, the Pawnee tribe decided to abandon their traditional hunting grounds in Nebraska and move to Indian Territory. The Pawnee population in 1879 was 1,440. (George Hyde's *Red Cloud's Folk*)

Fact #1247. Skirmishes between the Teton Lakota Sioux and the Crow to their West intensified in the first half of the 19th century, and by the 1850s, the Teton had driven the Crow out of Dakota and Wyoming and were pushing them (south) up the Yellowstone River in southwestern Montana.

Fact #1248. Six Crow scouts who had been part of Col. John Gibbon's Montana Column were assigned to accompany Custer's column because of their knowledge of the terrain; they were not expected to participate in any fighting. (*Encyclopedia of American Indian Wars*)

Fact #1249. Curly, a young Crow scout, is believed by some to be the last person to see Custer alive and live to tell about it. (*Encyclopedia of American Indian Wars*)

Fact #1250. The Standing Rock Indian Agency in Dakota Territory, and other Indian agencies from Wisconsin to Washington state, played an important role in Indian affairs. The leadership of the Sioux nation—chiefs, medicine men, warriors, and their families—moved in and out of this agency during the Indian wars from 1866 to 1890. Sitting Bull, leader of the Indian village along the banks of the Little Big Horn River in June 1876, is buried under a slender granite marker at the Roman Catholic Cemetery there.

Fact #1251. Certain of the Indian warrior societies were selected from time to time to act as "camp police." They were referred to as akicita.

Fact #1252. Wandering Indian bands learned that camping together usually meant enormous pony herds that cropped off the grass too quickly, so the bands tended to coalesce, drift apart, then coalesce again. (*Custer Battlefield*, Luce)

Fact #1253. "Societies and Ceremonial Associations in the Oglala Division of the Teton-Dakota" was published in 1912 as part of the American Museum of Natural History "Anthropological Papers."

Fact #1254. Forty-one Arikara scouts, known as Rees, marched from Fort Abraham Lincoln (D.T.) May 17, 1876, as part of the 7th Cavalry column. They were ancient blood enemies of the Sioux.

Fact #1255. The Arikara scouts' pay was $16 a month, $12 a month for the horse, and rations were furnished.

Fact #1256. In late April 1876, many "hostile" Indian bands left their camps along the Powder River to follow the buffalo southwestward and westward.

Fact #1257. Pvt. Peter Thompson (Co. C): "While we were at the Yellowstone, six Crow Indians joined us [as scouts], Half Yellow Face being their head man."

Fact #1258. By 3 p.m. on the afternoon of June 26, the Indians had all withdrawn from their surround of the Reno-Benteen position, and by late afternoon, the village had been dismantled and the Indians were moving (south) up the Little Big Horn valley. (Lt. W.S. Edgerly, Co. D)

Equipment

Fact #1259. At special events in the Indians' religious life, like the Sun Dance ceremony shortly before LBH, special costumes were involved. Memberships in various honor/warrior societies was indicated by the wearing of distinctive regalia.

Fact #1260. The caps of some "war bonnets" were sometimes trimmed with white fur, with a pair of horns in the center instead of eagle feathers.

Fact #1261. The love of heavy long tresses was a typical trait of the Plains Indians, and Sioux warriors, as well as Crow, adopted the pompadour style of upswept hair in front.

Fact #1262. The "warbonnet" was most commonly associated with the Lakota Sioux, although whether this tribe originated the long, feathered bonnet is not known. Crow Indians are, by some tribes, given credit for the "invention."

Fact #1263. Each of the tribes participating in the LBH, on both sides, had a custom of warrior societies or honor societies. Most were associated with animals, and some considered the animal cults as part of one great cult. It is true that the animal cults often held separate ceremonies at the same time, and joint ceremonies at other times, where they made a show of rivalry.

Fact #1264. The accessories of Crow warriors like those who served as scouts for the Army at the Little Big Horn often included elk teeth necklaces and adornments, deer hoof and hair tassel decorations on garments, and loop necklaces made of strung bone disks or of thongs wrapped with white beads.

Fact #1265. After an 1843 visit to America, Prinz Maximilian von Wied-Neuwied in *Travels in the Interior of North America* on the cultural adornment of the Sioux Indians: "If the enemy is killed with a musket, a small piece of wood is put in the hair, which is intended to represent a ramrod."

Fact #1266. Like the war bonnet, the war shirt trimmed with hair or weasel skins was considered to have great medicine power and could be worn on special occasions only by men in authority or those who had distinguished themselves in battle.

Fact #1267. Sioux and Cheyenne warriors at the Little Big Horn frequently used bison tails ("bull tails"), decorated with quillwork, as hair ornaments.

Fact #1268. After his adulterous liaison with Black Buffalo Woman, Crazy Horse was stripped of his honors adornments and rode into battle at the Little Big Horn with only a single feather, slanted down, in his hair, and no shirt at all or a non-fringed shirt.

Fact #1269. "Military Expedition Against The Sioux Indians," a "House Executive Document" of the 44th Congress, quotes Bad Wound as saying he "bought center-primed cartridges, calibre .50, at trader's by the box, 20 in a box, at $1 per box. He has bought cartridges at different times, and has seen other Indians buy ammunition at the same place."

Fact #1270. Crow warriors preferred close-fitting elkskin war shirts.

Fact #1271. Scalp locks were mere bundles of hair from the head of an enemy and were frequently used as decorations on the war shirt or on the leggings of a Plains Indian warrior.

Fact #1272. Many of the Indian warriors encamped along the Little Big Horn had firearms. Some even had Winchester rifles, obtained legally from traders and Indian agents for hunting. (1978 "Custer Battlefield" brochure)

Fact #1273. The Plains Indian war bonnet was constructed with a leather or felt base (a caplet), which could be covered with feathered hackles, down, split eagle plumes, or fur.

Fact #1274. While Sioux and Cheyenne warriors armed with rifles occupied vantage points all around the Reno-Benteen position, most of them were not good marksmen beyond point-blank range.

Fact #1275. While stains and dyestuffs used in the cosmetic ornamentation of Indian warriors generally came from organic sources, most "paints" were usually inorganic, coming from white, brown, red, yellow, and sometimes black clays.

Fact #1276. On the field of battle, the trailing "scarf" of a Dog Soldier was staked to the ground with a lance, which committed the warrior to a fight to the death unless one of his compatriot Dog Soldiers withdrew the lance.

Fact #1277. Many warriors at LBH were arrayed in a buckskin war shirt. Sometimes the entire shirt might be painted or stained. Sioux warriors often colored the top half blue and the bottom yellow, or occasionally green. Among some tribes the entire shirt was painted reddish brown.

Fact #1278. Maj. Marcus Reno testified (at the Reno Court of Inquiry in Chicago [IL] in 1879): "The Indians had Winchester rifles and the column made a large target for them and they were pumping bullets into it." Asked, "The Indians so far as you observed were armed with Winchester rifles?"; Reno answered, "Yes, sir." Asked, "Do you know that they had any other arms?"; Reno responded, "No, sir." Cartridge cases found on the battlefield tend to disprove this contention.

Fact #1279. Older Cheyenne warriors, like those who fought at the Little Big Horn, wore their breechcloths long in the front and the back, unlike the Sioux, who wore the clout longer in back. They wore moccasins with attached "tails." Their long braids were often cloth-wrapped.

Fact #1280. The Indian agent at Fort Peck (M.T.), W.W. Alderson, wrote in 1874: "I have taken special pains at different times to ascertain definitely to what extent the Indians belonging to this agency were provided with arms and ammunition, and have invariably found them poorly supplied with arms, and these a very inferior class and usually almost entirely destitute of ammunition. Very few breech-loading guns are to be found in their possession, yet those owning such contrive to obtain cartridges for them by some means."

Fact #1281. Scalp locks, small clumps of hair growing from the center of the scalp and often braided, were common for the men of many tribes, warriors wearing a scalp lock for every enemy killed. This was common to both friend and foe at the Little Big Horn, being found in Sioux, Crow, Cheyenne, and Arikara hairdos.

Fact #1282. About half the Indian warriors at LBH used bows and arrows in the battle. (*The Book of the American West*, prepared under the direction of Jay Monaghan, a Custer biographer)

Fact #1283. The accessories of the Lakota warriors included hair-pipe necklaces, hair-pipe breastplates (after 1870), chokers made of animal teeth, and hair tassels or feathers on garments. Many of the warriors at LBH would have been arrayed in some or all of these accessories.

Fact #1284. Indian war shirts were often called "scalp shirts" by whites, but, in fact, the hair used in trimming these shirts did not always come from enemy scalps, nor did each lock count for a slain enemy.

Fact #1285. Some of the guns used by the Sioux in the Dakota campaign against the cavalry were identified as having been given to them by the Indian Peace Commission at the conclusion of the Fort Rice (D.T.) Treaty (1868). (*The Book of the American West*)

Fact #1286. Older Lakota warriors, like those who fought at LBH, generally wore hide shirts, painted in two base colors; a breechcloth, long in the back; and a frontal lock of hair with long braids.

Fact #1287. The claws and teeth of animals were often incorporated into the decoration of Plains Indians costumes, particularly battle raiment.

Fact #1288. Reservation Indians—"friendlies"—were issued guns, ostensibly to kill buffalo and other game, even during the period of the Indian Wars. Trade guns were also part of the picture, and an impressive case can be made that Indians were frequently well-armed with guns, as at LBH. (*The Book of the American West*)

Fact #1289. If guns in the hands of Indians ever achieved a "great victory," it was at LBH. Experts have estimated that about half the warriors at the Little Big Horn had guns, and about half of those had repeating rifles. Those with repeating rifles probably outgunned Custer's soldiers, who were armed with Springfield single-shot breech-loading carbines. (*The Book of the American West*)

Fact #1290. Coloring materials for war decorations were obtained from a variety of sources. Among various tribes tamarack bark, spruce cones, and sumac fruits yielded reds, while yellow came from wolf or fox moss, sumac roots or pith, goldthread roots, cottonwood buds, certain lichens, sunflower or cornflower petals, buffalo berries or the roots of black willow.

Fact #1291. Prinz Maximilian von Wied-Neuwied in *Travels in the Interior of North America* on the cultural adornment of the Sioux Indians: "The Sioux highly prize personal bravery, and therefore constantly wear the marks of distinction which they have received for their exploits; among these are, especially, tufts of human hair attached to the arms and legs, and feathers on their heads."

Fact #1292. While the Indians at LBH did have some repeating rifles, "their greatest firepower probably came from captured 7th Cavalry carbines and pistols." (*Custer Battle Guns*, John S. du Mont)

Fact #1293. Assuming that Custer's command traveled seven miles in the hour between leaving Reno and beginning the final phase of the first day's battle on Last Stand Hill, the Custer squadron (Cos. C, E, F, I, L) engaged in what would be considered "rapid marching in any army or country and must have involved much extended trot and gallop, not considering the wild dashes to charge or escape which must have marked the end of that fatal conflict." (Nye, 1941 article in the *Veterinary Bulletin*)

Fact #1294. Mrs. Mary Eastman, writing in *Dahcotah* in 1849, commented on feather markings by the Sioux: a spot on the larger web of the feather denotes that the wearer has killed an enemy.

Fact #1295. "Among the Sioux an eagle's feather with a red spot, worn by a warrior in the village, denotes that on the last warpath he killed an enemy, and for every additional enemy he has slain he carries another feather painted with an additional red spot about the size of a silver quarter." (George P. Belden, *Belden, the White Chief, or, Twelve Years Among the Wild Indians of the Plains*)

Fact #1296. A number of wood shavings stained with vermilion and worn in the hair of a warrior denotes the number of wounds the warrior has received in battle. (Boller, *Among the Indians*)

Fact #1297. Writing in "The Religion of the Dakotas," part of the Minnesota Historical Society *Collections*, James W. Lynd explained the symbolism of warriors wearing four scalp feathers for each enemy slain in battle: "To the human body the Dakotas [Sioux] give four spirits. The first is supposed to be a spirit of the body, and dies with the body. The second is a spirit which always remains with or near the body. Another is the soul which accounts for the deeds of the body, and is supposed by some to go to the south, by others to the west, after the death of the body. The fourth always lingers with the small bundle of the hair of the deceased kept by relatives until they have a chance to throw it into the enemy's country, when it becomes a roving, restless spirit, bringing death and disaster to the enemy whose country it is in." Thus, four scalp-feathers, one for each soul.

Fact #1298. Prinz Maximilian von Wied-Neuwied in *Travels in the Interior of North America* on the cultural adornment of the Sioux Indians: "Whoever first discovers the enemy and gives notice to his comrades of their approach is allowed to wear a small feather which is stripped except towards the top."

Fact #1299. "Paint," or coloring/staining material was an important component in the Indian warrior's war kit. Many of the warriors at LBH delayed their entry into the conflict until they could apply the proper decorations to their face and body.

Fact #1300. Hair pipes, long tubular beads which were used as adornments by eastern Indians in the late 1700s, arrived on the Plains in the early 1800s. The most popular early use was as hair ornaments, but they were also used for ear pendants, necklaces, and breastplates. They had spread to the western Sioux by 1870, and would have been part of the "war costume" worn by some warriors at the Battle of the Little Big Horn.

Fact #1301. The Crow Indians, who served as scouts for Custer's column and the Montana column, sometimes decorated grizzly-claw necklaces with circular pieces cut from bleached bison shoulder blades polished and smeared with white clay. Prior to LBH, Crow scouts, along with their Arikara colleagues, paused to prepare themselves cosmetically for battle.

Fact #1302. Many of the warriors at LBH were in too much of a hurry to respond to the surprise attack to "deck themselves out" with much symbolic regalia, but it's entirely probable that they would have done so for the victory dance on the night of June 25, 1876, and at other celebrations before and after the battle.

Fact #1303. Buffalo hair or horse hair (which was better) was often used to lengthen a warrior's natural hair.

Events

Fact #1304. After fighting infantry and cavalry troops under Gen. George Crook to a standstill at Rosebud Creek, south and east of the Little Big Horn, the Indians moved west to the Little Big Horn valley.

Fact #1305. The water in the valley of what is now known as Reno Creek was "exceedingly scarce. . .but as we knew that the latter was short we had hopes of something better when we got out of it. We found, as we proceeded, that the camping places of the Indians were but a short distance apart showing that they were travelling in a leisurely manner for the purpose of giving their ponies an opportunity to feed; or it might have been that each tribe camped by itself." (Pvt. Peter Thompson, Co. C, *Belle Fourche [SD] Bee*)

Fact #1306. Most of the casualties at the Reno-Benteen position on June 26, 1876, the second day of the battle, were not caused by Indian rifle fire from the ravines and coulees leading to the besieged position, but rather from long-range rifle fire from the ridges to the north and east, which were higher than the Reno-Benteen position. Many Indians in the ravines and coulees surrounding the position shot large numbers of arrows into the air, some of which found blue-coat targets as they fell.

Fact #1307. At about 2 p.m., on the north side of what later came to be called Reno Creek, the two columns (Reno's and Custer's) came upon a single stand-ing Indian tent, "the Lone Tipi," which contained the body of Old She Bear, a Sans Arc Sioux killed at the Rosebud fight. The Indian scouts in advance of the column had counted coup on the lodge with their quirts, cut it open, and looted its contents.

Fact #1308. In 1868, at Fort Laramie (W.T.), representatives of the Sioux, Cheyenne, and other tribes of the Great Plains, signed a treaty with the U.S. Government by which a large area in western Dakota Territory and part of eastern Wyoming Territory was declared a permanent reservation.

Fact #1309. Four Cheyenne warriors confronted Custer's column as it rode toward Minneconjou Ford, and the column halted "as if in fear. Whether he feared a trap or not I do not know—I know only that he stopped there before Bob-Tail Horse and his three friends. The four Cheyennes fired at the soldiers as fast as they could work their guns, and the soldiers fired back without charging upon them. Five Sioux joined the Cheyennes, and together these nine

Stronghearts stood off the whites until warriors from all the camps came rushing downriver [north] to rub out the soldiers." (Charging Bear)

Fact #1310. When the Indians at Custer Hill observed the approach of cavalry companies toward Weir Point from the Reno-Benteen position on June 25, warriors began a frantic ride to head off the advancing cavalry. (*Custer Battlefield*, Luce)

Fact #1311. "So closely did the Indians approach our skirmishers at times that they inflicted several wounds from battle axes, lances and arrows, and in one or two instances they closed in upon a brave soldier and got his scalp before comrades would rush forward to the rescue." (Robert Strahorn, a correspondent with Gen. Crook at the Battle of the Rosebud just over a week before the same Indians defeated Custer at LBH)

Fact #1312. The Sioux response to the Custer thrust down Medicine Tail Coulee was to form two "battle groups." One was led by Gall, Crow King, Spotted Eagle, and Hump consisting of Hunkpapa, Sans Arc, and Minneconjou warriors, who charged across Minneconjou Ford at the base of Medicine Tail Coulee, and up Deep Coulee, hurling itself at Custer's right wing (Cos. E and F). (*The Black Hills War 1876-1877*, Benson)

Fact #1313. Pvt. Peter Thompson, Co. C, saw Reno's charge from up on the ridge east of the Little Big Horn River, where he had ridden with Custer's column (C, E, F, I, L companies). He noted that as the cavalry rode in to the village, there was a brief halt, ". . .for the Indians came rushing towards them in great numbers. At this juncture the dry grass caught on fire threatening the destruction of the village, but the squaws fearless as the braves themselves fought the fire and tore down the teepees which were in danger of burning."

Fact #1314. Charging Bear, a young Sioux warrior at LBH, recounted that after stopping Reno's charge and chasing him and his men back across the river to the bluffs, his war party received the message that more soldiers were coming (north) toward a higher ford. "Swiftly we rode downriver to defend our women and children, but we could see that we were too far away to stop these new enemies before they reached the river."

Fact #1315. The second "battle group" responding to Custer's thrust down Medicine Tail Coulee was made up of Oglala and Cheyenne and led by Crazy Horse, He Dog, and Two Moon. (*The Black Hills War 1876-1877*, Benson)

Fact #1316. Almost all Indian accounts of LBH agree that Reno's attack on June 25, 1876, at the (southern) upper end of the village was a complete surprise; but Gall, among others, said the soldiers were expected.

Fact #1317. Shortly before LBH, a large Sun Dance ceremony was held some distance from the banks of the Little Big Horn. The Sun Dance was an annual, summer ceremony involving most members of the tribe, lasting several days. It was frequently marked by ritualistic self-torture and self-mutilation by warriors seeking honor. The men who took the Sun Dance vow were painted on the face and body, and wore an eagle wing-bone whistle around their necks.

"The Last Command: Custer and the 7th Cavalry at Little Big Horn," by Kirk Stirnweis. *Americana Historical Art*

Chapter 4

Facts About the Literature

Individuals

Fact #1318. Sitting Bull's cousin, Pte-San-Waste-Win, was one of the women digging turnips near the Indian village along the Little Big Horn River on the morning of June 25, 1876. She later said she had seen the soldiers some six to eight miles distant. She was quoted in *Bury My Heart At Wounded Knee*: "We saw the flashing of their sabers and saw that there were very many soldiers in the party." In fact, the 7th Cav. had not carried sabers onto the field on this expedition.

Fact #1319. Thomas LeForge was born "an Ohio American" who chose to "die a Crow Indian American." He was with Gen. Terry at the time of LBH. (Marquis, *Memoirs of a White Crow Indian*)

Fact #1320. Individuals at the Little Big Horn have been the subject of many literary works; among the early compilers of these persons' lives was Kenneth Hammer, who authored *Little Big Horn Biographies* for the CBH&MA in 1964. Hammer expanded this into a later work, also for CBH&MA, *Men With Custer: Biographies of the 7th Cavalry*, edited by Ronald H. Nichols.

Fact #1321. Pvts. William Slaper, Francis Neely, and William Morris, all of Co. M, dragged their mortally-wounded comrade Pvt. Henry Klotzbucher into a clump of heavy underbrush before rejoining their comrades on Reno's frenzied retreat to the bluffs. "After the battle we found the body of Koltzbucher [sic] where we had dragged him. He was not mutilated, and consequently had not been discovered by the Indians or their squaws in their fiendish work of killing and mutilating. . ." (*Troopers With Custer*, Brininstool)

Fact #1322. Crow scout White Man Runs Him, who survived the battle, later wrote a book entitled *E-Sack-Wartee Stories*, which used a coyote to recount Indian folk tales.

Fact #1323. Author Usher Burdick wrote *The Last Battle of the Sioux Nation* in the 1930s.

Fact #1324. Pvt. Slaper (Co. M) just before the valley fight: "Our horses were scenting danger before we dismounted, and several at this point became unmanageable and started straight for the opening among the Indians, carrying their helpless riders with them. One of the boys, a young fellow named [George E.] Smith of Boston [MA], we never saw again, either dead or alive." (*Troopers With Custer*, Brininstool)

Fact #1325. Lt. E.S. Godfrey (Co. K), in *Century* magazine, January 1892: "Many corpses were found scattered over the field between Custer's line of defense, the river, and in the direction of Reno's Hill. These, doubtless, were of men who had attempted to escape; some of them may have been sent as couriers by Custer. One of the first bodies I recognized and one of the nearest to the ford was that of Sergeant [James] Butler of Tom Custer's troop. Sergeant Butler was a soldier of many years' experience and of known courage. The indications were that he sold his life dearly, for near and under him were found many empty cartridge shells."

Fact #1326. Lt. Francis Gibson (Co. H) wrote his wife Katherine Garrett Gibson on July 4, 1876, about LBH. This letter was published in the book, *With Custer's Cavalry: From the Memoirs of the Late Katherine Gibson*, written by Gibson's daughter, Katherine Gibson Fougera (Caxton Printers, Caldwell, Idaho; 1940).

Fact #1327. Dr. Thomas Marquis' published works include *Wooden Leg, a Warrior Who Fought Custer*, *Keep the Last Bullet for Yourself*, and, with Thomas LeForge, *The Memoirs of a White Crow Indian*. The Indians apparently trusted Dr. Marquis and told him things they would reveal to no one else.

Fact #1328. Mark Kellogg, the itinerant frontier newspaperman who accompanied Custer's column as a correspondent for the *Bismarck Tribune* (despite the rule against journalists being with the column), was riding a mule with the Custer column on June 25, 1876, dying not far from the Little Big Horn River. In his journal, he had written: "We leave for the Rosebud [River] tomorrow, and by the time this reaches you, we will have met and fought the red devils, and with what results remains to be seen. I go with Custer and will be at the death."

Fact #1329. Walter S. Campbell, better known through his "pen name" Stanley Vestal, was a distinguished writer about the West, including biographies of such Western figures as Sitting Bull, Jim Bridger, and Kit Carson, and other pieces about the Old West.

Fact #1330. Robert J. Ege, in his book, *Settling the Dust*, credits Dr. Thomas B. Marquis with opening the door to what he called "reliable" Indian testimony with the publication of *A Warrior Who Fought Custer*, the story of Northern Cheyenne warrior Wooden Leg.

Fact #1331. The classic *Legend Into History* by Dr. Charles Kuhlman was published in 1951 by the distributor of *1876 Facts About Custer & The Battle of the Little Big Horn*, Stackpole Books of Harrisburg (PA).

Fact #1332. Lt. E.S. Godfrey (commanding Co. K at LBH) authored an article for *Century* magazine in 1892, "Custer's Last Battle."

Fact #1333. Pvt. Jacob Hetler (Co. D) was interviewed in 1931 for articles in *Winners of the West* in 1931 and 1935. He served at the Reno-Benteen position with Benteen and was wounded in the left leg on June 25 and in the back on June 26.

Fact #1334. On May 2, 1877, the *Bismarck [D.T.] Tribune* reported: "R.N. Price, Robt. E. Cox, late of the U.S.A., classmates of Lt. [Benjamin H.] Hodgson at West Point arrived on Saturday and will proceed on the *Far West* to the Little Big Horn and endeavor to recover the body of Lt. Hodgson, killed in that unfortunate conflict last summer."

Fact #1335. The story of Pvt. Jacob Horner (Co. K) is told in *Jacob Horner and the Indian Campaigns of 1876 and 1877* by Usher L. Burdick and E.D. Hart.

Fact #1336. Author Robert J. Ege reports that Col. William A. Graham, a 35-year student of LBH who was often critical of Custer's actions, commented to Kuhlman on his book *Legend Into History* by saying, "You and your damn' logic."

Fact #1337. *The Sunshine Magazine*, September 1930, published an article by Charles Windolph (Pvt., Co. H), "The Battle of the Little Big Horn," in which he referred to the fatal wounding of Sgt. George Lell (Co. H) at the Reno-Benteen position on June 26, 1876. "A smile came to his face as he saw the beautiful fight the Seventh was making. Then they laid him down and he died soon after."

Fact #1338. Dr. Henry Rinaldo Porter's account of the LBH was published in *Compendium of History and Biography of North Dakota*, 1900. Dr. Porter rode with Reno's battalion and supervised the field hospital at the Reno-Benteen position.

Fact #1339. Civilian scout Charles Alexander Reynolds kept a diary of the 1876 Sioux Expedition, which can be found at the Minnesota State Historical Society.

Fact #1340. *The Sunshine Magazine*, September 1930, carried an article by Daniel Newell (Pvt., Co. M) which told of an exploit by "Crazy Jim" Seivers [sic]: "While the fight was the thickest [in the advance from the hilltop towards Custer's position] one of the pack mules with a load on its back started to leave. He had gone maybe a hundred yards when he was overtaken by a man we called 'Crazy Jim' Seivers [sic] who brought him back. He was exposed to fire of the

Sioux from the minute he started until he got back. I saw this and it was a mighty brave deed but Seivers [sic] never got any medal of honor for it that I know of." James Severs was a private with Company M, who, in fact, was not rewarded for his heroic effort.

Fact #1341. After LBH, 2d Lt. W.S. Edgerly, Co. D, wrote of Pvt. James Wynn: "We had in our troop a corpulent old tailor, known throughout the regiment as 'Jimmy' Wynn, was riding an old horse, blind in one eye, and ordinarily very quiet. The instant he mounted, his horse started for the rear at full speed and one of the most laughable sights I ever saw was 'Jimmy' pulling at the reins with both hands, his carbine dangling at his side, a veritable fat John Gilpin. He wasn't able to stop until he reached the horses of the rest of the command."

Fact #1342. Shortly after LBH, Henry Wadsworth Longfellow wrote a poem, "Revenge of Rain-In-The-Face," which charged the Sioux warrior Rain-In-The-Face with cutting out Custer's heart, and carrying it high as a trophy of the Indian's victory. The story was later modified to say that the Custer heart cut out by the ferocious Sioux was Tom's, not George's. Pvt. Charles Windolph (Co. H), who accompanied the party to the Custer battlesite on June 27, 1876, for the purpose of identifying the slain officers, later wrote: "I saw the body of Tom Custer. . .and must say that the story of his heart having been cut out by Rain-In-The-Face is not so."

Fact #1343. *Men With Custer: Biographies of the 7th Cavalry* by Dr. Kenneth Hammer, edited by Ronald H. Nichols, and published by the Custer Battlefield Historical & Museum Association, Inc. (1995), offers a handy reference on every member of the 7th Cavalry on June 25, 1876, even those on sick leave or detached duty. For serious students, this is a "must-have" book.

Fact #1344. Capt. Frederick W. Benteen came under intense criticism after LBH, along with Maj. Marcus Reno. "Both officers have been vilified by Custer supporters for failing to support the ill-fated battalion, thereby ensuring its ultimate destruction." (*Encyclopedia of American Indian Wars*)

Fact #1345. In *Troopers With Custer* by E.A. Brininstool, William Slaper wrote about Saddler Michael Madden, one of the water carriers' detail who was not awarded the Medal of Honor: "In our venture to the stream, we found Trooper Mike Madden lying in the coulee, shot through the ankle. Mike was a big husky fellow and had accompanied the first detachment [of water carriers]. He lost his leg in the [field] hospital, where it was amputated. An amusing incident happened in connection with it. Before amputating the member, the surgeon gave Mike a stiff horn of brandy to brace him up. Mike went through the ordeal without a whimper, and was then given another drink. Smacking his lips in appreciation, he whispered to the surgeon, 'Doctor, cut off me other leg!'"

Fact #1346. "Early in the morning of [June] 26th [1876] the Sioux got to pressing pretty close to Benteen's company which was guarding the south side of the hill [at the Reno-Benteen position]. Benteen decided to charge and M Company came over from the north to re-enforce him. They charged and drove the enemy back but [Pvt. James J.] Tanner out of my company was badly wounded in the charge. He was carried back to the hospital [by 1st Sgt. John Ryan] and I said to him, 'Poor old Tanner they got you.' 'No,' he gasped, 'but they will in a few minutes.' To this day I choke every time I try to tell of his death." (Pvt. Daniel Newell, Co. M, in the September 1930 issue, *The Sunshine Magazine*)

Fact #1347. An original manuscript by Pvt. Peter Thompson of Co. C, who survived LBH, is in the possession of the North Dakota State Historical Society. A typescript copy, "The Experience of a Private Soldier in the Custer Massacre," is in the LBBNM archives.

Fact #1348. "I had made the trip for water with a young comrade named Jim Weeks. On our way back, Jim was hailed by Capt. Moylan, requesting a drink. I was surprised to hear Jim blurt out, 'You go to hell and get your own water; this is for the wounded.' Nothing more was said but I know this must have been a hard pill for Moylan to swallow." Weeks was not on the list of "water carriers" who received the Medal of Honor in 1878, probably because he deserted in 1877. (Pvt. William C. Slaper, Co. M, E.A. Brininstool's *Troopers With Custer*)

Custer

Fact #1349. "Custer stood alone for an instant after all his men had fallen around him; then killed an Indian as he fell." (Bates, June 20, 1926, column for the *New York Times*' commemoration of the 50th anniversary of the LBH)

Fact #1350. Controversy over whether Custer disobeyed the marching orders given him by Gen. Terry on June 21 centers on two phrases: "The Department Commander [Terry] places too much confidence in your zeal, energy and ability to wish to impose upon you precise orders which might hamper your action when nearly in contact with the enemy," but "desires that you conform to them [Terry's views] unless you shall see sufficient reason for departing from them." Custer did not make the wide sweep called for in Terry's orders, and critics claim he speeded up his march in order to grab the glory before Terry and Gibbon could arrive. Supporters of the Boy General point to incidents during

the march which seemed to show that the Indians had discovered the column, making it necessary for Custer to attack at once to prevent their escape. Terry's, and Custer's, greatest fear was that the Indians would escape.

General Alfred Terry

Generals in Blue

Fact #1351. Railroad executive Walter Camp sought Elizabeth Custer's assistance for his research into LBH.

Fact #1352. "It is very easy for critics to write of Custer, now that he is dead, that he was needlessly rash. But we point with pride to the indications which history gives him. He took more prisoners, more cannon and more rebel supplies during the war than any officers of the army of a command any ways near equal to his, and, more remarkable still, he never lost a gun or a color. This is the first defeat he ever sustained. And it was under the orders of his enemy, Terry. We knew him well, and nobler heart never throbbed." (*Cadiz [OH] Sentinel*, July 13, 1876)

Fact #1353. "Stars of the first magnitude did not appear often in the galaxy of military heroes. Custer was one of the few." Capt. J.H. Kidd, 6th Michigan Cav., at the unveiling of the Custer Equestrian Statue in Monroe (MI) in June 1910.

Fact #1354. W. Donald Horn of West Orange (NJ), a long-time guiding force in the Little Big Horn Associates organization, compiled a book of quotes about George A. Custer in 1981 and published it as *Witnesses for the Defense of General George Armstrong Custer*. Horn has been a leading defender of Custer's image for nearly 40 years.

Fact #1355. "There was a time after the battle of the Little Big Horn when I could not have said this, but as years have passed I have become convinced that the Indians were deeply wronged," the widowed Elizabeth Custer wrote in 1927.

Fact #1356. Information in this book on the aliases of 7th Cavalry personnel came from *Men With Custer: Biographies of the 7th Cavalry*, by Dr. Kenneth Hammer, edited by Ronald H. Nichols, and published by the CBH&MA (1995).

Fact #1357. Adjutant Jacob Green who served in the Michigan Brigade with Custer during the Civil War wrote to author Cyrus Townsend Brady: "Did this man, this soldier, whose service throughout the Civil War and a long career of frontier warfare was for over eighteen years unequaled for efficiency and brilliancy within the range of its opportunities and responsibilities, who never failed his commanders, who never disobeyed an order or deceived a friend—did this man, at the last, deny his whole life history, his whole mental and moral habit, his whole character, and willfully disobey an understood order, or fail of its right execution according to his best judgement; and what is worse—and this is what his detractors charge—did he not only disobey, to deceive his commander who trusted him, in order that he might get the opportunity to disobey?"

Fact #1358. "Custer had been fooled. He thought that the Indian village was in flight; it was not. He thought that the regiment might be facing 1,500 warriors; they faced closer to 4,000. He thought Major Reno would press his attack on the valley floor; he had not. Finally, Custer had sent Captain Benteen the urgent message to hurry to him, and Benteen never came." (Don Horn, *Witnesses for the Defense of General George Armstrong Custer*)

Fact #1359. A self-evaluation of Custer was published in *Custer's Indian Battles*, by Col. Charles Bates in 1936. Custer wrote: "I am not impetuous or impulsive, I resent that. Everything that I have ever done has been the result of the study that I have made of imaginary situations that might arise. When I became engaged in a campaign or battle and a great emergency arose, everything that I had ever read or studied focused in my mind as if the situation were under a magnifying glass and my decision was the instantaneous result. My mind worked instantaneously, but always as the result of everything I had ever studied being brought to bear on the situation."

Fact #1360. Theodore Davis, writing in "With Generals in Camp Homes" in the 1946 *Brand Book* of the Chicago (IL) Corral of Westerners, attributed this comment to George A. Custer: "I should not do all of my duty to allow one of my command to place himself in a position of risk except service to the Government is involved."

Fact #1361. Norman Wiltsey, in his book *Brave Warriors*, claimed that when Gen. Alfred Terry, commander of the Sioux Expedition, identified Custer's body, he stood over the corpse and cried, "Damn him! Damn him!" and "turned away with tears blinding his eyes."

Fact #1362. "Everyone at Fort [Abraham] Lincoln [D.T.] was fond of the general's wife. Libbie [Custer] could not do enough for others. She interested herself in the problems and needs of the troopers' wives and children, and when there was anything of a party going on in officers' circles, she could be counted on to perform minor miracles." (Merrill, *Spurs To Glory: The Story of the United States Cavalry*)

Fact #1363. During the 19th century, the United States Army fought many battles with the Indian tribes of the far West. Outstanding military leaders were involved in these wars, and there were a number of memorable engagements, including some in which sizable bodies of troops were annihilated by their Indian foes. But for the American public, says Kent Ladd Steckmesser in *The Western Hero in History and Legend*, one soldier and one battle have come to symbolize all these campaigns. George Armstrong Custer is the soldier and his "Last Stand" on the Little Big Horn River, June 25, 1876, has become the archetypal Indian fight of the Trans-Missouri West.

Fact #1364. The *New York Herald*, July 13, 1876, published a story about LBH stating that a Sioux warrior named Rain-in-the-Face, who had been arrested by Capt. Tom Custer for murder two years before the Battle at the Standing Rock Agency, had cut out Custer's heart, put it on a pole, and done a dance around it. The newspaper story laid the groundwork for a growing, but untrue, legend.

Fact #1365. The renowned American poet Henry Wadsworth Longfellow published a poem not long after LBH, "Revenge of Rain-in-the-Face," which said, "But the foemen fled in the night, And Rain-in-the-Face, in his flight, Uplifted high in the air As a ghastly trophy, bare The brave heart, which beat no more, Of the White Chief with yellow hair."

Fact #1366. *The Dashing Dragoon, or, The Story of Gen. George A. Custer from West Point to the Big Horn*, was published by Beadle's Boy's Library of Sport, Story and Adventure in New York in 1882, number 36 in the Beadle's Boy's Library.

Fact #1367. The *Chicago [IL] Tribune* of July 7, 1876, evaluated Custer in its editorial on LBH: "Custer. . .was a brave, brilliant soldier, handsome and dashing, but he was reckless, hasty and impulsive, preferring to make a dare-devil rush and take risks rather than to move slower and with more certainty, and it was his own mad-cap haste, rashness and love of fame that cost him his own life, and cost the service the loss of many brave officers and gallant men. . . He preferred to make a reckless dash and take the consequences, in the hope of making a personal victory and adding to the glory of another charge, rather than wait for a sufficiently powerful force to make the fight successful and share the glory with others. He took the risk and he lost."

Fact #1368. Elizabeth Custer joined the "hero makers" club when she published her books *Boots and Saddles* (1885) and *Following The Guidon* (1890), eulogizing her dead husband.

Fact #1369. The final answer to the question, "Did Custer disobey orders?" is "largely one of sentiment." Lt. E.S. Godfrey (Co. K) (*Century* magazine, 1892) answered the charge by pointing out that Gen. Alfred Terry, commander of the Sioux Expedition, had given Custer a free hand. Others disagreed.

Fact #1370. Gen. Nelson A. Miles sprang to Custer's defense after LBH disagreeing with those who suggested that Custer had disobeyed Terry's orders. "I have no patience with those who would kick a dead lion." (*Personal Recollections*, 1896)

Fact #1371. Col. Robert P. Hughes in an article in 1896 in the *Journal of the Military Service Institution of the United States* argued that however permissive and courteous the phrasing of an order, it is still an order. Some discounted Col. Hughes' position because he was Gen. Alfred Terry's brother-in-law, others said that detracted nothing from his logic.

Fact #1372. Custer was an individual whose words and whose actions are often contradictory. Even without the dramatic finale at the Little Big Horn, he would have been a formidable figure in Western legend because he was adept at self-dramatization. He was one of the few articulate frontier heroes. (Steckmesser, *The Western Hero in History and Legend*)

Fact #1373. The Custer saga attracted the attention of motion picture producers, beginning with Col. William Selig's production of a one-reeler entitled "Custer's Last Stand" in 1909.

Fact #1374. In *Custer's Last Campaign*, John Gray offered his theory of the timing of Reno's charge and retreat: the charge began at 3:05 p.m.; after a two mile, 15 minute gallop, the soldiers encountered heavy resistance, halting about 3:18 p.m. A retreat of about one mile, at about 3:53 p.m., brought the survivors to "Reno Crossing" at 4 p.m. (noted by Lt. G.D. Wallace's [Co. G] timepiece). The duration of the halt was about 35 minutes, 15 minutes skirmishing in the open and 20 minutes in the timber. The final half-mile climb to Reno Hill took about another 10 minutes, with the first troops arriving there at 4:10 p.m. (These times, Gray says, only apply to the advance elements of the column; a disorganization spread through Reno's column as time went along.)

Fact #1375. Officers who testified in the 1879 Reno Court of Inquiry in Chicago (IL) "agreed that there was no plan of attack, or if there had been one, it had died with Custer himself." (Steckmesser, *The Western Hero in History and Legend*)

Fact #1376. Dr. Thomas B. Marquis was unable to find a publisher for his third book, *Keep The Last Bullet For Yourself*, which remained unpublished and almost unnoticed for over 40 years. It was rediscovered, and published in 1976, the 100th anniversary of the battle.

Fact #1377. "General Custer on this occasion appeared in a beautiful crimson robe (red flannel *robe de nuit*), very becoming to his complexion. His hair was worn *au naturel*, and permitted to fall carelessly over his shoulders. In his hand he carried gracefully a handsome Spencer rifle. It is unnecessary to add that he became the observed of all observers." (Custer, *My Life On The Plains*) No better self-(word) portrait of Custer can be found.

Fact #1378. The first book out about the Battle of the Little Big Horn was probably Frederick Whittaker's *A Popular Life of Gen. George A. Custer* published in New York in 1876.

Fact #1379. Custer wrote (*My Life On The Plains*) of an experience by Dr. Coates, a physician who had accompanied his column on the Hancock Expedition: "The doctor. . .snuffed the savory odors which arose from the dark recesses of the mysterious [camp] kettle [found in a deserted lodge]. 'I have often desired to taste of the Indian mode of cooking..what do you suppose this is?', holding up a dripping morsel. . . .the Doctor. . .set to with a will and ate heartily of the mysterious contents of the kettle. 'What can this be?'. . .'" The scout Guerrier provided the answer, Custer said. "Fishing out a huge piece. . .he was not long in determining what the doctor had supped so heartily upon. His first words settled the mystery: 'Why, this is dog.'"

Fact #1380. The year 1933 marked the beginning of a new era in the Custer legend, according to *The Western Hero in History and Legend*. "The death of Elizabeth Custer in that year removed restraints upon criticism of the General." Criticism was soon embodied in Frederic F. Van de Water's *Glory-Hunter*, published in 1934, exemplifying "the debunking spirit which affected much of the biographical writing of the period."

Fact #1381. On his scouting mission for the Hancock Expedition in the summer of 1867, Custer and his 7th Cav. had "a detachment of white scouts, or Plainsmen, and one of friendly Indians, the latter belonging to the tribe of Delawares [Lenai Lenape Indians], once so famous in Indian wars." (Custer, *My Life On The Plains*)

Fact #1382. Steckmesser in *The Western Hero in History and Legend*: ". . .it is pretty well agreed that Mrs. [Elizabeth] Custer [the widow] exercised an inhibitory influence upon criticism of the General." She lived until 1933, outlasting almost all of Custer's contemporaries and critics.

Fact #1383. At Fort Riley (KS), the historic home of the United States Cavalry and the U.S. Cavalry Museum, visitors can find Custer's Headquarters, adjacent to the Cavalry Museum. Many of the memoirs written after LBH by Elizabeth Bacon Custer, widow of the fallen commander, center on their life at Fort Riley.

Fact #1384. Libbie Custer's description of the column leaving Fort Abraham Lincoln (D.T.) contained no portent of the tragic outcome of the 1876 Sioux Expedition: "The wagons themselves seemed to stretch out interminably. There were pack mules well laden and the artillery and infantry followed, the cavalry being in advance of all. The column totaled 985 men, including citizens, employees and Indian scouts. As the column passed by the barracks, the band struck up 'The Girl I Left Behind Me'. . ."

Fact #1385. "Exactly what happened after Custer led his battalion into the Little Bighorn Valley is not certain. The enigma of its annihilation spurs students of military history to infinite speculations over exactly why and how Custer met with such a catastrophe. But one thing is certain. By suffering one of the worst defeats in the history of the Indian wars, he won for himself and his regiment an immortality that no victory, however brilliant and decisive, could ever have achieved." (*Soldier and Brave*)

Fact #1386. "Round and round Custer's little band, a Gibraltar of courage, whirled and circled ever nearer and nearer the war-mad Sioux and Cheyenne horsemen, Ogallalas, Brulé and Hunkpapas. Little could be seen of the enemy except flashes of fire from Indian rifles lighting up the dust clouds. But above all the smoke and flame and blinding dust there tossed and tossed the ever rising tide of war bonnets." (Bates, 1926, *New York Times*)

Fact #1387. "As we were about to bury the last of [Custer's] men, we found the body of General Custer on a gravel knoll. He was shot in two places, one bullet having struck him in the right side of his face and passing through to the other side, the other in the right side of his body, passing through to the left side, and which, I understood at the time, one of the soldiers took from his body. Custer was not scalped." (John M. Ryan, 1st Sgt., Co. M, *Hardin [MT] Tribune*, 1923)

Fact #1388. *Our Wild Indians*, written in 1882 by Col. Richard Dodge, argued that Custer's body was not mutilated because Indians never touched a suicide.

Fact #1389. Hardorff, in *The Custer Battle Casualties:* ". . .the top of [Custer's] corpse had turned black from exposure to the sun, while the bottom parts had been reddened by the settlement of blood. Both the chest and the stomach cavities were bloated from the expansion of trapped gases. Decomposition had set in, while the maceration was accelerated by the myriad of flies attracted by the fetid odor. . ."

Fact #1390. As Reno crossed the Little Big Horn near the point where today's Reno Creek empties, and formed his command on the left bank, "Many of the horses had scattered in crossing in their frantic efforts to drink. However no halt was made for watering and a hastily snatched swallow here and there was all the desperately thirsty animals got. Reno had about two-and-a-half miles to cover between the ford and his first position of attack." (Nye, 1941, *Veterinary Bulletin*)

Fact #1391. ". . .the clothes of all the party had been carried away; some of the bodies were lying in beds of ashes, with partly burned fragments of wood near them, showing that the savages had put some of them to death by the terrible tortures of fire. The sinews of the arms and legs had been cut away, the nose of every man hacked off, and the features otherwise defaced so that it would have been scarcely possible for even a relative to recognize a single one of the unfortunate victims. . . .Each body was pierced by from twenty to fifty arrows, and the arrows were found as the savage demons had left them, bristling in the bodies." (*My Life On The Plains*, Custer recalling the discovery of the remains of Lt. Lyman S. Kidder [2d Inf.] and his 10 man patrol, who had been searching for Custer's column near the forks of the Republican River during the Hancock expedition)

Fact #1392. Custer's mission was not a scouting mission, nor was it an attempt to drive a hostile force to a particular, pre-determined site. It was a mission of war, to find and destroy the enemy. (Ege, *Settling the Dust*)

Fact #1393. Bates closed his 50th anniversary commemoration column in the June 25, 1926, *New York Times* by saying: "'The Price of a Battle Won Is Ever a Battle Lost.' It may be that only by such a sacrifice as that of Custer and his men could the Government have been brought to a right policy in dealing with its Indian population. Fifty years have passed since the bluffs above the Little Big Horn heard the whiz of arrows, the crack of rifles and the war cries of charging red men. Still on the hills above that Indian River waves an invisible guidon, the honor guidon of the Seventh, saved by the courage of a regiment which fired its own last proud salute."

Fact #1394. Elizabeth Bacon Custer contributed significantly to the literature inspired by her late husband and LBH that made him famous in American history. Motivated by both the inadequacy of her pension and her strong desire to protect her husband's memory against detractors, she wrote several books about him.

Fact #1395. The literature on Custer and LBH is exceeded in American history only by literature on the Battle of Gettysburg. Whittaker's *A Popular Life of Gen. George A. Custer* (1876) set the standard for later pro-Custer writers. Not until 1934 did debunker Frederic F. Van de Water weigh in with *Glory-Hunter*. Most books are somewhere in between with a slight bias toward pro-Custer. Recent scholarship has focused more on the battle, relying on scientific approaches to the interpretation rather than personalities or "legends."

Fact #1396. The case in Custer's favor, with regard to his "disobeying" Terry's orders, is weakened by his conduct at West Point, in the Civil War, at Fort Wallace (KS), on the Yellowstone Expedition of 1873, and on the Reno scout during the Sioux Expedition. Custer's record offers ample demonstration of his disregard for book regulations. (Steckmesser, *The Western Hero in History and Legend*)

Fact #1397. Estimates by the Indians and the Indian Bureau put the population of the village at LBH at not more than 3,000 people, according to Milligan in *Dakota Twilight*. Not more than 600-800 warriors could be mustered, Milligan said, "including all the able-bodied males fourteen and over." This estimate, he said, "corresponds with the estimates of One Bull, Whitebull, Two Bulls, and other participants in the fight."

Fact #1398. One of the giants of Custeriana is the late W.A. Graham, Col., USA Ret., who, over the years published *The Story of the Little Big Horn* (1926), the first book devoted solely to the battle; *The Official Record. . .of the Reno Court of Inquiry* (1951); *The Custer Myth: A Source Book of Custeriana* (1953); *The Abstract of the Reno Court of Inquiry* (1954); and *Custer Battle Flags* (1974).

Fact #1399. It was "the combination of events that defeated Custer and the 7th Cavalry that day in 1876: 1) the widely accepted idea that Indians would not stand and fight, but would scatter when attacked; 2) Custer's own command style, centered around chasing Indians; and 3) the phenomenon of intellectual vertigo [the brain believing what it wants to believe and not what it is told by its senses]. What if Custer had accepted the evidence of the size of the village? He could have saved his command and his honor by merely following Terry's order to go farther south and to avoid the valley of the Little Big Horn. In the end, Custer did not and could not fully believe his scouts." (Robert Church, 1991 CBH&MA Symposium)

Fact #1400. The best biography of Custer so far is thought by many to be Robert M. Utley's *Cavalier in Buckskin: George Armstrong Custer and the Western Military Frontier* (1988).

Fact #1401. *Custer: The Life of General George Armstrong Custer* by Jay Monaghan was the standard biography of Custer for many years, devoting more attention to Custer's career and less to LBH.

Fact #1402. Dozens of juvenile books, starting with dime novels, have been published over the years about LBH and Custer. *The Western Hero in History and Legend* devotes a whole chapter (15 pages) to these literary efforts. "The components of Custer's world—dogs, horses, uniforms, Indians, battles—are all things which boys understand. . . .Custer clearly stands as a symbol of certain traits which are particularly associated with boyhood: courage, enthusiasm, love

of animals, the enjoyment of physical action. Thus the history of Custer interpretation in dime novels, juvenile biography, and boys' fiction is to some extent
a record of American ideals."

Fact #1403. The *Encyclopedia of American Indian Wars*, by Jerry Keenan,
published in 1997, described Custer as a "fine physical specimen," and said, "A
superb horseman, Custer could spend hours in the saddle and required little
sleep to restore his depleted energy level."

Fact #1404. A *Biography* series program devoted to George Armstrong Custer is available from the A&E Network for $29.95 plus shipping and handling;
1-800-423-1212 (phone).

Fact #1405. W. Donald Horn, past president of the Little Big Horn Associates study group, offered the opinion that, while Custer might not have won at
LBH, he could have avoided defeat. "Custer was badly fooled at the Little Big
Horn. He believed the village was in flight and gambled everything on that
assumption. If Custer knew the village would still be standing and the occupants
full of fight when he reached it, he surely would have kept the regiment together
and all segments of it under his direct command."

Fact #1406. Northrop reported this incident in his 1890s book, *Indian Horrors, or, Massacres of the Red Men*: the young Crow scout Curly, purportedly
with Custer until almost the end, "mentioned one little incident which adds new
lustre to the aureole of glory that already encircles the brow of Custer. [Curly]
said that when it became evident that the party was to be entirely cut to pieces,
he approached the general and begged that he would permit him to show a way
of escape, which his powerful thoroughbred horse could easily have aided him
to accomplish. Custer dropped his head upon his breast. . .in thought. . . He
looked silently at Curly for an instant, then motioned him away with his hand,
and went back to die with his men."

Fact #1407. "The whole story of [Custer's] military life shows a brutal
disregard of the well-being of his men and animals. There can be no doubt that
this contributed, in part, to his tragic end beside the 'Greasy Grass.'" (Nye, April
1941 issue of *Veterinary Bulletin*)

Fact #1408. Elizabeth Custer and Margaret Custer Calhoun, wife of 1st Lt.
James Calhoun (commander, Co. L, LBH) rode out from Fort Abraham Lincoln
(D.T.) on May 17, 1876, accompanying their husbands and the Dakota Column
on the first day's march. The wives spent that first night with their husbands,
then returned to the fort the following morning, as the column moved westward
toward the Little Big Horn.

Fact #1409. One of the best of the recent "popular" histories of LBH is
Wayne Sarf's entry in Combined Books' "Great Campaigns" series, *The Little*

Big Horn Campaign (1993). The narrative is interspersed with informative essays on a variety of relevant topics.

Fact #1410. Commenting on Custer's performance at LBH in the *Encyclopedia of American Indian Wars* (ABC-CLIO, 1997), author Jerry Keenan said, "Contrary to much popular opinion, his [Custer's] judgement as a field commander, especially at the Little Bighorn, does not merit the censure earlier accorded to him, as recent studies have shown."

Fact #1411. Col. Elwood L. Nye (1941 article in *Veterinary Bulletin*), after noting that Custer's scouts had covered from 10-25 miles more than the regular troops, with the possible exception of Varnum and those in Benteen's battalion, stated "Military necessity cannot be urged as the motive for [Custer's] abuse of men and animals. Custer was to have arrived on the Little Big Horn to cooperate with Gibbon on the 26th; instead he reached the objective about 24 hours too soon. Had this additional time been allotted for the marches, men and animals would not have reached the scene of action in the exhausted state which was theirs."

Fact #1412. When Reno's battalion was formed on the left bank of the Little Big Horn, about two-and-a-half miles from his point of attack at the (southern) upper end of the village, he and his men began at a trot, then quickly went to a gallop, pushing the tired horses to their limit. (Nye, 1941, *Veterinary Bulletin*)

Fact #1413. Sitting Bull (*Buffalo [NY] Courier*, 1885) said he had "consented to come and see the great scout and warrior, Buffalo Bill, because he hoped to travel with him and to see the new White Father at Washington (DC), and his long-haired chief from the hot south (referring to Secretary [of War] Lamar)."

Fact #1414. "Controversy has raged more hotly over the battle of the Little Big Horn than over almost any other battle in our history. It became almost a political issue. Custer had aroused the resentment of the Republican Administration at Washington (DC) by his criticism of Secretary of War Belknap. His *War Memoirs* published that year had highly praised General George B. McClellan, and this was regarded as promoting McClellan's chances for gaining the Democratic nomination for the Presidency. Democrats attacked the Republican Administration for its responsibility for the Custer disaster, and Republicans felt impelled to assail Custer to defend the Administration." (June 20, 1926, *New York Times*, Bates)

Fact #1415. "Military experts have long conjectured what might have happened had Custer continued his galloping charge straight through the Indian village instead of halting his men at the river ford. Conceivably, he might have won by staking everything on this daring gamble in the dashing manner of other Custer battles. The Indians themselves admitted after the fight that such a headlong attack would have thrown them into great confusion. Why didn't Custer take that gamble?" (*Brave Warriors*, Wiltsey)

Fact #1416. The life of a cavalry soldier was hard, the rewards were few, and the military capability of the average enlisted man was mediocre at best. (Katcher, *The U.S. Cavalry on the Frontier 1850-1890*)

Fact #1417. "At the foot of this knoll, we dug a grave about 18 inches deep, and laid the body of the General in it. We then took the body of Tom [Custer], and laid him beside the General. Then we wrapped the two bodies in canvas and blankets, and lay them side by side in this shallow grave, and then covered them with earth. We took a blanket from an Indian travois, turned it upside down, put it over the grave, and laid a row of stones around the edge to keep the wolves from digging them up." (John M. Ryan, 1st Sgt., Co. M, *Hardin [MT] Tribune*, 1923)

Fact #1418. Peter Panzieri's *Little Big Horn 1876: Custer's Last Stand* is indispensable to the serious student of LBH. It was published in 1995 as part of Osprey Military's "Classic Battles" series.

Fact #1419. A personal favorite about LBH in the fiction category is *No Survivors* by the late Will Henry (Henry C. Allen), published in 1950. It begins with a marvelous quote: "What happened to Custer that 25th day of June 1876, from the time he disappeared with his 225 troopers into the twisted hills which flanked and straddled Sitting Bull's great war camp on the Little Big Horn, has preoccupied historians ever since. It is at best an endless riddle, for the tongue of silence is the language of the dead, and the only living thing found on the field forty-eight hours later, was Captain Keogh's horse, Comanche."

Fact #1420. The first serious time-and-motion approach to LBH was undertaken by John S. Gray in his *Custer's Last Campaign: Mitch Boyer and the Little Bighorn Reconstructed* (1991). Gray's preceding book, *Centennial Campaign: The Sioux War of 1876* (1976) earned plaudits as the best critique of the activities of Custer's three columns on June 25.

Fact #1421. The ground-breaking study of the Cheyenne was published in 1923 by Yale University Press: *The Cheyenne Indians, Their History and Ways of Life*, two volumes by George Bird Grinnell.

Fact #1422. *The Journal of the Indian Wars*, published by Savas Publishing Company in association with the Order of the Indian Wars, was begun in order to "interpret the American Indian Wars." This quarterly journal will, over time, be the source of much Battle of the Little Big Horn material. Edited by Dr. Michael Hughes, the quarterly can be contacted c/o Dr. Michael Hughes, Managing Editor, 814 East 6th St., Box E, Ada OK 74820; or e-mail at <mhughes@mailclerk.ecok.edu>; 580-436-3089 (phone).

Fact #1423. "The officer ranks of the 7th Cavalry were composed of several competent and capable leaders in one of the most petty and bizarre command climates on record. . . .Custer is reported to have kept strict control. . ." (*Little Big Horn 1876: Custer's Last Stand*, Panzieri)

Fact #1424. Author Daniel Magnussen, in *Peter Thompson's Narrative of the Little Bighorn Campaign 1876*, writes that if any subordinate should be criticized for not going to Custer's aid, it should be Capt. Frederick Benteen and not Maj. Marcus Reno. Benteen had received an order from Custer to take action (Bring the pack train) and made no effort to comply, instead sending the messenger on to Capt. Thomas McDougall, who was in charge of the pack train escort. (McDougall and Lt. Edward Mathey, who was in charge of the pack train, both denied ever receiving the message, although Sgt. Daniel Kanipe [Co. C], the messenger, said he had delivered it.) Then Benteen heard from Custer again, via Trumpeter John Martin ("Bring Pacs!" [sic]) and did nothing. Reno's last communication from Custer, via Adjutant W.W. Cooke, informed Reno that he would be supported by the whole outfit, which didn't oblige him to support action.

Fact #1425. "Some writers have asserted that Custer dismounted his men and fought them intelligently and under orders. . . This is not supported by Indian testimony which declares that he had absolutely no opportunity to give orders or do anything but fight desperately for life after the ambush was discovered." (Robinson, 1904, *History of the Dakota or Sioux Indians*)

Fact #1426. Gen. Nelson A. Miles, later Commanding General of the Army, who, with his 5th Infantry, had joined the Montana Column on June 27, 1876, wrote in *Serving The Republic*, that Terry's "Orders" to Custer were simply a list of "suggestions, advice, at the most, instructions."

Fact #1427. *The Western Edge: Fort Abraham Lincoln and the 7th Cavalry in the 1870s* is a video available from the Fort Abraham Lincoln Foundation, 401 W. Main St., Mandan ND 58554. The Foundation is a private non-profit support organization for Fort Abraham Lincoln State Park near Mandan.

Fact #1428. An "interview" with Sitting Bull was published in the 1885 Buffalo Bill's "Wild West" program: "During the ride out to the driving park, a good opportunity was afforded for holding a second-hand conversation with the veteran redskin, warrior, and statesman. The substance of this conversation carried on between the reporter, aided by Interpreter Halstead and Maj. Burke, and Sitting Bull, was as follows. Asked as to his satisfaction with the journey and its incidents, he said: 'Have much pleasure and much fatigue. Great difference between prairie travel on horse and foot and on the wagons drawn by the vapor horse. Major Burke very kind, all persons very kind. Think all the pale faces feel kind to the Sioux soldier. Believe they know why he held all his braves and all his people to starve rather than submit to what was wrong. . .'"

Fact #1429. "When appraising the historical value of an uncorroborated statement concerned with the battle of the Little Big Horn, it is the part of wisdom to bear always in mind that those diabolical twins, The Great American Faker and the Great American Liar, have been celebrating a continuous Field Day ever since the 25th of June 1876, and that General Custer and his Last Fight have furnished the inspiration for some wondrous and fantastic tales. . ." Col. W. A. Graham, USA-Ret., noted military author and historian.

Fact #1430. "Had [Reno] remained where he was [in a skirmish line in the timber] he would undoubtedly have held a great number of Indians in check. Altho [sic] his numbers were less, his advantages were greater. The grove of timber was not so large but that his men could have defended all of it and by this means engaged a sufficient number of Indians to give General Custer an opportunity to cross over the river and come to his assistance by attacking the Indians in the rear." (Pvt. Peter Thompson with the Custer column) Thompson was almost certainly mistaken.

Fact #1431. "The pale faces want the corn, the trees, the sky," Sitting Bull said (*Buffalo [NY] Courier*, 1885). "[Sitting Bull] only wanted for himself and his people a wide prairie where he could live among his tepes [sic] with his tribe in safety, and that the pale faces should not disturb him, but let him die in peace, and let people bury him undisturbed."

Fact #1432. The Battle of the Little Big Horn "was the sensational moment of truth in the war of the plains, at least for the Americans. It was the kind of humiliating defeat that simply could not be handed to a modern nation of 40,000,000 people by a few scarecrow savages. . . .The Custer defeat was, in effect, the end of the wars of the plains, and Crazy Horse and Sitting Bull lost by winning." (*The American Heritage Book of Indians*, William Brandon)

Fact #1433. In *The Almanac of World Crime*, by Jay Robert Nash, can be found this totally unsubstantiated "fact": The deaths of the Custer command at LBH, "were, in a large way, attributable to cannabis." Nash contends that, after splitting off Benteen and Reno, Custer's column proceeded toward the river along a "sacred" ridge, where the Indians had planted their hemp (cannabis), used to produce "the colorful puberty dreams of apprentice braves." This desecration of the sacred hemp ridge so enraged the Sioux, according to "some Indian tales," that they just killed every one of the soldiers.

Fact #1434. According to a *Buffalo [NY] Courier* news story in 1885, a "thrilling and romantic encounter between redskin and pale face chieftains" occurred at a local railroad depot. "As the Atlantic express over the Lake Shore road pulled into the depot at 3:40 yesterday, there was no evidence that any passenger of particular notoriety was likely to arrive at that time. And yet there came one of the most remarkable figures in the domestic history of the nation during the past quarter of a century. This was no other than the great Sioux warrior, the king of the Dakota Indians, the unconquered commander of twenty battles. 'He is ours. I have captured him. He is Buffalo Bill's guest. But I've had a tough time in getting him here,' said Major Burke to the *Courier* reporter, of his charge, Sitting Bull, Medicine Chief of the Teton Lakota Sioux."

Fact #1435. Daniel O. Magnussen, in *Peter Thompson's Narrative of the Little Bighorn Campaign 1876*, theorized that the order of march for Custer's column, after it divided from Reno's command and ascended the hillside east of the Little Big Horn River, was F, C, E, I, and L companies. Peter Panzieri, in *Little Big Horn 1876: Custer's Last Stand*, further postulates that Custer, at the head of Medicine Tail Coulee, divided the command into two "wings": the left wing, E and F companies, under the command of Capt. George Yates; and the right wing, C, I, and L companies, under Custer's direct command.

Fact #1436. Gen. Alfred Terry, commander of the Sioux Expedition of 1876, "lacked precise military intelligence" in four very significant areas: 1) knowledge of terrain, based on inadequate maps; 2) knowledge of the numerical strength of his enemies; 3) knowledge of the defeat of Gen. Crook's force at the Rosebud on June 17, and Crook's subsequent withdrawal to Goose Creek (W.T.), which effectively removed him from the expedition's strategic and tactical plans; and 4) knowledge of what the Indians would do—would the always unpredictable Indians fight or flee? (Ege, *Settling the Dust*)

Fact #1437. White scout George Herendeen had been temporarily transferred to the 7th Cavalry from the Montana Column, in order to report back to the column regarding Tulloch's Creek, which Custer was supposed to "thoroughly examine" according to Gen. Terry's "orders." Herendeen's statement, published in the January 4, 1878, *Bozeman [M.T.] Herald*: "On the morning of the 24th of June, 1876, we broke camp at 5 o'clock and continued following the [Indian] trail (south) up the stream (Davis Creek). Soon after starting Custer, who was in advance with (Mitch) Bouyer (a half-Sioux scout who was scouting for the 7th Cav.) called me to him and told me to get ready, saying he thought he would send me and Charlie Reynolds to the head of Tulloch's fork to take a look." But he did not report back to Gibbon.

Fact #1438. In an interview for the 1885 Buffalo Bill's "Wild West" program, Sitting Bull told a *Buffalo [NY] Courier* reporter that he was tired, but had enjoyed his trip, and that his escort, Major Burke was "very kind." He said he believed "pale faces respect him [Sitting Bull, the Sioux 'soldier'] for his hard fights and do not wish to hurt him because he had to kill the pale faces when he was fighting. No wish to fight now. Always spoken truth to the pale faces and always been deceived."

Fact #1439. Reading fiction about George A. Custer and LBH is "not only an exercise in historical imagination; it is also an experience in impassioned argument." (Steckmesser, *The Western Hero in History and Legend*)

Fact #1440. ". . .the most astounding military tragedy in the annals of our western frontier warfare was caused by an unbridled collapse of soldier morale resulting in a general self-extinction," Dr. Thomas Marquis wrote in the early 1930s.

Fact #1441. In 1917 in *Red Cloud's Folk: A History of the Oglala Sioux*, George E. Hyde noted: "That the [Sioux] showed no desire to stay and fight Terry was not surprising. They had had enough fighting for one summer. Their defeat of Crook, their great success in the battle with Custer, and the immense amount of plunder they had taken seem to have satisfied them. They had fought hard, and now they wished to be left alone, to dance and feast, to gloat over the plunder, and to quarrel over its division. Occupied with these ideas, they left the Little Big Horn and headed for the mountains, seeking seclusion and a period of freedom from military annoyance."

Fact #1442. "The battles of Little Bighorn and Isandhlwana [in South Africa] bear a number of similarities. In each conflict, armies considered inferior made use of superior tactics, numbers, and in the case of the Sioux, weapons, to crush the adversary. The western armies, in each instance, counted on the military support of indigenous collaborators—the United States relied on Crow, Pawnee, and Arikara scouts. . . Officers divided their commands in each encounter, thus weakening their forces in the face of an enemy of unknown strength and inviting a multitude of retrospective criticism. Finally, in both situations, officers failed to exercise adequate reconnaissance and thereby seriously misjudged the size, strength, location, and temper of the enemy." (*The Dust Rose Like Smoke*, Gump)

Fact #1443. Books on LBH, Custeriana, and the Indian Wars period and people can be obtained through the Custer Battlefield Historical & Museum Assn., Box 902, Hardin MT 59034, or at: www.cbhma.org.

Fact #1444. ". . .the Indian, taught the warlike arts from childhood, was man for man greatly the soldier's superior at scouting, tracking, living off the land, and fighting as an individual. A superb horseman, he might average 50 miles a day while being pursued. . ." (*The Little Bighorn Campaign*, Sarf)

Fact #1445. Pvt. Peter Thompson's (Co. C) version of Reno's charge and subsequent retreat back across the river says Reno, after setting up a skirmish line in the cottonwood timber upstream (south) from the village, ". . .made a blunder. Instead of secreting his men, as he should have done, he ordered them to mount their horses and led a retreat which not only proved fatal to a number of his men, but also to Custer." Of course, in hindsight, one suspects that if Reno had remained in the timber, his command, also, would have been wiped out; the Custer tragedy would have been compounded.

Fact #1446. Sitting Bull, according to *Wild Life On The Plains and Horrors of Indian Warfare*, enjoyed a strategic advantage in his war against the advancing Army in the mid 1870s because of the existence of Indian agencies—Cheyenne Agency, Brulé Agency, Grand River Agency, Standing Rock Agency, Fort Berthold (D.T.) and Fort Peck (M.T.), and several other places in D.T.—"all full of friendly Indians, supported by the government, and ready to join the hostiles in the summer, bringing arms and ammunition with them." The Missouri River "describes nearly a perfect circle around the country of the 'hostiles' and all the Indian agencies are on this river." This is, the book contends, what is meant by the "strategic advantages" of Sitting Bull.

Fact #1447. Out of print, rare, or previously-owned books on Custer and the Little Big Horn can be obtained from the following dealers (among others): Jim Mundie Books, 12122 Westmere Drive, Houston TX 77077, 281-531-8639 (phone); Broken Arrow Books, 3131 Monroe Way, Costa Mesa CA 92626, 714-546-7563 (phone), 714-546-0804 (fax), <maj.reno@prodigy.net> (e-mail); Upton & Sons, 17 Hillcrest St., El Segundo CA 90245, 800-859-1876 (phone), <richardupton@worldnet.att. net >(e-mail). Send them your wants.

Fact #1448. "The Experience of a Private Soldier in the Custer Massacre" was published in 1913-14 by Peter Thompson, Pvt., Co. C, LBH. The account was re-published in 1924. Thompson's manuscript was re-discovered in 1969, and came to the attention of Daniel Magnussen, a one-time seasonal ranger at the Custer Battlefield National Monument. Magnussen researched Thompson's writing, and published it, along with his editorial comment and analysis, in 1974, as *Peter Thompson's Narrative of the Little Bighorn Campaign 1876*, Arthur H. Clark Company, publisher.

Fact #1449. "It is ungracious to attempt to place the blame of this sad event upon any single individual. But after a careful review of the facts it is impossible to avoid the conclusion that there were some to be censured, and that the responsibility for the disaster must be divided. Custer was undoubtedly too rash and intrepid. On the other hand, if Reno had fought with the veteran courage of Custer and his men, and if Benteen had obeyed Custer's orders to hurry forward, it is certain that the day would have been disastrous to the Indians." (Northrop, *Indian Horrors, or, Massacres of the Red Men*)

Environment

Fact #1450. Custer followed his orders precisely up to the evening of June 24, pursuing the trail of the Indians for 72 miles, 70 along the Rosebud, in two-and-one-half days (just under the prescribed 30 miles a day). He was right on schedule. (Gray's analysis in *Custer's Last Campaign*)

Fact #1451. "In a tumult of shouting and in blinding clouds of dust, Custer and his men fought till their last cartridge was gone. A terrible sense of loneliness swept over them. For a soldier to die bravely is one thing: to die calmly and with perfect discipline when he knows himself abandoned is quite another. Custer's men fell company by company as they stood." (Bates, *New York Times*, 1926)

Fact #1452. The cavalry column halted at 2 a.m. on June 25, 1876, in a deep defile close to the "divide" between the Rosebud watershed and the Little Big Horn watershed. "The men built small fires for coffee but the alkaline water was so distasteful the coffee was, for the most part, wasted." (Monaghan, *Custer: The Life of George Armstrong Custer*)

Fact #1453. There is no certainty as to the time Custer's command's participation in LBH ended on the afternoon of June 25, 1876. Indian witnesses have estimated half an hour or less, although other evidence clearly indicates about an hour. "If we accept an hour for the engagement and that it terminated about 4:30 p.m., then Custer's squadron covered about 7 miles of very rough going between 2:30 p.m., (after separating from Reno) and 3:30 p.m., or in about an hour." (Nye, *Veterinary Bulletin*, 1941)

Fact #1454. At the 1879 Reno Court of Inquiry in Chicago (IL), Lt. E.S. Godfrey (Co. K) was the only officer who failed to approve Reno's conduct, characterizing it as "nervous timidity." (*The Western Hero in History and Legend*)

Fact #1455. "Someone failed to do his duty. It may be out of place to criticize, but the duty that Major Reno owed to General Custer is too plain to be misunderstood. According to military rule it was Reno's duty to report to his superior officer, whether he had failed or succeeded in his mission. . ." (Pvt. Peter Thompson, Co. C)

Fact #1456. The famous "lone tepee," which contained the body of a Sioux warrior mortally wounded on June 17 in the fight with Crook's column at the Rosebud, was a landmark remembered by many of the soldiers in the cavalry column advancing toward the Little Big Horn River. The tepee stood on the north bank of Reno Creek opposite the mouth of the South Fork. (*Custer's Last Campaign*, Gray)

Fact #1457. "Major Reno. . .and his troops were soundly beaten [in the valley fight], the major leading a gallant retreat across the river and up the cliffs to a craterlike position which he hoped to defend. The much maligned Reno really had little choice. He was completely outnumbered and the promised support from his commander, the willful and arrogant General George Armstrong Custer, failed to materialize. . . .Custer, in splitting his command, brilliantly failed in his promise to reinforce Reno. And poor Reno spent the rest of his life feebly defending himself as the scapegoat for Custer's impetuousness." (Royal B. Hassrick, former Curator of the Southern Plains Indian Museum)

Fact #1458. "How much better it would have been had [Reno] with his seven companies gone to the assistance of Custer. He would no doubt have been successful and the loss of life would not have been so great." (Pvt. Peter Thompson, Co. C)

Fact #1459. "Terry supposedly set the meeting time of the two columns at the mouth of the Little Big Horn for June 26, yet would call his troops into camp at 5 p.m. on the 24th after barely crossing to the south side of the Yellowstone. Though he started out bright and determined on the morning of the 25th, he would suddenly call for an unscheduled detour over uncharted land that would immeasurably slow his march. What if the Indians had decided to strike at Terry's column, separated and more disorganized on the 25th than Custer's command ever was?" (Barbara Zimmerman, 1991, CBH&MA Symposium)

Fact #1460. "That Reno disobeyed his orders [regarding the scouting assignment] there can be no doubt." (Taunton, "Sufficient Reason," English Westerners Society, 1977)

Fact #1461. The 7th Cavalry's horses were "played out" by the time they reached the Little Big Horn River. ". . .on the day of the battle those who had to walk because they had no horse to ride did not get to the battle in time to get killed." (Milligan, *Dakota Twilight*, 1976)

Fact #1462. In a 1941 article by Col. Elwood L. Nye published in the *Veterinary Bulletin*, Col. Nye offered a "day-to-day evaluation of the uses, abuses, and conditions of the animals" on the Sioux Expedition of 1876. Nye noted that "Custer and Reno's battalions marched over 60 miles from 5 o'clock in the morning of the 24th to approximately 2 o'clock in the afternoon of the 25th, Benteen, upwards of 70 miles and the pack train and its escort over 55 miles, in a period of 33 hours, including halts, with very little sleep or food, hardly any water, and but few oats for the animals." Col. Nye repeated this last quote from *The Custer Tragedy* by Fred Dustin.

Fact #1463. "The 7th Cavalry was under-strength when it started up the Rosebud on June 23; it numbered 31 officers, 566 enlisted men, and 13 quartermaster employees, including five scouts and six packers. There were also 35 enlisted Indian scouts (six Crows, 25 Rees, and four Dakota Sioux). Finally, the presence of news correspondent Mark Kellogg, and Custer's nephew, Autie Reed, brought the strength of the column to 640 officers and men." Most of the regiment's fresh recruits had been detached at the Powder River depot. (*Custer's Last Campaign*, Gray)

Fact #1464. In early June, the camps of the "roamer" Indians who were now deemed "hostile" because they had not returned to the reservation by the Army's January deadline began moving slowly (south) up the Rosebud toward the Little Big Horn.

Fact #1465. War parties from the camps along the Little Big Horn River converged along the Rosebud on June 17, 1876, and engaged Gen. Crook's column from Wyoming in fierce battle. Crook's advance was halted by the battle, and he withdrew his battered troops south to the site of present-day Sheridan (WY), no longer a factor in the Sioux Expedition of 1876. Following the battle, the Indian warriors returned to their camps along the Little Big Horn, to enthusiastically celebrate their "victory."

Fact #1466. If Capt. Frederick Benteen had not taken decisive action to rejoin the rest of the column; if he had, in fact, been where Custer had every reason to expect him to be—scouting the hills and valleys to the left of the main column's advance, his order to rejoin the column, brought by Pvt. John Martin, might have taken many hours to deliver, if Martin was even successful in finding the Benteen battalion. Had this been the case, Reno's command atop the bluffs would most likely have also been wiped out along with Custer's column. Benteen, when Martin arrived with Custer's famed "last message," rode to the sound of the guns, and in so doing, provided support to Reno's shattered battalion atop the bluffs. (Nye, 1941, *Veterinary Bulletin*)

Fact #1467. Author Daniel O. Magnussen's book, *Peter Thompson's Narrative of the Little Bighorn Campaign 1876*, is "A critical analysis of an eyewitness account of the Custer debacle."

Fact #1468. Edgar I. Stewart in *Custer's Luck* stated that Capt. Yates took charge of companies C and E (Yates' own company was F), while Capt. Keogh took charge of I, F, and L, with Custer accompanying. Scholarly disagreements over unknown "facts" speckle the landscape of Custeriana.

Fact #1469. Magnussen, in *Peter Thompson's Narrative of the Little Bighorn Campaign 1876*, proposes the theory that Custer, leading a column consisting of companies C, E, F, I, and L, further split his command in two, sending Capt. George W. Yates along the left (west) side of the long, high ridge east of Weir Point with companies F, C, and E (F was Yates' company), and accompanying Captain Myles Keogh with I and L companies.

Fact #1470. In the 122 years since LBH, there have been many critics of Maj. Marcus Reno and his handling of the attack on the Indian village and the retreat of his three-company (A, G, M) battalion back across the river to the bluffs. One of these critics was Pvt. Peter Thompson (Co. C) who claimed to have seen the entire action, from attack to retreat, from a ridge high above Little Big Horn River, upon which Thompson rode with Custer's column on the afternoon of June 25, 1876. Writing in a memoir published nearly 40 years after the battle, Thompson traced Reno's early action, which ended with a skirmish line at the edge of some cottonwood timber about a mile south of the valley. The skirmish line was formed to await the counterattacking enemy, ". . .who soon appeared in great numbers. The shots were few, and here, to my mind is where Major Reno made a blunder."

Fact #1471. Doane Robinson, Secretary of the South Dakota Department of History, wrote in 1904 in *History of the Dakota or Sioux Indians*, that Reno's men at the Reno-Benteen position began digging rifle pits and barricading the dish-shaped area atop the bluffs which the seven companies (A, B, D, G, H, K, M) occupied on the night of June 25, 1876. "All night the men worked while the Indians held a scalp dance just below them in the valley and in their hearing. By 2:30 a.m. the camp was reasonably prepared for defense, and at that moment the attack of the Indians was renewed with a fury seldom equaled. Every rifle seemed to be handled by an expert and skilled marksman and with a range that exceeded that of the carbines of the cavalry. It was simply impossible to show any part of the body before it was struck."

Fact #1472. Pvt. Peter Thompson, Co. C: "But here [Reno] was, nearly three hours had elapsed since his retreat from the river bottom and during all this time Custer had been fighting against fearful odds; his men melting away; and his ammunition running shorter and shorter every moment until the last round is fired." There is no evidence Custer's command ran out of ammunition. Most historians agree that Custer's main problem was the overwhelming number of Indians he had to contend with.

Fact #1473. While Rain-in-the-Face, Lt. Edward S. Godfrey (Co. H), historian Col. William A. Graham, author Cyrus Brady, and others have said that there was a huge celebration in the Indian camp on the night of June 25, 1876, Wooden Leg, author Stanley Vestal, and others, say there was not. This is among the many disputed points in LBH discussions.

Equipment

Fact #1474. During the engagement at the northern end of the battlefield on the afternoon of June 25, 1876, ". . .many casualties naturally occurred among the animals. Numbers of them, frantic with fear broke away from the horse holders and dashed away to be gathered up by the Sioux. Mute evidence on the stricken field showed plainly that troopers and officers had shot their mounts to form a breastwork behind which the last desperate minutes were passed." (Nye, 1941, *Veterinary Bulletin*)

Fact #1475. Custer was offered a battery of Gatling guns at the Terry-Gibbon meeting on the supply steamer *Far West* on June 21, but declined them, saying these guns, drawn by condemned cavalry horses, would slow the advance of his cavalry. (Camp, *Custer in 76*)

Fact #1476. Most warriors at LBH carried war clubs of one type or another and a bow, some also carried lances. (*Little Big Horn 1876: Custer's Last Stand*, Panzieri)

Fact #1477. Custer has been indirectly responsible for a perplexing question about Colt history: a photograph of Custer's three Indian scouts, taken with him on the Black Hills Expedition of 1874, shows each of the scouts holding Colt Single-Action six-shooters, with 7½" barrels that appear to be nickel-plated. It is not known how many of these Colt SA models were nickel-plated. (*The Saga of the Colt Six-Shooter*, Virgines)

Fact #1478. "The writer does not have the numbers of the horses killed, destroyed, or lost during the [1876 Sioux Expedition] campaign. He does, however, risk the statement that the loss was excessive, far greater than it would have been, had Custer conformed his marches and attack to the plans of [Gen. Alfred] Terry [commander of the 1876 Sioux Expedition]." (Nye, 1941, *Veterinary Bulletin*)

Fact #1479. Custer's Indian scouts were equipped with Colt Single-Action six-shooters. (*Arikara Narrative of the Campaigns Against the Hostile Dakotas, June 1876*, Libby)

Fact #1480. Why didn't Custer accept the offer of two Gatling guns? Design and lack of maneuverability, according to author John S. du Mont (*Custer Battle Guns*). The Gatling gun in 1876 was, in effect, a 10 barrel musket, mounted on a carriage similar to that used by artillery, with a limber and ammunition box. The barrels were cranked by hand like a revolver. It was, in modern terms, a rapid-firing multi-barreled gun with magazine feed.

Fact #1481. Pvt. Charles Windolph (Co. H), giving an enlisted man's view of LBH, said, "It has generally been accepted that all the red warriors were armed with the latest model repeating Winchester rifles and that they had a plentiful supply of ammunition. For my part, I believe that fully half the warriors carried only bows and arrow and lances, and that possibly half the remainder carried odds and ends of old muzzle-loaders and single shot rifles of various vintages. Probably not more than twenty-five or thirty per cent of the warriors carried modern repeating rifles." (*I Fought With Custer*, Robert and Frazier Hunt)

Fact #1482. "Gen. Carlin informs us that he has received through Indians the watch belonging to Lieutenant B.H. Hodgson, 7th Cavalry and two other watches from Sitting Bull's camp. Descriptions of the watches carried by officers or soldiers should be sent by friends to Gen. Carlin to the end that the other watches may be recognized. . ." (*Bismarck [D.T.] Tribune*, November 1876)

Fact #1483. "No less than 56 cases of arms, or 1,120 Winchester and Remington rifles, and 413,000 rounds of patent ammunition went there [to the Indian agencies] on these steamers, besides large quantities of loose powder, lead, and primers. These shipments were all for issue to Indians, through Indian agents or for sale through Indian traders. . . .These shipments, moreover, were as nothing to those of previous years, and especially those of the summer of 1876, when more than a million rounds of ammunition and several thousand stands of arms were sent through." (*Wild Life on the Plains and Horrors of Indian Warfare*)

Fact #1484. The Sioux and Cheyenne were well-armed at LBH, better than the cavalry, having secured rifles from the Chippewa, the Cree, and the Métis who lived near the border of the U.S. and Canada. (Milligan, *Dakota Twilight*, 1976)

Fact #1485. Custer's enemies at the Little Big Horn were armed with over 30 different types of firearms. "Rifles and pistols were objects of great prestige for warriors, but they were considered the least honorable tool for combat." (Panzieri, *Little Big Horn 1876: Custer's Last Stand*)

Fact #1486. The Indians secured all the cavalry horses possible after the destruction of Custer's command on the northern end of the battlefield, and many [horses] were seen later under Sioux riders attacking the Reno-Benteen position. (Nye, 1941, *Veterinary Bulletin*)

Fact #1487. The Indians' advantage regarding arms and military intelligence "can be seen, as first shown in the Yellowstone expedition of 1873. This expedition started from Fort Rice [D.T.] in the summer of 1873, and moved off at a leisurely pace, due west. Indian runners at the same time started off up and down the Missouri to carry the news. Many of them travelled luxuriously by. . .steamers. . . By the time [Gen.] Stanley had reached the Missouri River, every [Indian] agency all along the line of the river was informed of his movements, and parties of warriors on their war ponies, with no burden save arms, ammunition, and food, were starting away from the circumference of the quarter circle [the line of the Missouri River] to find Sitting Bull and have a little fun." (*Wild Life On The Plains and Horrors of Indian Warfare*)

Events

Fact #1488. The best movie based on Custer's Last Stand which did not invoke the name of Custer was the John Wayne/Henry Fonda/John Ford production of *Fort Apache* (1948), available at a video store near you.

Fact #1489. As Custer positioned his battalion for a blow from the east, Reno's battalion attacked the village from the south. Benteen's command, and the pack train, having been diverted when the command was divided, were still coming up. Unfortunately for the Army, LBH did not unfold in a conventional manner. (Hedren, *The Great Sioux War*)

Fact #1490. "As they felt for their last cartridges his men looked in vain for the long line of blue-coated troops which never galloped up. There is no doubt that Custer's men, with dogged courage, fought long and well. Their resistance must have lasted at least two hours." (Bates, June 20, 1926, *New York Times*)

Fact #1491. As Custer's left wing (Cos. E and F) moved down Medicine Tail Coulee toward Minneconjou Ford, there is disagreement as to the extent of the advance. Gall claims that the column was intercepted about a half mile up the bed of the coulee, others claim that the column reached the ford before turning back, still others say the column crossed the river before turning back. Gump, in *The Dust Rose Like Smoke*, says it seems "probable," from the testimony of the Crow scouts who left Custer around 3:15 p.m., that the two companies, led by Custer, were moving down the coulee with the intention of crossing the river into the village.

Fact #1492. Historian Walter Camp addressed the Order of Indian Wars of the United States in January 1920 on "Some of the Indian Battles and Battlefields." He was named the first Honorary Member of the organization, established as a genealogical group for the officers and descendants of officers who served during the Indian Wars era.

Fact #1493. The fate of Custer and his men was not foreordained (Bates, June 20, 1926, *New York Times*): "The issue of the battle was more than once in doubt, according to the Indian accounts. The squaws in the village began to take down the tepees, preparing for flight. At this period of the battle Chief Two Moons [sic] said he could not break the gray horse troop—the company near Custer. Crazy Horse saw his warriors fall before the desperate resistance of Custer's men. He rallied them with the cry: 'Come on, Dakotas! There never was a better day to die.' Sitting Bull, who took no part in the fight, said when he recounted the story he had heard from his braves: 'They [the soldiers] kept in pretty good order. Some great chief must have commanded all the time.'"

Fact #1494. When listing similarities between the 1876 Battle of the Little Big Horn and the 1879 Battle of Isandhlwana (in South Africa), lecturer Terry Karselis told the 1991 CBH&MA Symposium that the white field commanders who were eventually defeated—Custer and Pulleine—appear to have underestimated not only the size but also the fighting ability of the forces which faced them, and further compounded that mistake by fragmenting their immediate commands without knowledge of the enemy's strength and location.

Fact #1495. *Wild Life on the Plains and Horrors of Indian Warfare*, by "a Corps of Competent Authors and Artists," was published in 1891, and purported to tell the American public "A Complete History of Indian Life, Warfare and Adventure in America." "The Whole Forms An Authentic And Complete History Of The Savage Races In America—Their Illustrious Leaders, Their Beliefs, Manners And Customs, Comprising Terrible Battles, Wonderful Escapes, Thrilling Tales of Heroism, Daring Exploits, Wonderful Fortitude, etc., etc." About four pages of this 592-page book are devoted to LBH, but extensive coverage is also given to Sitting Bull and other battles on the Plains between whites and Indians. The book was republished in 1969 by Arno Press, Inc.

Fact #1496. The famed "first scalp for Custer" event stemmed from a fight between Buffalo Bill and a Cheyenne "warchief" forever after known as "Yellow Hand" along the banks of Warbonnet Creek in northern Nebraska, July 17, 1876. Cody dramatized this event for years in his "Wild West" show, not telling his audiences that his translation of the dead Cheyenne's name, Hay-o-wei, was incorrect; the correct name was "Yellow Hair" (which really would have made for a better advertising pitch: He took a scalp for Yellow Hair from Yellow Hair.)

Fact #1497. *Archaeology, History, and Custer's Last Battle*, by Richard Allan Fox, Jr., offers fresh perspectives on LBH based on archaeological excavations and investigations at LBBNM in 1984 and 1985.

Fact #1498. *Indian Horrors, or, Massacres by the Red Men* was published toward the turn of the century and included information on LBH. Written by Henry Davenport Northrop, D.D., it was typical of the florid Victorian prose of the time.

Fact #1499. Speaking to the Order of Indian Wars of the United States in 1920, historian Walter Camp said: "As for the battle of the Little Bighorn, you know that the site has been marked by a monument on which are inscribed the names of the men killed with both Custer and Reno, 263 in all, of whom 207 were killed with General Custer. This was a battle in three fights, the one in which Custer fell and where the monument stands being known as the engagement on Custer ridge. The sites of Reno's fight in the river bottom, where he lost twenty-nine men killed, and on the bluffs where he lost twenty-seven more killed and some sixty wounded, have not been marked but should be. Leaving Custer's part of this fight out of consideration, these two fights under Major Reno were about the hottest affairs of the kind, where the troops got out of it still in shape to fight, that the historians will find opportunity to study."

Fact #1500. In a presentation to the CBH&MA's 1991 Symposium, Terry Karselis pointed out that both the battle in Montana Territory, against the Sioux and Cheyenne, and the battle in what is now South Africa against the Zulu, occurred on warm, dry Sunday afternoons, fought against "savage hostiles" who were the eventual victors.

Fact #1501. Several authors, including Doane Robinson, Secretary of the South Dakota Department of History, in *A History of the Dakota or Sioux Indians*, and Edward A. Milligan in his *Dakota Twilight: The Standing Rock Sioux 1874-1890*, say that Custer's immediate command did not survive half an hour after he first led the attack down Medicine Tail Coulee toward the village.

Fact #1502. If Benteen "and Reno had done their duty, it is quite probable that the Indians could have been held in check until the arrival of General Terry, and the massacre [at the Little Big Horn] would have been avoided." (Northrop, *Indian Horrors, or, Massacres of the Red Men*) This theory was prevalent for several decades after the 1876 battle.

Fact #1503. Custer "had refused to take with him two Gatling guns (the first machine guns) because he thought they were 'uncavalrylike.' The Gatling guns would, beyond doubt, have saved his life. Custer ordered his troops to dismount and fight. This was a fatal mistake, for the Indians stampeded his horses, leaving him afoot and surrounded. And each man had only 100 rounds of ammunition. The Indians apparently waited until the fire slackened, and then attacked." (*Soldiers on Horseback: The Story of the United States Cavalry*, Butterworth)

Fact #1504. "That there were more than ten warriors for every soldier in Custer's column, concentrated directly in his path, and who instantly surrounded him is beyond question. All accounts that the fighting was continued until late in the afternoon are purely speculative and without foundation." (Robinson, *History of the Dakota or Sioux Indians*)

Chapter 5

Facts About the Aftermath

Individuals

Fact #1505. Capt. Holmes O. Paulding, M.D., served in the Medical Corps of the United States Army, and was the only surgeon with the Montana Column in the 1876 Sioux Expedition. He kept a diary with many references to LBH.

Fact #1506. "After Sitting Bull had waited in the hot sun with characteristic Indian patience, word came to his carriage that the great hunter, Buffalo Bill, was ready to meet him. Bull simply grunted his assent, but his eyes twinkled in a very lively manner. Then the carriage moved along the track towards the grand stand. As the Indian chieftain was seen he was loudly and repeatedly cheered. The carriage was suddenly stopped. Up the track, near the grand stand, was seen the tall form of Buffalo Bill standing motionless. Major Burke descended from the carriage, and Sitting Bull, with his interpreter and the *Courier* representative, also alighted. Major Burke went towards Buffalo Bill and shook him heartily by the hand." (1885, *Buffalo [NY] Courier*)

Fact #1507. Seven Medal of Honor recipients are buried at Custer Battlefield National Cemetery.

Fact #1508. "He did not wear his long hair as he used to wear it. It was short but it was the color of the grass when the frost comes. . . When the last stand was made, the Long Hair stood like a sheaf of corn with all the ears fallen around him." (Sitting Bull, quoted in *Custer: The Life of George A. Custer*)

Fact #1509. Capt. Charles A. Varnum, commander of the Detachment of Indian Scouts at LBH, was awarded the Medal of Honor for his conduct at Wounded Knee (SD) in 1890.

Fact #1510. Even though Comanche, Capt. Myles Keogh's horse, was designated as the "lone survivor" of the Battle of "Custer's Last Stand," at least two surviving cavalry horses were found on the battlefield after the battle.

Fact #1511. On July 19, 1876, Capt. Lewis Thompson (Co. L, 2d Cav.) of the Montana Column committed suicide in camp by shooting himself in the heart with a pistol. The brevet major had been suffering from "neuralgia and nervous prostration." He was buried with full military honors.

Fact #1512. The body of 2d Lt. John J. Crittenden (Co. G, 20th Infantry, temporarily assigned to Co. L, 7th Cavalry), which had been buried on the battlefield immediately after the battle, was not removed to the mass graves in 1881, at the request of his family, but was left in its original resting place until 1931, when it was exhumed and buried in CBNC.

Fact #1513. In a July 15, 1876, story in the *Helena [M.T.] Herald*, Lt. James H. Bradley, 7th Infantry, Montana Column, was interviewed about his discovery of Custer's fallen soldiers: "It would be in place at this juncture to state that Lieut. Bradley, with his [Indian] scouts, on the morning of the 27th of June, crossed to the opposite [east] side of the Little Horn [sic] from which the command was searching, and deployed out through the hills in a skirmish line," where they found the bodies of Custer's command.

Fact #1514. Two of the founding members of the Custer Battlefield Historical & Museum Association in 1953 were Mike Reynolds and George Osten, both of whom had attended the 1926 Semi-Centennial Observance. Nationally-known artist J.K. Ralston, lifelong Custerian student John A. Popovich, and Stella Foote and her son John, possessors of one of the great collections of Western artifacts in the world at that time, were also members, as were Joe Medicine Crow, a respected tribal leader, and Don Rickey, Jr., a former Custer battlefield historian and a leading writer on the history of the Army in the West.

Fact #1515. As Buffalo Bill and Sitting Bull approached their first meeting, a reporter from the *Buffalo [NY] Courier* was there. Maj. Burke, Sitting Bull's traveling companion and "warden," approached Cody: "'I am here, governor. I've got him. Come and shake hands. He's a fine fellow. See, he is coming.'Cody hesitated for a moment. At this time Sitting Bull who had advanced several paces, also halted. There was a strange pause and then the famous redskin and the equally noted white hunter, pressed by the interpreter and Major Burke, advanced, and Buffalo Bill, drawing himself up and assuming a very striking and really handsome pose, stuck out his hand to the redskin warrior."

Fact #1516. According to an interview in the *Helena [M.T.] Herald* on July 15, 1876, Lt. James Bradley, 7th Infantry, Montana Column, scouted with his Indians on the morning of June 27, 1876, seeking Custer's command. As he rode over a rise, he spied a large number of "white" objects, which turned out to be dead cavalrymen. "Lieut. Bradley rode hurriedly over the field, and in a few minutes time counted one hundred and ninety-seven dead bodies."

Fact #1517. Comanche, Capt. Myles Keogh's horse, which was known as the "lone survivor" of the "Custer Massacre," was nursed back to health at Fort Abraham Lincoln (D.T.) and placed on the retired list by regimental order. No person was allowed to ride or work the horse, which was saddled, bridled, and paraded at every ceremony of the 7th Cavalry regiment.

Fact #1518. Cpl. Bernard McCann (Co. F, 22d Inf.) was awarded the Medal of Honor for "conspicuous gallantry and meritorious service" at Cedar Creek, Redwater Creek, and Wolf Mountain (M.T.), engagements fought between October 1876 and January 1877 under General Nelson Miles. He is buried at CBNC.

Fact #1519. After LBH, Capt. Frederick W. Benteen (Commanding, Co. H) engaged in the Nez Perce campaign of 1877, and commanded a battalion against hostile Indians in 1878.

Fact #1520. Sgt. Wendelin Kreher (Co. C, 5th Inf.) was awarded the Medal of Honor for "conspicuous gallantry and meritorious service" at Cedar Creek, Redwater Creek, and Wolf Mountain (M.T.), engagements fought between October 1876 and January 1877 under Gen. Nelson Miles. He is buried at CBNC.

Fact #1521. In his 1885 article (*Buffalo [NY] Courier*) the reporter also wrote about the interpreter who traveled with Sitting Bull on his journey to the East to join the "Wild West" show and the government agent assigned to Sitting Bull in New York: "The interpreter, William Halstead, is a quiet, intelligent half-breed, and is implicitly trusted by Sitting Bull, as also is Paul Blum, the government agent who accompanies him here."

Fact #1522. In 1895, Capt. Charles A. Varnum (Co. A, LBH, in command of the Detachment of Indian Scouts) was placed on detached service and detailed as Professor of Military Science at the University of Wyoming in Laramie until the opening of the Spanish-American War in 1898.

Fact #1523. After the Little Big Horn, both Capt. Myles Moylan (Co. A) and 1st Lt. E.S. Godfrey (Co. K) participated in the campaign against the Nez Perce in 1877 and were severely wounded in the battle of Snake Creek near the Bear Paw Mountains (M.T.). Both received the Medal of Honor for gallantry in action.

Fact #1524. The two officers who fought at LBH who are now interred at the Custer Battlefield National Cemetery are Marcus A. Reno (Maj.), second-in-command of the 7th Cavalry at the Battle, and 2d Lt. John J. Crittenden (Co. L).

Fact #1525. The Custer Battlefield Historical & Museum Association was founded in 1953, at a time when Custer Battlefield was a quiet, almost sleepy outpost of the NPS. Among the members were Mike Reynolds, whose father had been the agent at Crow Agency in the early 1900s; Edwin C. Bearss, who grew up within a few miles of the Battlefield and later became the Chief Historian of the National Park Service; Col. Elwood L. Nye and R.G. Cartwright, of Nye-Cartwright Ridge (a significant landmark in battlefield interpretation) fame; "Slim" Kobald, owner of much of the Rosebud Battlefield; Mrs. Evelyn Luce, wife of the most famous superintendent of the Battlefield, E.S. Luce; and Don Russell, one of the founders (in 1940) of Westerners International, which began with the Chicago (IL) Corral. Plus, it had more American Indian representation than the organization would ever have again.

Fact #1526. Capt. William Logan (Co. A, 7th Inf.) was awarded the Medal of Honor for heroism at the Battle of the Big Hole (M.T.). He is buried at CBNC.

Fact #1527. Following Sitting Bull's introduction to the crowd at Buffalo Bill's "Wild West" show, which the Sioux chief joined in Buffalo (NY) in the summer of 1885, Cody and Sitting Bull went for refreshments and dinner with the Sioux [warriors who were] already a part of the show. The *Courier* reporter wrote: "[Dinner] was followed by a curious meeting between the newly-arrived Sioux and Pawnees, and other Indians in camp. At first there appeared to be a sort of hesitancy or jealousy, but this seemed to wear off, and Sitting Bull was the recipient of a large amount of hero worship from those of his own race."

Fact #1528. Thomas Custer (Capt., Co. C), James Calhoun (1st Lt., Co. L), Algernon Smith (1st Lt., Co. E), and George Yates (Capt., Co. F) all of whom died with Custer at the Battle of the Little Big Horn, are buried at Fort Leavenworth National Cemetery (KS).

Fact #1529. Two Moon, one of the Cheyenne war leaders at LBH, lived until 1917.

Fact #1530. The Montana Column rode (south) up the Little Big Horn Valley on the morning of June 27, 1876, and discovered an abandoned Indian camp, then the abandoned Indian village along the river. (Dr. Paulding's *Surgeon's Diary*)

Fact #1531. Crow Indian scout Curly (Curley) served in the Detachment of Scouts for six months and was discharged September 1876.

Curley, a Crow Indian, served as a scout for the army at Little Big Horn

Fact #1532. After LBH, Lt. Winfield Scott Edgerly (Co. D) was promoted 1st Lt. and served on frontier duty until 1883 when he was sent to Cincinnati (OH) for recruiting duty.

Fact #1533. Cpl. John Haddo (Co. B, 5th Inf.) was awarded the Medal of Honor for "conspicuous gallantry and meritorious service" at Cedar Creek, Redwater Creek, and Wolf Mountain (M.T.), engagements fought between October 1876 and January 1877 under General Nelson Miles. He is buried at CBNC.

Fact #1534. Maj. Marcus Reno, by virtue of his Civil War Brevet Brigadier General (Volunteers) rank, is the highest ranking officer buried in the Custer Battlefield National Cemetery, and one of only two 7th Cavalry officers buried there.

Fact #1535. On the day he first joined the Buffalo Bill "Wild West" show in Buffalo (NY) Sitting Bull was introduced by Cody to the large crowd awaiting his arrival; then the two had dinner with other Indians in the show, and later Sitting Bull was introduced to the new Indian members of the cast, with good results. (*Buffalo [NY] Courier*)

Fact #1536. In 1902, Winfield Scott Edgerly (a 2d Lt. at LBH, now a Lt. Col. 7th Cavalry) was promoted Col., 2d Cav., and took the regiment to the Philippine Islands.

Fact #1537. Maj. Reno's remains were buried for 78 years in a pauper's grave in Washington (DC) before being reinterred at CBNC.

Fact #1538. As Sitting Bull and Buffalo Bill clasped hands, a large audience of spectators and "Wild West" show performers looked on. So did a Buffalo (NY) reporter from the *Courier*: "Buffalo Bill and Sitting Bull vigorously grasped and both seemed to say to the other, 'I can trust you.'"

Fact #1539. After LBH, 1st Lt. Edward S. Godfrey (Co. K) participated from October 15-November 16, 1876, in an expedition "to disarm and dismount" agency Indians.

Fact #1540. Medal of Honor recipient Richard P. Hanley (Sgt., Co. C), who was in the pack train escort at the Reno-Benteen site, retired as a Sgt. and lived in Boston (MA) for many years.

Fact #1541. In his *Surgeon's Diary*, Dr. Holmes O. Paulding told of coming upon the abandoned Indian village along the Little Big Horn River on June 27, 1876: "The camp [of two tepees and many bare lodge poles] covered thickly a valley at least 4 miles square. . .I think that 1900 lodges was not much of an over-estimate for this village."

Fact #1542. After LBH, 2d Lt. Luther Hare (Co. K) was promoted 1st Lt. in Co. I and was engaged in the 1877 Nez Perce campaign.

Fact #1543. Sgt. Aquila Coonrod (Co. C, 5th Inf.) was awarded the Medal of Honor for "conspicuous gallantry and meritorious service" at Cedar Creek, Redwater Creek, and Wolf Mountain (M.T.), engagements fought between October 1876 and January 1877 under General Nelson Miles. He is buried at CBNC.

Fact #1544. Telling the story of Frisking Elk, one of Sitting Bull's companions in Buffalo Bill's "Wild West" show in 1885, a Buffalo (NY) reporter for the *Courier* wrote about Frisking Elk being severely wounded by a cavalry patrol, "but he stoically endured the fatigues of a journey of 126 miles on a travoix before he reached Standing Rock, where his right leg was amputated by Dr. Quinlan. Though he now only has one leg, he is one of the best horsemen of the Sioux nation."

Fact #1545. "A History of Sitting Bull" was published in the program for Buffalo Bill's "Wild West" in the 1885 season: "Tatonka-i-Yotanka (Sitting Bull), a Huncpapa Sioux, was born on the Missouri near Grand River in 1830. In early life he was noted as a hunter and a warrior, and in early middle age he gained prestige as a Medicine Man (the Sioux order of priesthood) and Counselor. . ." Sitting Bull was a great draw for Cody's extravaganza.

Fact #1546. Sgt. James Fegan (Co. H, 3d Inf.) was awarded the Medal of Honor for single-handedly fighting off a group of desperados trying to free a deserter. Sgt. Fegan was serving on the escort detail for a powder train and some deserters. He shot two of the desperados, put the others to flight, and brought the train and prisoners to safety. He is buried at CBNC.

Fact #1547. During an 1885 interview with the *Buffalo [NY] Courier* as he was about to join Buffalo Bill's "Wild West" show, Sitting Bull said "the Great White Fathers had not helped him or his people, who were being pushed across the prairies and must perish with hunger among the barren mountains."

Fact #1548. Christian Barthelmess, an immigrant from Bavaria, is buried at Custer Battlefield National Cemetery.

Fact #1549. Pvt. Charles Windolph (Co. H), the last survivor of those who fought at the Reno-Benteen position, pointed out the places where Pvt. Thomas Meador (Co. H) and Pvt. Julien Jones (Co. H) were killed. Remains unearthed in that general area in 1958 point to the probability that those two were buried in the trench line on July 26, 1876, and their bodies were not recovered by contemporary burial parties.

Fact #1550. In an 1885 *Buffalo [NY] Courier* article, the reporter described Sitting Bull's "costume" in some detail: "His pantaloons were of buckskin neatly trimmed with blue and white beadwork, and his feet were encased in moccasins trimmed with porcupine work tastefully colored. In his hand he carried a long calumet trimmed with ribbons and decorated with porcupine mosaic work. He also had with him a bow and arrows in buckskin cases trimmed with beads and porcupine work."

Fact #1551. Sgt. Thomas Kelley (Co. I, 5th Inf.) was awarded the Medal of Honor for gallantry in action at Upper Wichita (TX) on September 9, 1875, and is buried at CBNC.

Fact #1552. Capt. William Judd Fetterman is buried at CBNC, along with most of the men who died with him on December 21, 1866, in what has become known as the Fetterman Massacre (W.T.).

Fact #1553. 1st Lt. John C. Jenness is buried at CBNC. He was a member of the garrison at Fort Phil Kearny (W.T.) shortly after the Civil War, and was second in command at the Wagon Box Fight (W.T.) August 2, 1867.

Fact #1554. Maj. Marcus A. Reno, Custer's second-in-command, blamed for Custer's defeat, and plagued by charges of cowardice, dereliction of duty, and disobeying orders, requested a Court of Inquiry which was held in Chicago (IL) in 1879. Although he was cleared of all charges, the criticism continued. Former friends kept their distance to keep from being associated with a man still under a cloud of suspicion.

Fact #1555. Curly, a Crow Indian and one of Custer's scouts at LBH, is said to have watched the battle from a distant ridge. When he arrived at the steamer *Far West* the next day, there was great interest in Curly's story, but since he spoke no English, his words may have been shaped by what his listeners wanted to hear.

Fact #1556. Goes Ahead, a Crow scout with the Custer column, is buried at CBNC. He was married to Pretty Shield, who was the subject of a biography by that name.

Fact #1557. Clothing belonging to two 7th Cavalry officers whose remains were never found were discovered by Surgeon Holmes O. Paulding, who described the finds in his *Surgeon's Diary*. "I picked up a buckskin shirt from which the skin had been stripped, marked PORTER. Poor fellow, there was a hole under the right shoulder & blood over the rest. Found 'Yates 7th Cav.' marked on a pair of gloves - underclothing of Jack Sturgis, with his spurs, & traces of other old friends of that gallant regiment."

Fact #1558. The reporter for the *Buffalo [NY] Courier* in 1885, after Sitting Bull joined Buffalo Bill's "Wild West" show, wrote that "The warriors with Sitting Bull have strong peculiarities. Perhaps the most noteworthy is Crow Eagle, who has known Bull from his youth up. He is so doggedly attached to him that three years ago he left his wife and family at Popular Creek and insisted on remaining with the Sioux chieftain at the Standing Rock agency, and could not be induced to leave him when he started his eastern trip."

Fact #1559. White Man Runs Him, a Crow scout assigned to the Reno battalion, is buried at CBNC. He survived the valley fight and the action at the Reno-Benteen position and, with White Swan, joined Gibbon's column, then returned to Crow Agency in western Montana (not the present town near the battlefield).

Fact #1560. Vincent Charley, a native of Switzerland and a farrier (horseshoer) for Co. D, KIA at LBH, is buried at CBNC.

Fact #1561. Pvt. John Burkman (Co. L and Custer's orderly) is buried at Custer Battlefield National Cemetery.

Fact #1562. According to He Dog, the aged Sioux war chief interviewed by Eleanor Hinman in 1930 at Oglala (SD): "It was many years after our first battles before we were made chiefs. A man had to distinguish himself in many fights and in peace well before he could be chosen as a chief."

Fact #1563. When Sitting Bull traveled to New York in 1885 to join Buffalo Bill's "Wild West" show, "His black hair was braided in long scalplocks, with two main plaits twined with strips of otter skin. Around his neck was a large brass chain from which depended a crucifix." (*Buffalo [NY] Courier*)

Fact #1564. Cpl. John Noonan (Co. L) is buried at Custer Battlefield. Noonan was not at LBH, being on detached duty at the Yellowstone Depot. He was married to a Mrs. Nash, a post laundress who had a succession of soldier husbands. In October 1878, Mrs. Noonan died, and when the ladies of the post prepared the body for burial, they discovered that Mrs. Noonan was a man. Noonan suffered so much scorn and ridicule that he shot himself with a rifle on November 30, 1878.

Fact #1565. "Frisking Elk has long been one of Sitting Bull's most sagacious and reliable spies. He was several times captured by the government troops and escaped. On one occasion he was surrounded and refusing to surrender was fired at simultaneously by an entire squadron of cavalry under Major Galbraith. His horse was killed instantly and sadly riddled. Frisking Elk was terribly wounded." (*Buffalo [NY] Courier*)

Fact #1566. Lt. J.J. Crittenden (2d Lt., 20th Inf.) is buried at Custer National Battlefield. Assigned to Co. L, 7th Cav., for the Sioux expedition, he died with Custer's men, was buried where he fell, and was left there at the request of his father. In 1932, the Army routed the road along Custer Ridge and Calhoun Hill, so Crittenden's remains were moved to the National Cemetery. Some believe the road was the excuse for the Army policy of not having scattered graves on the battlefield.

Fact #1567. White Swan, a Crow scout assigned to Reno's battalion, is buried at CBNC. One of the least publicized of the scouts, White Swan expressed himself about the battle through "ledger art" that appears in prestigious galleries around the country, including the Smithsonian.

Fact #1568. Margaret A. Littlejohn is buried at CBNC. Of all the women on a frontier Army post, only the laundresses were accorded official recognition. Even officers' wives had no official status. Laundresses, however, were provided fuel, rations, housing and medical services, in addition to the money they received for their labors. Despite the material rewards, the laundresses gave more than they received by providing homes for their families, nursing the sick, and helping others in time of need. Margaret Littlejohn died in 1872 at the age of 36 at Fort Buford (D.T.). As a lasting expression of their esteem, the soldiers had her headstone inscribed, "Laundress for Co. I, 6th U.S. Infantry."

Fact #1569. "I and Crazy Horse were born in the same year and at the same season of the year. We grew up together in the same band, played together, courted the girls together, and fought together. I am now 92 years old, so you can figure out in what year he was born by your calendar. When we were 17 or 18 years old we separated. Crazy Horse went to the Rosebud [Brulé] band of Indians and stayed with them for about a year. Then he came home. After he had been back awhile, I made inquiries about why he had left the Rosebud band. I was told he had to come back because he had killed a Winnebago woman." (He Dog in interview, June 1930, by Elizabeth Hinman, with Thomas White Cow Killer acting as interpreter) The woman was presumably killed in sight of the fighting men of her tribe, acceptable to Oglalas, not so to Brulé.

Fact #1570. Watching the dramatic moment in 1885 when Sitting Bull and Buffalo Bill met for the first time, prior to the Sioux chief joining the "Wild West" show, a *Buffalo [NY] Courier* reporter was there: "They grasped hands. For several seconds they eyed each other. It was truly a dramatic spectacle and entirely unrehearsed in its striking effects. Drawn up at the inner fence opposite the grand stand were all the Indians, Mexicans, and cowboys of the 'Wild West' show; the outside of the track was lined with carriages, and the grand stand as well as the space a long distance along the stretch was crowded with spectators, all watching with breathless interest the novel and interesting interview."

Fact #1571. Two Whistles, a member of a band of insurgent Crows under the Crow prophet Swordbearer, is buried at CBNC.

Fact #1572. Pvt. Frank Braun (Co. M) is buried at CBNC. He has the dubious distinction of being the last soldier to die from wounds received at the Battle of the Little Big Horn.

Fact #1573. Oglala war chief Low Dog told Gen. Nelson A. Miles in 1878, "If Reno and his warriors had fought as Custer and his warriors fought, the battle might have [gone] against us." (Gump, *The Dust Rose Like Smoke*)

Fact #1574. After Sitting Bull's introduction by William F. Cody to the huge crowd gathered at Buffalo Bill's "Wild West" show in Buffalo (NY) in 1885, "Buffalo Bill and Sitting Bull then entered a carriage and were driven to the new club house where they were followed by the rest of the Dakota party of Indians," wrote the *Courier* reporter from Buffalo. "After resting there a while and partaking of very modest refreshments in the form of pop and sandwiches, the whole party adjourned to the camp, where a hearty dinner was served. Sitting Bull ate very moderately, but Crow Eagle, Crow's Ghost, and Iron Thunder disposed of truly enormous quantities of broiled steak, potatoes, coffee, and bread."

Fact #1575. "Custer's Last Lieutenant" was Charles Albert Varnum, whose Army career spanned more than 50 years of our nation's history. Jay Kanitz noted in a paper for the CBH&MA Symposium in June 1991, "[Varnum] was born in 1849, during the California Gold Rush, and he died in 1936, just as the United States was preparing for the Axis threat of World War II. . . .he died in San Francisco, California, at age 86."

Fact #1576. Several Indians who had known the Oglala Sioux war leader Crazy Horse were interviewed in 1930 by Elizabeth H. Hinman, a stenographer at the University of Nebraska who was studying Crazy Horse's life. Miss Hinman, 30, was accompanied by Mari Sandoz, then 36, who had at this time written nothing about Indians, and by Helen Blish, a Lincoln (NE) friend who had interviewed elderly Sioux for her graduate thesis. They employed John Colhoff, a professional interpreter for the Pine Ridge Agency. Hinman's interviews, taken on the Pine Ridge and Rosebud Sioux reservations in South Dakota, were given to the Nebraska Historical Society.

Fact #1577. At the Court of Inquiry held in 1879, Capt. Frederick Benteen testified, "When I received my orders from Custer to separate myself from the command, I had no instructions to unite with Reno or anyone else. There was no plan at all. . . If there had been any plan of battle, enough of that would have been communicated to me so that I would have known what to do under certain circumstances. In General Custer's mind there was a belief that there were no Indians and no village." The fact that Custer did not send a surgeon with Benteen's column may have meant that Custer didn't expect Benteen's men to see any action.

Fact #1578. In his *Surgeon's Diary*, Dr. Holmes O. Paulding, the only surgeon with the Montana Column, wrote on June 27, 1876: "[Lt.] Bradley [Chief of Scouts, 7th Inf.] found the bodies of 200 & over soldiers on the bluff opposite the main village, among them [Lt. Col. George] Custer, [Capt. Myles] Keogh [Co. I], [Lt. Algernon] Smith [Co. E], [1st Lt. William W.] Cooke [HQs Adjutant], [Capt.] Tom Custer [Co. C], Bos [Boston] Custer [civilian, brother of

George and Tom], [1st Lt. James] Calhoun [Co. L], [2d Lt. Henry Harington] Harrington [Co. C], Dr. [1st Lt., Asst. Surgeon, Edwin] Lord [HQs], [Lt. James] Porter [Co. I]. . ." (Lord, Porter, and Harington, as well as Capt. George Yates [Co. F], were missing; the remains of Porter and Harington were never recovered. Several enlisted men were also missing.)

Fact #1579. "Ladies and Gentlemen: To me this hour is a most peculiar one, as on your beautiful fair grounds [in Buffalo (NY)] I meet a warrior whom I, backed by the active army forces of the government, sought a personal conflict with in the campaign of 1876, but he evaded us most successfully. Without egotism, I can point with pride to my own record, if you will excuse the use of the only phrase I know to explain it, as an Indian fighter; but I have never been insensitive to the abstract rights that civilization, as our progress is called, has perhaps unconsciously trodden upon, and in time of peace, I am strongly the red man's friend." (William F. Cody's introduction of Sitting Bull in 1885 at Cody's Buffalo Bill's "Wild West" show)

Fact #1580. Col. John Gibbon, commander of the Montana Column, personally discovered the body of newspaperman Mark Kellogg on the morning of June 29, 1876, near the river, away from the main group of slain soldiers on the hills.

Fact #1581. Dr. Henry R. Porter (HQs) was with Reno's battalion, tending to the wounded at the Reno-Benteen position. He was the only surgeon among the three doctors with the 7th Cavalry to survive the battle. 1st Lt. Edwin Lord, an assistant surgeon, was with Custer's command, and Dr. James M. DeWolf also rode with Reno and was killed during the retreat to the bluffs, being scalped in view of other Reno survivors who made it to the top of the hill.

Fact #1582. Dr. Holmes O. Paulding wrote in his *Surgeon's Diary* for June 27, 1876, after arriving at the site of the Custer battle, "Custer had lost the whole of his 5 cos. & his staff. Went up with [Dr. John W.] Williams [chief medical officer, Dakota Column] to Reno's position on the bluffs and helped [Dr. Henry R. Porter] with his wounded—50—Lts.[Benjamin] Hodgson [Reno's adjutant] & [Donald] Mcintosh [Co. G] were lost with 41 men from Reno's. Custer's battalion lost about 210 men & 14 officers, besides 3 or 4 of the wounded died subsequently within a few days."

Fact #1583. The Sioux war chief He Dog, interviewed by Elizabeth Hinman in 1930 at Oglala (SD) talked about Crazy Horse's name: "Less than a year after Crazy Horse left [the Oglala] camp, I joined in a trip against the Crow Indians. When I got home, the crier was announcing that Crazy Horse was back in camp. Only his name was not Crazy Horse at the time. He had three names in different times of his life. His name until he was about 10 years old was Curly Hair. Later, from the time he was 10 until the time he was about 18 years of age, he was called His-Horse-on-Sight, but this name did not stick to him. When he was about 18 years old there was a fight with the Arapahos. . .although he was just a boy he charged them several times and came back wounded with two. . .scalps. His father—whose name was Crazy Horse—made a feast and gave his son his own name. After that the father. . .was called by a nickname, Worm."

Fact #1584. Gen. Nelson A. Miles, who, with his 5th Infantry, joined the Montana Column shortly after LBH, offered this succinct comment on the "mysteries" of the Little Big Horn: "No commanding officer can win victories with seven-twelfths of his command remaining out of the engagement when within the sound of his rifle shots."

Fact #1585. One "Colonel" Alvarez Allen made an agreement with Sitting Bull that he would see to it that the chief got to talk to the Great White Father in Washington (DC), if he would agree to appear on a tour of 15 U.S. cities in 1884. But Allen didn't keep his end of the bargain. He carted the chief around the country as "the slayer of General Custer," and as Sitting Bull, who spoke no English, greeted his audiences in Sioux, Allen interpreted his friendly words as a lurid description of how the Sioux had destroyed the Army at the Little Big Horn.

Fact #1586. Most of the officers who testified at the Reno Court of Inquiry in Chicago (IL) (1879) agreed that Reno's retreat to the bluffs, although badly managed, had undoubtedly saved the lives of what was left of the regiment. (Steckmesser, *The Western Hero in History and Legend*)

Fact #1587. With the death of Sitting Bull, "The dying embers of the Seven Council Fires had been extinguished, and the death knell of the Sioux Nation had been sounded." (*Dakota Twilight*, Milligan)

Fact #1588. The story of the Crow scout Curley escaping from the Last Stand by disguising himself in a Sioux blanket (on a cruelly hot day) is, according to Col. W.A. Graham, a learned authority on the battle, ludicrous. Graham said, "A Crow amongst the Sioux would be about as inconspicuous as a man in white tie and tails among a crowd of one piece bathing suits."

Fact #1589. After LBH, Capt. Thomas McDougall, who had commanded Co. B, the pack train escort, remained in the 7th Cav. until he retired for disability June 1890.

Fact #1590. Thomas Francis McElroy was born in March 1874, just 16 months before his father, Trumpeter Thomas McElroy, was killed with Co. E at LBH. The widow later married John Furey (Co. E, 7th Cav.) and the boy took his stepfather's name, becoming known as Thomas Francis Furey.

Fact #1591. The widow of Archibald McIlhargey (Pvt., Co. I) who was killed with Custer on June 25, later married Sgt. Michael C. Caddle (Co. I, 7th

Cav.). McIlhargey's daughter was 18 months old when her father died; his son was born five months after the death of his father.

Fact #1592. He Dog told Eleanor Hinman in 1930, through the interpreters John Colhoff and Thomas White Cow Killer, "When we were young men, the Oglala band divided into two parts, one led by Red Cloud and one led by Man-Afraid-of-His-Horse, the elder. I and Crazy Horse stayed with the part led by Man-Afraid-of-His-Horse."

Fact #1593. Capt. E.S. Godfrey (1st Lt. commanding Co. K at LBH) wrote of Sitting Bull years after the battle: "Sitting Bull, an Uncpapa Sioux Indian, was the chief of the hostile camp; he had about sixty lodges of followers on whom he could at all times depend. He was the host of the Hostiles, and as such received and entertained their visitors. These visitors gave him many presents, and he was thus enabled to make many presents in return. All visitors paid tribute to him, so he gave liberally to the most influential, the chiefs, i.e., he 'put it where it would do the most good.' In this way he became known as the chief of the hostile Indian camp, and the camp was generally known as 'Sitting Bull's camp.'"

Fact #1594. Writing in his *Surgeon's Diary*, Dr. Holmes O. Paulding, wrote regarding the morning of June 27: "There were immense fresh trails of lodge poles leading toward the ravines & bluffs & along all of them packs, travoises, lodge poles & utensils dropped or hastily cut loose when the Indians ran out on our approach the night before - Oh! why did we not march only 6 or 8 miles further! All this told the tale - Custer had been literally cut to pieces."

Fact #1595. "Sitting Bull was a heavy-set, muscular man, about five feet eight inches in stature, and at the time of the battle of the Little Big Horn was forty-two years of age." (Capt. E.S. Godfrey, January 1892, *Century* magazine)

Fact #1596. ". . .a short time previous to the battle, [Sitting Bull] had 'made medicine,' had predicted that the soldiers would attack them and that the soldiers would all be killed. He took no active part in the battle, but, as was his custom in time of danger, remained in the village 'making medicine.'" (Capt. E.S. Godfrey, January 1892, *Century* magazine)

Fact #1597. Apparently basing his opinions on conversations with various Indian warriors at the 10th anniversary of LBH in 1886, Capt. E.S. Godfrey, who had commanded Co. K as a 1st Lt. on June 25-26, 1876, wrote: "Personally [Sitting Bull] was regarded as a great coward and a very great liar, 'a man with a big head and a little heart.'"

Fact #1598. Crazy Horse, the Oglala Sioux warrior who, some say, led the final charge against Custer and his troops on Last Stand Hill, is being memorialized at Crazy Horse Mountain, five miles north of Custer (SD) on US 16, by a mammoth carving planned by the late sculptor Korczak Ziolkowski. The equestrian statue of Crazy Horse, being literally carved out of the mountain top, is planned to be the largest statue in the world when finished: 563 feet high and 641 feet long—not just a bas-relief carving like Mount Rushmore and Stone Mountain. How big is that? An eight-room house will reportedly fit in the pony's nostril.

Fact #1599. Col. John Gibbon of the Montana Column sent out a party of mounted infantry on the morning of June 27, 1876, to search for Custer. This patrol found the remains of a huge encampment along the banks of the Little Big Horn River, and near the center of the encampment they discovered three lodgepoles standing upright in a triangle. At the foot of each pole were inverted kettles. Underneath the kettles were the decapitated heads of cavalrymen John McGinniss (Co. G) who had been with Reno's battalion in the valley fight, John Armstrong (Co. A) also with Reno in the valley, and an unidentifiable head. On the bank of the river lay the body of another soldier, whose features had been mutilated beyond recognition.

Fact #1600. A mounted infantry patrol, sent out from the Montana Column on the morning of June 27, 1876, to look for Custer's command, found evidence that at least two of Custer's officers had been casualties in a battle. They found the bloody underclothing of Lt. James Garland Sturgis (Co. M, but attached to Co. E during the battle). They also found the buckskin jacket of Lt. James Porter (Co. I) with a bloody hole on the side which covers the heart.

Fact #1601. Responding in an 1896 letter to artist Edgar S. Paxson, who was seeking information on the "scene" at Custer Hill for his forthcoming painting, "Custer's Last Stand," Gen. Edward S. Godfrey (1st Lt. commanding Co. K, LBH) wrote about Tom Custer: "He was found near the top of the hill, and a few yards from the General, lying on his face; his features were so pressed out of shape as to be almost beyond recognition; a number of arrows had been shot in his back, several in his head, one, I remember, without the shaft, the head bent so that it could hardly be withdrawn; his skull was crushed and nearly all the hair scalped. . ."

Fact #1602. Little Big Horn Associates has an Adopt The Grave Program, devoted to finding and caring for the graves of soldiers who were with the 7th Cavalry in 1876. Around 300 graves have been located with headstones placed over several graves that had none. There are still around 100 graves to be found and identified. If you would like to participate in this effort, contact Guy Orseno, Adopt-A-Grave Program/LBHA, 43630 Middle Ridge Rd., Lorain OH 44053.

Fact #1603. A Sioux chief, Long Wolf, fought the 7th Cavalry at LBH and was later a member of Buffalo Bill's "Wild West" show.

Fact #1604. Capt. Frederick W. Benteen transferred to the 9th Cavalry following the 1877 Nez Perce Campaign. (*Encyclopedia of American Indian Wars*)

Fact #1605. Custer Battlefield National Monument was established in 1893, under the jurisdiction of the War Department. Andrew Nathan Grover was the first superintendent, July 11, 1893, to April 1906.

Fact #1606. The National Park Service took over responsibility for the Custer Battlefield National Monument, currently the Little Bighorn Battlefield National Monument, in 1940, after nearly 48 years of War Department administration. Edward S. Luce was the first NPS superintendent.

Fact #1607. Dr. Holmes O. Paulding, the only surgeon to accompany the Montana Column, had reported for duty at Fort Abraham Lincoln (D.T.) in May 1875, and was under the direct command of Lt. Col. George A. Custer for two months, during which time he had his picture taken with a group of Custer's officers and some wives at a picnic. In July he was ordered downriver to Fort Randall (D.T.), where he served until October on detached service with a battalion of the 1st Infantry.

Custer

Fact #1608. In the *Army and Navy Journal* of November 14, 1877, Sitting Bull was quoted as saying, "It is better to be afraid than too brave like Custer."

Fact #1609. The worst portrayal of Custer in the movies (so far) was in *Little Big Man* (1970), a satirical look at an evil, demented Custer whose demise was cheered by the audiences.

Fact #1610. It was reported that Custer's body, discovered on "Last Stand Hill," was neither scalped nor mutilated, which may have been the "official" story to spare his wife. He had been struck twice by bullets, either of which could have been fatal, once in the breast and once in the right temple. (Luce, *Custer Battlefield*)

Fact #1611. "This battle wrecked the lives of twenty-six women at Fort [Abraham] Lincoln [D.T.], and orphaned children of officers and soldiers joined their cry to that of their bereaved mothers." (Elizabeth Custer, *Boots and Saddles*, 1885)

Fact #1612. Gen. Philip H. Sheridan, speaking of the cavalry's defeat at LBH, said, "It was an unnecessary sacrifice due to misapprehension and superabundant courage—the latter extraordinarily developed in Custer."

Fact #1613. Fort Custer (M.T.) was named for George A. Custer as were Custer State Park (SD), Custer County (MT), and other places throughout the

U.S. Fort Custer was evacuated in 1898 and the buildings were sold, the structures forming the nucleus of present-day Hardin (MT) two miles west.

Fact #1614. On July 5, 1876, Elizabeth Custer was informed of the death of her husband George, his brothers Tom and Boston, his nephew Harry Armstrong Reed, and her sister-in-law's husband Lt. James Calhoun, all killed at LBH. She died in April 1933 in New York City, having spent most of her life defending and enhancing the memory of her husband.

Fact #1615. The famed Cassilly Adams painting of "Custer's Last Stand" depicts a long-haired Custer (his hair was cropped) waving a sword (he didn't even have a saber with him) amidst blue-jacketed soldiers (most of whom would have doffed their "blouses" because of the heat) and Indians carrying Zulu-style shields and Seminole- and Apache-style headgear. But other than that. . .

Fact #1616. The American people—nearly 40 million of them proudly reviewing a century of progress since the signing of the Declaration of Independence—were stunned out of their Centennial Celebration exhilaration by news from Montana of the death of the Boy General, their hero Custer. The story dominated the burgeoning news industry like nothing since Civil War days.

Fact #1617. *The Harrisonian* is the annual publication of the Harrison County Historical Society, Cadiz (OH). The 1989 issue commemorated the 150th year of the birth of George Armstrong Custer (1839-1876). The Society has a large collection of Custeriana.

Fact #1618. The *Cadiz [OH] Sentinel*, on July 13, 1876, (p. 2) ran a lengthy column from Chicago (IL) on "the Custer massacre," which began: "CHICAGO, July 7—The following account of the Custer massacre has been received here: SIOUX EXPEDITION, MOUTH OF THE LITTLE BIG HORN, July 1, via Bismarck, Dak., July 6—Long before the arrival of the dispatch you will have heard of the tragedy which has been enacted here. At noon on the twenty-second of June, General Custer, at the head of twelve veteran companies left the camp at the mouth of the Rosebud to follow the trail of a very large band of hostile Sioux leading up the river and westward in the direction of the Big Horn. The signs indicated that the Indians were making for the eastern branch of the last named river, marked on the map as the 'Little Big Horn.'" Custer had taught school in Cadiz.

Fact #1619. Elizabeth Custer, with her sister-in-law Margaret Custer Calhoun, had ridden out with Custer's column on the first day of the Last March, May 17, 1876. They returned to Fort Abraham Lincoln (D.T.) with the paymaster the next day, and she then had a premonition of disaster such as she had never felt before. She wrote many years later that there had "been silence as the column left the garrison. Alas, the closed houses they left were as still as if death had set its seal upon the door, no sound but the sobbing and moans of women's breaking hearts."

Fact #1620. Lt. James Bradley (7th Infantry), scouting for Gibbon's Montana Column, was the first to discover the fallen bodies of Custer and his men on June 27: "Probably never did heroes who had fallen upon the field of battle appear so much to have died a natural death. [Custer's] expression was rather that of a man who had fallen asleep and enjoyed peaceful dreams than that of a man who had met his death amid such fearful scenes as that field had witnessed, the features being wholly without ghastliness or any impress of fear, horror or despair. He died as he lived, a hero." Some believe Lt. Bradley exercised considerable literary license in this description.

Fact #1621. On the evening of July 5, 1876, Capt. McCaskey, the post commander at Fort Abraham Lincoln (D.T.), and Dr. Middleton, the post surgeon, went to the rear entrance of Lt. Col. Custer's post quarters, and asked the maid to call Mrs. Custer, Mrs. Calhoun (Custer's sister), and a sister of young Autie Reed, Custer's nephew. Quietly the news of the disaster was broken. The three women sank to their knees, clinging to each other in their shattering grief.

Fact #1622. President Theodore Roosevelt wrote Elizabeth Custer: "I need not tell you that General Custer has always been a favorite of mine."

Fact #1623. "A typical soldier, a great commander whose memory brings out of the past the greatest cavalry commanders of the world—Prince Ruprecht, Murrat, and others—he stands equal with all. Brigadier General at twenty-three, Major General at twenty-five, he showed in his youth that genius and force that we have at the same age in the great commanders of the world." (President William Howard Taft, at the unveiling of the Custer Equestrian Statue in Monroe [MI] June 1910)

Fact #1624. "I will never cease to cherish the memory of General Custer. I knew him well and loved him and I think I can truthfully say he reciprocated some of my admiration for him. His boyish pranks—but harmless-frolics kept him in constant hot water. . . .He was beyond a doubt the most popular boy in his class." Gen. E. Van Arsdale Andress, U.S.A. (West Point classmate of Custer wrote Elizabeth Custer, 1905)

Fact #1625. Chief of Staff of the Army, Gen. William T. Sherman, commented a month after the Battle in a letter to Sen. I.T. Christancy on charges that Custer was too "hasty" in his attack: ". . .in all our former experience in that region, and in similar cases, success was only possible by rapid movements, so as to catch the warrior whilst encumbered with lodges and families."

Fact #1626. Noted Indian fighter Brig. Gen. George Forsyth, wrote after LBH: "In the opinion of the writer, he [Custer] was within his orders, and fully justified from a military stand in [attacking the village]."

Fact #1627. Gen. Nelson A. Miles, later Commanding General of the Army, joined the Sioux expedition with his 5th Infantry not long after LBH. He wrote to his wife: "The more I see of movements here [along the Little Big Horn River], the more admiration I have for Custer and I am satisfied that his likes will not be found very soon again."

Fact #1628. James McLaughlin, Indian agent at the Devil's Lake and Standing Rock Sioux reservations (D.T.) wrote of Custer: "General Custer was not the dashing, devil-may-care, hard-riding and fast-fighting mounted soldier that the romancers have made him out. He was a careful, painstaking man and officer, devoted to his profession of arms and properly appreciating the tools he had to work with."

Fact #1629. Custer probably was not scalped because he had been to the barber before leaving Fort Abraham Lincoln (D.T.) and had his thinning hair close-cropped.

Fact #1630. According to *Brave Warriors* by Norman Wiltsey, Custer's body was stripped but not scalped. Although Lt. James Bradley (7th Inf., Chief of Scouts for the Montana Column) was probably the first white man to see Custer's body after his death, and reported that he was not mutilated, some believe that this description, by Lt. Bradley and others, was based on respect for the widow and the wish to spare her feelings. All agree that he was shot twice, in the left breast and the left temple; either wound would have been mortal. He may have been slightly mutilated—a slash on one thigh, a fingertip cut off, awl punctures in both ears (mutilations which were a common practice of Sioux women), and a gash in his left side.

Fact #1631. Indian agent James McLaughlin, who served at the Devil's Lake and Standing Rock Sioux Reservations (D.T.), said of Custer: "He might go into an undertaking when he knew the chances were against him, but he would not do it in a spirit of bravado."

Fact #1632. After the battle, Custer's friend and mentor Gen. Philip Sheridan said, "Had the 7th Cavalry been kept together, it is my belief that it would have been able to handle the Indians at the Little Big Horn and under any circumstances it could have at least defended itself; but separated as it was into three detachments, the Indians had largely the advantage, in addition to their overwhelming numbers." (Merrill, *Spurs to Glory*)

Fact #1633. "I regard Custer's massacre as a sacrifice of troops, brought on by himself, that was wholly unnecessary. He was not to have made the attack but effect the juncture with Terry and Gibbon. He was notified to meet them on the 26th [of June 1876], but instead of marching slowly as his orders required to effect the junction on the 26th, he entered a forced march of eighty-three miles in twenty-four hours, and thus had to meet the Indians alone on the 25th." (President U.S. Grant, shortly after LBH)

Fact #1634. After receiving a June 27, 1876, message from Gen. Alfred Terry to ready the steamer *Far West* for transport of wounded soldiers from Reno's and Benteen's commands to Fort Abraham Lincoln (D.T.), over 700 miles east on the river systems, Captain Grant Marsh, skipper of the *Far West*, converted the boat into a floating hospital. Eighteen inches of prairie grass was spread on the decks, then covered with tarpaulin. All available medical supplies were made ready. Then they waited for the wounded to arrive at the mouth of the Little Big Horn, several miles from the battle site.

Fact #1635. Before the Sioux Expedition of 1876, Gen. Philip Sheridan, commanding general, Division of Missouri, sent a telegram to Gen. Alfred Terry, commander of the Sioux Expedition and Dakota Column: "Advise Custer to be prudent, not to take along any newspapermen, who always make mischief, and to abstain from personalities in the future."

Fact #1636. William F. "Buffalo Bill" Cody staged "Custer's Last Stand" as the climax of his "Wild West" show, which played before thousands of people in this country and across Europe.

Fact #1637. Custer apologists have argued that Custer could not have disobeyed Gen. Terry's orders, because those orders were "discretionary" rather than "obligatory." Since Terry could not give precise orders, lacking knowledge of the situation—enemy location, strength, etc.—Custer could not "disobey" those orders in any manner that would involve dereliction of duty.

Fact #1638. The Custer Headquarters House Museum at Fort Riley (KS) (home of George and Elizabeth while stationed there) has many items of civilian historical interest as well as military relics.

Fact #1639. From Fort Abraham Lincoln (D.T.) Lt. Col. George A. Custer led his 7th Cavalry regiment as part of the 1876 Sioux Expedition on May 17, 1876. Custer commanded the post (which is now a state park just southeast of Bismarck-Mandan [ND] on state highway 80), from 1873-1876.

Fact #1640. Present-day Custer (SD) is supposedly where the Black Hills gold rush began in 1874 after one of the prospectors with Custer's Black Hills Expedition found "dirt" that would pay off as gold.

Fact #1641. "General Custer was stripped with the exception of his sox. He had a gunshot wound in his head and another in his side, and in his left thigh there was a gash about eleven inches long that exposed the bone. Custer was not scalped nor otherwise mutilated, and I am sure he did not commit suicide. . . There were no powder burns on Custer's face and, in those days of black powder, it would have been next to impossible for a man to hold a gun far enough away from his face to escape such burns when committing suicide." (Pvt. Jacob Adams, Co. H)

Fact #1642. Gen. Edward S. Godfrey (1st Lt. commanding Co. K at LBH) disclosed to his close friend Col. Charles Bates many years after the battle that Custer had been mutilated by having an arrow forced into his penis, a common practice among Indians. This defilement of Custer's body was not revealed during Mrs. Custer's lifetime. (*The Custer Battle Casualties*, Hardorff)

Fact #1643. "Custer had no clothing on whatever, nor none of the soldiers. There was nothing left but a foot of a boot, the leg of this being gone, on Custer. There was no mutilated soldiers at this point, except [Lt. W.W.] Cooke [the regimental adjutant], and the mutilation of him was just a gash on one of his thighs. Custer's wound was in the left breast, near the heart, just one shot." (Daniel Kanipe, Sgt., Co. C, at LBH, writing to historian and researcher Walter M. Camp some years later)

Fact #1644. "I will explain that [Custer was] wounded: he had 2 bullet wounds—one in the right temple and one in the right breast and a knife wound about 6 inches long in the thigh. I think the wound in the temple killed him as it had bled and run down his face, and the other wounds had not bled any, and he was stripped of all his clothes except his socks and was not scalped." (Co. H Pvt. Jacob Adams writing to Gen. E.S. Godfrey [1st Lt. commanding Co. K at LBH] some years after the battle)

Fact #1645. "I had just identified and was supervising the burial of Boston Custer, when Major Reno sent for me to help identify the dead on Custer Hill," wrote Gen. Edward S. Godfrey (1st Lt. commanding Co. K at Little Big Horn, June 25, 1876). "When I arrived [at Custer Hill], General Custer's body had been laid out. He had been shot in the left temple and the left breast. There were no powder marks or any signs of mutilation. [The civilian interpreter Fred] Girard. . .found the bodies of two soldiers, one across the other, and Custer's naked body in a sitting position between and leaning against them, his upper right arm along and on the topmost body, his right forearm and hand supporting his head in an inclining posture like one resting or asleep. . ." (*Century* magazine, 1892)

Fact #1646. Artist Edgar S. Paxson, seeking verisimilitude for his painting-in-the-works, "Custer's Last Stand," contacted Gen. Edward S. Godfrey (1st Lt. commanding Co. K at LBH) in 1896, asking for details on the after-the-battle scene at Custer Hill. Gen. Godfrey responded: "The General was not mutilated at all; he laid on his back, his upper arms on the ground, the hands folded or so placed as to cross the body above the stomach; his position was natural and one that we had seen hundreds of times while taking catnaps during halts on the march. One hit was in the front of the left temple, and one in the left breast at or near the heart."

Fact #1647. Jerry Keenan, author of the *Encyclopedia of American Indian Wars*, notes that, "Given the sensational nature of the [Battle of the Little Big Horn] and the attention it received, it is not surprising that the Custer legend began to take shape immediately. But more than anything else, it was Custer's widow, Elizabeth. . .who devoted the remainder of her considerable life to glorifying her husband's image. . ."

Fact #1648. In an 1896 deposition Cpl. John E. Hammon (Co. G at LBH), stated: "Custer's body was found at the western end of the field on a little knoll, a little to the south of its crest. . . There was a dead soldier lying under the calf of his right leg alongside [a] dead horse. Three bullet holes were found on his person: one in the left under the heart in the ribs; one in the left side of the head in the ear; the other in the right forearm. . . Four men in G Troop buried Custer's body where it lay; and I signed the proofs of death for the life insurance company. . .some six weeks or thereabouts afterward."

Environment

Fact #1649. News of the shocking disaster in the hills of southeast Montana, along the banks of the Little Big Horn River, was heralded under big headlines by the press of the day, bringing repercussions from many parts of the country.

Fact #1650. On June 27, 1876, Capt. Frederick Benteen (Co. H) was detailed to Custer battlefield to try to identify the slain officers. He was accompanied by Capt. Thomas Weir (Co. D), Lt. Francis M. Gibson (Co. H), Lt. Charles DeRudio (Co. E, but attached to Co. A during the battle), and Lt. Henry Nowland (Acting Quartermaster for the Dakota Column), along with a detail of 14 Co. H soldiers, and a detail of Ree scouts, commanded by Lt. Charles A. Varnum (Co. A). The detail was guided by Lt. James A. Bradley, 7th Infantry, head of the Montana Column's Crow Indian scouts.

Fact #1651. In the Foreword to "Custer's Last Battle," by Captain Edward S. Godfrey, 1st Lieutenant commanding Company K at LBH, Battlefield Supt. Richard T. Hart wrote: "[The Battle of the Little Big Horn] was a tragedy for the United States Army and a victory for the Indians, although they too suffered losses. The Army was there because of depredations on the part of the Indians against white settlers and installations in the region. The Indians were there because they preferred their former life to that of the reservations. Some have said the only 'sin' of the Indians was that of his pride in his lifestyle and his culture. But Godfrey does not moralize even this much, maintaining apparently complete military reserve. Nevertheless, people will be quick to perceive the human issues that were involved in this battle—basically a contest over land possession. . ."

Fact #1652. In an interview with Western photographer D.W. Barry 10 years after the battle, Gall, the Hunkpapa war chief, who led his warriors against Custer on Last Stand Hill, said, "The smoke and dust was so thick that we could not always see the soldiers. The soldiers were fighting on foot, so finally we rode over them with our ponies."

Fact #1653. Gen. Terry described the various phases of LBH in his June 27, 1876, telegram to Division headquarters in Chicago (IL). After remarks on the Valley fight, he continued, "Captain Benteen, who, with three companies, D, H, and K, was some two miles to the left of Reno when the action [in the valley fight] commenced, but who had been ordered by General Custer to return, came to the river, and rightly concluding that it was useless for his force to attempt to renew the fight in the valley, he joined Reno on the bluffs. Captain McDougall, with his company, B, was at first some distance in the rear, with the train of pack-mules; he also came up to Reno. Soon this united force was nearly surrounded by Indians, many of whom, armed with rifles of long range, occupied positions which commanded the ground held by the cavalry—ground from which there was no escape."

Fact #1654. The property encompassing part of the Reno-Benteen position was added to the battlefield holdings April 14, 1926, (the Fiftieth Anniversary of the Battle) as "Reno-Benteen Battlefield."

Fact #1655. In 1882, Frederick Benteen was charged with drunkenness and sentenced by a court martial to dismissal from the Army, according to the *Encyclopedia of American Indian Wars*.

Fact #1656. The Custer Battlefield Preservation Committee, Inc., is a 501(c)(3) non-profit, Box 7, Hardin MT 59034; <jimcourt@juno.com> (e-mail).

Fact #1657. The Custer's Battlefield Reservation, including the National Cemetery, Last Stand Hill, and the Reno-Benteen position, was redesignated Custer Battlefield National Monument in March 1940, and transferred from the U.S. War Department to the National Park Service July 1, 1940.

Fact #1658. "The Custer battlefield today is a national monument, administered by the National Park Service as part of the nation's historic heritage. It exists not to take sides on the battle long past, but to preserve and present the story of this episode in history, so that you and all Americans may better ponder the moral issues on your own, relate them as you may to the aspirations in that most humanistic form of government yet conceived by man, and grope for common meanings in our past, so often diverse, so that we may then all grope together, but in our separate ways, for a better common future." Richard T. Hart,

Superintendent, Custer Battlefield National Monument, written for *Century* magazine, 1892; reprinted as an undated booklet in the 1930s.

Fact #1659. The steamer *Far West* began its epic "mercy voyage" on July 3, 1876, down the Big Horn River to the Yellowstone, thence to the Missouri and Fort Abraham Lincoln (D.T.). Double-shifts of sweating firemen kept the boilers supplied with wood while Captain Grant Marsh and pilot Dave Campbell took four-hour shifts at the wheel around the clock.

Fact #1660. In the fenced area west of the Custer memorial at the Little Bighorn Battlefield National Monument, are the spots where Lt. Col. Custer fell, along with his closest companions in death, who included his brothers, Captain Thomas Ward Custer and Boston Custer, and their nephew, Henry Austin (Autie) Reed. Boston Custer and Autie Reed were civilians.

Fact #1661. In the early morning hours of June 30th, the wounded from Reno's command were loaded on the steamer *Far West*, docked where the Little Big Horn River entered the Big Horn River. The boat moved (north) downriver to the Yellowstone River, where it spent two days ferrying Col. Gibbon's troops across the Yellowstone.

Fact #1662. Four 7th Cavalry officers serving at LBH attained the rank of General in their Army career: one, Maj. Marcus A. Reno (HQs staff) received a brevet promotion to brigadier general (USV) March 13, 1865.

Fact #1663. The Custer Battlefield National Cemetery is located to the rear of the visitors' center/museum, and is of interest to many visitors. Within the national cemetery are buried many who died in other Indian Wars battles. Among those of historic interest are Capt. (Bvt. Lt. Col.) William Judd Fetterman and his command of three officers, 76 enlisted men, and four civilians who were slain at the Fort Phil Kearny Fight (W.T.), also known as the "Fetterman Massacre," December 21, 1866.

Fact #1664. In September 1883, the "last great buffalo hunt on the plains" was held with Sitting Bull as a participant. A herd of 10,000 buffalo had been discovered between the Cannonball and Moreau rivers in Dakota Territory, and the Sioux had been "allowed" to share in the activity along with a horde of white hunters. The whites killed 20-60 animals a day, per man, with their modern repeating rifles; the Indians averaged one kill per day per man. In less than two months, the herd was wiped out. With heavy hearts, Sitting Bull and his hunters rode back to Standing Rock Agency (D.T.).

Fact #1665. Little Bighorn Battlefield National Monument lies within the Crow Indian Reservation in southeastern Montana, two miles south of the town of Crow Agency, 15 miles south of Hardin, on I-90.

Fact #1666. The officers and men of Reno's command were stunned to learn that "Custer's entire command had been annihilated, and our companions in arms of years standing were lying butchered on their last battlefield only three short miles distant." (Lt. W.S. Edgerly, Co. D)

Fact #1667. At 11 p.m. on July 5, 1876, the steamer *Far West* docked at Bismarck (D.T.). Captain Grant Marsh's little riverboat had averaged nearly 350 miles a day on the 710 mile journey, a record that remains unbroken to this day. A race against death had been won, except for one badly wounded soldier who had died en route—Pvt. James C. Bennett (Co. C), who had been wounded at the Reno-Benteen site.

Fact #1668. In the summer of 1885, Sitting Bull and Buffalo Bill met in a dramatic moment at the Buffalo (NY) fair grounds, and Cody introduced the Sioux chief to the audience at the "Wild West" show: "The man who stands before you today has been a great warrior; his deeds, divested of our personal feelings to the victims of his success, occupy the blood-red pages of this nation's history. He, from his standpoint, fought for what he believed was right and made a name for himself to be known forever. The man I now introduce to you is Sitting Bull, the Napoleon of the red race, who has journeyed thousands of miles to be present with us here today."

Fact #1669. Four 7th Cavalry officers serving at LBH attained the rank of General in their Army career: one was 2d Lt. Winfield Scott Edgerly (Co. D) who was appointed brigadier general on June 28, 1905.

Fact #1670. The Little Big Horn Days festival, sponsored by the Chamber of Commerce and the Custer Battlefield Preservation Committee, Inc., is held on the weekend closest to the June 25 anniversary of the Battle, and features a live-action re-enactment of Custer's Last Stand (started in 1990) on land near Hardin, as well as an arts, crafts, and books fair, a public symposium sponsored by the CBH&MA, and various other activities. It is one of Montana's top summer tourist attractions. E-mail for more information: custertours@juno.com.

Fact #1671. The Custer Battlefield Preservation Committee, Inc., was formed in 1982 as a result of private attempts to build permanent facilities on two areas surrounding the Battlefield. With the approval of the Secretary of Interior, the Committee was formed and raised over $2 million. The Committee has purchased or obtained permanent scenic easements on approximately 2,200 acres of land (the National Park Service owns 700+ acres), and has plans to purchase the Village site, all of the land involving the Reno Valley fight, including the retreat, and additional acres along the highway frontage.

Fact #1672. Traversing the Park Service road leading south from the memorial monument at Little Bighorn Battlefield National Monument, some of the marble markers placed where soldiers' bodies were found after the battle cannot be seen for they are concealed by the rolling contours of the slope. Beyond these markers and across the river is the location of the Indian encampment which early reports said spread over three miles along the flatter west bank of the river; later research has shown that the length of the village was about a mile.

Fact #1673. After LBH, Lt. James Bradley (7th Infantry) wrote the editor of the *Helena [M.T.] Herald*: "I was sent to guide Colonel [Capt.] Benteen of the 7th Cavalry to the field, and was a witness to his recognition of the remains of Custer. Two other officers of that regiment were also present and they could not be mistaken, and the body so identified was wholly unmutilated. Even the wounds that caused his death were scarcely discoverable (though the body was entirely naked) so that when I afterwards asked the gentlemen whom I accompanied whether they had observed his wounds, they were forced to say they had not." Lt. Bradley obviously altered reality because of compassion for Mrs. Custer, as did the other witnesses.

Fact #1674. The Monument headquarters/visitors' center/museum is located just west (down the hill) from the memorial monument and can be visited before or after touring the battlefields. Here is found a graphic story of the battles, told by maps, photographs, dioramas, artifacts, and National Park Service historians/interpreters.

Fact #1675. Accounts vary as to what percent of the bodies at Custer's battlefield was scalped and/or mutilated. Much of the clothing and personal belongings were missing.

Fact #1676. Reno's men, after the battle, were told "the only person said to have survived the 'Custer Massacre' was a Crow Indian scout who, it is said, got a Sioux blanket and escaped in disguise," according to Lt. Francis Marion Gibson (Co. H). This is obviously a fanciful tale.

Fact #1677. On June 28, 1876, three days after the battle, all that was left of the 7th Cavalry marched to Custer's battlefield "and buried his noble dead, whose memories are still green in the homes and hearts of comrades and friends." (Lt. Francis Gibson, Co. H)

Fact #1678. "The empty shells that surrounded the dead gave very strong evidence of the brave and desperate stand they made. Some of the bodies were much mutilated, and were believed to have been the work of blood-thirsty squaws, who, however, did not disturb the body of Genl. Custer. This I know to be the case, for to the men under my command fell the sad duty of laying to rest our gallant leader." (Lt. Francis Gibson, Co. H)

Fact #1679. Four 7th Cavalry officers serving at LBH attained the rank of General in their Army career: one was 2d Lt. Luther Rector Hare (Co. K) who was appointed brigadier general (USV) on June 1, 1900.

Fact #1680. The first graves for Custer and his men were dug in great haste, over the entire battlefield, where the dead had fallen. In 1881, as many of the graves as could be found were reopened and the bodies reinterred in a common grave around the base of the memorial now found on "Last Stand Hill" at Little Bighorn Battlefield National Monument. Many of the officers were reinterred in various places.

Fact #1681. Bvt. Maj. Gen. Wesley Merritt was promoted Colonel of the 5th Cavalry on July 1, 1876, taking command of the regiment as it was scouting near the Black Hills. News arrived of the Little Big Horn disaster and Merritt was ordered to join Gen. Crook's command on Goose Creek (W.T.), where Crook had withdrawn after the Battle of the Rosebud on June 17. At the same time, however, Merritt received word of some 800 Cheyenne who had fled the Red Cloud agency in Nebraska, presumably to join Sitting Bull. Merritt prepared an ambush for the oncoming Cheyenne, but the ambush was spoiled by the arrival of two couriers who were attacked by Cheyenne scouts. William F. "Buffalo Bill" Cody, scouting for the 5th Cavalry, along with seven or eight scouts and soldiers, rode to rescue the couriers, and Cody shot and scalped a Cheyenne war chief, Yellow Hand. This episode was publicized as the taking of "the first scalp for Custer."

Fact #1682. "When I went to Tom Custer's body it had not been disturbed from its original position. It was lying face downward, all the scalp was removed, leaving only tufts of his fair hair on the nape of his neck. The skull was smashed in, a number of arrows had been shot into the back of the head and body. I remarked that I believed it was Tom, as he and I had gone swimming together and the form seemed familiar. . . His belly had been cut open and his entrails protruded." Positive identification was made by the discovery of a tattoo, "T.W.C." and "the goddess of liberty and flag." (*Century* magazine, 1892, Edward S. Godfrey, 1st Lt. commanding Co. K at LBH, now a Captain)

Fact #1683. The Custer Battlefield National Cemetery was established on the eastern slope above the Little Big Horn River by "General Orders No. 78" in 1879, to protect the graves of the 7th Cavalrymen who fell at LBH.

Fact #1684. On the steamer *Far West*'s record-breaking voyage east on the Big Horn, Yellowstone, and Missouri Rivers to Fort Abraham Lincoln (D.T.), 710 water miles away, at one point where the river narrowed, a small band of Sioux raced apace with the boat, firing their rifles at the "fireboat" (Peyta Watah). One blast on the boat's whistle and the Indian ponies stampeded away from the deafening noise.

Fact #1685. On Tuesday, June 27, 1876, Gen. A.H. Terry, commanding the Dakota Column and the 1876 Sioux Expedition, wrote in his private diary: "Reached Reno's position about 11 o'clk. Troops encamped in bottom some distance below Reno's bluff. Wounded brought down to camp in bottom. Removal completed shortly after night fall. Supplies brought down. Sent messenger [sic] to find Steamer with orders in evening."

Fact #1686. Indian losses at LBH are generally accepted to be no more than 100 men killed (plus an undetermined number of non-combatant women and children). The Indians removed most of their dead from the battlefield when the large village broke up. (1978 "Custer Battlefield" brochure)

Fact #1687. On the (east) left side of the Park Service road leading south from the memorial monument at the Little Bighorn Battlefield National Monument are white markers for Co. I and Co. F, showing approximately where the bodies of the slain soldiers were found after the battle, and first buried. All the bodies have now been removed from the field, and most are buried in the single grave beneath the memorial.

Fact #1688. Pvt. Charles Windolph (Co. H) accompanied the detail on June 27, 1876, to identify the remains of the officers, and later wrote: "It was a horrible sight. There the bodies lay, mostly naked, and scattered over a field maybe half a mile square. We went among them to see how many we could recognize. . . I have read that Lt. Bradley later wrote that the bodies were not badly mutilated. That was kind of him to spare the feelings of their relatives, but they were badly mutilated, some of them too bad to tell about. . . .Col. [Capt.] Benteen took a little piece of wood, hollowed it out on one side and wrote Custer's name on it and stuck it in the ground near Custer's body."

Fact #1689. In December 1886, the National Cemetery at Custer's Battlefield Reservation was established. In 1940 it became the Custer Battlefield National Cemetery, and is now designated the Custer National Cemetery.

Fact #1690. "The Ree [Arikara] scouts, who had not been very active for the past day or two, were together [on the morning of the battle] and the 'medicine man' was anointing them and invoking the Great Spirit to protect them from the Sioux. They seemed to have become satisfied that we were going to find more Sioux than we could well take care of." (Capt. E.S. Godfrey, *Century* magazine, 1892)

Fact #1691. After the Battle of Slim Buttes (September 9, 1876), cavalrymen under Capt. Anson Mills were enraged to find evidence directly linking inhabitants of the village to LBH: a swallow-tailed guidon (flag), a gauntlet marked with the name of Capt. Myles Keogh (Co. L), several McClellan saddles, three 7th Cavalry horses, several orderly books, an officer's blouse, some letters written by and to 7th Cavalry soldiers, and a large amount of U.S. currency.

Fact #1692. On the morning of June 27, 1876, Col. John Gibbon, commander of the Montana Column, rode through the devastated, abandoned Indian encampment along the banks of the Little Big Horn River after receiving the report about the dead soldiers on the nearby hillside. Reaching the area near Reno's crossing, he and his staff discovered several more bodies of dead soldiers. Near this place, he said, "The command was placed in camp. . .and details at once set to work to haul away the dead horses and bury the men, both of which were already becoming offensive. Then mounting my horse, I proceeded to visit Colonel [Maj.] Reno's command. As I rode a few hundred yards up the river towards the ford, bodies of men and horses were seen scattered along at intervals, and in the river itself several dead horses were lying."

Fact #1693. "Implied in war is an ability for social organization and a community of interest in each of the opponent groups, and also the realization by each that those things which they hold dear are worth the risk of dying for. This itself is an abstract concept probably unique in man among the earth's creatures. . . .War is, for those involved, and at the time of their involvement, a great adventure. But war takes a tragic toll, at a price far too high—and whether the dead or maimed be Indian, white soldier, or other. For after 'victory', what?" (Hart, in his foreword to "Custer's Last Battle," by Capt. Edward S. Godfrey)

Fact #1694. Between the time just after the battle, when bodies were buried where they were found, and 1881, when as many graves as could be found were reopened, and the remains placed in a common grave at the top of "Last Stand Hill," the bodies of 11 officers and two civilians had already been exhumed for reburial elsewhere at the request of relatives.

Fact #1695. Little Bighorn Battlefield National Monument in southeastern Montana memorializes the last major effort of the Northern Plains Indians to preserve their ancestral way of life in battle.

Fact #1696. After a march of 29-30 miles on June 26, 1876, the men of the Montana Column were "very weary and daylight was fading," according to Gen. Terry's telegraphed report to Division headquarters on June 27. "The column was therefore halted for the night, at a point about eleven miles in a straight line above the mouth of the stream. This morning the movement was resumed, and, after a march of nine miles, Major Reno's intrenched [sic] position was reached. The withdrawal of the Indians from around Reno's command and from the valley was undoubtedly caused by the approach of General Gibbon's troops. Major Reno and Captain Benteen, both of whom are officers of great experience, accustomed to see large masses of mounted men, estimate the number of Indians engaged at not less than twenty-five hundred. Other officers think that the number was greater than this."

Fact #1697. Custer's body, hastily buried on "Last Stand Hill" after the battle, was disinterred in 1877, and buried in the historic cemetery at the U.S. Military Academy in West Point (NY) in October of that year.

Fact #1698. "For a long time [after the Battle of the Little Big Horn] the Indians would not talk about this battle, for fear of being held responsible for the mistreatment of the wounded. Therefore their version of the battle was unknown at the time the official reports were written. The almost unvarying account given later by the Indians is that, while Custer's approach was looked for and his numbers accurately known, the form of his attack was a complete surprise. They had not counted on its being made by daylight, and they had not expected him to divide his force." (Bates, June 20, 1926, *New York Times*)

Fact #1699. Non-fiction videos about LBH include *Touring Custer Battlefield* (1989) from Old Army Press, and *Red Sunday*, an older production, shown for many years at the Custer Battlefield National Monument. These and others are available from the Custer Battlefield Historical & Museum Association, PO Box 902, Hardin MT 59034.

Fact #1700. On the evening of June 29, the Terry column set out again, now with the wounded on mule litters. Although the march was intended to be a short one, information was received that the steamer *Far West* was at the confluence of the Little Big Horn and Big Horn rivers, and it was decided to push on to that point. By 2 a.m. on June 30, all the wounded were safely on board the boat.

Fact #1701. Garryowen (MT), just off I-90 south of the exit for the Little Bighorn Battlefield National Monument, has a historical marker which points out the area where LBH began on June 25, 1876, where Reno's battalion started its charge on the Indian village. "Garryowen" was the marching song of the 7th Cavalry.

Fact #1702. The first Superintendent, Andrew Grover, attempted to beautify the barren, sage-covered National Cemetery grounds by planting grass, but his efforts were hampered by the lack of water.

Fact #1703. Rumors had reached Gen. Edward S. Godfrey (1st Lt. commanding Co. K at LBH) concerning remarks purportedly made by Capt. Frederick Benteen on June 27, 1876, when he led the detail to identify the bodies of the 7th Cavalry officers slain on June 25. Gen. Godfrey had heard that, when Capt. Benteen first saw Custer's dead body, he exclaimed, "There he is, God damn him, he will never fight anymore!" so he contacted former Co. H private Jacob Adams, who had also been on the detail. Adams replied: "In regard to what Captain Benteen said on that day: I called him when I found General Custer and he came up and dismounted and walked over and looked and said, 'By God that [is] him,' and mounted and rode away and never said another word. It makes no difference what they say he said nobody was in hearing distance but me at the time."

Fact #1704. On the day after the battle, Col. John Gibbon (commander, Montana Column) reported seeing the body of one stripped, scalped, and mutilated soldier in the bend in the creek below the Reno-Benteen position, then said, "Close by was another body, also close to a dead horse, but partially clothed, and this was recognized by one of our officers as the body of captain [1st Lt. Donald] McIntosh [Co. G]."

Fact #1705. Little Big Horn Days is an annual event in the town of Hardin (MT), just 12 miles from the Battlefield. It began when Jerry Russell of the Order of the Indian Wars registered the name with the Montana Secretary of State in 1985, and Jim and Virginia Court of Hardin (Jim Court was superintendent of the Battlefield for nearly eight years [1978-1986]) persuaded the Hardin Chamber of Commerce to take on the project and ramrodded the effort in the early years.

Fact #1706. The men at the Reno-Benteen position on the night of June 25, 1876, "knew [the Indians] were having a scalp dance [in their camp along the Little Big Horn River]," according to Capt. E.S. Godfrey (1st Lt. commanding Co. K at LBH) in *Century* magazine in January 1892. ". . .the question has often been asked 'if [the Indians] did not have prisoners at the torture [scalp dance]?' The Indians deny that they took any prisoners. We did not discover any evidence of torture in their camps. It is true that we did find human heads severed from their bodies, but these probably had been paraded in their orgies during that terrible night."

Fact #1707. "Ordered Lt. McGuire with one company of cavalry as escort to make survey of battlefield. Ordered pols [sic] to be prepared to make a full compliment [sic] of horse litters. Litters completed & fording commenced & march commenced at 6½ p.m. Reached boat [*Far West*] about 2 a.m. of the 30th. Litters a great success." (Gen. Alfred H. Terry's private diary, Thursday, June 29, 1876)

Fact #1708. Four 7th Cavalry officers serving at LBH attained the rank of General in their Army career: one was 1st Lt. Edward Settle Godfrey (Co. K) who was appointed brigadier general on January 17, 1907.

Fact #1709. From "Last Stand Hill" one can see most of the battlefield and the valley in which the Indian village was located. On the west side of the hill, just below the memorial shaft, a cluster of 52 markers shows as nearly as possible where the remnants of Custer's battalion gathered for the "last stand." Custer, his brothers Tom and Boston, and his nephew, "Autie" Reed, were all found in this group.

Fact #1710. At 9 a.m. on June 27, the troops at the Reno-Benteen position, no longer under siege, discovered a dense dust cloud rising about five miles due north. Doubts about the cause of the dust produced anxiety, but the men were soon relieved to learn those approaching were with Col. Gibbon's Montana Column, according to Francis Gibson's narrative published after the battle.

Fact #1711. Gen. Alfred Terry, commander of the Dakota Column and of the 1876 Sioux Expedition, accompanied Col. Gibbon's Montana Column as they

Little Bighorn Battlefield. The white markers on the knoll variously known as Custer Hill, Monument Hill, or "Custer's Last Stand" Hill mark the approximate locations where Custer, some of his staff, and the men of Company F fell and were initially buried. The marker for Custer has a darkened inset. *C. Lee Noyes*

---

approached the Reno-Benteen position, bearing word of the death of Custer and his men.

Fact #1712. The Custer National Cemetery was established January 29, 1879, to accommodate burials for those slain at LBH.

Fact #1713. A description of the situation at the Reno-Benteen site was included in the telegram sent June 27, 1876, by Gen. Terry to Division headquarters in Chicago (IL): "Rifle pits were dug, and the fight was maintained [on the afternoon of June 25, following the valley fight], though with heavy loss from about half past two o'clock of the 25th until 6 o'clock of the 26th, when the Indians withdrew from the valley, taking with them their entire village."

Fact #1714. As the frontier era came to a close, the role of the Custer National Cemetery was expanded. An 1886 executive order by President Grover Cleveland defined and set aside a larger area "for military purposes." The following decade saw the abandonment of numerous forts throughout Montana, Wyoming, and the Dakotas. The remains of military personnel and others, buried originally in the various post cemeteries, were moved here.

Fact #1715. In his official report after LBH, Gen. Philip Sheridan stated, "There was nothing official or private to justify an officer to expect that any detachment [of the 1876 Sioux Expedition] would encounter more than 500, or at the maximum, 800, hostile warriors."

Fact #1716. Sgt. Daniel Kanipe (Co. C), in a letter to historian Walter Camp: "The horses were killed and scattered all over the hill, and at the point where Custer lay showed it to be the last stand. There was not hardly any horses around where he was lying when found. The soldiers lay thick at this point. Custer was lying across two or three soldiers, just a small portion of his back touching the ground. There was no such thing as them arranging to corral their horses, or to make a fortification out of their horses, as there was nothing to show this."

Fact #1717. An 1890 detachment of 7th Cavalry soldiers, commanded by Capt. Owen J. Sweet, erected 249 marble markers on the "Custer Battlefield" portion of LBBNM, markers which punctuate the landscape today, with 242 remaining. Only 210 men died on this portion of the battlefield with Custer. Whether the surplus markers were intended for the Reno Battlefield, where the graves had never been adequately marked, or because civilian scout James Campbell, who had placed stakes at the original graves sites in 1881, was misinterpreting the sites of the old graves is not known, according to *Digging Into Custer's Last Stand* by Sandy Barnard, a participant in the 1985 "dig." But, as Barnard notes, "A baffling puzzle had been created for future historians."

Fact #1718. The National Cemetery of Custer's Battlefield Reservation (formerly Custer National Cemetery) was established December 7, 1886, to accommodate the burials of the dead from campaigns and wars other than LBH, and was under the jurisdiction of the War Department.

Fact #1719. "There were a number of Sioux Indians who never went to an agency except to visit friends and relatives. They camped in and roamed about the Buffalo Country. Their camp was the rendezvous for agency Indians when they went out for their annual hunts for meat and robes. They were known as the 'Hostiles,' and comprised representatives from all the different tribes of the Sioux nation. Many of them were renegade outlaws from the agencies. In their visits to the agencies they were usually arrogant and fomenters of discord. Depredations had been made upon the commerce to the Black Hills, and a number of lives taken by them or by others, for which they were blamed. . . . hence the Sioux War." ("Custer's Last Battle," Capt. E.S. Godfrey, commander Co. K at LBH)

Fact #1720. Custer Battlefield National Monument was re-named by the National Park Service in December 1991, and is now officially the Little Bighorn Battlefield National Monument and Custer National Cemetery.

Fact #1721. Capt. Anson Mills' attacking column discovered a number of 7th Cavalry-related items from LBH in the captured village of Sioux chief

American Horse after the Battle of Slim Buttes, September 9, 1876. Later, some Indians would say that visiting Oglalas had brought and left the items, and that American Horse's Minneconjou followers had been victimized by association.

Fact #1722. About one-half mile south of the memorial monument at LBBNM, along the Park Service road, on a loop road to the (east) left, is an interpretive sign at the position where Co. L made its last stand with Lt. Calhoun, brother-in-law of Lt. Col. Custer, commanding the company. According to those who buried the soldiers on June 28, 1876, the bodies of these men showed the most clearly drawn skirmish line on the battlefield.

Fact #1723. The Little Bighorn Battlefield National Monument is administered by the National Park Service, U.S. Department of Interior. A superintendent (PO Box 39, Crow Agency MT 59022) is in charge.

Fact #1724. In 1877, the bodies of the officers slain at the Little Big Horn were removed to such places of burial as their relatives selected. Lt. John J. Crittenden's body remained on the field, and his father Gen. Thomas L. Crittenden placed a monument on the field to mark the spot Lt. Crittenden fell with Co. L. (Lt. Crittenden was later reinterred at the Custer Battlefield National Cemetery when the tour road on top of Custer Ridge was built.)

Fact #1725. Terry's column made camp on the evening of June 26, 1876, near the present site of Crow Agency (MT), about two miles north of the Little Bighorn Battlefield.

Fact #1726. Early estimates placed the Indian dead from the two-day battle at about 36, and 600 wounded, according to Lt. W.S. Edgerly (Co. D). Other estimates of Indian dead ranged from 600-1,000.

Fact #1727. "For two or three days [the Indian] camp had been pitched on the site where they were attacked. The place was not selected with the view to making that the battlefield of the campaign, but whoever was in the van[guard] on their march thought it a good place to camp, put up his tepee, and the others as they arrived followed his example. It is customary among the Indians to camp in bands. The bands usually camp some distance apart, and Indians of the number then together would occupy a territory of several miles along the river valley and not necessarily within supporting distance of each other. But in view of the possible fulfillment of Sitting Bull's prophecy the village had massed." ("Custer's Last Battle," written after the 10th anniversary of the battle by Capt. E.S. Godfrey [1st Lt., Co. K at LBH])

Fact #1728. For the best understanding of LBH, visitors should begin at the Reno-Benteen Battlefield, following the road back to the memorial monument at Custer Battlefield, so the story of the battle can be studied in the chronological order of events. Then, make the stops at the visitors' center/museum and the national cemetery. Guided tours are available by bus at the battlefield.

Fact #1729. Army losses from the two-day battle were 255 killed and 52 wounded, in early estimates cited by Lt. W.S. Edgerly (Co. D).

Fact #1730. Near the mouth of the Little Big Horn River on the morning of June 26, Terry's troops had sign talk with three Crow Indians who had been scouts with Custer. The Indians told them all the white men had been killed. None of the soldiers fully believed the story.

Fact #1731. The steamer *Far West* started (east) down the Yellowstone River on July 2, after Gibbon's column had been ferried across to the north bank of the river, and then hurried on to the Missouri River, reaching Fort Abraham Lincoln (D.T.) (710 miles) in 54 hours. Captain Marsh of the *Far West* made a record never equaled again by packet boats on the Missouri River.

Fact #1732. At Fort Stevenson (D.T.) on the Missouri River, Captain Grant Marsh of the steamer *Far West*, ferrying wounded soldiers from Reno's and Benteen's commands to Fort Abraham Lincoln (D.T.), halted the boat to take on badly-needed supplies and drape the steamer's derrick and jackstaff in mourning black. Following a brief prayer service conducted on deck, the riverboat again cast off for its final destination.

Fact #1733. By the morning of June 27, no more Indians were seen by the men of the Terry column, and, following breakfast, the march southward continued, still seeking to connect with Custer and the 7th Cavalry.

Fact #1734. As news of the Custer disaster spread, investigations were demanded; accusations and insinuations concerning the blame for what happened led from Fort Abraham Lincoln (D.T.) to Washington (DC).

Fact #1735. In camp at the mouth of the Rosebud on Wednesday, August 26, 1876, Gen. Terry, commanding the 1876 Sioux Expedition reported in his private diary: "At 2 o'clk steamer *Durfee* arrived with Genl [Nelson A.] Miles six companies of 5th Inf & 150 cavalry recruits. At same time, *Josephine* arrived back with supplies & guns & 64 horses."

Fact #1736. On Friday, July 7, Gen. A.H. Terry, commanding the Dakota Column and the 1876 Sioux Expedition, wrote in his private diary: "A party of seven Crows came into camp today searching for information of friends. Report that General Crooks forces had a fight with Sioux about the 17th of June on Little Tongue River. Sioux at first successful afterward driven back. I think that only Crooks advance guard engaged Main body in fight. Reported that Crook fell back to his wagon train after his fight. One days march. Crook identified as commanding by shoulder straps and by beard."

Fact #1737. Going south on the Park Service road from the memorial monument at Little Bighorn Battlefield National Monument, past the loop road at Calhoun Hill, the road turning to the (west) right leads to the Reno-Benteen Battlefield entrenchments, four miles to the southeast. In a short distance, this road leaves Little Bighorn Battlefield and passes over Indian reservation land, before returning to NPS land. Those driving to the Reno-Benteen Battlefield portion of LBBNM must return by the same route, a round trip of approximately 10 miles.

Fact #1738. The bodies remaining at Custer battlefield after the exhumation party under Capt. Sheridan had done its work in July 1877 were carefully reburied in one large grave within the enclosure on which a large granite memorial now stands, with the exception of 2d Lt. John J. Crittenden (Co. G, 20th Infantry, temporarily assigned to Co. L, 7th Cavalry).

Fact #1739. The principal feature of Little Bighorn Battlefield National Monument is the battlefield, marked by the memorial which stands over the grave of most of the slain victims of this battle. This memorial is about one-half mile beyond the main entrance to the area. From near this fenced, granite shaft can be obtained an excellent view of the field over which occurred the final stages of Custer's battle. White markers, scattered over the hillsides, show as nearly as possible where the dead were found after the struggle was over.

Fact #1740. The reburials in the Custer Battlefield National Cemetery of remains from numerous forts throughout Montana, Wyoming, and the Dakotas abandoned during the 1890s, found in Sections A and B, constitute a unique aspect of the cemetery. Here can be found the pageant of the West reflected in the graves of soldiers killed in action at the Fetterman Massacre (W.T.), the Wagon Box Fight (W.T.), the Little Big Horn (M.T.), the Big Hole (M.T.), Bear Paw Mountains (M.T.), and other skirmishes on the Northern Plains. More numerous by far are the graves of military personnel and their families, who died from disease or by accident at isolated frontier posts. Here, too, are the graves of Indian scouts who served with the Army.

Fact #1741. When the steamer *Far West* reached the Missouri River on its epic journey to deliver Reno's and Benteen's wounded to the hospital at Fort Abraham Lincoln (D.T.), the steamer docked briefly to allow a wounded Indian scout to disembark at Fort Buford (D.T.), then swung quickly away from the wharf.

Fact #1742. "Of the 206 bodies buried on the field, there were very few that I did not see, and beyond scalping, in possibly a majority of cases, there was little mutilation. Many of the bodies were not even scalped, and in the comparatively few cases of disfiguration it appeared to me rather the result of a blow than of a knife. . ." (Lt. James Bradley, July 27, 1876, *Helena [M.T.] Weekly Herald*)

Fact #1743. The progress of Terry's column away from the battlefield was so slow and tedious that it only moved four and one half miles during the night of June 28.

Fact #1744. As the besieged men at the Reno-Benteen position waited through the night of June 25, 1876, Capt. E.S. Godfrey reported in an article published in January 1892 that "Of course everybody was wondering about Custer—why he did not communicate by courier or signal. But the general opinion seemed to prevail that he had been defeated and driven down the river, where he would probably join General Terry, and with whom he would return to our relief. Quite frequently, too, the question, 'What's the matter with Custer?' would evoke an impatient reply."

Fact #1745. President Grant regarded the loss of Custer and most of his command at the Little Big Horn as a "sacrifice of troops" by Custer. Others condemned Reno and Benteen. Some of the mystery occasioned by the battle on June 25, 1876, remains unsolved.

Fact #1746. "After dark [on June 25, 1876] the troops [at the Reno-Benteen position] were arranged a little differently," according to Capt. E.S. Godfrey in *Century* magazine, 1892. "The horses were unsaddled, and the mules were relieved of their packs; all animals were secured to lariats stretched and picketed to the ground." Capt. Godfrey, as a young 1st Lt., commanded Co. K at LBH.

Fact #1747. The memorial which is the principal feature of the Little Bighorn Battlefield National Monument is a small group of markers within a fenced area, indicating the sites where Lt. Col. Custer and those nearest him in battle were found.

Fact #1748. Most of the day June 29 was spent by the men of Terry's column destroying the enormous amount of camp equipment and supplies left behind by the Indians.

Fact #1749. At the Little Bighorn Battlefield National Monument, a NPS road leads from the memorial marker on "Last Stand Hill" generally south along the ridge, from which can be seen the rough terrain over which the soldiers of the 7th U.S. Cavalry and their Indian warrior opponents fought.

Fact #1750. Lt. James Bradley, Co. B, 7th Inf., was sent on special scout duty to the east side of the Little Big Horn River on the morning of June 27. He soon returned, bringing the first official news of the tragic loss of Lt. Col. Custer and his entire immediate command.

Fact #1751. The original (1896) wooden flagpole at Custer Battlefield National Cemetery was destroyed by lightning in 1907 and replaced the following year by the present steel structure.

Fact #1752. Proceeding generally south from the grave memorial monument on "Last Stand Hill," visitors will see groups of white markers to the right, toward the Little Big Horn River, which graphically display the story of how Co. C and Co. E fought to their death. A number of bodies were found in some of the ravines near the river. The bodies were buried where found, immediately after the battle. All have now been removed, most to the single grave at the monument.

Fact #1753. Before Terry's column arrived on June 27, the Indians had carried away and cared for most of their dead from the June 25 and 26 battles along the Little Big Horn River. The loss of the Indians has never been satisfactorily determined. Published figures have ranged from 30 to 300.

Fact #1754. Besides the members of Fetterman's command killed in the Fetterman Fight (W.T.) of December 1866, others buried at the Custer Battlefield National Cemetery include those slain in the Hayfield Fight, near Fort C. F. Smith (M.T.), August 1, 1867; the Wagon Box Fight, near Fort Phil Kearney (W.T.), August 2, 1867; the Battle of the Big Hole (M.T.), August 9, 1877; the Bear Paw Mountains (M.T.), September 30, 1877, and other battles and skirmishes of lesser importance.

Fact #1755. Following the 1983 grassfire at Custer Battlefield National Monument (now Little Bighorn Battlefield National Monument), the battlefield superintendent James V. Court asked a neighbor, archaeologist Richard Fox, to assess the potential of a productive archaeological study of the battlefield. After 10 days of study, tramping the charred ground, Fox's answer was affirmative, and a systematic, controlled archaeological study was planned.

Fact #1756. Most of the actual ground involved in the Little Big Horn battlefield is in private hands. The federal government owns two significant portions of the battlefield, known as the Custer and Reno-Benteen battlefields (about 700 acres). Over 2,000 acres are owned in trust by the Custer Battlefield Preservation Committee, Inc., a private, non-profit group.

Fact #1757. Col. W.A. Graham, noted military historian and author, offered this "Word to the Wise" regarding Indian testimony: "In considering the weight to be given Indian accounts concerned with any event that involved differences with white [accounts], one should be wary. One should make sure, so far as that be possible, that the accounts are authentic; that they are in truth and in fact correct truthful renderings into English of what the Indians concerned actually said, whether by word of mouth or by sign language."

Fact #1758. Weir Point, two miles southeast of Medicine Tail Coulee, on the tour road between Custer Battlefield and Reno-Benteen Battlefield at the LBBNM, affords a fine view of the portion of the Little Bighorn valley where Maj. Reno's battalion fought and of its retreat route up the bluffs.

Fact #1759. The 1984-85 archeological survey project following the 1983 grass fire at Custer Battlefield National Monument (now Little Bighorn Battlefield National Monument) was funded mostly by the Custer Battlefield Historical & Museum Association, Inc., a national volunteer support group for the battlefield. The purpose of the project was to address some of the unanswered questions about the battle through archaeological research.

Fact #1760. At the Reno-Benteen position on the night of June 25, 1876, the men didn't get much rest. "Although our dusky foes did not molest us with obtrusive attention during the night, yet it must not be inferred that we were allowed to pass the night in perfect rest; or that they were endeavoring to soothe us into forgetfulness of their proximity, or trying to conceal their situation," according to Capt. E.S. Godfrey (1st Lt., Co. K, LBH) in *Century* magazine in January 1892. "They [the Indians] were a good deal happier than we were; nor did they strive to conceal their joy. Their camp was a veritable pandemonium. All night long they continued their frantic revels; beating tom-toms, dancing, whooping, yelling with demoniacal screams and discharging firearms."

Fact #1761. Having been informed by three Crow scouts on the evening of June 26 that the Custer command had been "cut to pieces," Lt. James H. Bradley, 7th Infantry, Montana Column, went out the next morning, seeking the Indians and/or Custer's column. One of Bradley's Indian scouts reported seeing a dead horse in the hills above the west bank of the Little Big Horn. "The Lieutenant found it to be a dead cavalry horse, and going a few yards further on, to the brow of the hill, looking into the valley below, a terrible scene was presented to view. It was literally strewn with the dead of the gallant Seventh Cavalry." (July 15, 1876, *Helena [M.T.] Herald*)

Fact #1762. After the Indians had traveled about 50 miles south from their Little Big Horn encampment, they went into camp "and held a consultation, where it was determined to send into all the agencies reports of their success and to call upon them to come out and share the glories that were to be expected in the future. Wherefore, we may expect an influx of impudent Indians to urge, by force perhaps, an accession to Sitting Bull's demands," said the Commanding Officer of the Standing Rock Reservation (D.T.). (*The Custer Myth*, Graham)

Fact #1763. Indians coming into the Standing Rock Reservation (D.T.) just a few weeks after LBH reported that "There is a general gathering in the hostile camp from each of the agencies on the Missouri River, Red Cloud and Spotted Tail's, and also a great many Northern Cheyenne and Arapaho (lila ota—a great many)," according to Capt. J.S. Poland, 6th Infantry, Commanding, Standing Rock Agency.

Fact #1764. Following a serious grass fire at Custer Battlefield in August 1983, two archaeological digs were held, in 1984 and 1985, using volunteers under the direction of professional archaeologists. Four books resulted from these surveys: *Digging Into Custer's Last Stand*, by Sandy Barnard, AST Press, Terre Haute (IN), 1986; *Archaeological Insights Into The Custer Battle*, by Douglas D. Scott and Richard A. Fox, Jr., University of Oklahoma Press, Norman (OK), 1987; *Archaeological Perspectives on the Battle of the Little Big Horn*, by Douglas D. Scott, Richard A. Fox, Jr., Melissa A. Connor, and Dick Harmon, University of Oklahoma Press, Norman (OK), 1989; and *Archaeology, History, and Custer's Last Battle: The Little Big Horn Re-Examined*, by Richard Allan Fox, Jr., University of Oklahoma Press, Norman (OK), 1993.

Fact #1765. The July 8, 1876, *New York Herald* quoted an unidentified officer in the Montana Column (commanded by Col. John Gibbon): "The Montana column felt disappointed when they learned that they were not to be present at the final capture of the great village, but General Terry's reasons for according the attack to General Custer were good ones. First, Custer had all cavalry and could pursue if they attempted to escape, while Gibbon's column was half infantry, and in rapid marching in approaching the village, as well as in pursuing the Indians after the fight, General Gibbon's cavalry and infantry must become separated and the strength of the column be weakened. Second, General Custer's column was numerically stronger than Gibbon's and General Terry desired the strongest column to strike the Indians."

Fact #1766. Leaving the southeastern boundary of Little Bighorn Battlefield National Monument, the Park Service road becomes a private road across the Crow Reservation. The road drops down very near to the Little Big Horn River. It was at this point (Minneconjou Ford), which was near the center of the Indian encampment, that the Hunkpapa Chief, Gall, crossed to make his first attack on Custer's battalion (C, E, F, I, L companies), meeting the soldiers about three-fourths of a mile northeast of this ford.

Fact #1767. In their three fights with the Sioux expedition (Rosebud, Reno-Benteen, Custer), Indians reported to their relatives at the agencies that "they have captured over 400 stand of arms—carbines and rifles (revolvers) not counted—and ammunition without end; some sugar, coffee, bacon, and hard bread," according to the July report from Standing Rock Reservation (D.T.).

Fact #1768. Indians after LBH claimed "to have captured, from the whites this summer, over 900 horses and mules. I suppose this includes operations against soldiers, Crow Indians, and Black Hills miners." (From a report by the Commanding Officer at Standing Rock Reservation [D.T.], Capt. J.S. Poland, 6th Infantry)

Fact #1769. Just west of the Memorial Monument on Last Stand Hill at Little Bighorn Battlefield National Monument is an enclosure surrounded by an iron fence which was erected in 1930; within the enclosure are 52 white markers, representing the places where Custer and the last of his command were killed.

Fact #1770. Reviewing the actions taken by him and his command prior to LBH, Gen. A. H. Terry, commander of the Sioux Expedition of 1876, made these comments in his telegram to Division headquarters on June 27: "At the mouth of the Rosebud, I informed General Custer that I should take the supply-steamer *Far West* up the Yellowstone to ferry General Gibbon's column over the river, that I should personally accompany that column; and that it would, in all probability, reach the mouth of the Little Big Horn on the 26th instant. The steamer reached General Gibbon's troops, near the mouth of the Big Horn, early in the morning of the 24th, and at 4 o'clock in the afternoon all his men and animals were across the Yellowstone."

Fact #1771. Describing the movement of the Montana Column on June 24, 1876, in his telegram to Division headquarters on June 27, Gen. Terry said, "At 5 o'clock the column, consisting of five companies of the Seventh Infantry, four companies of the Second Cavalry, and a battery of three Gatling guns, marched out to and across Tullock's Creek. Starting soon after 5 o'clock in the morning on June 25th [the day of the battle], the infantry made a march of twenty-two miles over the most difficult country which I have ever seen. In order that scouts might be sent into the valley of the Little Big Horn, the cavalry, with the battery, was then pushed on thirteen or fourteen miles farther, reaching camp at midnight." The cavalry and the Gatling guns, over very difficult terrain, advanced 35 miles that day.

Fact #1772. On the battlefield tour route leading from the monument at the Custer Battlefield portion of the Little Bighorn Battlefield National Monument, to the Reno-Benteen Battlefield portion, the road is cut through the high point (Weir Point) from which Capt. Thomas Weir viewed the Custer battle on the afternoon of June 25. Lt. Edgerly took Co. D north beyond Weir Point but Capt. Weir signaled him to return as Indians approached. The advance party then retreated south back to Reno Hill. A descriptive sign marks Weir Point.

Fact #1773. Scouts from the Montana Column were sent out from their camp in the lower (northern) end of the valley of the Little Big Horn at 4:30 a.m. on June 26, 1876. Gen. Terry, commander of the 1876 Sioux Expedition, recounted their progress in his telegram to Division headquarters in Chicago (IL) on June 27: "They soon discovered three Indians, who were at first supposed to be Sioux, but when overtaken they proved to be Crows, who had been with General Custer. They brought the first intelligence of the battle. Their story was not credited. It was supposed that some fighting, perhaps severe, had taken place, but it was not believed that disaster could have overtaken so large a force as twelve companies of cavalry."

Fact #1774. Fort Abraham Lincoln State Park is four miles southeast of Mandan (ND) on State Hwy. 80. Lt. Col. George A. Custer commanded this post 1873-1876. It was the base for Custer's 1874 Black Hills expedition, resulting in the announcement of gold discoveries which attracted hordes of prospectors to the Black Hills, claimed as sacred by the Sioux (who had taken the land from the Crow).

Fact #1775. Sections A and B in the Custer Battlefield National Cemetery are the oldest sections, containing the remains of soldiers, their family members, and Indian scouts, who died during the frontier era. Other sections of the cemetery contain the remains of veterans of other conflicts, from the Spanish-American War to Viet Nam. These men and women represent the tapestry of America, yet they share one thing in common: they served the nation, and in many instances gave their lives so that we might enjoy its freedoms.

Fact #1776. "It was well-known to the Indians that the troops were in the field" in late June of 1876, according to an article by Capt. E.S. Godfrey in *Century* magazine January 1892. ". . .a battle was fully expected by [the Indians]; but the close proximity of our column was not known to them until the morning of the day of the battle. Several young men had left the hostile camp on that morning to go to one of the [Indian] agencies in Nebraska. They saw the dust made by the column of troops; some of their number returned to the village and gave warning that the troops were coming, so the attack was not a surprise."

Fact #1777. Early reports from Crow scouts who had been with Custer as to the extent of the disaster were not believed by the advance elements of the Montana Column, when the Crow were encountered early on June 26. Gen. Terry reported by telegram to Division headquarters in Chicago (IL) on June 27: "The infantry, which had broken camp very early [on the morning of the 26th], soon came up, and the whole column entered and moved up the valley of the Little Big Horn. During the afternoon, efforts were made to send scouts through to what was supposed to be General Custer's position, to obtain information of the condition of affairs; but those who were sent out were driven back by parties of Indians, who, in increasing numbers, were seen hovering in General Gibbon's front. At twenty minutes before 9 o'clock in the evening, the infantry had marched between twenty-nine and thirty miles."

Fact #1778. The quarterly *Custer/Little Bighorn Battlefield Advocate* was born in 1993, inspired by a controversial NPS plan to "privatize" the Battlefield. Its "mission statement" notes opposition to "the twin evils of overdevelopment and 'political correctness,'" and promises to "dish out the real skinny" on various practices at the Battlefield which the *Advocate* finds offensive. Those interested can contact *C/LBB Advocate*, Box 792, Malibu, CA 90265, or Custer Battlefield Update website at: http://members.aol.com/Custerfact/index.html.

Fact #1779. The earliest film on "the Custer Battle" was made in 1909, but the earliest film available on videotape is the 1912 *Custer's Last Fight*.

Fact #1780. Gen. Terry reported that the Indian encampment which had been attacked on June 25, 1876, by the 7th Cavalry column was "about three miles in length and about a mile in width," in his telegram to Division headquarters in Chicago (IL) on June 27. "Besides the lodges proper, a great number of temporary brushwood shelters was found in it, indicating that many men besides its proper inhabitants had gathered together there. Major Reno is very confident that there were a number of white men fighting with the Indians. It is believed that the loss of the Indians was large. I have as yet received no official reports in regard to the battle; but what is stated herein is gathered from the officers who were on the ground then and from those who have been over it since. Alfred H. Terry, Brigadier-General."

Fact #1781. Despite the fears of Terry and Custer that the Indians would discover the cavalry advance and flee, Indian accounts generally agree that their scouts had not discovered the soldiers' approach and that the attack came as a surprise (*The Book of the American West*). Although some panic did ensue, because of Reno's, and later Custer's, attacks, it may simply have been that the village was too big for the Indians to even try to run away—they had to stand and fight.

Fact #1782. As of 1997, there were about 4,950 burials in reserved spaces at the Custer Battlefield National Cemetery, with spaces for about 50 more. The cemetery is presently closed except for instances where deceased individuals reserved sites for spouses. Since the cemetery lies entirely within a historic site, an Act of Congress would be required to expand its borders.

Fact #1783. Fort Abraham Lincoln, now the site of a state park southeast of Mandan (ND), originally called Fort McKeen for Col. Henry Boyd McKeen who had been killed in the Civil War battle of Cold Harbor in 1864, was built on the site of an ancient Mandan Indian settlement known as Slant Village, and was located on the river bluffs. The post has been partially restored, including the Custer Home, which is interpreted daily by Park personnel.

Fact #1784. Gen. Terry's private diary entry for Wednesday, June 28: "Reno abandoned hill in morning. Moved down ridge & buried officers and men of Custer's five companies. Then came into valley & encamped on the right of Gibbon. Moved camp about four miles down valley at 8:00 p.m. Great trouble for hand litters. Horse litters reported as doing well."

Fact #1785. Col. John Gibbon, commanding the Montana Column, rode through the abandoned Indian village on the morning of June 27, 1876, after receiving the report regarding 197 soldiers' bodies on the nearby hillside. Col. Gibbon then discovered two bodies near the Reno Crossing, and noted: "More bodies of both men and horses were found close by, and it was noted that the bodies of men and horses laid almost always in pairs, and as this was the ground over which Colonel [Maj.] Reno's command retired towards the hills after its charge (north) down the valley, the inference was drawn that in the run the horses must have been killed first, and the riders after they fell."

Fact #1786. Only 765.34 acres of federal land are included in the Little Bighorn Battlefield National Monument. The Custer Battlefield Preservation Committee, Inc., owns an additional 2,200 acres of land contiguous to the Battlefield which is to be presented to the National Park Service.

Fact #1787. The Custer Battlefield Historical & Museum Association, Inc., was formed in 1953 to serve as the cooperating association for the National Park Service at Custer Battlefield National Monument. The Association served in that capacity for 40 years and raised almost a million dollars for the battlefield. The CBH&MA left the battlefield in 1993 to become an active non-profit independent educational organization whose purpose is now to encourage interest in the Battle of the Little Big Horn, and to protect the Little Bighorn Battlefield National Monument from commercial exploitation. For further information about the Association, write: CBH&MA, Box 902, Hardin MT 59034-0902.

Fact #1788. Capt. E.S. Godfrey, in his article "Custer's Last Battle," written from the vantage point of a company commander at that battle (he was a 1st Lt., Co. K, in June 1876) and of one who had met with many veterans of the battle, red and white, at the 10th anniversary in 1886, stated, "Major James McLaughlin, United States Indian Agent, stationed at the Devil's Lake Agency, Dakota, from 1870 to 1881, and at the Standing Rock Agency [D.T.] from 1881 to the present time, has made it a point to get estimates of the number of Indians at the hostile camp at the time of the battle. In his opinion. . .about one-third of the whole Sioux nation, including the northern Cheyennes and Arapahoes, were present at the battle."

Fact #1789. There is another Custer National Cemetery at Monroe (MI), Custer's "home town."

Fact #1790. White marble markers dot the Little Bighorn Battlefield today throughout the "Custer Battlefield" portion of the National Park Service site, but 249 were placed in 1890 while only 210 men fell under Custer's immediate command. Fifty-two stones mark grave sites around Custer Hill, where only 43 bodies were discovered. More than 50 markers can be seen between Custer Hill and Deep Ravine, although observers said no more than a dozen bodies were discovered there. And no marble headstones were placed in Deep Ravine, where almost every contemporary account says more than 28 soldiers fell. According to Sandy Barnard, a participant in the 1985 "dig," in his book *Digging Into Custer's Last Stand*, ". . .some students of the battle wonder if those men might still be buried somewhere in the twisting, bramble-choked coulee" known today as Deep Ravine.

Fact #1791. William H. "Buffalo Bill" Cody, who was scouting for Gen. Crook's column, rode into Gen. Terry's camp along the Rosebud on Thursday, August 10, according to Terry's private diary.

Fact #1792. The first hasty burials on Little Big Horn Battlefield were made three days after the battle wherever a body was found. Identified officers and some civilians were removed in 1877 for private burials in the East, and in 1881 all the remaining shallow graves were opened and the remains placed in a mass grave around the base of the large granite memorial placed on Battle Ridge in the "Last Stand" area. Today those original grave sites are symbolically preserved by the marble markers dotting the battlefield.

Fact #1793. Upon the arrival of the first superintendent of Custer Battlefield National Cemetery, Andrew N. Grover, in 1893, construction was begun on a home for him and his family. The present brownstone lodge, known today as The Stone House, was completed the following year. The building was one of the first permanent structures in eastern Montana and is now listed on the National Register of Historic Places.

Fact #1794. When the first wooden flagpole was erected at Custer Battlefield National Cemetery in 1896, the local Crow Indians began calling the superintendent the "ghost herder." They believed that as he lowered the flag in the evening, the dead soldiers' spirits rose from the graves and their spirits returned to the graves when he raised the flag the next morning.

Fact #1795. Over the years, skeletal remains of 7th Cavalrymen who fell at LBH have been uncovered near the battlefield and reburied in the Custer Battlefield National Cemetery as unknown soldiers.

Fact #1796. In 1958, remains of three soldiers from the Reno-Benteen Battlefield were moved to the Custer Battlefield National Cemetery.

Fact #1797. "Custer lost his fight against the Indians, but he did not lose his fight against corruption in the administration of Indian affairs and against the sale of ammunition to the Indians. The Government stopped immediately, so far as it could, the sale of arms and ammunition. Better treatment of the different tribes also resulted from the focusing of public opinion on the causes of the Sioux War. These were in large part the breaking of treaties by the whites and the cheating of Indians in the issuance of supplies." (C.F.Bates, June 20, 1926)

Fact #1798. "Information was despatched from General Sheridan that from one [Indian] agency alone about eighteen hundred lodges had set out to join the hostile camp [along the Little Big Horn River]; but that information did not reach General Terry until several days after the battle." (Capt. E.S. Godfrey, 1st Lt., Co. K, at LBH, writing years after the battle)

Fact #1799. "The story of Sitting Bull's being induced to come east on this trip is full of interesting incidents, which illustrate alike the enterprise of Messrs.

Cody & Salsbury, and the clever diplomacy of their manager, Major Burke," wrote the *Courier* reporter after Sitting Bull had arrived in Buffalo (NY) to join Buffalo Bill's "Wild West" show.

Fact #1800. In July 1881, Lt. Charles F. Roe (7th Cavalry) supervised the erection of a suitable monument on Last Stand Hill, where the remains of many of the fallen cavalry soldiers had been buried in 1877 and 1879. The 36,000-pound granite shaft with the names of most of the dead carved upon it stands there now, overlooking the Little Big Horn River.

Fact #1801. Civilian scout James Campbell, who had restaked the original grave sites at the "Custer Battlefield" in 1881 when the bulk of the remains gathered from various spots in the battlefield had been reinterred into the mass grave at the base of the monument, returned to the battlefield in 1890. He assisted a detachment commanded by Capt. Owen J. Sweet (7th Cav.) which installed the marble markers which still decorate the battlefield, denoting the spots where soldiers fell during the battle. Lamentably, the detachment erected 249 stones while only 210 men died with Custer's battalions.

Fact #1802. "It was believed that the Indians were on the head of the Rosebud or over on the Little Horn, a divide or ridge only fifteen miles wide, separating the two streams. It was announced by General Terry that General Custer's column would strike the blow, and General Gibbon and his men received the decision without a murmur. There was great rivalry between the two columns and each wanted to be in at the death. General Gibbon's cavalry [2d Cav.] had been in the field since the 22nd of last February. . .and the infantry [7th Inf.] had been in the field and on the march since early last March. They had come to regard the Indians as their peculiar property." (July 8, 1876, *New York Herald*)

Fact #1803. A message was sent on June 27, 1876, from Gen. Alfred Terry, commander of the 1876 Sioux Expedition, to Captain Grant Marsh of the supply steamer *Far West*, asking Capt. Marsh to prepare for a speedy trip to Fort Abraham Lincoln, near Bismarck (D.T.), over 700 miles away, to transport wounded soldiers from Reno's and Benteen's commands to a hospital.

Fact #1804. In 1882, the U.S. Army changed the designation of the basic cavalry unit from "company," also used for infantry units, to "troops." Writers on LBH after 1882 often refer to these units as "troops," although they were not called "troops" at the time of the battle. (In this book, "troops" refer to bodies of men; cavalry units are referred to as "companies.")

Fact #1805. Testimony from officers and men during the 1879 Reno Court of Inquiry in Chicago (IL) made it clear that most of the men at the Reno-Benteen site didn't feel like they had abandoned Custer, but, rather, that Custer had joined Terry's column, abandoning them.

Fact #1806. During LBH, 1st Lt. Edward S. Godfrey was the commanding officer of Co. K in Benteen's battalion. Over a decade after the battle, now-Capt. Godfrey wrote "Custer's Last Battle" for one of the popular magazines of the day. In the foreword, Battlefield Supt. Richard T. Hart notes that "Captain Godfrey tells this story of Custer's last battle from the military side, as that is the side he was on. It appears as an objective account from this point of view, and does include information from interviews with Indian participants following the battle, the only source left who could report on the demise of Custer and the men caught with him. Godfrey and his cavalrymen had taken position on another section of the battleground, with no knowledge of Custer's straits, and although harassed badly, managed to avoid annihilation until relief came."

Fact #1807. Summing up a presentation in 1977, Francis B. Taunton, a member of the English Westerners' Society in London, offered the following judgement about "Terry's Celebrated Order To Custer": "Custer had been given his chance; Terry had no intention of taking the blame because he had thrown away that chance." Taunton's article was published in a limited edition of *Special Publication No. 5*, entitled: "Sufficient Reason?"

Fact #1808. A historical marker at the junction of the Big Horn and Yellowstone Rivers, on US Hwy. 10 in southeastern Montana, one mile west of Big Horn Station, denotes the spot from which Gen. Alfred E. Terry and Col. John Gibbon started up the Big Horn and Tullock Creek to aid Custer's column in seeking the Indian village reported to be in the vicinity. The column arrived on the banks of the Little Big Horn on June 27, 1876, two days after LBH.

Fact #1809. Fort Custer in Big Horn County (MT) one mile west of I-90 and two miles southeast of Hardin (MT), was established July 4, 1877, on a bluff above the confluence of the Big Horn and Little Big Horn rivers, to control the Sioux and other Indians. It was originally called Big Horn Post or Big Horn Barracks, but was designated Fort Custer in November 1877. A D.A.R. marker designates the site, which is on the Crow Indian Reservation.

Fact #1810. The 1991 miniseries *Son of the Morning Star* was well-done except for the accuracy of the script, the comprehensibility of the script, and the casting of Gary Cole as Custer—that is to say, the scenery was great and the movie made as much sense as the book.

Fact #1811. The web page for the Little Bighorn Battlefield National Monument can be found at: nps.gov/libi/.

Fact #1812. Maj. James McLaughlin, a long time Indian agent, after years of research, estimated the number of Indians at the camp along the Little Big Horn River in late June 1876 "as between twelve and fifteen thousand; that one out of four is a low number in determining the number of warriors present; every male over fourteen years of age may be considered a warrior in a general fight such as was the battle of the Little Big Horn; also, considering the extra hazards of the hunt and expected battle, fewer squaws would accompany the recruits from the agencies. The minimum strength of their fighting men may then be put down as between twenty-five hundred and three thousand," wrote Capt. E.S. Godfrey in his article, "Custer's Last Battle," published in *Century* magazine, January 1892. As a 1st Lt., Capt. Godfrey had commanded Co. K in Benteen's battalion on June 25-26, 1876.

Fact #1813. Camp Supply (I.T.), from which Custer launched his strike against the Cheyenne village on the Washita River in November 1868, later Fort Supply, is now occupied by the Western State Hospital. Some buildings survive from the Army period: a brick guardhouse, a log fire station, and a few others. It is part of a registered historic district.

Fact #1814. Gen. Philip Sheridan developed his theories of "total war" during the Civil War, serving as Gen. U.S. Grant's cavalry commander in Virginia, and overseeing the devastation of the Shenandoah Valley late in the War. Writing in 1878 about the Indians, he said, "We took away their country and their means of support, broke up their modes of living, their habits of life, introduced disease and decay among them, and it was for this and against this they made war. Could anyone expect less?"

Fact #1815. Continuing interest in the military history of the American West sparked the formation of many "hobby" organizations to study that history. One of these is The Order of the Indian Wars (OIW), "a spiritual descendant" of the military organization for officer veterans of the Indian Wars, the Order of Indian Wars of the United States (OIWUS), organized near the turn of the century and recently revived. The modern organization (OIW), established in 1979, has a newsletter and an annual "Assembly" at various Indian Wars sites. (PO Box 7401, Little Rock AR 72217; indianwars@aristotle.net (e-mail).

Fact #1816. According to *Soldier and Brave*, edited by Robert G. Ferris, in the stunning victory by the Sioux and Cheyenne at LBH "lay the roots of Indian defeat. The Nation demanded that Custer's death be avenged and the Army poured troops into the Sioux country. The alliance of tribes fragmented, and through the winter General [George] Crook and Colonel [Nelson] Miles hounded them across the frozen land. By spring, after several battles and great suffering, most of the Sioux and Cheyennes had returned to their agencies. Only Sitting Bull scorned surrender. He and some diehard followers took refuge in Canada. They held firm until 1881, when hunger at last compelled their capitulation." Sitting Bull and his followers returned to the U.S.

Fact #1817. "The officer in charge of the mounted infantry, in the hills to the north of us, rode up to where General Terry and I sat upon our horses, and his voice trembled as he said, 'I have a very sad report to make. I have counted one hundred and ninety-seven dead bodies lying in the hills!' 'White men?' was the first question asked. 'Yes, white men.' A look of horror was upon every face, and for a moment no one spoke." (Col. John Gibbon's record of the report from the 7th Infantry, 1st Lt. James Bradley commanding, sent on patrol to scout for Custer on the morning of June 27, 1876)

Fact #1818. Col. John Gibbon, commanding the Montana Column, recorded his impressions of the abandoned village on June 27, 1876: "Nearly the whole valley was black and smoking with the fire which had swept over it, and it was with some difficulty I could find grass sufficient for our animals, as it existed only in spots close enough to the stream where too green to burn. Except the fire, the ground presented but few evidence of the conflict which had taken place. Now and then a dead horse was seen; but as I approached the bend of the creek just below the hill occupied by the troops, I came upon the body of a soldier lying on his face near a dead horse. He was stripped, his scalp gone, his head beaten in and his body filled with bullet-holes and arrows."

Fact #1819. The Little Big Horn Associates, founded in 1967, is based on the study of "the life and times of George Armstrong Custer." The organization has built a solid reputation for scholarship over the years, striving to "seek the truth" about Custer, the 7th Cavalry, and Custeriana. The group holds an annual meeting at locations related to Custer's life and times (including his Civil War career), and publishes a newsletter and a semi-annual *Research Review*. LBHA, 105 Bartlett Pl., Brooklyn, NY 11229; http://www.lbha.org (website).

Fact #1820. Testifying at the Reno Court of Inquiry in 1879, 2d Lt. George D. Wallace (Co. G) stated, "[The 7th Cavalry] had been marching for three or four days, making many of the marches at night, and they moved that morning [June 25, 1876] with little or no breakfast. The men were tired and the horses worn out." Col. Elwood L. Nye quoted this testimony in his 1941 article in the *Veterinary Bulletin* to advance his case that part of the blame for Custer's defeat could be blamed on his "abuse" of the men and animals of his command.

Fact #1821. The heroic portrayal of Custer in the movies reached its peak in 1941, with the never-yet-topped *They Died With Their Boots On*. Custer scholar and historian Dr. Brian Dippie has commented, "after Errol Flynn's 'last stand', there was really nothing more to say on the subject."

Equipment

Fact #1822. Figuring time and distance it appears that after Reno separated from the main column and, with his battalion, crossed the Little Big Horn about 2:30 p.m. to advance toward the attack on the upper end of the village, Custer and the five companies (C, E, F, I, L) under his immediate command, rode nearly seven miles to the final action in less than two hours. (Nye)

Fact #1823. In the late 1960s there were two Colt Single-Action six-shooters in the H.N. Sherwood Collection at El Paso (TX) that may have been associated with Custer's Arkiara scouts, according to *The Saga of the Colt-Six Shooter*, published in 1969. The revolvers were properly martially marked with "US" and inspector's markings, possessed the serial numbers 13201 and 13185, had all matching numbers and ivory grips, and were nickel-plated. Both barrels have been cut down to 4¾".

Fact #1824. Artist Edgar S. Paxson who painted one of the better-documented depictions of the "Last Stand," had received a detailed account of the arms and equipment, issue and non-standard, used during the battle, by 1st Lt. Edward S.Godfrey (commander Co. K, Benteen's battalion on June 25, 1876) in a letter from the soldier to the artist dated January 1896.

Fact #1825. "I have the honor to report that in the engagement of 25 & 26 June between the 7th Cav'y & the hostile Sioux that out of 380 carbines in my command six were rendered unserviceable in the following manner. . .failure of the breechblock to close, leaving a space between the head of the cartridge & the end of the block & when the piece was discharged & the block thrown open, the head of the cartridge was pulled off & the cylinder remained in the chamber, whence with the means at hand, it was impossible to extract it. I believe this is a radical defect, & in the hands of hastily organized troops, would lead to the most disastrous results." (Maj. Marcus Reno's report, July 11, 1876, to Chief of Ordnance Brig. Gen. Stephen Vincent Benet, about the difficulties with the 1873 Springfield carbine experienced by his men at LBH)

Fact #1826. Complaints about the effectiveness of the 1873 Springfield carbine were not limited to the 7th Cavalry; Capt. J.W. Reilly, chief ordnance officer for the Military Division of the Missouri, wrote headquarters July 20, 1876: "Sir, My reason for asking for so little carbine ammunition, in comparison with rifle ammunition for the Department of Dakota, is that it is the general impression in the Army that the latter is superior to the former for both arms. The trajectory of the carbine ball is too much curved, and the range not long enough to cope with the rifle in the hands of Indians. Old huntsmen on the plains tell me they invariably use the 70 grain cartridge with the carbine, and find the recoil not too much."

Fact #1827. The Chief Ordnance Officer of the Division of the Missouri, Capt. J.W. Reilly, expressed his criticism of the Springfield 1873 carbine in a July 20, 1876, letter to the Chief of Ordnance in Washington (DC): "Within short ranges the carbine shoots too high, while its extreme range is insufficient. I respectfully recommend for your consideration the propriety of using the same cartridge (70 grains powder) in both [rifles and carbines]. This would require a corresponding alteration in the rear sight of the carbine. When our rifles fall into the hands of rifle clubs and huntsmen, the powder charge is invariably increased in the cartridge to 80 or 85 grains. The complaint against the feebleness of the carbine cartridge is almost universal."

Fact #1828. The commander of the National Armory in Springfield (MA) commented on the discussion regarding the merits of increasing the powder charge in carbine bullets, stimulated by a complaint from Maj. Marcus Reno on July 11, 1876, about the effectiveness of the carbines used by his troops at LBH. "As the [Ordnance] Department is aware, the only reason for not issuing the rifle cartridge for the carbine was the very general complaint from line officers on the severity of the recoil. As there seems to be a change of opinion on this subject, I hope it may lead to the adoption of the rifle cartridge for both rifle and carbine. The difference in range between the two cartridges in the carbine is not, however, very great up to 500 yards. After that there is a slight falling off in favor of the rifle cartridge. . . .I think, therefore, that the rifle cartridge may be issued at once. . ."

Fact #1829. Maj. Marcus Reno's critical report to the Chief of Ordnance on the Springfield 1873 carbine in July 1876 was endorsed by Lt. Col. J.G. Benton, the commander of the National Armory in Springfield (MA): "As the carbines which Col. [sic—Reno's brevet rank] Reno refers to as being unserviceable from defects of manufacture, or from use, will probably be replaced by others which are serviceable—I recommend that they be sent to this Armory for examination—with samples of the cartridges used in the engagement [LBH], if there be any remaining."

Fact #1830. Frederick W. Benteen, Jr., of Atlanta (GA), only son of Capt. Frederick W. Benteen, told author John du Mont (*Custer Battle Guns*) that his father had owned a nickel-plated Colt Model "P" revolver, cased in a wooden box with cartridges in bored holes. He said this was the only pistol his father had, and that it had been destroyed in a fire. The weapon, Benteen, Jr., said, had belonged to Maj. Marcus Reno and was carried by him at LBH. Reno had given it to Capt. Benteen, who had, himself, carried the U.S. Regulation issue Colt revolver on June 25-26, 1876.

Fact #1831. William A. Allen, who visited the Custer battlefield in 1877, noted the evidence of forked sticks along the Indian's firing line around the Reno-Benteen position, an indication that the buffalo hunter's method of steadying his weapon had been used by Indian marksmen using newly-captured Springfield carbines. (John S. du Mont, *Custer Battle Guns*)

Fact #1832. Col. Elwood L. Nye, who advanced a strong argument in a 1941 article in the *Veterinary Bulletin* that Custer's men and mounts were worn out even before LBH began, wrote, "We know that during this approach march at least four troopers dropped out of the column because their mounts were so exhausted they could not be goaded forward. We know this could be the only reason, for in a country then seen to be swarming with enemy Indians, no man would be left behind who could do anything to prevent it. Two of these men later succeeded in joining Reno. The fate of the others is not known."

Fact #1833. "What if Custer had chosen to accept the offer of [Maj. James F.] Brisbin's four companies of [2d] cavalry and the two Gatling guns offered during their [June 21] shipboard conference? A tremendous effect could have resulted as the guns might well have slowed Custer to the degree his command would have been the one to arrive at the river meeting place late on the 26th." (Lecturer Barbara Zimmerman, 1991 CBH&MA Symposium)

Fact #1834. Testimony at the Reno Court of Inquiry in 1879 in Chicago (IL) produced statements that the 1873 Springfield carbine had an "effective" range of 1200 yards, but "range" and "accuracy" are two different things. Capt. Frederick Benteen stated in his March 1874 "Ordnance Report" that the carbines issued to his company were "altogether too short for accurate shooting at long range." Being able to shoot a bullet 1200 yards is not the same as being able to hit something at 1200 yards. Few carbines are accurate long range weapons, and the 7th Cavalry soldiers at the Little Big Horn were armed with carbines.

Fact #1835. Maj. Marcus Reno sent a report to the Chief of Ordnance on July 11, 1876, criticizing the performance of the 1873 Springfield carbines used by his troops at LBH. The biggest problem, he said, was jammed breeches. "I send you these observations," Maj. Reno wrote, "made during a most terrific battle & under circumstances which would induce men to fire with recklessness, as our capture was certain death & torture, & the men fully appreciated the result of falling into the hands of the Indians, & were not as cool perhaps as they would have been fighting a civilized foe."

Fact #1836. At the reburial of the soldiers' bodies in 1878, Gen. Nelson A. Miles is said to have conducted firing tests to see if volley firing could be heard on Custer Hill from Reno Point; the results were affirmative. Cavalry exercises were held on the battlefield after Fort Custer (M.T.) was established in 1877, and hunters and Indians roamed the area for many years. All the cartridges found on the battlefield in "modern" times are not necessarily from LBH.

Fact #1837. Testimony at the Reno Court of Inquiry (Chicago [IL], 1879) eventually caused the Army Ordnance Department to test captured Indian arms to determine if they were superior to the Army weapons. The 1873 Springfield carbines were specifically eliminated from the tests, which did include Sharps buffalo rifles and carbines, Henry and Winchester rifles and carbines, Spencer carbines, Lemat and Hawken "plains rifles," double-barrel shotguns, and Parker trade muskets—in all, 17 breech-loaders and 12 muzzle loaders, with a few assorted percussion pistols thrown in. The Ordnance Department was "amazed that anyone, even an Indian, would fire guns in such condition," and some could not be made to fire at all. (John S. du Mont, *Custer Battle Guns*)

Fact #1838. "I also desire to call attention to the fact that my loss would have been less had I been provided with some instrument similar to the 'Trowel bayonet'—& I am sure had an opponent of that arm been present with my command on the night of June 25th, that he would have given his right hand for 50 bayonets. I had but 3 spades and 3 axes & with them loosened the ground which the men threw in front of them with tin cups & such other articles as could in any way serve the same purpose. Very Resp'y, M.A. Reno, Maj. 7th c'vy, Comd'g Regt." (Closing of Reno's report to the Chief of Ordnance, July 11, 1876, in the earlier portion of which he criticized the performance of the Springfield carbines used by his troops at LBH)

Fact #1839. Custer's Last Stand in 1876 was an important event in the history of U.S. Army weapons, because the Army's reloading improvements program began just after that battle and was an important correction. At that time, there was a real need for improved marksmanship in the military. Analysis of the defeat of a popular general and all his command by ill-equipped "savages" highlighted the Army's monthly allotment of 10 rounds per man for target practice. Improvements were obviously needed, and with this tragic example, improvements were undertaken. (James Zupan, *Tools, Targets, and Troopers*)

Events

Fact #1840. On June 28, the 7th Cavalry proceeded to the battlefield to locate, count, and bury the bodies of their comrades. Four officers and 14 enlisted men were found to be missing, but none was found alive.

Fact #1841. When the Custer Battlefield Historical & Museum Association was founded in 1953, among the charter members were Joe Medicine Crow, Henry Old Coyote, Lloyd G. Old Coyote, and William Watt, son of William White who was the first "unofficial" guide at the Battlefield and a veteran of the Custer Campaign. Percentage-wise, the Association had more American Indian representation in the group than it ever would have again.

Fact #1842. Many anniversaries of the battle have been celebrated since the first commemoration in 1877. On the 10th anniversary (1886), several Army and Indian veterans of the fight returned to the battlefield for an elaborate observance, including Capt. Benteen, Lt. Godfrey, trumpeter Penwell, and Chief Gall of the Hunkpapa Sioux. (1978 "Custer Battlefield" brochure)

Fact #1843. Army Surgeon Holmes Offley Paulding, who served with Gibbon's Montana Column, wrote his mother on June 28: "We reached here yesterday morning to find that Custer's command had attacked an immense village extending along the valley from here up and down several miles each way. His command divided into 3 battalions attacking at different points on the 25th. He, with five whole companies, was literally annihilated, not an Officer or man escaping." (*The Great Sioux War*)

Fact #1844. When the mammoth village along the Little Big Horn broke up, the tribes and families scattered, some to the north, others to the south. Most returned to the reservations and surrendered in the next few years.

Fact #1845. After LBH, Col. Nelson A. Miles was given the task of blocking the escape route of the fleeing Indians. By the end of September 1876, most of the Army units involved had returned to their posts but Miles pressed on, outfitting his men for a winter expedition, and caught up with Sitting Bull at Cabin Creek (MT). Miles had 394 soldiers, Sitting Bull had 1,000 warriors. After several days of fighting, over 2,000 Sioux men, women, and children surrendered to the Army, but Sitting Bull escaped and made his way to Canada.

Fact #1846. In 1926, at the 50th anniversary of the famous Battle of the Little Big Horn, some 30,000 people attended an impressive ceremony. Indians in full regalia greeted 7th Cavalry soldiers in uniform, splendidly mounted, as the United States Army Air Corps conducted a fly-over. It was a never to be forgotten event, and, unfortunately, a never to be repeated one. In 1976, the 100th anniversary of this battle, fewer than 600 persons attended a ceremony sadly lacking in any semblance of pageantry or direction. The speakers' platform was given over to an endless number of Indians, each castigating those present and entailing grievance on top of grievance. Without passing judgement on the validity of the Indians' remarks, it can, nonetheless, be said that those who come to this battlefield did not come to be verbally assaulted. (*Custer Centennial Observance*, Old Army Press, 36650 Canal, Ft. Collins, CO 80524)

Fact #1847. At the "Court of Inquiry in the Case of Major Marcus A. Reno, Concerning His Conduct at the Battle of the Little Big Horn River on June 25-26, 1876," held in Chicago (IL) in 1879, 23 witnesses testified.

Fact #1848. The Custer Battlefield National Monument (now the Little Bighorn Battlefield National Monument) was ravaged by a grassfire in 1983, as the flames raced up Deep Ravine and across the arid, dry-grass hillsides and swales, destroying years of dense grass and sagebrush cover that had grown up since the 1876 battle.

Fact #1849. The Custer Battlefield Historical & Museum Association was organized in 1953 as a closed club with about 60 members. Once a year the members met at the Stone House (formerly the home of the Battlefield Superintendent) with a business meeting and a report by the Battlefield Historian, before adjourning to the Superintendent's home (at the Battlefield) for a potluck picnic. Most of the members were from the local area.

Fact #1850. On the 50th anniversary of the Battle of the Little Big Horn (1926), Chief White Bull led a group of 80 Sioux and Cheyenne survivors of the fight to the battlefield. Six years later, in 1932, White Bull claimed to noted author Stanley Vestal that he was the slayer of Custer, a "secret" Vestal kept until 1957, long after White Bull's death.

Fact #1851. The actual field work on the 1984-1985 archaeological "digs" at Custer Battlefield National Monument, resulting from a 1983 grassfire which denuded much of the landscape, making it accessible to archaeological research, was done by 62 individuals, including students from Sheridan Girls School, under the direction of archaeologists Douglas D. Scott and Richard A. Fox, Jr. Many of the volunteers were members of the Custer Battlefield Historical & Museum Association, Inc.

Fact #1852. At the 100th anniversary of the Battle of the Little Big Horn, National Park Service Assistant Director Robert M. Utley stated, in his official speech on June 24, 1976, ". . .let us not infuse this battlefield with a modern meaning untrue to the past. Let us not bend it artificially to serve contemporary needs and ends, however laudable." Yet this is exactly what the Park Service allowed to happen, according to *Custer Centennial Observance*, published by Old Army Press, which stated that this action "not only denied the American public of a meaningful Centennial Observance, it also tore apart one of the National Parks' best cooperating associations" and finally destroyed the relationship when the Association opposed NPS plans to allow an adjacent theme park.

Fact #1853. H.R. Porter, M.D., who served as the 7th Cavalry's physician and surgeon at LBH, was among the witnesses at the Reno Court of Inquiry in January and February 1879 in Chicago (IL).

Fact #1854. "Comanche," Capt. Myles Keogh's horse, was found alive on the battlefield after the battle, and thereafter designated the "lone survivor" of the Custer Battle. Wounded in seven places, Comanche was transported to Fort Abraham Lincoln (D.T.) and nursed back to health.

Fact #1855. After the steamer *Far West*, carrying the wounded from LBH, arrived at Bismarck (D.T.), telegraph operator J.M. Carnahan took his seat at the telegraph key and for 22 hours he hardly moved from his chair, telling the nation and the world about the tragedy at the Little Big Horn. Upon completing his original message, he remained another 60-odd hours at the key without sleep sending newspaper dispatches throughout the country.

Fact #1856. The news of the Army's disaster on the banks of the Little Big Horn River on June 25, 1876, swept across the plains like a grass fire. At Pine Ridge Reservation (D.T.) a large group of Cheyenne rode out on the warpath, scenting plunder, scalps, and honor. Col. Wesley Merritt's 5th Cavalry, with William F. "Buffalo Bill" Cody as chief scout, made a 30-hour forced march to cut off the fleeing Cheyenne at War Bonnet Creek (NE). It was here that the Cheyenne chief Yellow Hand was killed by Cody in a frontier incident almost as controversial as "Custer's Last Stand."

Fact #1857. One year after LBH, during the summer of 1877, Co. I, 7th Cavalry, under the command of Capt. Michael V. Sheridan, returned to the battlefield. The bodies of 11 officers and two civilians were exhumed and shipped to the homes of relatives of the deceased. Lt. Col. Custer's remains were sent to the post cemetery at the United States Military Academy at West Point (NY) and reburied October 10, 1877.

Fact #1858. After discovering Custer's body surrounded by dead cavalrymen at the crest of a hill overlooking the west bank of the Little Big Horn, Lt. James H. Bradley, 7th Infantry, Montana Column, immediately reported to Col. John Gibbon, "the first intelligence of the battle received." A few moments later a scout arrived from Reno's command, asking for assistance, and Gen. Terry and Col. Gibbon pushed forward to the rescue.

Fact #1859. At the age of 30, the horse Comanche, the "last survivor" of Custer's command, died at Fort Riley (KS) where the 7th Cavalry regiment was then stationed. The horse's body was prepared by Prof. L.I. Dyche of the University of Kansas, and is now displayed at the Dyche Museum of the University of Kansas in Lawrence.

Fact #1860. The first movie ever produced about LBH was *On the Little Big Horn, or, Custer's Last Stand.*

Fact #1861. Eleven 7th Cavalry Regiment officers testified as witnesses during the 26-day Reno Court of Inquiry, held in Chicago (IL) in January and February of 1879: Maj. Marcus Reno, Capt. F. W. Benteen, Capt. Myles Moylan, Capt. T.M. McDougall, Capt. E.G. Mathey (a 1st Lt. at LBH), Capt. E.S. Godfrey (a 1st Lt. at LBH), 1st Lt. G.D. Wallace, 1st Lt. C.A. Varnum (a 2d Lt. at LBH), 1st Lt. Luther Hare (a 2d Lt. at LBH), 1st Lt. W.S. Edgerly (a 2d Lt. at LBH), and 1st Lt. C.C. DeRudio.

Fact #1862. The numerous artifacts found on Calhoun Hill during the 1984 archaeological "dig" at Custer Battlefield National Monument, indicate, in terms of cartridge pattern, that organized resistance had taken place in the area. (*Digging Into Custer's Last Stand*, Sandy Barnard)

Fact #1863. The Custer Battlefield visitor center and museum was dedicated on June 25, 1952.

Fact #1864. In 1926, a 50th anniversary celebration of the Battle of the Little Big Horn was held. In connection with this, a column, "Lost and Won: Custer's Last Battle," was published in the *New York Times* of June 20, 1926: "On June 25 there will be a celebration by Indians and white man alike of the fiftieth anniversary of Custer's fight with the Indians on Little Big Horn River. In that fight, the unbeaten Custer, four members of his family and 200 troopers of the Seventh Cavalry rode boldly to their death against Sioux and Cheyenne warriors, while the greater part of his regiment fumbled his plan of battle and failed to respond to his call for reinforcements."

Fact #1865. On June 27, 1876, Gen. Alfred H. Terry, commander of the 1876 Sioux Expedition in southern Montana, sent the following telegram from the field to the Adjutant-General's Office in Chicago (IL): "It is my painful duty to report that day before yesterday, the 25th instant, a great disaster overtook General Custer and the troops under his command. At 12 o'clock of the 22d, he started with his whole regiment and a strong detachment of scouts and guides from the mouth of the Rosebud. Proceeding up that river about twenty miles, he struck a very heavy Indian trail which had previously been discovered, and, pursuing it, found that it led, as it was supposed that it would lead, to the Little Big Horn River. Here he found a village of almost unexampled extent and at once attacked it with that portion of his force which was immediately at hand."

Fact #1866. Ten years after LBH, Hunkpapa chief Gall told western photographer D.W. Barry, "Our ponies were well rested and fast runners, but the soldiers' horses [at Last Stand Hill] were so hungry that they were eating grass while the battle was going on and our braves had no difficulty catching all of them. While making our way to Poplar River these horses were not much good and we left a lot of them on the Missouri River."

Fact #1867. The four volunteer sharpshooters and 15 of the 16 volunteer "water carriers" at Water Carriers' Ravine on June 26, 1876, earned individual Medals of Honor for their gallant conduct in the effort to procure water for the wounded at the Reno-Benteen position, according to the "Reno-Benteen Entrenchment Trail" brochure (LBBNM). Actually, there were three "water carriers" in the party who did not receive Medals of Honor.

Fact #1868. Assistant Surgeon Holmes O. Paulding was with the relieving column under Gen. Terry and Col. Gibbon, which arrived in the Little Big Horn valley on the morning of June 27, and wrote in *Surgeon's Diary*, "All the men were—when I got there—in spite of all their hardships and sufferings, cheerful and apparently as cool and nonchalant as though nothing much had happened and though the announcement of Custer's fate fell upon them like an unexpected shock, they soon rallied. . . .They appear to be just beginning to realize what it all means."

Fact #1869. The Terry-Gibbon column bivouacked on the flats immediately west of the Little Big Horn River, where the village had been located, on June 27. They were soon joined by the 344 survivors of the 7th Cavalry, plus the civilian packers and guides. On June 28, the Custer dead were counted, identified to the extent possible, and given a hurried burial on the field. Litters were rigged for the seriously wounded from the Reno-Benteen position, and that evening the entire force moved slowly back (north) down the Little Big Horn to its mouth, where the steamer *Far West* awaited at the confluence of the Big Horn River, near the present town of Hardin (MT). About 30 badly wounded were placed on board the *Far West* for transport back to Fort Abraham Lincoln (D.T.).

Fact #1870. Four civilians—packers B.F. Churchill and John Frett, interpreter F.F. Girard, and scout George Herendeen—testified as witnesses before the 1879 Reno Court of Inquiry held in Chicago (IL).

Fact #1871. Pvt. Elijah J. Strode (orderly for Lt. Charles Varnum, Co. A, Detachment of Indian Scouts), who was wounded in the valley fight, was discharged from the Army June 1877 as a private; enlisted September 1877 and appointed Sgt. (Co. D); fought in the Snake Creek Fight (M.T.) against Chief Joseph's Nez Perce. According to one source he was murdered February 1881 at Fort Yates (D.T.); another source says he was killed by a man named Brody at Sturgis (SD); while another states he died a natural death at Belle Fourche (SD).

Fact #1872. On August 9-10, 1983, a rampaging grass fire swept across Custer Battlefield National Monument. Flames 15 feet high and half a mile wide were whipped by winds, which, fortunately, changed before the Visitors Center, the Stone House, the maintenance sheds, and the park housing were engulfed. This led the way to two archeological digs, in 1984 and 1985, done by volunteers under the direction of professional archaeologists, which have added considerably to knowledge about the battle.

Fact #1873. At the 50th anniversary of Custer's Last Stand in 1926, hundreds of mounted Indians in full war dress, preceded by 80 Sioux and Cheyenne survivors of the fight, followed Chief White Bull to meet the 7th Cavalry column as it arrived at the granite monument on the battlefield. Chief White Bull raised his hand in the peace sign, and Gen. E.S. Godfrey (1st Lt. commanding Co. K, Benteen's battalion, at LBH) sheathed his sword. They shook hands, the Chief gave the General a fine blanket, and the General gave the Chief a large American flag.

Fact #1874. Four military officers not connected to the 7th Cavalry Regiment testified as witnesses in the Reno Court of Inquiry (Chicago [IL] 1879): Col. John Gibbon, commander of the Montana Column during the 1876 Sioux Expedition; LTC Michael Sheridan, Military Secretary to the Chief of Staff of the

Army, Gen. W.T. Sherman; Capt. J.S. Payne, 5th Cavalry; and 1st Lt. Ed Ma-
guire, Corps of Engineers.

Fact #1875. Seventeen miles northeast of Harrison (NE) on US 20, a historical marker points out the site of the War Bonnet Creek battlesite, where William
F. "Buffalo Bill" Cody purportedly took "the first scalp for Custer" in an alterca-
tion between soldiers of the 5th Cavalry and their scout, Buffalo Bill, and a
party of Cheyenne led by "chief" Yellow Hand, on July 17, 1876. Cody publicized this event internationally in his "Wild West" show.

Fact #1876. For the cavalry troops in the field after the Custer battle, there
was little rest until the Indians, so completely victorious at the Little Big Horn,
were subdued; as the "hostiles" dispersed, some were pursued and defeated in
the Battle of Slim Buttes, others escaped, and, with Sitting Bull, took refuge in
Canada where they remained for several years. The campaign would continue
but the Battle of the Little Big Horn had passed into history.

Bibliography

Anderson, Harry H. "Cheyennes at the Little Big Horn - A Study of Statistics." *North Dakota Historical Society Quarterly* 27.2 (1960).

Barnard, Sandy. *Digging Into Custer's Last Stand*. Terre Haute, 1986.

Bates, Charles F. *Custer's Indian Battles*. Bronxville, 1936.

Bates, Charles F. and Fairfax Downey. *Fifty Years After the Little Big Horn Battle*. Grand Rapids, 1973.

Belden, George P. *Belden, the White Chief, or Twelve Years Among the Wild Indians of the Plains*. New York, 1870.

Benson, D. S. *The Black Hills War 1876-1877*. Chicago, 1983.

Bland, T. A. "Brief History of the Late Military Invasion of the Home of the Sioux." NC., 1891.

Boller, Henry A. *Among the Indians*. Philadelphia, 1868.

Bostwick, Bob. *Henry Bostwick: Mountain Man—Army Scout*. N.P. n.d.

Brininstool, E. A. *Troopers With Custer: Historic Incidents of The Battle Of The Little Big Horn*. Harrisburg, 1952.

Brown, Dee. *Bury My Heart At Wounded Knee*. New York, 1970.

Burdick, Usher L. *The Last Battle of the Sioux Nation*. Stevens Point, 1929.

Burdick, Usher L. and Eugene D. Hart. *Jacob Horner and the Indian Campaign of 1876 and 1877*. Baltimore, 1942.

Butterworth, W. E. *Soldiers On Horseback: The Story Of The United States Cavalry*. New York, 1967.

Carroll, John M., ed. *The Gibson and Edgerly Narratives*. Bryan, n.d.

— *I, Varnum: The Autobiographical Reminiscences of Custer's Chief of Scouts*. Glendale, 1982.

Carter, William H. *Horses, Saddles And Bridles*. Leavenworth, 1895.

Church, Robert. "Did Custer Believe His Scouts?" *5th Annual Symposium Custer Battlefield Historical & Museum Assn.*, held at Hardin, Montana, on June 21, 1991: 61.

Constable, George, ed. *Time Life Books: The Old West*. New York, 1990.

Cromie, Alice. *Tour Guide to the Old West*. New York, 1977.

Custer, E. B. *Boots and Saddles, or Life in Dakota with General Custer*. New York, 1885.

—. *Following The Guidon*. New York, 1890.

—. *Tenting on the Plains or General Custer in Kansas and Texas*. New York, 1874.

Custer, George A. *My Life On The Plains or Personal Experiences with Indians*. New York, 1874.

—. "The Redman." *The Harrisonian* 2.1, 1989.

Daly, H. W. *Manual of Pack Transportation*. Santa Monica, 1981.

Davis, Theodore. "With Generals in Camp Homes," *Brand Book*. Chicago, 1946.

DeMallie, Raymond. *The Sixth Grandfather: Black Elk's Teachings Given to John G. Neihardt*. Lincoln, 1984.

Dodge, Richard I. *Our Wild Indians*. Hartford, 1882.

du Mont, John S. *Custer Battle Guns*. Ft. Collins, 1974.

Eastman, Mary. *Dahcotah*. New York, 1849.

Ege, Robert J. *'Settling The Dust': A Brief for a Much-maligned Cavalryman*. Great Falls, 1968.

Fougera, Katherine G. *With Custer's Cavalry*. Caldwell, 1940.

Fox, Richard A., Jr. *Archaeology, History, And Custer's Last Battle*. Norman, 1993.

Godfrey, Edward S. *Diary of the Little Big Horn*. Portland, 1957.

Graham, W. A. "Custer Battle Flags," *The Westerners Brand Book*. Los Angeles, 1950.

—. *The Story Of The Little Big Horn*. New York, 1926.

Graham, William A., ed. *Abstract of the Official Record of Proceedings of the Reno Court of Inquiry*. Harrisburg, 1954.

—. *The Custer Myth: a Source Book of Custeriana*. Harrisburg, 1953.

—. *The Official Record of a Court of Inquiry. . .upon the Request of Major Marcus A. Reno, 7th U. S. Cavalry, to Investigate His Conduct at the Battle of the Little Big Horn*. Pacific Palisades, 1951.

Gray, John S. *Centennial Campaign: the Sioux War of 1876*. Ft. Collins, 1976.

—. *Custer's Last Campaign: Mitch Boyer And The Little Bighorn Reconstructed*. Lincoln, 1991.

Greene, Jerome A. *Slim Buttes, 1876: An episode of the Great Sioux War*. Norman, 1982.

Gump, James O. *The Dust Rose Like Smoke: The Subjugation Of The Zulu And The Sioux*. Lincoln, 1994.

Hammer, Kenneth, ed. *Custer In '76: Walter Camp's Notes On The Custer Fight*. Provo, 1976.

Hammer, Kenneth. *Little Big Horn Biographies*. Brookings, 1964.

—. *Men With Custer: Biographies Of The 7th Cavalry*. Hardin, 1995.

Hardorff, Richard G. *The Custer Battle Casualties: Burials, Exhumations, And Reinterments*. El Segundo, 1989.

Hedren, Paul L., ed. *The Great Sioux War 1876-1877: The Best From Montana The Magazine of Western History*. Helena, 1991.

Henry, Will. *No Survivors*. New York, 1950.

Hinman, Eleanor. "Oglala Sources on the Life of Crazy Horse." *Nebraska History*, 57.1 (1976).

Horn, W. Donald. *Witnesses For the Defense of General George Armstrong Custer*. Short Hills, 1981.

Hunt, Frazier and Robert Hunt. *I Fought With Custer: the Story of Sergeant Windolph, Last Survivor of the Battle of the Little Big Horn*. New York, 1947.

Hutchins, James S., ed. *Boots & Saddles At The Little Bighorn*. Ft. Collins, 1976.

Hutton, Paul A. *Phil Sheridan And His Army*. Lincoln, 1973.

Hyde, George. *Red Cloud's Folk: a History of the Oglala Sioux Indians*. Norman, 1937.

Johnson, W. Fletcher. *Red Record of the Sioux*. Philadelphia, 1891.

Kanitz, Jay F. "Varnum: The Later Years of Custer's Last Lieutenant." *5th Annual Symposium Custer Battlefield Historical & Museum Assn.*, held at Hardin, Montana, on June 21, 1991: 19.

Karselis, Terry C. "Disaster in Duplicate: An Examination of the Similarities Between the Battle of Isandhlawana and the Little Big Horn," *5th Annual Symposium Custer Battlefield Historical & Museum Assn.*, held at Hardin, Montana, on June 21, 1991: 45.

Katcher, Philip. *US Cavalry On The Plains: 1850-90*. London, 1985.

Keenan, Jerry. *Encyclopedia Of American Indian Wars: 1492-1890*. Santa Barbara, 1997.

Koch, Ronald P. *Dress Clothing of the Plains Indians*. Norman, 1977.

Koury, Michael J., ed. *Custer Centennial Observance 1976*. Ft. Collins, 1978.

Kuhlman, Charles. *Legend Into History*. Harrisburg, 1951.

—. *Did Custer Disobey Orders at the Battle of the Little Big Horn?* Harrisburg, 1957.

Lamar, Howard R., ed. *The Reader's Encyclopedia of the American West*. New York, 1977.

Lavender, David. *The American Heritage History of the Great West*. New York, 1965.

Libby, Orin G., ed. *The Arikara Narrative of the Campaign Against the Hostile Dakotas, June 1876*. Bismarck, 1920.

Lynd, James W. "The Religion of the Dakotas." Minnesota Historical Society *Collections*, Vol. II, Part 2 (1922).

Manion, John S. *General Terry's Last Statement to Custer*. Monroe, 1983.

Magnussen, Daniel O., ed. *Peter Thompson's Narrative of The Little Bighorn Campaign 1876*. Glendale, 1974.

Marquis, Thomas B. *Keep The Last Bullet For Yourself: The True Story of Custer's Last Stand*. New York, 1976.

—. *Memoirs of a White Crow Indian Thomas H. LeForge*. New York, 1928.

—. *She Watched Custer's Last Battle*. Hardin, 1933.

—. *Which Indian Killed Custer?*. Hardin, 1933.

—. *Wooden Leg: A Warrior Who Fought Custer*. Lincoln, 1931.

Meketa, Ray. *Luther Rector Hare, A Texan With Custer*. Mattituck, NY and Bryan, TX, 1983.

Merington, Marguerite, ed. *The Custer Story: The Life and Intimate Letters of General George A Custer And His Wife Elizabeth*. New York, 1950.

Merrill, James M. *Spurs to Glory: The Story of United States Cavalry*. Rand McNally, 1966.

Miles, Nelson A. *Personal Recollections*. Chicago, 1896.

Miller, David H. *Custer's Fall: The Indian Side of the Story*. New York, 1957.

Milligan, Edward A. *Dakota Twilight: The Standing Rock Sioux, 1874-1890*. Hicksville, 1976.

Monaghan, Jay. *Custer: The Life of General George Armstrong Custer*. Boston, 1959.

—, ed. *The Book Of The American West*. New York, 1963.

Nash, Jay R. *Almanac of World Crime*. New York, 1981.

Neihardt, John G. *Black Elk Speaks: Being the Life Story of a Holy Man of the Oglala Sioux*. Lincoln, 1961.

Nichols, Ronald H., ed. *Reno Court of Inquiry: Proceedings of a Court of Inquiry in the Case of Major Marcus A. Reno Concerning His Conduct at the Battle of the Little Big Horn River on June 25-26, 1876*. Hardin, 1996.

Northrop, Henry Davenport. *Indian Horrors or, Massacres By the Red Men*. Philadelphia, n.d.

Nye, Elwood L. *Marching With Custer: a day-by-day evaluation of the uses, abuses, and conditions of the animals on the ill-fated expedition of 1876*. Glendale, 1964.

Panzieri, Peter. *Little Big Horn 1876: Custer's Last Stand*. Hong Kong, 1995.

Paulding, Dr. Holmes Offley. *Surgeon's Diary*. 1876.

Rickey, Don, Jr. *History of Custer Battlefield*. Hardin, 1967.

Robinson, Doane. *A History of the Dakota or Sioux Indians*. Minneapolis, 1904.

Sandoz, Mari. *Crazy Horse: the Strange Man of the Oglalas*. New York, 1942.

—. *The Battle of the Little Bighorn*. Philadelphia & New York, 1966.

Sarf, Wayne M. *The Little Bighorn Campaign: March-September 1876*. Hong Kong, 1993.

Scott, Douglas D. and Richard A. Fox, Jr. *Archaeological Insights Into the Custer Battle: An Assessment of the 1984 Field Season*. Norman, 1987.

Scott, Douglas D., Richard A. Fox, Jr., Melissa A. Connor, and Dick Harmon. *Archaeological Perspectives on the Battle of the Little Big Horn*. Norman, 1989.

Steckmesser, Kent Ladd. *The Western Hero In History and Legend*. Norman, 1965.

Stewart, Edgar I. *Custer's Luck*. Norman, 1955.

Taunton, Francis B. *Custer's Field: "A Scene of Sickening Ghastly Horror"*. London, 1986.

—. *"Sufficient Reason?"* London, 1977.

Terrell, John and George Walton. *Faint the Trumpet Sounds*. New York, 1966.

Terry, Alfred H. *The Field Diary of General Alfred H. Terry: The Yellowstone Expedition - 1876*. Bellevue, 1969.

Utley, Robert M. and Wilcomb E. Washburn. *The American Heritage History of the American Indian Wars*. New York, 1977.

Utley, Robert M. *Cavalier In Buckskin: George Armstrong Custer And The Western Military Frontier*. Norman, 1988.

—. *Custer and the Great Controversy: The Origin and Development of a Legend*. Los Angeles, 1962.

—. *Custer's Last Stand: With a Narration of Events Preceding and Following*. Dayton, 1949.

—. *Frontier Regulars: The United States Army and the Indian, 1866-1891*. New York, 1973.

Van de Water, Frederick F. *Glory-Hunter: A Life of General Custer*. Indianapolis, 1930.

Various. *Wild Life on the Plains and Horrors of Indian Warfare*. New York, 1969.

Vestal, Stanley. *Sitting Bull: Champion of the Sioux*. Norman, 1932.

U.S. Department of the Interior, National Park Service. "Custer Battlefield" (brochure). GPO, 1978.

—. *Custer Battlefield National Monument*, by Edward S. and Evelyn S. Luce. GPO, 1952.

—. *Custer Battlefield Official National Park Handbook*, by Robert M. Utley. GPO, 1988.

—. "Custer National Cemetery." Southwest Parks & Monuments Association, 1997.

—. "Little Bighorn Battlefield National Monument, 1998 Summer Program." GPO, 1998.

—. *Indian, Soldier, And Settler: Experiences in the Struggle For the American West*. Jefferson National Expansion Historical Assoc., 1979.

—. "Reno-Benteen Entrenchment Trail." Southwest Parks & Monuments Association, 1996.

—. *Soldier And Brave: Indian And Military Affairs In The Trans-Mississippi West*, Robert G. Ferris, ed. GPO, 1971.

Virgines, George E. *Saga of the Colt Six-Shooter and the Famous Men Who Used It*. New York, 1969.

Wied-Neuwied, Prinz Alexander Philip Maximilian von. *Travels in the Interior of North America*. Translated by H. Evans Lloyd. London, 1843.

Whittaker, Frederick. *Popular Life Of Gen. George A. Custer*. New York, 1876.

Wiltsey, Norman E. *Brave Warriors*. Caldwell, 1963.

Wycoff, James. *Famous Guns That Won The West*. New York, 1966.

Zimmerman, Barbara. "Gibbon's Montana Column" *5th Annual Symposium Custer Battlefield Historical & Museum Assn.*, held at Hardin, Montana, on June 21, 1991: 1.

Zupan, James. *Tools, Targets, And Troopers*. Mattituck, 1985.

Various Period Newspapers and Magazines as shown in the text.

Various Government and Military Documents as shown in the text.